AMERICA'S ATONEMENT

Studies in the Postmodern Theory of Education

Shirley R. Steinberg
General Editor

Vol. 476

The Counterpoints series is part of the Peter Lang Education list.
Every volume is peer reviewed and meets
the highest quality standards for content and production.

PETER LANG
New York • Bern • Frankfurt • Berlin
Brussels • Vienna • Oxford • Warsaw

Aaron David Gresson III

AMERICA'S ATONEMENT

Racial Pain, Recovery Rhetoric, and the Pedagogy of Healing

SECOND EDITION

PETER LANG
New York • Bern • Frankfurt • Berlin
Brussels • Vienna • Oxford • Warsaw

Library of Congress Cataloging-in-Publication Data
Gresson, Aaron David.
America's atonement: racial pain, recovery rhetoric, and the pedagogy of healing /
Aaron David Gresson III. — 2nd edition.
pages cm. — (Counterpoints: studies in the postmodern theory of education; vol. 476)
Includes bibliographical references and index.
1. United States—Race relations—Psychological aspects—Study and teaching.
2. Racism—United States—Psychological aspects—Study and teaching.
3. Loss (Psychology)—Study and teaching. 4. English language—United States—Rhetoric.
5. Rhetoric and psychology. I. Title.
E185.625.G65   305.800973—dc23   2014048958
ISBN 978-1-4331-2878-3 (paperback)
ISBN 978-1-4539-1509-7 (e-book)
ISSN 1058-1634

Bibliographic information published by **Die Deutsche Nationalbibliothek**.
Die Deutsche Nationalbibliothek lists this publication in the "Deutsche
Nationalbibliografie"; detailed bibliographic data are available
on the Internet at http://dnb.d-nb.de/.

Cover design by Lisa Barfield
Cover photo of Vietnam Women's Memorial in Washington, D. C.:
created by Glena Goodacre, 1994.

The paper in this book meets the guidelines for permanence and durability
of the Committee on Production Guidelines for Book Longevity
of the Council of Library Resources.

© 2015 Peter Lang Publishing, Inc., New York
29 Broadway, 18th floor, New York, NY 10006
www.peterlang.com

All rights reserved.
Reprint or reproduction, even partially, in all forms such as microfilm,
xerography, microfiche, microcard, and offset strictly prohibited.

Printed in the United States of America

For Robert Williams, Bernie O'Brien, and Rosaline Griffin;
and the memories of
Joe, Robert, and Elbert,
colleagues, friends, and brothers

The man who has tripped between death's legs and then
Recovers himself and breathes again,
Can only laugh or only weep:
He has not the heart to mourn.

—Charles Vildrac

One of the most important insights of modern socio-biology is that self-deception is the handmaiden of deceit: in hiding the truth from ourselves, we are able to hide it more fully from others. Therefore, like deceit, self-deception lies at the core of our humanity.

—David Livingston Smith

A good deal of time and intelligence has been invested in the exposure of racism and the horrific results on its objects. But that well-established study should be joined with another, equally important one: the impact of racism on those who perpetuate it.... The scholarship that looks into the mind, imagination, and behavior of the slaves is valuable. But equally valuable is a serious intellectual effort to see what racial ideology does to the mind, imagination, and behavior of masters.

—Toni Morrison

CONTENTS

A Personal Preface
The Dance of Agency in the 21st Century   XI

Preface to the Second Edition   XVII

Acknowledgments   XXIII

Part One
Racial Pain and its Discontents

Chapter 1. Introduction
America's "Atonement" and the Right
to a Non-Spoiled Identity   3

Chapter 2. Racial Pain in the 21st Century
Spoiled Identities and Traumatized Relations   29

Part Two
White Pain and the Dance of Agency

Chapter 3. Narcissism and White Pain
The White Male and the Masculinity Crisis—Again   59

Chapter 4. White Studies and Racial Pain in the Academy
The Plight of the Neo-Liberal Agenda
in the Existential Moment   91

Chapter 5. Mediating White Pain
Ritual Recovery, Yellow Ribbons, and Patriotic Wars   119

Part Three
The Pedagogy of Healing

Chapter 6. Multiculturalism and Social Justice
White Pain and the Search for a Non-Oppressive
Cultural Turn   151

Chapter 7. Toward a Psychopedagogy of Healing
Mourning and Mending Difference
in the New Millennium   179

Chapter 8. Postscript
Relational Justice and the Pedagogy
of the Wounded Healer   215

Notes   233
References   253
About the Author   277
Index   279

A PERSONAL PREFACE

The Dance of Agency in the 21st Century

USA—God Bless Her... We'll Defend Her.
Anonymous 9/11 slogan

What does agency mean? What is its relevance for the new century in American society? These questions are at the core of this book. But because the subject matter—race, identity, power, and healing—is not immediately understood in terms of agency, I want to use this preface to introduce both the subject matter and the intention of *America's Atonement*.

Simply put, *agency* is the primal cry *I am somebody*! Look up the term in, say, *Webster's II New World College Dictionary*, and you will see that the word comes from the Latin, *agens*, and means "effective," "action," "power." The difference between my simple definition and the more official idea is important: my own, which hints at Jesse Jackson's mantra for black Americans of another generation, represents a recent effort by some in American society to insist that the average person, Everyman, has a voice and a personal motive and agenda. The dictionary term harks back to when one acted on behalf of another in whom power and authority resided.

The difference between these two understandings is critical, as they represent two sides of the human condition in which one is either passive or active, giving or taking, losing or winning. Although life is often depicted as either one or the other, we recognize that a truer, less Manichean view depicts us as moving back and forth between these two circumstances. This is why I refer to *the dance of agency*. But why do I suggest that this dance has some special importance in contemporary America?

I began *America's Atonement* in the mid-1990s shortly after the publication of my *The Recovery of Race in America*. Encouraged by the apparent success of this work—it received both national and international honors—I began where this work left off, arguing that a racial recovery was occurring and that we must closely monitor and manage it lest we return to the racist past. But there was an irony in my thesis: if I were correct, there was a good chance that my own work would become problematic and thus marginalized. This occurred when the publisher, having fired its minority acquisitions editor, decided to let my book go out of print despite its relative success.

The firing of my editor was part of a major debate carried in *The Chronicle of Higher Education*.[1] Although he had claimed racism toward himself and other minorities in publishing who did not follow the party line, the University of Minnesota Press "found no evidence of racial discrimination." I felt both guilty and powerless as a result of these events. I felt guilty because I had unfairly and unfeelingly accused my editor of abandoning me when the publisher had tried to suppress my title's message: *racialism continues in America*. I felt powerless because I could help neither my editor nor myself. Indeed, under new leadership in late 1999, the press dropped my book from its list without explanation or encouragement.

What is the point of this story? By 1999, I had been working on this book for nearly four years. Most of the material was collected and drafts had been rewritten. But I could not finish or release what I had already written. Not even the kind, persistent chiding of my friends and editors, Shirley Steinberg and Joe Kincheloe, or the fact that my publisher repeatedly promised on Amazon.com a forthcoming volume gave me the energy and motivation to finish this work. Even my headlong rush toward a broken contract—anathema to a serious author—could not move me. I was deeply wounded and silenced by the fate of my editor at Minnesota and my award-winning book's short life in print.

My writing and publishing a critique of racial relations in the late 20th century had been an act of agency. The silencing of my work seemed to me an act of counteragency. Both acts imply power. My act represented a belief that

I had come far from the Old South where I rode on the back of the bus; called all whites "sir" and "ma'am"; shined shoes for poor, white sailors outside the segregated USO in Norfolk, Virginia; and dreamed of nothing much at all. I confess that I have sometimes said and written things that I would not have done had it not been for the radical 1960s. Like so many, I had found in that decade a burst of freedom, a new voice.

Whatever its motive, the publisher's actions had the effect of reminding me of where I had come from and where I really stood. Sending my work into out-of-print status was for me a renewal of the older meaning of agency, for the press effectively acted on the behalf of powerful others who would rather not have such ideas circulating in society. (In Chapter 2, I present material indicating how certain "blind reviewers" of a textbook that I was commissioned to write attempted to suppress my voice by reducing my work to "white man bashing.") Together, my and my publisher's actions constitute a dance of agency.

Recent events, including a resurgence of racial discord at my alma mater and employer, Penn State University, have renewed my sense of agency. The recovery of race I foretold in my *Recovery of Race in America* has become the recovery of racism. The concerns I had when writing *America's Atonement* have come of age. But as some have noted, the swinging back of the pendulum from racial consciousness and conscience to the other side does not mean the same old racism. On the contrary, something decisive has occurred, partly because of the mass media and the global political economy and the resulting global cultural condition.

This is a more complex America we now live in: we are unified but complicatedly so, and our relations both at home and around the world are a dance of agency. The dominant television media—CNN, MSNBC, and Fox News—daily play out the nuances of this dance. The written media also reflect this dance. For instance, on December 22, 2001, the (Baltimore) *Afro-American* reported the federal government's filing of a $100 million lawsuit against the Cracker Barrel restaurant chain, under charges of systematic racial discrimination in 175 cities and 30 states. But in the same edition of this paper, we learn that Richard D. Parsons, a black liberal Republican, protégé of former New York governor Nelson Rockefeller, now controls the media conglomerate AOL Time Warner.

The contemporary racial context is indeed complex. This global cultural condition underpins how we Americans seek to fuse power and pragmatism in the 21st century. It is symbolized by the triad of George W. Bush/Dick

Cheney, Condoleezza Rice, and Colin L. Powell. It does not allow for slogans and declarations of either "the end of racism" or "a renewed runaway racist assault." Rather, we are fed a diet of accommodation and annihilation.

September 11, 2001, and the resulting "war on terrorism" are perhaps the best illustrations of this dance of accommodation and annihilation. There are many "sidebars" to the war on terrorism:

- Muslims as targets of "patriotic anger"
- The national debate about ID cards and privacy
- Mourning antiwar marchers
- The minority presence in the antiwar effort
- Rising unemployment
- Stock market agitation
- Erosion of the national surplus
- Executive encroachment on congressional powers

Whatever we understand and feel regarding the attack on our country and the destruction of human life on September 11, it is clear that some people feel terrorism is essential to relieve perceived wrongs and that others feel that it is never acceptable. Clearly terrorism, while unquestionably extreme and perverse, is the birthright of humans and is not unknown in this country: think of the bombings of abortion clinics, Oklahoma City, and so on. But it is perhaps in the war-on-terrorism discourse that we can best see the complex unfolding of the Us/Them mentality underpinning racism and so many other forms of human oppressiveness. The actions taken to remove terrorism from the planet have stimulated a series of "dances," such as the simultaneous dropping of bombs and care packages on Afghanistan.

Death and dying may or may not change human nature. I have known people whose sickness and imminent death gave them deeper wisdom, compassion, and serenity. And I have seen—even among these individuals—occasions when the darker side seemed to dominate. Nations are much like individuals in this regard. On September 11, 2001, numerous stories of heroism among the victims, their families, and fellow citizens surfaced. Then there were the scandals: some people received more relief money than others; some received none; some people scammed, trying to get money they didn't deserve; the Red Cross itself came under fire and had to apologize for mishandling funds. Nor did the matter of racism escape all reference during this time. For instance, plans to erect a tribute to the heroism associated with September 11 resulted in the so-called Firefighters' Memorial scandal.

There is a broader significance to this debate over who should be memorialized. In Chapters 3 and 4, I elaborate on similar dramas, especially over the Vietnam and Vietnam Women's memorials. Here my point is to note that September 11 exposed not only the positives of our national character but also the negatives. The healing, the reach for a higher plane, is often compromised by past tendencies and conflictive propensities. For instance, consider the so-called psychological warfare in Afghanistan. The Bush administration has been accused of lacking cultural sensitivity because of the "doctored" photo of bin Laden on the leaflets dropped into that country after the bombing. Even retired general Wesley Clark questioned the thinking and wisdom of this strategy. More recently, President Bush's labeling of three foreign countries as forming an "axis of evil" led to similar doubts. Former president Jimmy Carter described Bush's "mantra" as "over-simplistic, counter-productive,... [an action] that will take years to correct."

These cases hint at the complex role of agency and counteragency regarding racial and related matters of social justice sparked by September 11. What they seem to share is an undercurrent of pain, which I focus on in *America's Atonement*. It is because the pain generated by September 11 fuses so often with the pain traditionally associated with racial and social justice issues that I have completed this work. I have come to believe that my silence—my refusal to complete this book—represents a loss. All is not well and no amount of chanting "United We Stand!" can long conceal the many divisions within, divisions our enemies correctly apprehend, even if they fail to understand how we "dismiss" such differences when under siege.

The slogan opening this preface announces the tension and the challenge taken up in this book. We say God is the "first cause" and "final solution" to matters such as "blessing" our nation, but we recognize the need for personal action. This is agency. This is the human condition. This is the dialectical. This book is a refusal to be silent; it is a celebration of hope based on evidence of the possibility for both personal and social growth, even as we surrender to the reactionary and destructive moments marking one side of the dance of agency.

PREFACE TO THE SECOND EDITION

In the winter of 2013 I met up with Chris Myers, managing director of Peter Lang (USA), at one of the national education conferences. At this time he encouraged me to consider a second edition of *America's Atonement*. I was especially enthusiastic about the invitation because I was just about to visit the University of Virginia to speak with students who were studying the book. Later, Chris further enhanced my growing enthusiasm with an observation: "The world is such that your argument about the state of things is well supported by reality." I agreed with him. But what of it? What might be said that has not; and to whom might it be directed? These two questions have figured greatly in the revisions and expansions made to this second edition.

In the first edition of *America's Atonement*, I focused on racial pain, its rhetorical expressions, and some of the opportunities they provided for racial healing. I paid particular attention to white racial pain both because of its under-examination and centrality to any comprehensive and meaningful movement toward greater social justice. I therefore looked at the objective and subjective character of white racial pain across several settings, notably academia and the multicultural classroom. I further examined popular cultural expressions of efforts to recover from this massively felt psychomoral pain through the cinema and cultural movements. By turning a critical lens on these phenomena, I hoped to further what I termed a "pedagogy of healing," a compassionate invitation to participate in the furtherance of greater social justice for both self and other.

In the first edition, I also argued that a dance of agency animates racial relations in contemporary race relations in the United States. I suggested white pain is a critical though inadequately examined facet of this dance of agency, especially among proponents of multiculturalism and social justice pedagogy. White pain continues to be an organizing concept for the book. But through my experience at the University of Virginia in 2013, I recognized the need to give a more complete statement of racial pain in general: some students wondered if blacks and other minorities felt "racial pain."

The greater necessity for this enlarged discussion of racial pain is due, however, to a newer, more insistent "atonement" attitude in the contemporary United States. I call it the "non-apology" white identity discourse. It embraces but transcends white pain as a motive for maintaining and, in some instances, regaining the white supremacist past. Although a new urgency characterizes this attitude, it is not a really new idea. James Owens (1999) echoed its central vision shortly before the new millennium:

> The Euro-white race, with its unparalleled achievements of mind and innovation throughout history, still contains the unmatched capability to preserve its race and culture—if the will for it can be revived. But, by pathological apathy and altruism, whites are fast abandoning that essential will. And, as all history proves, that is the ultimate determinant for survival—in war or peace.

This attitude has gained complexity during the past decade or more and now finds expression in both the social-media and social-justice-oriented classrooms as a demand for *existential* recognition. Buttressed by institutional supports—from the Supreme Court and the Criminal Justice Enterprise to Corporate America—the demand for being accepted for whom and what one is, or chooses to be, has gained momentum across the society. This attitude has accounted for two particular tensions taken up more fully in the revised edition.

First, there is the *dance of racialized identities* where people are seen shifting back and forth among imposed or embraced racial views of themselves. This "dance" may be seen as contributing to the increased presence of white race discourse, especially among students, that simultaneously rejects crude racism but embraces structural racist practices. To recognize these shifting, negotiated identities is an incipient step. Second, there is the increasing demand to pay greater attention to the emotions—the *affective turn*—which was central to the first edition. In the second, I introduce several newer pedagogical efforts responding to the emotional aspects of social justice education.

In this edition, I have benefitted from critical input of readers of the earlier work—students and their teachers, as well as reviewers and other critics. I have tried, where possible, to respond to their reflections without an awkward break in the flow of the arguments I made then. Toward this end, the footnotes for this edition have grown significantly and tend toward the intertextual; that is, a dialogue with some of the readers and critics of the first edition. I hope that this improves ideas presented in the first edition without compromising its foci.

Finally, readers of the first edition will note that the book has been enlarged as well as updated. In particular, Chapters 1, 2 and 8 represent major additions. In Chapter 1, I expand the discussion of America's "atonement" as a specialized concept. In Chapter 2, I have moved toward a broader psychopolitical emphasis on "traumatized" racial identities for blacks, whites, and others caught within the racialization net. Recognizing and reflecting on the psychological effects of war on children in the Middle East and elsewhere (Boothby, 2008; Boothby, Strang, & Wessells, 2006; Wessells 2006, 2009), we need to understand that trauma is also very real in American society. As noted in a recent task force report from the American Psychological Association (2008):

> ...the United States is a highly diverse society comprising many different racial and ethnic groups. There is no doubt that because of poverty and discrimination, racial and ethnic minority youth and families are more likely to be subjected to traumatic events, and immigrant youth and families may be particularly at risk. Cultural context and background, as well as membership in a minority group, will affect how individuals perceive a traumatic event and its impact and how the community can assist in recovery.

Here, one may immediately think of the trauma characterizing the lives of the residents, black, whites, and others, living through the nightmare in Ferguson, Missouri: the trauma associated with seeing the body of the young black youth, Michael Brown, lying on the streets for hours as police and neighbors looked on; and the trauma due to the militarization of police that led Amnesty International to come to town, and the leaders of Egypt and Iran to caution the United States on human rights violations.

Within this context, although written before the Ferguson crisis, Chapter 2 argues that "spoiled racialized identities" are also sources of trauma that may intensify the use of violence and other forms of aggression. The implications of this assertion are taken up in Chapter 8, where I extend the conversation of Chapter 7 on the psychological aspects of healing and reconciliation. In particular, I focus on the pedagogical requirements for greater "cultural" (read humanitarian) sensitivity to racial pain and its resistance to social justice pedagogies. I especially reaffirm the need for social justice educators to *use self* in the pedagogical engagement of their students around issues of social justice. In this regard, I forefront two different but convergent pedagogical trajectories: Henri Nouwen (1972) in *The Wounded Healer* and Paulo Freire (1994) in *Pedagogy of Hope*. Each of these men, one from a theological tradition, the other from a community organization/activism tradition, invited helpers to transcend their own inherited biases and vulnerabilities; and use their acquired compassion to guide others toward greater engagement with social justice initiatives.

Writing a second edition can be both an exciting and a humbling experience. For me, this has been both and more. My turning to Nouwen and Freire in the conclusion to this second edition perhaps signals the "more." Let me briefly explain: as one gets older (and hopefully wiser), there can be a reluctance to engage with the enthusiasm and "innocence" of youth. Throughout the months that I worked on this revision, I struggled with "why bother?" Perhaps this was merely the fatigue of a life in the social change/justice trenches; perhaps too much wine, which, like the aging Don Corleone in *The Godfather*, I have grown increasingly fond of. But I believe that there was something else occurring that is important to share here: I was acknowledging at some deeper level that the issues taken up in both editions of *America's Atonement* belong to the young in a special, nay, existential way. The fact is that even though I continue to be engaged, even outraged at the injustices around me, I have achieved a degree of detachment. This is due, in part, to the *necessary losses* that accompany advancing years: I look at most things through the lens of time remaining. This, of course, increases my sense of urgency to witness to those around me. Others who have both inspired and gone on before me shared this sense of urgency. And while this sense of urgency in the aging can be an annoyance or "white noise," it remains, I feel, an essential ingredient in the collective human project of greater kindness to each other in the pursuit of fuller social justice for all.

But events like the current crisis in Ferguson, Missouri, re-energize all committed social activists, for we see that the young must continue to glean wisdom and experience compassion from those of us who have been "wounded" by experience but continue to survive and thrive. The near hopelessness that conditions in Ferguson (and other parts of the nation) have brought to the fore explain, in part, the racial rage and pain of those who feel disempowered and disregarded. By joining with the young on "ground zero," where they live lives of traumatized wretchedness, we can share our lived experience of hopefulness that positive change can take place. It is within this spirit, then, that I offer this second edition of the book to a younger generation, one hopefully not yet exposed to too many of the necessary losses of life to seize the reins of individual and collective power.

Aaron D. Gresson
Owings Mills and Baltimore, Maryland
August 2014

ACKNOWLEDGMENTS

This second edition has a somewhat shorter list of people to whom I am grateful, but it goes without saying, perhaps, that I continue to be thankful to those mentioned in the first edition since this volume builds on it. I would like to mention once again my thanks to Shirley Steinberg and Chris Myers for their support and encouragement. To Derrick Alridge and his students from the Curry School of Education at the University of Virginia, I owe special thanks for inviting me to their campus to work through some of the ideas added to this edition. Mark McPhail of the University of Wisconsin (Whitewater), John Hatch of Dubuque University, and Donal E. Mulcahy of Wake Forest University have offered very helpful insights into my thinking on racial pain—thanks to each of you. Michael G. Lacy has been both generous in his assessment of my efforts and inspiring in his important work on critical race rhetorics; and I thank him for this. As always, I am thankful for the love and support of my family, especially my life partner and wife, Pat.

I also want to recognize three people—master clinicians and mentors—whose guidance and support have aided my transition from academe into private life and clinical work. Drs. Robert Williams, Bernie O'Brien, and Rosaline Griffin have contributed to helping me find "a room of my own" within which I have been able to do the revisions to this book. Dr. Griffin, especially, has been most helpful in providing the collegial exchange that can be so critical in the writing process. My gratitude and thanks to all of you.

Finally, I remain grateful in a profound way to three men who have gone on to the ancestors: Joe L. Kincheloe, Robert E. Haskell, and Elbert McKeithan. In life, I drew strength from their brilliance, joy for life, and loving compassion for humanity. I miss them deeply; and I continue to draw courage and inspiration from their lives.

Part One

RACIAL PAIN AND ITS DISCONTENTS

... men are not gentle creatures, who want to be loved, who at the most can defend themselves if they are attacked; they are, on the contrary, creatures among whose instinctual endowments is to be reckoned a powerful share of aggressiveness. As a result, their neighbor is for them not only a potential helper or sexual object, but also someone who tempts them to satisfy their aggressiveness on him, to exploit his capacity for work without compensation, to use him sexually without his consent, to seize his possessions, to humiliate him, to cause him pain, to torture and to kill him.
... Anyone who calls to mind the atrocities committed during the racial migrations or the invasions of the Huns, or by the people known as Mongols under Jenghiz Khan and Tamerlane, or at the capture of Jerusalem by the pious Crusaders, or even, indeed, the horrors of the recent World War—anyone who calls these things to mind will have to bow humbly before the truth of this view.

– Sigmund Freud, *Civilization and Its Discontents* (1930/1961: 58)

... the pain-free, white American body exists easily in the cultural imagination and cultural productions of social agents within the United States. Even the most horrific wounding experiences are allowed invisibility, as if this mythological white body is cloaked within a magic circle. As an historical and everyday (or commonplace) sign

of suffering, the pounded black body is walled off "legally, socially, and ideologically to benefit those within the magic circle and protect the national body from [pain's] contamination" (Rogin [1996]: 12).

– Debra Walker King, *African Americans and the Culture of Pain* (2008: 5)

· 1 ·

INTRODUCTION

America's "Atonement" and the Right to a Non-Spoiled Identity

Sacrifice is par excellence the means of restoring the ethnic balance; and in this capacity it is never without a basic sense of loss and surrender.

– Susanne Langer (1984: 133)

When enough men have died, then perhaps there will be redemption, renewal... until then, we mourn.

– Anonymous

They thought that they would be able to heal their wounds if they went against Baghdad.
– Saddam Hussein

Prologue: The Dance of Spoiled Identities—The Million Man March Meets the Tea Party

In 1995, the Million Man March captured the national imagination. Several hundred thousands of black males came to the nation's capital for a three-day conclave. Their purpose, according to Louis Farrakhan and other black leaders, was to make a public expression of atonement and reconciliation. Through this cultural event, black leaders and the men participating in the March hoped to affirm their racial integrity: to acknowledge before each other, black women, the Black Family, and the world that they recognized their individual and collective failures but to also affirm that black men had a long history of racial love, solidarity, and uplift (Adelekan, 2000). In this cultural display—the speeches, seminars, concerts, and communal meals—these men were publicly exposing and expressing their "racial pain." Through their speeches, shared stories, and fellowship, they atoned and began a healing process.

Ostensibly a positive event, the March drew some negative press: for its failure to include black female and black gay participation (Carboda, 1999); and for its implicit indictment of white America for racism and discrimination.[2] Additionally, some white males had a particularly telling reaction; it took the form of a question: "Are you atoning for your actions against us, too?" On the surface, this attitude seemed misinformed if not a bit duplicitous. As one African American critic wrote: "The white male commentariat's responses to the Million Man March evidenced 'buck passing.' Since the March was billed as an atonement for black men, these white men had nothing to atone for, engaging in a phony effluvia of congratulations to black men for finally getting themselves together" (Reed, 1999: 46).

"Buck passing" may have been part of the motivation of these white males. This attitude, however, was traceable to the 1960s and gained momentum during the Reagan era as various civil-rights reforms came under siege (Gresson, 1995). What the Million Man March revealed, in fact, was a deep anger and resentment towards black males, in particular, that went far beyond their self-display during the March. Nowhere, perhaps, was this attitude more in evidence than in jokes generated by the March:

- What was good about the million man march? Only three people missed work. (Warped Network)
- What was missing from the Million Man March? About a thousand miles of chain and an auctioneer! (Niggermania.net)

The traditional myth regarding black reluctance to work ("be a good slave") and the essential righteousness of slavery (Genovese & Fox-Genovese, 2011) are implicit in these two jokes. These jokes also expose a deeper grievance: *the white race under siege*. Within this larger context, white men are victims of black and minority wrongdoings, as seen in this 2009 blog:

> I would like to start a million man march with white men only, will people call it racist? I would invite only taxpaying white men who are tired of supporting people who stay at home and have babies and need the government to take of them all the time. And deadbeats who don't want to work and beat their women for the hell of it. (Yahoo Answers, 2009)

Cataloguing a number of racialized "grievances," this blogger identifies blacks as offenders of "taxpaying white men." From this view, a *counter-atonement* march is desirable as retribution. But something more is involved here besides retribution. We gain a sense of this in a 2011 blog, where the writer, using the March as a rallying point, laments the unfairness of being called racist for having racial pride: "In the Million Man March, you believed that you were marching for your race and rights. If we marched for our race and rights…you would call us racist" (Yahoo Answers, 2011). To be denied the right to "race pride" can be painful both because of the denial itself *and* the insistence that racial self-affirmation is racist.

This sense of unfairness, while a longstanding belief, conveys a more insistent grievance. Each of the above bloggers expresses both beliefs about racial injustice and racial pain toward those forces within society that seemingly insist that whites bear a negative identity—racist—for expressing perceived racial pride. These bloggers also echo sentiments more recently associated with the so-called Tea Party, which was created partly by the traumatic economic, emotional, and institutional losses of the 2008 recession. Although racial minorities were economically more adversely affected than whites by the financial collapse of 2008, the upsurge in massive anger, depression, and outrage has been largely associated with working, middle-class, and older white Americans.[3] Within this context, the Tea Party has emerged as a metaphor for white pain. This pain has found expression in renewed populist rhetoric against a variety of perceived antagonists, including President Barack Obama, Congress, Wall Street, immigrants, women, and "undeserving minorities."

Some, like Adam Dyer (2013), have seen the Tea Party's pain—and pitfall: "I see you Tea Party; I see who you are and I will not let your fear bring us all down. I will acknowledge your pain, for we all share in the trauma…." Despite popular concerns with some aspects of its social activism, the Tea Party has been politically effective through mobilizing its pain into a winning power bloc in Congress. It has also, through social policies championed by its political representatives and political rallies, stirred up claims of racism. Whether true or not, this racial tension has led some to wonder if the Tea

Party is just a gathering of angry, selfish, older white people. Dyer (2013) expresses this tension when he declares: "I will call you out on your crap. Just remember that ultimately I will love you all the same, as I ask you to love me, because ultimately that is the only way this cycle will end."

Both the Million Man March and the Tea Party record pain and reflect atonement seeking. They are expressions of *spoiled identity*. They represent people, loosely defined as a group, who have felt pain associated with their views of themselves—and others. They have been constituted as collective identities that seek to make a statement, to display agency, and to accomplish particular ends. But their actions are held as suspect, partly because of tradition and partly because of new events that take place. They thus experience devalued identities. Accordingly, a white might now view her- or himself as devalued or spoiled both because of an event like the Million Man March *and* the sense of impotence to launch a white Million Man March without fear of accusations of white racism.

Spoiled identity has been traditionally viewed as mainly the fate of the minority person or group (Goffman, 1963; Gresson, 1982). This is so partly because of tactics such as self-deception and collective forgetting that can help conceal the emotional scars oppressive societies exact on the dominant group.[4] But social oppression may also affect an entire society. For instance, Nancy Scheper-Hughes (2006: 360) found in the study of racism in South Africa that "Apartheid not only shaped social self-identities in South Africa, but it spoiled those identities, filling people of all races with feelings of disgust and self-loathing, even after the antiapartheid struggle had begun."

Closer to home, Angie Maxwell (2014) makes a parallel argument in *The Indicted South: Public Criticism, Southern Inferiority, and the Politics of Whiteness*. According to her, the South has long struggled with a racialized inferiority complex rooted in *public criticism* for slavery, the Civil War, and other forms of racial oppression. It is, moreover, a negative public assessment of the South's racial behavior, combined with perceived limited opportunities to change the public perception that has undergirded the oppressive social policies and practices in the South. From Maxwell's view, then, the South has a spoiled identity. One ongoing expression of this has been the rhetoric of the "white victim."

But this regionalized spoilage is perhaps even more pervasive: writing on the romanticization of the South, Joe Kincheloe (2006: 28–29) deftly describes the *rhetorical reversal*—white victimhood—that fans out across the nation, proclaiming its spoilage:

Many white Southerners in the contemporary socio-cultural landscape prefer to focus on the wounds inflicted on them rather than on the injustices they have imposed on others. Here rests a central force driving contemporary American socio-political life. As working-class and numerous middle-level jobs have been outsourced to parts unknown, many white males have been introduced to a situation African Americans and other people of color have suffered with for a long time—a declining domain for individual development and progression. In this new context fewer white men are going to college. In this twenty-first-century context some of these southern (and of course American in general) men are sensing a decline in the traditional privileges accorded them. At the same time they feel this loss, they are watching media images and representations of them as the subjugators of African Americans, Latinos, Native Americans, women, and others. For a majority of these men, history and its influence on the present is not a topic understood or deemed important.

In this dehistoricized context the representation of white male as victim can be promoted in a way that resonates with the larger society to such a degree that it alters the political landscape. With the image of white male as racial victim firmly entrenched, any discussion of racism in the national political discourse or even in classrooms can be characterized as a personal attack on white people and their "traditional values." When this is the case a new form of racial politics dominates the cultural landscape.

From this view, spoilage is culturally induced, but it becomes personal as it mobilizes a range of defenses, including distorted beliefs, values, and perceptions of what is real and what is appearance. Contemporary society is teeming with precisely these dynamics, not in a unique, but certainly in a profound way. The national malaise, the sense that the nation is on the wrong track, and similar descriptions of American society, are expressions of this condition. Furthermore, whatever one's views of the Million Man March or the Tea Party, they are expressions of a nation struggling with spoilage. Racial pain and atonement are ways of thinking about and organizing some of the dimensions of this condition.

Philosopher Susanne Langer (1984) placed these emotions at the center of the "ethnic balance." She described this balance as a relationship among the members of the community. More precisely, it pertained to the traditional understanding of who owed whom obedience, respect, and loyalty. Originally, the individual owed these sentiments—ethnic balance—to the kin group. But as times changed, individuals increasingly separated from family and kin group, creating a relational tension (not unlike that among racial-ethnic groups in American society). As Langer observed, for individuals to reconnect or renegotiate a satisfactory balance with the larger group, there is an element of sacrifice. This sacrifice may entail, moreover, the experience of loss and surrender. As it pertains to race matters, the loss of this "ethnic balance" has given rise to America's "atonement."

What Is America's "Atonement"?

There are many definitions for the term "atonement." Douglas George-Kanentiio (n.d.), a Native American scholar and activist, has provided one of the most insightful definitions of atonement. He writes, "Atonement is the making right, the reestablishing of balance, the restoration of sanity, alleviation of grief and the resumption of life." From this view, the Million Man March as atonement directed toward the "Black World" meant black men were embarked on a "restoration of sanity" by confronting their drift into madness, the pathologies engulfing the black family, their adaptive but problematic adjustments to racism and oppression. Atonement also involves a recovery of a previous balance and "resumption" of previous ways of living. Of course, for blacks, the previous "balance"—slavery and racial oppression—is untenable. Thus, one aspect of the problem is conflicting, even opposing meanings for the term atonement. Herein is a possible clue to the white male query: are you apologizing for infractions against me, too?

Here also we get a different sense of what racially defined "atonement" activities might look like. Atonement, as I am using the term in *America's Atonement*, pertains to the "apology... not!" The non-apology is rooted in the perceived, experienced correctness of one's subjectivity—this is me—that springs forth. This emergent attitude is expressed powerfully by a Princeton freshman, Tal Fortgang, in an often-reprinted 2014 opinion piece from *The Princeton Tory*:

> There is a phrase that floats around college campuses, Princeton being no exception, that threatens to strike down opinions without regard for their merits, but rather solely on the basis of the person that voiced them. "Check your privilege," the saying goes, and I have been reprimanded by it several times this year. The phrase, handed down by my moral superiors, descends recklessly, like an Obama-sanctioned drone, and aims laser-like at my pinkish-peach complexion, my maleness, and the nerve I displayed in offering an opinion rooted in a personal Weltanschauung. "Check your privilege," they tell me in a command that teeters between an imposition to actually explore how I got where I am, and a reminder that I ought to feel personally apologetic because white males seem to pull most of the strings in the world....
>
> Behind every success, large or small, there is a story, and it isn't always told by sex or skin color. My appearance certainly doesn't tell the whole story, and to assume that it does and that I should apologize for it is insulting. While I haven't done everything

for myself up to this point in my life, someone sacrificed themselves so that I can lead a better life.⁵ But that is a legacy I am proud of.
I have checked my privilege. And I apologize for nothing.

There is something both attractive and compelling about this man's narrative. It carries *existential* depth and persuasiveness—for some, perhaps for most. Few of his points can be attacked frontally, for they are narrative and subjective. In this, they certainly resonate, if not universally, for an old American value—meritocracy—and a currently ascendant "libertarian" impulse. And his conclusion is significant: *I apologize for nothing*.

Now consider one response to his commentary, printed in the *Huffington Post*:

> I realize now, as I hope Tal can someday realize: white privilege isn't about me *individually*. It's not a personal attack. White privilege is a *systemic cultural reality* that I can either choose to ignore, or choose to acknowledge and attempt to change. It has nothing to do with my worth as a person or my own personal struggle. (Howerton, 2014)

This response, and dozens of other responses to Tal Fortgang, may be cogent. But they cannot easily face off with a non-apologetic insistence where there is no shared narrative regarding the *identity underpinnings of white privilege*—or for that matter, of any privilege that an individual may embrace as her or his "inheritance" and "entitlement."

Moreover, this young man has obviously captured in a compelling manner—*Time* magazine also reprinted his commentary—something about the individual and apology that has significance for the character of atonement around race matters in the 21st century.⁶ Here, I am reminded of an old western I saw recently in which the white antagonist tells the white hero's black male sidekick: "boy, I'm a different kind of white man—a real man."⁷ Implicit in this exchange (albeit fictionalized) is the fact that identity is a socially negotiated process and project; it entails embracing *and* performing, or not, a prescribed set of beliefs and behaviors (Bederman, 1995; Catano, 2001).

Today, the new "wrinkle" is the upsurge in white-pride rhetoric—a right to a non-spoiled identity. This was shown above in the reactions to the black Million Man March and the perception that whites cannot demonstrate a parallel "racial pride" without be named "racists." This is important because we see that the word does have power, at the subjective level, even though power relations—the system—remains very much intact. The consequence, "aversive racism," points to a dialectical discourse with a neutralizing effect; the stalemate in Congress between Republicans and Democrats is illustrative here: the disproportionate power of the "extreme Right" (Tea Party) when allied with the NRA, the Chamber of Commerce, and so forth to change state policies regarding public unions, voting, abortion, immigration, and gun safety.

Traditional multicultural pedagogies have significantly underexamined the emotional underside of "white privilege" and its implications for social change and justice. Such pedagogies have, implicitly at least, operated from an assumption that "reason" or rational discourse alone could change hearts and minds. The arrival of the so-called cultural turn points to the new implications of the *affective* for such pedagogies.[8] A critical racial pedagogy must now address the rhetoric of perceived loss of identity and atonement activities that seek to regain the foundation for the desired identities. *America's "atonement" is a metaphor for the combined rhetorics and politics of contemporary racial relations.* To understand how precisely these factors appear together, let me quote a passage from *Letters Across the Divide*:

> Given the premise that unresolved anger leads to resentment and prolonged resentment leads to rage, we can then answer the question: Where did the rage of black Americans come from? Did it originate from racism experienced during the 1990s or has it festered from years of unresolved anger and racism?
>
> My friend, I do not understand why blacks are so angry, nor why blacks have been so angry for so long that their anger has become rage.[9] Cannot blacks see all the tremendous advances toward eliminating racial discrimination that have been made in the last thirty years? *Why the hatred of whites? Slavery was a long time ago and as best as I can tell, life for blacks as a whole today is better in America than in any of the African countries their ancestors were kidnapped and enslaved from.* So why so much rage? I watched in amazement the riots in South Central Los Angeles. I just do not understand how anyone could be so full of rage that they would destroy their own community. I cognizantly understand that unresolved anger is self destructive—but these riots seemed to be an extended lapse of reason, even insanity. (Anderson & Zuercher, 2001: 32, italics added)

The speaker is Brent Zuercher; the context is a series of letters written by him and his friend David Anderson to each other.[10] Anderson is a Protestant pastor and Zuercher, a professional CPA. Both are Christian; Anderson is black, Zuercher is white. In this particular chapter of their book, they are exploring black and white anger. What is remarkable about this passage is that it offers at least one reason why white men may see an apology from black men and people as just: *black behavior is not Christian, it is not rational, it is not justified.* Moreover, this view of collective black behavior as unjustified offers a partial context for understanding the place of relational justice in the pursuit of racial reconciliation, the focus of Part Three of this book. In the following passage, Brent Zuercher draws attention to the fact that any consideration of racial pain and atonement must consider the emotional and relational underpinnings of American society:

> For the first time I realized that I have been harboring anger in my heart. Anger that has gone unresolved long enough that it has grown into resentment, a resentment that is racially based, a resentment against blacks collectively, but not against blacks individually. I do not resent you, my friend, nor do I resent the accounting clerk in my office nor the friend I had in college from the inner city of Indiana nor do I resent the stranger I pass on the street. This leads me to believe that my frustration, anger, and resentment are founded on something other than my being a racist. I would expect a racist to dislike both the individual and the individual's racial group. I believe that my feelings are toward the responses and actions of a group of people rather than toward the genetics (i.e., being black) of the group...
>
> I do not think I fully understand yet the depth of my resentful feelings but I anticipate that as we correspond, the focal points will become obvious. There is one thing I am not so sure I know how to do, though—*how to stop being angry*. (Anderson & Zuercher, 2001: 34–35, italics added)

Of the many questions that might be asked of Brent Zuercher, one stands out: how did racial anger and resentment come to own a decent man in ways he feels unsure how to remove? Whatever the answers one might get, the emotions he expresses are both painful and the seeds for "atonement" directed outward. In this case, the black leaders who have failed to help blacks "get over it"—and the blacks who "hate whites"—are the basis for feeling aggrieved and in need of "atonement."

Now, it should be noted that Mr. Zuercher does experience a shift in his understanding of race matters in the course of the exchange of letters with his friend David Anderson. But many, many racially conflicted whites do not necessarily have a Christian or similar moral commitment to understand and reconcile race matters as Brent Zuercher. In fact, according to John Hatch (2009b: 489), quite the contrary predominates the average white person's racial imaginings:

> The rhetoric of contemporary racial injustice strikes many whites as disingenuous or contradicts what they feel to be common sense. As members of the majority culture in one of the world's most individualistic and future-oriented societies... white Americans believe almost religiously in the individual's power to transcend the

> constraints of both the group and the past. Add to the deflective nature of cultural perception the defensive character produced by the social psychology of whiteness, especially in the post–civil rights era, ..."discrimination" and "reverse racism," even as they unwittingly enjoy a legacy of white privilege....

Hatch is describing the implicit significance of emerging white race discourse research: at both individual and institutional levels, there has been a decisive turn away from effects of guilt, shame, sorrow, and repentance for "alleged" sins against the Other. Disbelief that the legacy of "white privilege" ought to be interrogated, moreover, increasingly fuels America's "atonement."[11]

I first used the expression America's "atonement" more broadly to describe the country's efforts to recover from the deep psychological and spiritual pain associated with the social upheaval and crises of the 1960s. Some people felt pain because we "lost" the Vietnam War. Others felt it because America fought the war, and I recall those men who expressed pain because they had been too young to participate in it. Many also felt pain because of the civil rights and black power movements, the peace and women's movements, the gay rights movement, and other social justice activism. The pain was diffuse within the society, and did not focus on any one issue or event. Yet, a peculiar quality characterized much of this societal pain. It seemed to entail more than a personal or group grievance with the social chaos and change of the moment. It seemed to have an otherworldly, theistic quality. Nowhere, perhaps, was this quality any more evident than in the following passage:

> Two of the things I believe the Seventies will NOT bring are (a) Black or Brown or Yellow Power schools supported by public tax money but run by various minority groups and (b) massed compulsory busing of children to achieve an artificial racial distribution within a given geographical area. Speaking both as an educator and as an individual, I've been waiting impatiently for the Seventies to get here. Alongside the Sick Sixties, almost any decade in history would look like Paradise Regained (Rafferty, 1970: xiii).

These lines concluded a 1970 book by Max Rafferty on education in America. At that time, Rafferty was a well-known conservative education leader in California, having served as state superintendent of education. As the passage indicates, he was both pained and angered by the social justice movements of the 1960s, especially multicultural education. Multiculturalism is a perspective, policy, and set of practices that forefront diverse cultural values and backgrounds. With roots in the liberation schools of the 1960s, multiculturalism has evolved to represent a perceived assault on dominant, Anglo-American culture. Ironically, Rafferty anticipated the arrival of diversity; and he imagined, moreover, even greater loss and pain if "Black or Brown or Yellow Power schools" gained prominence in American society. But it is his identification of these precursors of multiculturalism as an evil to be eliminated that constitutes the rationale for "atonement."

As if in response to the atonement so profoundly longed for by Max Rafferty, there have been widespread and consequential shifts amounting to a racial recovery (Gresson, 1995) and viewed by some as an updated return to white supremacy sentiments (Ikard, 2013). Some have seen what I call "white pain" as a reason for the rise of both recovery rhetoric and atonement activity (Hatch, 2006a, b); there is some truth to this reading of my meaning. However, I actually perceive "white pain" itself to be a socially constructed emotion that finds itself, so to speak, as individual whites connect with the already circulating rhetorics and recovery projects. White pain, like all racialized pain, is bound up in *spoilage*. That is, it comes about within social situations and relationships where bad things happen because of how people are defined and valued by each other. In and of itself, white pain is nothing more or less than the emotional underside of a "flawed" social identity. But herein lies the rub, or the problem: it's not that easy, nor desirable, to cast off these identities. Moreover, an identity that has been "called out," or publicly decried may yield a bitter consequence: identity spoilage that invades all who are touched by racialization. This consequence can be seen as emerging from sixties-era activism.

The radical sixties "blamed" whites collectively for much social injustice. One consequence was lost: both the moral and material power to "call a spade a spade." While younger generations may not feel this dual loss as keenly as their parents' generation, they do share in the inheritance: spoiled identity. Hence, the laments of the young who seek to proudly affirm their white identities but perceive a looming otherness waiting to name any suspect gesture "racist." This is probably why the internet has become a feeding ground for so many diverse expressions of racial injustice toward whites, perpetrated by the "other." For example, James S. Robbins (2013) recently collected and posted online pictures and stories of "black on white murder," arguing that these "prove" the one-sided racial violence of blacks toward whites. Perspectives like Robbins's undergird an alternative understanding of the proper nature of atonement: *those who blame whites, particularly white men, for the ills befalling blacks, women, and other oppressed groups, should atone. Moreover, the entire nation/culture should atone.*

Max Rafferty's "anti-affirmative action" discourse in 1970 also illustrates the early genesis of the atonement/recovery activity later associated with

Reaganism and the religious right. Rafferty's self-professed alienation from the social activism of the 1960s reveals an *existential moment*, a moment of personally, directly felt threat. It also reminds us that something very personal and subjective was at stake for millions of Americans challenged by the radical possibilities of the movements characterizing the 1960s. Max Rafferty's passionate outpouring is also evidence that the pain found in so many recent—Tea Party—representations of the social changes of the 1960s did not spring forth from nothing. Still, few would readily relate Rafferty's pain to recent discussions of multiculturalism, affirmative action, political correctness, and white male victims. Nor are we likely to see how the social activism of the 1960s later exposed millions of white youth, particularly those in multicultural learning situations, to a special kind of vulnerability: a forced encounter with minorities' often painful images of whites in relation to themselves and their past and present relations. But Rafferty's comments are related to these youth in both prophetic and pedagogical ways because of the forced vulnerability many feel. This vulnerability can be seen in these words written by one white male in my course on minority education in the United States: "Every Monday and Wednesday, I come in here to learn about what an asshole I have been throughout history."

This statement might be read as idiosyncratic, and it might be attributed to the failures of a specific teacher or the flaws of a given student. But the 1990s discussions about affirmative action and multiculturalism (Gresson, 1995; Kincheloe & Steinberg, 1997) revealed the link between individual expressions of racial pain and the social action of the 1960s and 1970s. The radical 1960s introduced a degree of shared vulnerability. It was no longer a given that whites were "right" and blacks had to "get back"; women were not automatically relegated to "second-class" status; gays and lesbians achieved a space for the open expression of their humanity and right to "come out of the closet"; and so on. True, blacks, women, gays, and others remained vulnerable to the power of those different from them, but now those previously privileged to assume that their views, values, and positions were "natural," "right," and "just" shared this vulnerability. Sometimes blacks, women, and gays even got public support for their experiences, visions, and demands. Further, my student's response revealed, in part, the pain many whites feel when forced to view as racism their identification as white. Recall the words of the young blogger introduced earlier who lamented: "If we marched for our race and rights…you would call us racist" (Yahoo Answers, 2011).

This sense of vulnerability is not new, but it is renewing. Throughout history there have been periods when the myth of white togetherness and race-wise well-being has been strained; at such times whites, notably those at the bottom, today's "Main Streeters," are in need of sympathy. And they receive it, if only in fiction—novels, movies, and memoirs (Charles, 2013; Mailer, 1968). In many ways, white victim discourse is an expression of this sympathetic impulse turned inward. But there is a new, emerging affect, suffused with self-sympathy, but stridently, aggressively combative.

White Privilege and "Atonement": "I apologize...not!"

The assertion of white identity and pride denied through accusations of racism adds an ominous potency to Max Rafferty's pain in 1970. It is particularly telling that Rafferty envisioned the post–Civil Rights era would be "Paradise Regained." "Paradise Regained" is the title of a 17th-century epic poem by John Milton, in which he chronicled the spiritual temptations or challenges encountered by Jesus Christ. It was a sequel to his earlier work, "Paradise Lost." As has been noted by scholars, "Paradise Regained" deals with reversals. Milton sought to reverse the "loss" of Paradise. To do this, he charted the path of recovery through *atonement*, a process involving sacrifice, loss, and suffering.

Max Rafferty's book, like Milton's poem, pursued a mission of reversal and recovery. But pain precedes atonement. Pain is grounded in *loss*. Rafferty placed loss with the rise of multicultural education. By naming multiculturalism as an evil to be eliminated, Rafferty offered a clue to the required recovery and the precise *character of atonement*, as he perceived it must be in order to regain paradise lost. The atonement he envisions is the turning away from affirmative action, multiculturalism, and "politically correct" practices. Atonement thus viewed is less about self-reflection, humility, and self-transformation than a return to some idyllic past. This past is achieved through what Harold Isaacs (1975) called "retribalization." A dominating feature of this retribalizing is taking the side of the in-group over all others, right or wrong. This kind of atoning behavior may have a decidedly violent or aggressive quality. But more centrally, it entails a reframing—implicit in "atonement"—of who is the true victim. For example, *The Right Stuff* (TRS) blogger Michael Enoch (2014) reframes and instructs on the idea of "white privilege":

> The seemingly ubiquitous meme of "White Privilege" has been a favorite topic of TRS since we began. It has been explored at length on this site by myself and other authors and tackled from several different angles and we've had a lot of fun with

it. I have suggested in previous writings that one sure way to fluster Social Justice Warriors, Tumblristas and "more progressive than thou" lefties in the course of argument is to accept their "white privilege" narrative without guilt or shame and challenge them to make their next rhetorical point. They can't, because the narrative relies on whitey balking at the concept and arguing against it out of a desire to cleanse himself of the existential guilt implied by the accusation of privilege. I stand by this as an effective argumentative technique that sabotages the progressive narrative and could potentially lead to some valuable reflection both on the part of the leftist as well as their intended white victim.

There is probably no way to accurately estimate what percentage of the population in America, or elsewhere sees itself as "victim" (although 2012 presidential candidate Mitt Romney's now famous reference to the 47% might be read as attempting precisely this). What is evident, however, is the increasing presence of the image of the "white victim" of social justice initiatives that seem intent upon dismantling "white privilege." Perhaps more than the dramatic and blatant reversals of affirmative action practices in state and national legislatures, this rhetoric of white racial victimage and recovery has dominated the past decade of race discourse. Moreover, this aspect of white race discourse has a decided atonement quality—but with a twist. Another *The Right Stuff* blogger, Alexander McNabb (February 2014), reacting to an article by a black female on the *BlackGirlDangerous* blog site (McKenzie, 2014), offers an "addendum" to fellow blogger Michael Enoch in this way:

> This ...[article] features the new phenomenon of seeing a normal state of affairs as privilege. If you don't need a wheelchair, apparently you are privileged. (I was once in a wheel chair, does this mean I get Oppression Points to cash in?) She claims that if an event does not cater to disabled people, you shouldn't go no matter what, because "not being a dick" is super hard and stuff but you gotta make the sacrifice. Once again, why should I push back against my "privilege" to walk on two feet? Is this some kind of self-flagellation that I must perform to atone for my sins? What the fuck am I getting out of this shit?

Several emergent and highly emotional themes are evident in this response: the references to sacrifice and self-flagellation are especially notable. They point to the observation made by Susanne Langer in the opening epigraph: achieving *the ethnic balance* is hard work. Social justice, as a pursuit and process, entails achieving precisely this balance.

Yet, it is precisely because of the sacrificial dimension attending social justice initiatives that some recognize atonement as a two-sided, highly negotiable matter. Accordingly, the above blogger has uttered the increasingly strident if not novel idea: "White privilege *is* normal!" Implicitly, "abnormality" is the "balls" to ask the white man to surrender anything to anybody for any reason. The "abnormal" is the surrendering of power, *however attained and retained*. It is, I believe, precisely this *affective* aspect of contemporary white race discourse that is increasingly leading to the emphasis on white anger and aggression, especially, but not solely, in the social network world.[12]

The rhetorical power of "white privilege is okay" notwithstanding, to use it requires a degree of self-deception. This is so because "the system is rigged against the average person" is a populist stance that clashes with "privilege is okay" reasoning. To promote privilege is, implicitly, to not only recognize but also affirm a corrupt system, and the partisan, unfair arrangements and practices that prevent the average person from "lifting oneself up by his bootstraps." Self-deception involves, in part, lying to oneself in order to be able to lie to another (Smith, 2004). The topic or issue of "white privilege" has traditionally suffered from this very dialectic. But as seen in the preceding passages from the blogger sphere, there are those who have sidestepped this latent contradiction by simply saying, "I do not apologize—like it or lump it." The precise sentiment and dynamic I am calling attention to at the intersection of atonement and white victimhood is seen in a billboard (Fig. 1) I saw in the Harrisburg, Pennsylvania, area in the early 1990s.

Fig. 1. Billboard near Harrisburg, Pennsylvania, circa 1990.

This particular billboard was apparently the reply to the public response to an earlier billboard that depicted these two male morning-radio talk-show hosts with a young blonde female sandwiched between them in a head-and-shoulder shot that over-exposed her breasts. I recall, upon seeing the earlier billboard, my own "puritanical" shock. I was therefore not the least surprised to see the billboard's relatively short lifespan. A short time after its removal, the billboard shown in Figure 1 appeared.

One remarkable message embedded in this artifact is the implicit fusion of the talk-show hosts' view of their actions with both innocence *and* defiance.[13] They are signaling a rejection of the then-emerging "politically correct" discourse of the period on sexism (Kilbourne, 2000). They are also performing this rejection through a seizing of traditional imagery of sacredness and innocence. This is a rhetorical move that has been increasingly associated with certain reactionary political positions around a number of seemingly discriminatory, oppressive policies: women's health rights, minority voting rights, gay and lesbian marital rights, etc. From this view, it might be argued that this billboard stands as a metaphor and prescient portrait of the "angry white male" (Kimmel, 2013).

In *Manliness and Civilization*, Gail Bederman (1995: 11) argues, "Manhood is an ideological construct which is constantly being made." From this view, the right of these talk-show hosts to portray themselves between a young buxom female in only a bra was more than a matter of good press: it said something to their listeners about the kind of men these radio stars were attempting to self-represent. To be challenged, therefore, was about more than differing political, social, or cultural tastes. It was about the "presentation of self" (Goffman, 1959) in the moment. The so-called masculinity crisis, in this view, is ongoing; each man is also moment-to-moment invited, even forced, to step forward and declare *what kind of man he is*. Of course, this does not mean that men get no time "off stage." But this perspective does offer a nuanced dimension to one's understanding of the confrontations that daily occur among men in public spaces. And it is within this broader context that contemporary manhood, notably "the angry white male," performs.

Scholars like Michael Kimmel (2013) feel that only a small but highly vocal minority actually evolves into the "angry white male"—characterized by "aggrieved entitlement." Elaborating on Willard Gaylin's (1984: 37) contention that a "smoldering rage" overcomes those who feel they have lost what was theirs, Kimmel says "It's misdirecting that anger to others that is the central dynamic of America's angry white men" (2013: 25). But Southern studies scholar Angie Maxwell (2014) offers a more sober assessment of the condition Kimmel documents. In *The Indicted South*, she writes:

> The continual construction of southern white identity, particularly the maintenance of white cultural supremacy and conservative political domination, required strict allegiance to self-promotional narratives of superiority. Such propaganda sensitized many white southerners to public criticism of their home region, criticism that became a staple of media rhetoric in the modern era and that unleashed a regional defensiveness capable of transforming moderate communities into reactionary forces.

Applying the psychological studies of Alfred Alder to white behavior in the South, she maintains that a powerful, even self-defeating inferiority complex affects Southern whites, and possibly whites beyond the South.[14] The South's will to racial superiority, Maxwell argues, resulted from the humiliation of the loss of the Civil War in conjunction with the poverty visited on the South writ large. In short, being so inferior made them claim superiority and set up affairs accordingly, including Klan violence and Jim Crow laws. Maxwell's focus on class orients us to the economic underpinnings of slavery and Southern political economics. Likewise, Michael Kimmel (2013: 25) writes:

> Ultimately, I argue that understanding white men's anger requires a focus on *class*—the ironic parallel that finds the United States more racially and gender equal than ever before in our history and more unequal in terms of class than at least the Gilded Age, if not ever. The tensions and anxieties produced by such dramatic increases in class inequality lead many to look at those who appear to have gained, while "we"—the white middle and working classes—have most assuredly been losing. While race and gender are certainly the defining features of today's angry American, it is the growing chasm between rich and poor that is the engine of that rage.

Kimmel echoes those who are increasingly treating economic inequality—the "shrinking" middle class and the growing income disparity—as critical national and international security crises.[15] Of course, there is a standard counter-rhetoric proffered to challenge these voices: "you're fermenting class warfare!"

But the pain of class difference cannot be effectively silenced by rhetoric. This is especially true for contemporary race relations. In an essay on racial hurt and recovery activism, Joe Kincheloe wrote: "The pain of the perception of a new psychological disprivilege within an old privilege gnaws at contemporary white people.... The new disprivilege emerges from the increasingly valued concept of difference and Whites' lack of it" (1999: 11, 15). Kincheloe illumines a pivotal idea: whites' lack of a sense of difference in an increasingly more differentiated world. In a related context, a growing number of critical scholars have seen a disproportionate impact of this affective condition on the lives of the marginalized, especially blacks. In *Blinded by the Whites: Why Race Still Matters in 21st-Century America*, David Ikard (2013: 8–9) implicitly links this "aggrieved entitlement" to the material condition of blacks:

> The stubborn persistence of economic inequality between blacks and whites, racial profiling among the police, the attendant prison industrial complex, zero-tolerance laws and policies in schools (and beyond) that disproportionately target black and brown folks, racial health disparities, and the like demonstrate what we are witnessing as this moment is not so much a radical shift in racial thinking but rather an updated version of white supremacist ideology.

An updated version of white supremacist ideology. To be sure, it is important to recognize and challenge specific policies and practices that result in social injustice. Often we don't understand difference as a right to be, a press/ pursuit of self-interests, dreams, and aspirations. The fear of being stereotyped— made the same, rigidified into sameness, non-different—underpins much white male pain and the push toward "white anger" and the recovery of "white pride" and "white identity" (Kimmel, 2013; Taylor, 2011). Chapters 3 through 5 illustrate aspects of this self-healing through the demonization of affirmative action, multiculturalism, and other ideologies and initiatives aimed at redressing an historical oppressiveness. But there are other understandings and expressions of healing. These, too, have a pedagogical message and facilitate an alternative relatedness. In Chapters 6 and 7 these alternative visions of healing are examined. Together, these chapters engage the notion of "white pain" and its recovery activism.

White Pain and Recovery

In Chapter 4, I examine multiculturalism from its position as a challenge to inherited understandings of whites and nonwhites and their respective places as students, achievers, and "inheritors of the earth." White pain is the organizing metaphor for this discussion. White males especially share this pain. I argue that much of the social, cultural, and political action of the past three decades has been directed at challenging the images of the white male as essentially evil. White men have recognized how the ideology and cultural practices privileging them have had a boomerang effect, resulting in their representation in the popular imagination as all-powerful and all-responsible for society's ills. Because of the vast power white men wield, comparatively, it has been difficult to give much credence to individual white male voices disavowing responsibility for various social oppressions. Subjectively, individual white males are not responsible for the structure of society, yet individually and collectively white males participate in the construction of our racial, sexual structure. This represents a paradox for a democratic society.

In *White Men, Women and Minorities in the Changing Work Force* (1997), Anthony Ipsaro reminds us that white men are as diverse and heterogeneous as women and minorities, and accordingly, they constitute multiple identities and infinite possibilities. A democratic society must recognize and nurture this fact. Still, white society has so effectively constructed the world around notions of white and "other" that most of us routinely accept as real these categories and the effects attributed to them. The "essentializing" of individuals and groups is in error and counterproductive for a democratic program of social change. But how do those who have been pre-eminent "essentializers" of "others" renegotiate their own humanity when this has been "stereotyped" into an "essence"? This renegotiation is what I have elsewhere described as the "recovery project" (Gresson, 1995). Here I refer to it as atonement activity to emphasize its "sacred" dimension.

It will be helpful to set the context for our analysis. In particular, what elements promote atonement activity? Given the preceding discussion, at least two conditions appear to enable recovery work: (1) a collection of reactionary images, and (2) media saturation of these images within an interpretive frame or context that concretizes the recovery ideology.

Reactionary Images

Once, in a classroom exchange, a white female student identified affirmative action on behalf of women and minorities as the basis for the greater number of suicides among white males compared with black females. Since the early 1970s, reactionary images have increasingly dominated the popular representation of race, gender, and class, as illustrated in the behavior of the young white female student defending the image of the besieged and betrayed white male. Her imagination had been so thoroughly dulled with respect to certain social justice matters that she was unable to entertain alternative visions and understandings of white male suicide. Furthermore, by resisting the idea of women and minorities as victims, she was unwittingly reaffirming the status quo. To be sure, women—including this woman—are not mere pawns; it has been repeatedly shown that such behavior has a conscious, self-interest motive (Blee, 1991; Ipsaro, 1997). Thus it has become preferable to view such incidents in terms of hegemonic dynamics: the collusion or confluence of individual and collective interests. Nonetheless, with or without women, privileged white men take measures to protect their own interests. According to Anthony Ipsaro, government initiatives on behalf of women and minorities have motivated this self-interested backlash:

> Faced with this confusion and overt onslaught by women and minorities, most White males have gone underground. White men use their present positions of power to defend themselves and covertly subvert women and minorities out of key meetings and informal discussions, and avoid mentoring them. Without this powerful network, many women and minorities fail to move into upper management. If they do move into managerial positions, women and minorities feel isolated, begin to make poor decisions, and move toward failure. (1997: 2)

Ipsaro reminds us of the obvious: white men, as humans, are likely to act to protect their interests, right or wrong. Moreover, since society, including the workplace, requires the sharing of information and knowledge for success, isolation or non-inclusion of white males in the diversity discourse leads to minority and female failure in organizations. But to succeed, these efforts to protect their real and symbolic power require the complicity of others. Enter the black male.

Recently, I participated in an exchange familiar to my clinical practice: a young black male preteen, diagnosed by the system as "oppositional," was venting: "I am not perfect...nobody is perfect...I am not a stereotype..." For his schoolteachers and officials, he *is*, unfortunately, precisely that: an oppositional black male youth—a stereotype. And he knows it, partly because his parents and I spend time reminding him that he must be extra careful—he cannot get away with what white boys do; and once he is labeled, he cannot easily recover from it. Of course, he knows this is true. I believe that is part of his "oppositional" problem: by being "oppositional" he both attempts to affirm subjectivity and to reject labeling. This is, unfortunately a flawed strategy because the behavior lacks institutional or cultural support (power).

The absence of this power, moreover, has contributed to construction of *the black male as the reactionary image par excellence*. When apprehending, or viewing, the black male, there is a range of long-standing images that may be called forth, "a coherent and meaningful set of metaphors, familiar words, and emotionally laden expressions" (Herf, 1987: 1). We need only recall the words of Zuercher, cited earlier in this introduction: "I believe that my feelings are toward the responses and actions of a group of people rather than toward the genetics (i.e., being black) of the group...."

"The responses and actions of a group of people" become the basis for a return to the past, and a recovery of past attitudes toward what must be done to the black body, what pain must be inflicted upon black (male) bodies in the name of an "existential crisis" (King, 2008). This was seen in the reactionary imagery called forth in the 2013 trial of George Zimmerman for killing Trayvon Martin, and, even more recently, in the 2014 trial of Michael Dunn for killing Jordan Davis. Zimmerman's lawyer apparently persuaded the nearly all-white female jury that Trayvon Martin was the aggressor, the "bad actor," and Zimmerman, a mere victim, guilty of nothing and undeserving of false accusations by those who would suggest race was relevant to anything. In Michael Dunn's trial, a similar portrayal of the young black male as the fearful thug was employed; and Dunn noted that even though he was the "victor," he was still the "victim."

These self-portrayals are not idiosyncratic or inconsequential, as evidenced by the acquittals but even more by the range of supportive arguments offered by various members of the public. Together, these types of incidents lend power to the observation made by Michele Fine (1997: 62): "Not Republicans, not global capitalists, not elites. African American men... are discursively imported to buffer the pain, protest the loss, and still secure the artificial privilege of whiteness."

The image conveyed by Fine's observation is scary—certainly for black men. But Debra Walker King (2008) recognizes a tremendously damning process in this discursive work of protecting whites from pain, loss, and insecurity. She calls it *blackpain*, to represent the ways images and representations of blacks in pain are used to insulate whites both from their own existential vulnerability to pain and participation in the creation of pain for blacks. Like *blackpain*, America's "atonement" includes the range of cultural activities that freed the killers of these black male youth and helps create the increasingly narrow space for demanding social justice in the face of such misdeeds.

To this point, recent work on white women's roles in the creation and support of "whiteness" (Blee, 1991; Fiske, 1994; Frankenberg, 1993) reminds us that very emotional and relational (parent, child, lover/mate, friend) forces influence the racial, class, and related societal decisions made by white women. Though various racial and ethnic stereotypes also participate in the reproduction of white male cultural dominance, I forefront one that has ancient roots. I call this stereotype the "Pietà Embrace" because it recalls Michelangelo's

"Pietà" (Mary and the crucified Christ), sculptured around 1500 C.E. The pose—a grieving female holding a fallen white male—is well known. As I argue in Chapter 5, the Pietà Embrace is a central feature of the Women's Vietnam Memorial, marking the reactionary sociopolitical climate of the 1980s and 1990s. The media's role in promoting a particular understanding of the memorial points to their larger participation in the atonement process, and in the manipulation of gendered images in non-liberatory ways (Kilbourne, 2000).

Media Saturation and Meaning Mediation

Few have to be reminded of the media's strong influence on our culture: from the traditional conversations regarding media and violence (Fiske, 1994) to recent self-examination by the media in the wake of the yearlong coverage of President Bill Clinton and Monica Lewinsky. John Fiske reminds us, for example, how the media figured in the widely viewed O. J. Simpson trial and Rodney King beating:

> The media do not just report and circulate knowledge; they are involved in its production. *Time* and *Newsweek* were actively involved in producing a particular truth of O.J. by using his mug shot for their covers, and *Time*'s blackening italicized it: the computer enhancement inclined the truth in the direction of white racism. In the same way, the computer enhancement of the video of Rodney King's beating was used by the defense to tilt its "truth" in the same direction. *The National Enquirer* published a computer- produced "photograph" of O.J. in the Bronco pointing a gun at his head and speaking into his car phone, an image that only a computer could produce, for no camera could have been present to take it. Yet this was not a "lie," but a mediatruth. (1994: xxiii)

The media "mediate" messages and meanings. The ways in which white males are represented and understood by the public at large are greatly influenced by the media. A society committed to "atoning" for highlighting white male privilege through various affirmative actions must find ways of balancing the tensions thus created. This is achievable only with the assistance of media that are prepared to favor certain ideologies that aid this process. As the "embedded media" in the Iraqi War illustrate, certain kinds of information receive greater representation: that which legitimizes the presumed imminent war. The vitally critical racial underside of this recovery is seen even with respect to the Iraq War: years ago I watched a human-interest segment on television, focusing on the only African American fighter pilot—in 2003 nonetheless—stationed at a Virginia Air Force base. The reporter promised to keep the audience abreast of the airman and his family during the ensuing conflict. Fusing the black male body to the battle—this time, a willing patriot in the Bush/Chaney war—deflected our collective attention from a war that later generations would declare not worth the loss of life and material resources.

Saturation of newspapers, radio, and television with certain images is the second element promoting atonement. As above, it can even work a largely devalued black male persona into a "worthy"—read "patriotic"—American. But the power of the media to contribute to a much more pervasive and negative representation of the black male cannot be overstated. Nor can the global reach of its mediating powers. In particular, the power of the media to chain this image of "minority evil" to "white innocence and civilization" was depicted in a recent documentary featuring Bishop Desmond Tutu and the African American historian John Hope Franklin.[16] In this video, young people from Africa, Europe, and the United States met in Senegal for a week of racial discussions and healing. One observation made in the documentary was that all the youth from Africa and Europe—both white and black—shared one dominant image of racial evil: the *young* black male.

The "atoning" character of America's "atonement" is conceived and constituted around, in part, the ongoing portrayal of the black male as an ever-fearful presence. The media do not necessarily construct the black male's image of himself, but they do play a pivotal role in circulating and interpreting preferred racial images. Nor is the atonement motive absent from the media when focusing on other subjects. In Chapter 5, white females are shown to be a primary mediated agent during the Yellow Ribbon movements of 1979 and 1991. But the media are not only active in creating; they are also created, in part, by the sociohistorical moment and the society within which they operate. Thus, there is a certain peculiarity and pathos to the media's apparent evolution into a continua of "liberal" (MSNBC), "conservative" (FOX), "in between"(CNN), "extreme" (Limbaugh et al.), and "alternative" (everybody else, especially the blogs).

Conclusion: Racial Pain and the "Postracial"

So to be white, through its invisibility, affords a certain privacy and privilege surrounding identity, and yet relinquishing that privacy does not necessarily result in disruption of the privilege but rather a claiming of existential status.

– Wendy Ryden and Ian Marshall (2012: 26)

It has been said that we are living in a "postracial" America. At least one view of this stance, if true, would suggest that "racial pain" is less significant today than in previous times. A full consideration of the postracial in contemporary race relations is beyond the scope of this book, although I take it up in a forthcoming volume. Still, it must be stated why a renewed look at racial pain is merited in the present so-called postmodern era. Regarding the postracial, Jonathan Rossing (2014: 16–17) has observed: "National narratives fail to confront honestly the unrealized promises of freedom and justice. Postracial attitudes reject racial truths and obscure the persistence of racial hierarchies and privilege in favor of the belief that race no longer matters ...."

What Rossing correctly identifies as the flaw of national race narratives—dishonesty—is a quality of human nature: the ambivalent, ongoing flight from despair over the continuing struggle against "sin" in a world that has largely jettisoned the notion of sin.[17] In their important rhetorical study of whiteness, Wendy Ryden and Ian Marshall (2012) document a subjectively experienced and affirmed outcome of this "dishonesty": the individual white insisting upon an identity rooted in the immediacy of the moment, the self unencumbered by allusions to the privilege that undergirds its racialized dance of agency. It is, existentially, in the moment of "being recognized" and labeled—hence, stereotyped—that pain is forced upon the agent-in-waiting. It is then that one either says, "I apologize…what next" or "I apologize …not!" This is the *dialectic of place*. It is, in part, because of this tension-filled contradiction that several prominent speakers have come forth affirming the right to reaffirm the righteousness of "racial privilege" as an aspect of "white identity." Thus, for instance, in the 1990s (and again in 2012, albeit from a different strategic position),[18] Charles Murray wrote:

> A large number of well-meaning whites fear that they are closet racists, and this book [*The Bell Curve*] tells them that they are not. It's going to make them feel better about things they already think, but do not know how to say.
>
> (Cited in Giroux, 1995: 342)

This dialectic of place (Rajendran, Walker, & Parnell, 2013) is the source of ongoing racial pain. It is precisely racial pain and its attendant effects—self-deception, complicity, existential agitation—that must be recognized as flying in the face of an already arrived "post society."[19] Latina blogger Rosana Cruz (2014) frames the situated contradiction of and challenge for the present "post society" in this way:

It's true, 2013 was a painful year in racial justice. Besides the George Zimmerman verdict, Paula Deen and Twerkgate, we witnessed numerous shootings of young people of color, including Renisha McBride in Michigan, Marshall Coulter in New Orleans and Israel Hernandez in Miami. My people, Cuban immigrants in Miami, have a saying that is particularly apt at this moment, *lo bueno de esto es lo malo que se seta poniendo*—which loosely translates to, "the good thing about this is how bad it is getting." Fewer people can ignore or deny the race problem in this country. With instant media glued to the palm of our hands, many of us are unable to turn away from the wounds in our communities. In 2013, many of us learned or were reminded, racism actually kills.

So what could my eternally optimistic Cuban outlook be? My own racial justice wish for 2014 is that we (re) turn to the spiritual and cultural resources all around us and use them to find solace and speak truth, to build community and understanding. I hope we dig into books, make meals together, listen to each other's voices lifted in song.

This writer offers a hopeful perspective on the "postracial" challenge. But there are other voices that articulate the "postracial"—from within "white pain"—in a significantly different way. In August 2014, for instance, Mississippi Congressman Mo Brooks accused the Democrats of waging a "war on whites" and implicitly undercutting his "postracial" vision in this way:

This [the immigration debate] is a part of the war on whites that's being launched by the Democratic Party. And the way in which they're launching this war is by claiming that whites hate everybody else. It's a part of the strategy that Barack Obama implemented in 2008, continued in 2012, where he divides us all on race, on sex, greed, envy, class warfare, all those kinds of things. Well that's not true. Okay?

And if you look at the polling data, every demographic group in America agrees with the rule of law, enforcing and securing our borders. And every one of them understands that illegal immigration hurts every single demographic group. It doesn't make a difference if you're a white American, a black American, Hispanic American, an Asian American or if you're a woman or a man. Every single demographic group is hurt by falling wages and lost jobs.

And so the Democrats, they have to demagogue on this and try and turn it into a racial issue, which is an emotional issue, rather than a thoughtful issue. If it becomes a thoughtful issue, then we win and we win big. And they lose and they lose big. And they understand that and as they get more desperate, they are going to argue race and things like that to a much heightened emotional state.... (Capehart, 2014)

The above thoughts were shared with conservative talk-show host Laura Ingraham and focused on the immigration issue and Republicans. The dialectic between Representative Brooks's and Ms. Cruz's take on the "postracial" is crucial: each offers a radically different view of what people are seeing and experiencing in contemporary race relations. Together, these contrasting perspectives frame the tensions taken up in this new edition of *America's Atonement*. Specifically, in the following chapters I consider several different themes—racial pain, whiteness, affirmative action, multiculturalism, mourning, and healing. These concepts pertain to the human desire for and press toward the achievement of social justice for everyone in the face of a persisting human resistance to see and accept the human condition as we experience it in day-to-day struggles for survival and perfection. I hope that one outcome of this exercise will be a clearer sense of the scope of the work that remains to be done, whatever the truth of the notion of a "postracial" America. I begin with a selective overview of the contemporary social context within which racial identity and racial pain are intertwined.

· 2 ·

RACIAL PAIN IN THE 21ST CENTURY

Spoiled Identities and Traumatized Relations

My answer is not right or wrong. It's your opinion [that's wrong].

– Black woman, March 15, 2002

Many [who write pain memoirs] …suggest … that the primary problem they face is … how to make readers receptive to stories of pain. Their question is not how to find words for pain, but rather, who will listen and what will they hear?

– Ann Jurecic (2012: 44)

Prologue

Pain Begets Pain When Identity Is Threatened

In the epilogue to the first edition of *America's Atonement*, I began with a recollection:

> Last Friday night I stopped in a neighborhood bar to have a drink and unwind with the fellows—middle-aged, middle-class black men. As is often the case, the conversation turned to racism. One man, a retired city policeman, was venting his rage at

white America. Another, a senior administrator at an urban high school, was chiding his lifelong friend because he knew this man was generally an even-tempered, solid citizen. However, another brother was very upset with the conversation's seemingly anti-American tone. Eventually, the battle came to that point familiar to many African Americans when we're challenged with the question: Are you an American or an African?

Of course, this generally leads to an affirmation: we love America, racism notwithstanding. When that night's "antagonist"—for in truth, we all have found ourselves in the role of "revolutionary African warrior"— proceeded to call us "Uncle Toms," the younger brother, a Vietnam veteran with a strong military-patriotic persona, left the group and approached a woman selecting songs at the nearby jukebox. He asked her how she felt about September 11 and our soldiers in Afghanistan. She took his question well, even though he had intruded into her own entertainment and group space (she had two other black women waiting for her at the bar). She answered, "I feel something in my heart for the people who were killed; I hurt for them and their families. But I wouldn't want my children over there. I don't think we should be over there."

To this response, with strong emotion and self-righteousness, the brother-soldier declared her unpatriotic and her answer as "wrong." Now showing her own emotion, she replied with the words opening this chapter.

I relate this little drama because it helps illustrate just how complex and nuanced are the elements constituting "cultural pain" and its near relative, "racial" pain. In particular, these two people indicate the vast gulf that may separate people, even those of the same race, class, and sociopolitical circumstances. Furthermore, the story illustrates how personal identity and subjective perspective are tied up with what we say about the world and how we choose to comport ourselves in it. Most of all, we see how a threatened identity can lead people to talk past each other and to cause pain in the process.

This passage is an excellent starting point for chapter 2. It powerfully illustrates the complicated character of racial pain and traumatized relations.[20] Its implications seem even more urgent to discuss today than they were a decade ago because of a recent experience I had. In the winter of 2013, my colleague and friend Derrick Alridge invited me to the University of Virginia to speak before his class on multiculturalism and social justice. He and co-instructor Carol Anne Spreen were using *America's Atonement* in their survey course, attended by some 170 students from across the campus. In preparation for my visit, students had been invited to submit questions that I might respond to. One of the most surprising, if not recurring, of these was, "Do African Americans and other minorities have 'racial pain'"?

Initially, I thought this question might have been raised because of the book's focus on "white pain" and a somewhat understated consideration of other forms of racial pain. But later, another possibility occurred to me: black pain is not perceived to be as real as white pain. Researchers have recently offered just such an explanation for what they call a "racial empathy gap" that has been found among lay people and professionals, and even among some blacks.[21] Insensitivity to others' pain, however, is broader than the matter of racial empathy. As Ann Jurecic has observed, pain is a difficult topic for people to relate to and discuss in our society. People do not readily know how to talk about pain; they often suppress awareness of it. So pervasive is this tendency that those suffering with various illnesses began, some years ago, writing their "illness memoirs" as a partial corrective to the neglect of their pain (Jurecic, 2012).

Still, people can and do repress much that is intuitively known. I admit it took me some time to consider the link between lack of empathy for some other's pain to "repression" rather than "denial." Both concepts have a history with Freudian-oriented psychologists: they are considered two of the more primitive or less sophisticated (socially useful) defense mechanisms. The first term assumes that there are things so painful or dreadful that people hide awareness of them from themselves; the second does not assume lack of knowledge, rather, it suggests that one simply refuses to acknowledge or accept things that are unpalatable. In this case, not seeing/feeling "black pain" frees one from dwelling on both another's or even the precise nature of one's own pain—we "live and partly live" as T.S. Eliot's Greek chorus put it in *Murder in the Cathedral*.[22]

The point is that daily life is full of painful moments and we live, in large measure, through "ignoring" them, both in others and ourselves. But it seems to me that this is at the heart of social injustice—ignoring the avoidable harm we cause to others and ourselves. The concept of "white pain" seeks to emphasize this point. Whites deserve to be seen as capable of hurt, pain, and distress due to a "spoiled" racial identity. This is beneficial to both whites and those who may suffer because of perceived white pain. Interestingly, this theme has been increasingly apparent in volumes dealing with white anger (Kimmel, 2013) and white racial endangerment (Taylor, 2011).

But the world is comprised of more than whites and blacks—or males and heterosexuals. There are many ways of being named or placed into categories; and pain is ubiquitous, felt personally in them all. Perhaps this is why we neglect it. But there is another possibility: *Numbness*. In an important but nearly forgotten study of Japanese survivors of Hiroshima and Nagasaki, psychiatrist Robert Jay Lifton concluded that the trauma of the H-bomb was so horrific that it "numbed" these people. In an interview years later, he explained this term further:

> I came upon the idea of what I call "psychic numbing," at first I called it "psychic closing off," in trying to understand what Hiroshima survivors were describing to me. They would say such things as, "the bomb fell"—or they would describe the experience they had: "I saw this array of dead and dying people around me. And I saw everything, but suddenly I simply ceased to feel anything." Some used the metaphor of a photographic plate that was overexposed. It was as though the mind was shut off. And I came to call that psychic numbing. (Lifton, 1999)

Lifton concluded that those of us living in the modern world were also significantly numbed. I sometimes sense this in others and myself. Daily I watch the horrific reports of mass and individual slaughter of humans by humans. We try to cry, to offer support, to rescue—and often we fall short; the United States cannot bomb the hell out of Syria, and free the suffering millions; we cannot pass sensible gun laws and defy the gun lobby—the NRA—and its constituents whose birthright seems to be the Second Amendment (an AK-assault rifle and a 200-round clip); and not even the massacre of 20 precious *white children* can move the nation to act. We are indeed numb. And it is within this numbed state that we pursue our daily life, including the *racialized dance of agency*. In this chapter, I want to sketch in some of the outline of the diversity characterizing this racialized dance of agency. It is within this larger context that white pain gains its fuller significance.

Racial Pain: A Perspective

Racial pain is pain caused by voluntary or forced identification with a "spoiled racial identity" (Goffman, 1963; Gresson, 1982). It can be viewed as a felt absence of power and the strong presence of guilt and shame. Many people express racial pain. I am an African American male, and I routinely feel racial pain. Some years ago a neighbor asked me whether I thought my race might be the reason that a house I have been trying to sell has not yet sold. I felt shame at his articulation of my vulnerability as a black man, for I indeed wondered whether this might be the reason my house has not sold. In fact, a day earlier, a Chinese family hastily went through my home after calling me to see it. As they departed, they remarked, in seeming amazement, "You have certainly kept it clean." I felt horrible for just a few minutes after this encounter. I knew that Asians are not necessarily prejudiced against African Americans; I also knew that this family might have meant nothing "racial" by their comment. Still, given the racial history of the United States and much of the world, their words symbolized more than they perhaps meant. I felt racial pain.

Racial pain is created, not inherited. Paradoxically, it is often created even as one seeks to enlarge or negate "race." For instance, when my daughter was barely four, she asked me whether one of her close friends was white. Although this child was from a biracial family, he did not seem to me to be difficult to identify as "black." Over the next several months my daughter asked me the same question regarding other light-skinned blacks. I soon got the idea that she was in the process of constructing race. Moreover, I saw that I was colluding with her by treating as absolute, factual, or essential something that she correctly failed to see as "self-evident."

The point is that we all can damage the identity formation and freedom of our young. And if we are not careful, this can promote confusion. I first noticed this confusion while conducting a psychological study of black female identity issues. In my book partly based on this study (1995), I presented the case of Eartha, a black woman conflicted about her value and worth as a black woman. Rejecting her inherited vision of reality, including racial reality, she tried to construct a privatized understanding of it. But she was unable to sustain this vision when her white friends relied on past ideologies to understand her and her behavior. Nor could she escape her gender labeling and her "matriarchal heritage." When I asked whether she thought being a black woman had been helpful to her, knowing that she had earlier disclaimed the meaningfulness of the label, she replied as follows:

> Yes, it has. It's helped me because black females don't have that many... people don't have too many expectations of where they are coming from or how they are. A black female is real hard for people to put in a... to define. There is an expectation but there really isn't. People don't really know what that expectation is.

Eartha was closing in on a generally under-examined idea: society's relative ignorance of black women because of the dominant expectations and stereotypes of them. She continued:

> Yeah, we don't know what to expect. I myself don't know what to expect from some black women!... I just don't know what to expect of people because I look at people. I don't know what to expect from a black man, I don't know what to expect from a

white man, I don't have that all laid out. I don't write scripts before I meet people to play through or run successfully. And I think a lot of the problems that we put ourselves in is that we write scripts even before we meet somebody. *A lot of this is us, it's us. We are writing our own scripts—we are fantasizing—what we expect or how we expect one to respond to us.* And the only way you can expect one to respond to you is to truly know how you are projecting yourself. To truly know yourself is to have an idea of what to expect, and it goes across the line with anyone. And a lot of people don't understand the chemistry we give off to a lot of people. (Italics added)

Eartha was a courageous and confident young woman. Above, we see the benefits of these attributes; she has ventured beyond her comfort zone and found acceptance as well as new knowledge. This "new knowledge" includes the fact that the "oppressed" can participate in their own entrapment. Rhetoric scholar Mark McPhail (1991) has called this joining with the oppressor "complicity," by which he means that both blacks and whites can act as if "things are black and white" only.

Eartha attempted to break free of this binary thinking and relating. However, caught in her own contradictions, which were tied to the larger societal contradiction, Eartha grappled with her mother's fears and her friend's caution regarding intimacy with a white male:

> I don't want to be any color. I want to be me. I am me. I am a female. I realize I have brown skin. I enjoy having brown skin. I am thankful to have this color when we talk about visual effects. I like my color, you know. I am proud of it. Artistically speaking, if I had a choice, I would keep this color because I think it is much more attractive. But that doesn't have anything to do with race.

Freed of collective context and support, such words become problematic. I asked Eartha to explain what her color pertained to if not race.

> Uh, my color?... I'm proud... I don't know how to explain it because I don't put things in a category. I can confuse myself when I try to understand it... how I look at it...I don't want to put labels on anything. I don't want to be labeled as a female, as a black person. I want to be labeled as an earthling. Maybe I want to go to another planet. I've had it with this planet; I mean it!

Many blacks struggle to renegotiate their space in a white- and male-focused world. How they go about this negotiation is not always easy to understand. In Eartha's case, the contradiction, her own sense of confusion (she can acknowledge it but can find no source for it), is balanced and sustained by the ideology of the black male's fear of black women. She defines herself as a strong but "ambiguous black woman." She disavows the force of race except as an aesthetic quality. But her narrative is shot through—as is true for all who identify as racialized blacks—with *racial pain*.

Unlike Eartha, other blacks may be more accepting of their "blackness," and aware of the oppressive forces around them. They too may express pain around some racialized quality. For example, take the case of black women's hair, about which much has been written (Cooper, 2014; Douglas, 2013). A recent military regulation about women's hairstyles has again refocused on black women, prompting the following recollection by a black female veteran:

> I am an African American woman, a Psychiatrist, and a former US Army Major, and I am dismayed by [the regulation regarding women's hair]. When I read the regulation and endured words like "unkempt" and "matted" used to define my natural hair, I was reminded of the pain and humiliation I, too, endured five years ago before I voluntarily departed the Army. Since then I've enjoyed the simple dignity of wearing my natural hair to work in a neat and professional manner. (Mitchell, 2014)

Yet the pain expressed by this woman or that Eartha felt is not wholly unique to blacks or any other racial or ethnic group. We all can feel hurt when we are treated unfairly or badly because of our group identification. Pain becomes racial pain through the linking, grafting, or fusing of the psychophysical to specific "racial" identities and socially meaningful occasions.

Racial pain as defined here has many nuances or dimensions; moreover, it is fluid, shifting, and indeterminate. One feature of racial pain with which I am concerned is vulnerability. I consider vulnerability as openness, awareness, or readiness for impact from without. Derived from the root word for wound, it signals a crucial relation to the experience and expression of pain and recovery. Let me illustrate using the case of white and black parents of biracial children.

A white father with biracial children refuses to acknowledge their racial history. Because they are growing up in a privileged, tolerant, white environment, he insists that race does not touch them. He rants and raves because his daughter's skin and features are not given greater positive social assessment because of his whiteness. Then, when she goes off to college, she has an identity crisis, based partly on the difficulty she has negotiating a white or mixed racial identity. A black father reveals a similar refusal: when his biracial son is unable to woo white females in his upper-middle-class New England town, the father grieves, finding exoneration only when his son "wins" an Asian American girlfriend.

Of course, many mixed racial parents can and do "acknowledge difference" (Kirk, 1964) without becoming bitter or alienated. The point is that racial pain is possible because most humans identify with racial categorizations, internalizing many of society's valuations—positive and negative—of the traits attributed to different racial groups. And even when they reject these labels in favor of others—like Eartha's self-soothing metaphor of *earthling*—they run the risk of being drawn into racialized encounters and exchanges. These exchanges involve individuals, aware of themselves as such, confronting spoiled identities as they try to maneuver traumatized relations. Consider Shakespeare's character, Shylock, in *The Merchant of Venice*. Many have declared Shakespeare a racist for his portrayal of Jews through the character of Shylock. Perhaps; but I have always been personally drawn to the humanity of the character, as seen in his soliloquy:

> He hath disgraced me,
> and hindered me half a million; laughed at my losses,
> mocked at my gains, scorned my nation, thwarted my
> bargains, cooled my friends, heated mine
> enemies; and what's his reason? I am a Jew. Hath
> not a Jew eyes? hath not a Jew hands, organs,
> dimensions, senses, affections, passions? fed with
> the same food, hurt with the same weapons, subject
> to the same diseases, healed by the same means,
> warmed and cooled by the same winter and summer, as
> a Christian is? If you prick us, do we not bleed?
> if you tickle us, do we not laugh? if you poison
> us, do we not die? and if you wrong us, shall we not
> revenge? If we are like you in the rest, we will
> resemble you in that. If a Jew wrong a Christian,
> what is his humility? Revenge. If a Christian
> wrong a Jew, what should his sufferance be by
> Christian example? Why, revenge. The villany you
> teach me, I will execute, and it shall go hard but I
> will better the instruction. (Act 3, Scene 1)

Here the merchant Shylock explains why he seems intent upon getting his just end from the Gentile society in which he lives. I believe his fatal flaw (all tragic heroes possess these) to be confidence in a just Gentile court. This notwithstanding, I see his words as a powerful affirmation, even in its vulnerability and naiveté, of the pain of racial stereotyping. They are reminiscent, ironically perhaps, of Sojourner Truth's famous lines: "Ain't I a Woman?"[23]

Sojourner, of course, was addressing a white audience of abolitionists; but, like Shakespeare's Shylock, she was asserting her subjectivity—personal agency—and her humanity—the strengths, weaknesses, hopes, fears, and courage common to all humans. Additionally, both Sojourner and Shylock were confronting spoiled identities and traumatized relations shaped by racial pain. Shylock, predictably, found tragedy for his insistence upon a human's, a citizen's rights: a "pound of flesh." Sojourner recognized a kind of victory: the abolition of slavery. Shylock and Sojourner, fictional character and historical giant, symbolize the ongoing struggle with racial pain. Each of these historical figures, moreover, reflects the trauma of injustice and the spoilage of identity. We do well to consider these a bit closer.

Spoiled Identity, Subjectivity, and Traumatized Relations

What makes for identity spoilage? The loss of *agency* is at the heart of spoilage. Agency is activity, engagement, and power. It is a sense of self asserted, taken seriously, not predefined into stereotypy. Isn't this ultimately the outrage of the male forced into invisibility, the white denied self-display, the rich despised? This said, racial pain is dialectic—a contradiction—and a fluid, ever-changing irony: identities and their values continue to change over time. Take, for example, "coloureds" in South Africa: they are neither white nor black, not at the top or the bottom. They live with a peculiarly "spoiled identity." According to Nancy Scheper-Hughes (2001), "this spoiled identity, while characteristic of all South Africans, is especially pathetic for the 'coloureds.'" As she explains further:

> One continuing dilemma of the new, non-racial South Africa is the legacy of apartheid which has "spoiled" all cultural and ethnic identities, although some are more spoiled than others. Zulu (because of its identification with the right-wing Inkatha Freedom Party), Afrikaner (because of its political history of institutionalized racism), and "Coloured" (because it is seen as a fictive category, as the "pure invention of apartheid") are perhaps the most "spoiled" today.

Identity is spoiled in South Africa because everyone can be seen as dangerous, to some degree. Some of this danger is rooted in the past, but some is based in ongoing relations that contain *trauma*: experience that is both deeply painful and depressing.

According to Debra Walker King (2008: 39) severe trauma can conceal truth about the conditions that create it, yet this truth "… exists in racial hurt. Pain is a personal experience, a feeling that is uniquely our own. … Racial hurt, however, is not something we own. Racial hurt owns us. It, not pain, attacks the soul and renders its victims wounded or worse—soul murdered." Consider Jews: identified as the killers of Jesus Christ, Jews have been repeatedly singled out and persecuted by various nation states over the centuries. The atrocities are well known and need not be rehearsed here. But there are continuing struggles Jews must endure in various contexts. For instance, there is the Wall Street scandal surrounding Bernie Madoff. This scandal is a powerful illustration of racial hurt for American Jews, in part, because it calls forth memories of traumatic injustices that seem impervious to "good works" by Jews:

> Michael Milken, Jack Abramoff, Ivan Boesky, Meyer Lansky and now we have Bernard Madoff to add to the Jewish Financial Hall of Shame. Historically we Jews have prided ourselves on financial acumen and success. Many of the prominent investment houses of 20th century America bore Jewish names. I believe that we can still be proud. Note how many in the Obama financial team marshaled to respond to the current fiscal crisis are Jewish. These are honorable men and women, who will be striving to do what is right. Then along comes Bernard Madoff, once Chair of NASDAQ, now a name of pain and embarrassment. (Loewy, 2008)

These reflections hint at the hurt individual feelings and the damage or trauma to relations among citizens. Rabbi Robert F. Loewy, in this passage, references both spoilage and the struggle to retrieve wholeness or identity integrity. The overriding awareness is that despite the legends of noble achievements in business and finance, Jews continue to be negatively portrayed. But there are other aspects of this tragic drama. Danielle Berrin (2011) reports on the "peripheral pain" caused by Bernie Madoff:

> Last week, Madoff's daughter-in-law Stephanie Madoff Mack released a book, *The End of Normal: A Wife's Anguish, A Widow's New Life*. Next up is a tell-all penned by Madoff's other son, Andrew, which is set to hit bookshelves Monday, and will be preceded by a *60 Minutes* interview with both Andrew and his mother, Bernie's wife Ruth Madoff. Why, all of a sudden, Madoff's relatives have chosen to come forward with their tails [sic] of woe seems oddly tied to the mythos of the moment in which Occupy Wall Street is railing against unequal distribution of wealth.
>
> Madoff himself tried to blunt the brunt of his crime by telling Barbara Walters, "The average person thinks I robbed orphans and widows. I made wealthy people

wealthier." Sure he feels bad for defrauding clients out of billions of dollars, but not that bad. "The gravy train is over," he told Walters. "I can live with that." But while Madoff's moral relativism may work when applied to his clients, the peripheral pain he caused his family cannot be quantified.

Not surprisingly, stereotyping individuals and treating them negatively contribute to racial hurt and trauma, and traumatic experiences can promote more stereotyping. Few of us, moreover, can easily escape this fate. Aymen Abdel Halim (2012), reflecting on the research of Dr. Khalil Gibran Muhammad, director of the Schomburg Center for Research in Black Culture at the New York Public Library, has argued:

> ... one of U.S. society's major afflictions when it comes to African Americans is that there is an "unspoken acceptance that there is something wrong with young black people, particularly young black men."

> In the 21st century, however, there seems to be an unspoken acceptance that something is wrong with Arabs and Muslims too, particularly young Arab and Muslim men. This widely held belief was cemented by 9/11 and subsequently led to legislation that made Arabs and Muslims suspect of criminality and subject to racial profiling.

Racial profiling is just one mode of racial hurt that traumatizes individuals who feel thrust into stereotypy. Ironically, the racial hurt of stereotyping increasingly touches whites. This is a huge part of the reactions of individual whites, insisting upon their right to the *existential me*—that is, a separate, individual presence, free, it would seem, from the shackles of labels and socially assigned realities and obligations. Resisting labels of racist, oppressor, or the like, these individuals are stressed and distressed—traumatized—by the seeming injustice of a race-conscious America. But there is a problem: institutional racism and race-based machinery intent upon it retain racialized privilege. Evidence that whites simultaneously disavow racism while affirming racist practices that retain their privilege (J. D. Foster, 2013; Ryden & Marshall, 2012) undercuts the pursuit of the existential me—at least in the minds of some minorities. For example, Ta-Nehisi Coates (2008) has argued:

> Racial resentment is just racial grievance—for white people. If it's absurd to hear Civil Rights era black folks attributing the entire fate of black people to racism, then it's just surreal to hear white folks chalking their problems up to Affirmative Action. One doesn't have to be pro-Affirmative Action to see the hypocrisy in those who say to blacks, heaving under a legacy of hate, "get over it" and then turn to Southern white "resenters," merely grappling with equality, and say "I understand."

This passage resists seeing white pain as the moral equivalence of the objective oppressive forces that underlay racial hurt (King, 2008: 38; 44). Here, white resentment is understood as merely white racism. Why? White "losses," though felt and validated by "white power" as oppression, are here seen as merely an excuse and effort to return to whites things stolen from others; namely, equitable access to society's resources, both material and cultural. To be sure, racial hurt occurs significantly in the eyes of the beholder, regardless of the material facts of the situation. Thus, individual whites do not necessarily feel "privileged" or "merely grappling with equality." They may feel a direct assault upon themselves as shown in Chapter 1. Efforts to achieve "equality" are, moreover, often felt as "reverse racism," a source of additional "white pain." But it is in the struggle to confront a spoiled identity—"Why do blacks and others hate my 'whiteness'?"—that further racial hurt is inflicted on various minorities. This fact undercuts the plea for recognition of white racial hurt in many contexts. But there is, nonetheless, substance to white claim for a share of the "racial hurt" narrative.

White Pain, Personal Identity, and Racial Hurt

Max Rafferty's self-professed alienation (in Chapter 1) from the social activism of the 1960s reminds us that something very personal or subjective was at stake for millions of Americans challenged by the radical possibilities of the movements characterizing the 1960s. His passionate outpouring serves also as a reminder that the pain found in so many recent representations of the social changes of the 1960s did not spring forth from nothing. Still, few would readily relate Rafferty's pain to recent discussions of multiculturalism, affirmative action, political correctness, white anger, and white male victims. Nor are we likely to see how the social activism of the 1960s later exposed millions of white youth, particularly those in multicultural learning situations, to a special kind of vulnerability: a forced encounter with minorities' often painful images of whites in relation to themselves and their past and present relations. This vulnerability can be seen in these words, cited earlier, by one white male in my course on minority education in the United States: "Every Monday and Wednesday, I come in here to learn about what an asshole I have been throughout history."

This is a personal or subjective aspect of "being white." It is, moreover, racial hurt (King, 2008). But why is it important to focus on this fact of *subjectivity*? Perhaps it would be helpful to consider the word itself. American history professor and blogger Mike O'Malley (n.d.) suggests:

> People use "subjectivity" to get at the way the sense of self is composed of social forces that bear on individuals. They also use it to describe the way the sense of self varies with circumstances: it isn't static. Disciplines like psychology or criminology invent new kinds of subjectivities: in the gilded age, a whole bunch of new "subjectivities" were made available/forced on people. For example, you could be a kleptomaniac or a nymphomaniac: you could be "normal" or "perverse." You could be this new thing just invented, a "homosexual." "Subjectivity" in this sense might be described as "a new way of thinking about people." And "a new set of possibilities or procedures for dealing with those people."
>
> So "subjectivity" implies not just the individual's sense of self, but the ways that sense of self is acted on and even made up by outside forces.

O'Malley's description of subjectivity is especially useful for a discussion of racism, including racial identities and pains. His comments add subtle but significant nuances to our understanding of the interplay of personal identity, racial pain, and atonement-seeking behavior. The profound, even pervasive, quality of this interplay of forces is seen in the discourse surrounding the idea of multiculturalism. This discourse has many features, particularly the outrage at affirmative action and related "preferential privileges." The pain and anger expressed by Max Rafferty in 1970 have grown like a cancer. Even in mid-2014, one candidate for governor of Idaho, Harley Brown, declared in the primary debate: "I don't like political correctness. Can I say this? It sucks! It's bondage...."[24] The "cure" for this "sickness" has been a series of social and political battles. It is as a corrective to so-called political correctness that America's "atonement" has found both political and pedagogical expression.

America's "atonement" has considerable impact on the pursuit of social justice. The changes required to bring about social justice may include revelations that are difficult to integrate with one's reference-group identity or subjective sense of self. The pedagogical significance of the role of the pain associated with this kind of learning is seen in the response to the discourse of multiculturalism.[25] It is especially evident in the challenges to the social reform policies metaphorically identified as "affirmative actionism" (Lynch, 1997). In an earlier work, Lynch told whites, "talk about the issues... widespread talk can be a potent instrument of change" (Gresson, 1995: 1). His words are both illustrative and instructive with respect to atonement as recovery pedagogy. These words also barely conceal a deep *racial pain*. To be sure, it seems merely "white pain," and hardly something that historically oppressed nonwhites are especially required to sympathize with even though we have always had to recognize and be wary of it. But to give life to the idea of "white pain" in isolation is both inaccurate and misleading. If white pain is anything at all, it is a part of a larger socially constructed *racial pain*. It is helpful to recognize this connection in order to better access and assess pleas like Lynch's call to stand firm against the onslaught of social justice policies, practices, and pedagogies. But such pleas conceal, nay, sidestep other racial hurts: that beyond black and white.

Racial Pain: Beyond Black and White

> ... as the nation's diversity increases over the 21st century, we will need to figure out how to discuss and think about race in America. The black white binary that dominated American racial thought—popularly and academically—seems to have little relevance in a nation where Asian American and Latino American residents seem to increase their numbers every year. Racism affects each of these groups, but in different manners and through different pathways. No one doubts the long established prejudice against Black citizens in America. The historical legacy of slavery and Jim Crow remain central aspects of our nation's history. Yet, Asian Americans and Latinos, notably Mexican nationals and Mexican Americans, have their own histories of struggle.
>
> –Ryan Reft (2012)

Years back, one of my white female students was explaining why she felt certain that she was "white." In her view, she was "white" because of her skin color. Moreover, she felt skin color also provided an unassailable explanation for the difference between herself and a darker-skin female whom she also "knew" was white: "she is white but less fair than me because she is Italian and I am Irish." I observed that others once saw Italians as "niggers." The Italian female responded that she had always been white, "although they [the Irish] didn't consider my ancestors as so."

These young women's exchange provides a powerful window on the ongoing negotiation of the white-black rule that has dominated race in the United States for centuries. If one was not "white," one was essentially a "nigger" (read as "black"). To be sure, there were exceptions to this cultural mandate. But by and large, people who recognized themselves as "ethnic" groups still struggled to gain recognition as "white" when it came to participating in "white privilege." However, the "white-black" formulation has increasingly lost its capacity to force people into fixed, stable racial or ethnic identities. One of the most critical developments taking place today is the necessity to "wrestle" with the fact that "race" is not only unstable or changeable but also a source of struggle that takes place all the time (Pollock, 2006).

Within this context, Ryan Reft (2012) has argued for the need to recognize that racism has affected different groups differently; accordingly, attention must now turn to dealing with the racial pain and traumatized relations of groups outside of the white-black narrative. From this view, for example, we may gain an enlarged understanding of the current escalation of debate around the use of Native American names for sports teams like the Washington Redskins. Some continue to see Native American activists pushing for this kind of change as "petty," but in doing so they are refusing to confront the character of the racial hurt (Ahmed, 2004; King, 2008) specific racialized groups have endured in the past and how the trauma continues even today.

But the reluctance to yield "the right" to name sports teams with references to Indians points to a deeper, dialectically profound racial pain that threatens to infect us all in an ongoing complicity. I had an existential moment with precisely this invitation to complicity to inflict racial pain last week. My wife and I were just outside Myrtle Beach, South Carolina. We recently closed a home there and were returning to get some personal items we had left behind. We decided to stop at one of those welcome centers common to tourist spots. The older white southerner who greeted us was very friendly and solicitous. But at one point in the conversation, he drifted onto the day's big news: the U.S. Patent and Trademark office canceled protection of the Washington team name: "Redskins" (June 18, 2014). Clearly bothered by this government action, our "host" invited us to join his view with the following narrative: earlier that day, he had met six Native American visitors—they identified themselves as Apache—who had responded to his questioning about the name change issue with "we could care less what name is used." From the gentleman's view, their response affirmed his take on the matter; and he clearly felt we should feel likewise. My wife turned away in irritation; I, however, felt pressure to affirm him yet express my own disagreement with his position. So I searched for a non-offensive answer for him that would not violate my own sense of integrity.

The importance of this episode is multilayered. First, it expresses what investment some whites have in being able to do and say what they choose with respect to racialized others; this is "white privilege" that is routinely denied because the individual white may not recognize the built-in offense and aggression in their "First Amendment right." Second, the continued collapsing of racialized others into neat but problematic categories of black and white was evident when this man failed to recognize or even suspect that my skin color meant I might be "Indian" and possibly offended by his view, or that my "Indian narrative" might be different from the "six Apaches" in his story. Third, my personal discomfort—I was born and raised in the "Old South"—in being "discourteous" to this man brought me face to face with my own racial past and ongoing racial pain when confronted with *active* racialized (if not necessarily racist) practices (Ahmed, 2004). That I felt bothered by this encounter is not just my problem, something to get over: it is or should be society's problem.

But there are other painful aspects of the issue raised by Ryan Reft, particularly the mutually traumatizing exchanges among minorities. Racial chauvinism, as many white commentators are quick to point out, is not unique to whites; and it is precisely the racial hurt among minorities that constitutes a *dialectics of betrayal* (Gresson, 1982). This betrayal is complex; it is painful; and it highlights the ubiquity of both spoilage and racial hurt. Consider a little discussed but eerie exchange involving Asian women and Jewish women and men. A recent episode of TV psychologist/host Dr. Phil (2010) featured a self-identified "traditional Jewish woman" who felt called upon to condemn for the Jewish community the alleged mad pursuit by Jewish men of Asian women. Dr. Phil and the young lady had a particularly complicated and racially painful interchange during one segment of the show:

> "You said, 'If a non-Jewish woman tries to steal my man, I would tell her she needs to know her place. A Jewish man wants a Jewish woman. When I see a non-Jewish woman trying to take my money or fame by dating a Jewish man, I get crazed and verbally abusive.'"
>
> "Absolutely," Josie answers. "It's like the African American community. When their men hit the top, and they are successful, they marry a white woman, and that's not fair. Same with the Jewish community."
>
> "Well, it didn't work, because you said, 'My ex left me for an Asian woman who looked like a sneaker soler from a Third World sweat shop.'"
> "And a happy ending massage. Absolutely."[26]

This young woman expresses considerable racial pain around the felt losts, the spoiled identity, of a desirable, worthy mate for "rich, Jewish men." Moreover, she very powerfully expresses her sense of self—her subjectivity—by identifying the felt loss of desirable Jewish men to Asian women, in a way that parallels, in her mind, black female loss of successful black males to white (including, presumably, Jewish) females.

But the dance of agency—implied self-other definition and negotiation—has many nuances. Thus, at a major Asian blog site, we find an Asian female involved with a white male and lamenting the "spoiled identity" imputed by the Jewish female above; she describes her initial rejection of a white suitor, then her eventual surrender to him in this way:

> After this emotional tug-of-war, I gave the relationship a chance, and I am grateful I did. But my entry into the white male/Asian female club does not mean I've gone on an "it's always about love" kick and that I blindly celebrate all the relationships that, on the surface, look like mine. There are the WM/AF relationships which I firmly believe are equal partnerships between two egalitarian, colorblind individuals who respect each other's cultures and beliefs.
>
> However, as someone recently reminded me, there are those kinds of WM/AF relationships that give the rest of us a bad name—the ones that are formed on the perhaps covert and destructive valuing of the white man's race and culture over the Asian woman's, where the white man has little regard for his partner's culture, or sees her as a trophy. Some pairings are just blatantly unequal, and as that someone commented, "Only an AF who is really un-self-aware and/or self-loathing would date or marry such a man." (Christina Tan, 2011)

What stands out immediately is this writer's sense of a shared Asian female "spoiled identity" and the racial pain embedded within it. This pain is different from, say, the Asian pain associated with being labeled the "model minority." Still, it carries an ache born of stereotyping that cannot be readily jettisoned because it does carry that "kernel of truth" so often found in stereotypes. The real concern, in such matters, is not the "truth" of the stereotype, but the negativity attached, unilaterally, to it. Thus, (some) Asians may indeed be extraordinarily committed to education, or whatever, and do excel proportionally; but this does not apply to *all* Asians, nor ought it to be concretized as an "essence."

But there are deep layers that perhaps all racialized peoples struggle with; and these "dialectical positions" can breed racial pain. Again, the Asian female blogger exposes her own implicit racial pain:

Asian women only suck when they don't think twice about saying things like:

- I have a cultural/aesthetic preference for white guys.
- Asian men have small penises, trust me, I'm Asian.

- White guys are much more physically attractive compared to Asian guys.
- Asian men are nerds and geeks and quiet losers.
- Asian men aren't romantic.
- White guys are hot and sexy, while Asian guys are just loyal friends.
- I will never date an Asian guy, I only date white guys.
- I can't date Asian men because they're like my brothers.
- Caucasian features are more attractive compared to the round face, olive skin, small squinty eyes Asian guys have.
- Etc. along the same lines.

I've heard enough Asian women say these things as if they were absolute truths, without questioning how they came to their racial preferences, and not realizing how much these seemingly flippant remarks harm Asian men, create a rift between Asian men and women, and breed negativity towards Asian women who don't hold these views.

Sometimes I wonder how an Asian woman can say she prefers white men because they are more aesthetically pleasing, when one day she might have a son who looks more like her side of the family than his father's. This is why I feel bad for the very angry Asian-looking hapa son who hates his white dad and Asian mom – if his mother did think all the bullet points above, it's no wonder her Asian-looking son is so resentful for being brought into a world where even his own mother could dismiss men with his features. (Christina Tan 2011)

What is evident in this blogger is the ongoing dialectics of position, or more precisely, the dialectics of sense of self (subjectivity) as one interacts with others in diverse spaces. This is an important point to understand as it pertains to historically marginalized people because it applies increasingly to whites, as we shall see in forthcoming chapters. In this instance, the Asian female is trying to create/affirm a place for herself as an Asian sympathetic female who happens to be with a particular white male. Yet she recognizes that the particular choice she has made, symbolically and perhaps substantively, feeds into the stereotypes she has rejected, and joins herself in a "sisterhood" with Asian women whose apologetics she has challenged.

What is perhaps even more remarkable about this Asian woman's reflection, or act of self-persuasion, is the awareness that Asian women may be willingly pursuing "unequal" relations with white men because of the financial rewards. Further, this writer even suggests that there may be actual disrespect of the Asian culture by the white males involved. Thus, she is struggling with a dual form of racial pain: both from within and without. This seems a partial motive for her blogging. But there is evident here a shared though unstated racial pain with any woman—Asian, black, or white (Jewish)—whose self-identity/esteem is complicatedly woven into the male's material and cultural capital: where he sits on the "food chain."

But even there, we must stop and consider yet another nuance to racial pain: the wealthy, older, white (Jewish) male. He too struggles with a complicated racial pain. For instance, Donald Sterling, former owner of the NBA's Los Angeles Clippers, told his girlfriend not to Instagram pictures of herself with black people and not to bring black people to his basketball games. TMZ posted an audio recording—with commentary—in which Sterling alleged said:

> "You can sleep with [black people]. You can bring them in, you can do whatever you want. The little I ask you is not to promote it on that ... and not to bring them to my games." Later, he makes the point specifically about Magic Johnson, telling her that "it's too bad you can't admire [Johnson] privately...bring him here, feed him, f*** him, I don't care. You can do anything. But don't put him on an Instagram for the world to see so they have to call me. And don't bring him to my games. Okay?" Sterling's comments about Johnson follow a long argument about his girlfriend—who says in the recording that she is half-black and half-Mexican—not understanding the cultural differences between white, black, and Hispanic people. At one point, Sterling asks her if she gets "a benefit" from associating with black people, and calls her "stupid" when she asks why the race of the people she associates with matters.

What is to be made of Don Sterling? Is he simply a "bad actor"? Does his past signify his essence, or tell the entirety of his story? Can he be seen—and empathized with—as a real person: conflicted, compassion, and certainly vulnerable to youth, beauty, envy?

These questions beg for answers because they orient us to the larger question: can one achieve a self-identity impervious to spoilage? Perhaps we can't. This is the nature of the dance that we all participate in, one way or the other. The answer, to the degree there is one, calls for us to be "heroic." That is, we must be able to balance the contradictions of life without escaping into fanaticism, on the one hand, or despair, on the other (Becker, 1964). Those who attack in a non-forgiving way Sterling's contradictions, vulnerabilities, and ugliness are perhaps too exacting; there has probably been more to the man than is captured in his "racist" proclivities. Similarly, those who excuse him because of age or wealth also engage in self/other deception: Sterling's racial identity vulnerabilities persist despite his wealth. He is exposed as pitiable. We see, perhaps unknowingly, his racial pain. This pain is his dependence on the younger "mixed-blood" woman for something he called "love." But he is a human being trying to make it in a world in which he has real but complicated choices. He is, in many ways, us.

An added dimension of this dance of racial agency is seen in Sterling's girlfriend's "naiveté" regarding her mixed racial identity.[27] She expresses confusion regarding Sterling's capacity to differentiate between her and non-mixed blacks. Her attitude is characteristic of a younger generation; and both she and Sterling probably fail to consider the importance of this fact in establishing the possibility of mutual understanding. The media pundits and public have largely sidestepped this point in favor of the more exciting focus on "racism." I will return later to this particular exchange between a wealthy aged Jewish male and his younger mixed-race female companion as we consider the cultural in racial pain. Before that, however, there is another dimension of racial pain among whites that has gained visibility, although its complicated features remain a problematic topic for reflection: *the class and gender tensions within whiteness.*

Class, Gender, and White Pain

Norman Mailer, winner of both a Pulitzer Prize and American Book Award, took on many themes in his 1968 *Armies of the Night*, including the anti-Vietnam 1967 clash at the Pentagon, where white college students, blacks, and "others" faced off against the "government" and its working-class white boys (policemen, guardsmen, and U.S. marshals). In a woefully neglected section of this often-cited work, Mailer (1968: 284) lets loose with his take on the psychic-sexual energies of white-on-white gendering:

> They looked across the gulf of the classes, the middle classes and the working classes. It would take the rebirth of Marx for Marxism to explain definitively this middle class condemnation of an imperialist war in the last Capitalist nation, this working class affirmation. But it is the urban middle class in America who always feel most uprooted, most alienated from America itself, and so instinctively most critical of America, for neither do they work with their hands nor wield real power, so it is never their lathe nor their sixty acres, and certainly never is it their command which is accepted because they are simply American and there, too, the urban middle class was the last class to arrive at respectable status and it has been the most overprotected (for its dollars are the great nourishing mother of all consumer goods) yet the most spiritually undefended since even the concept of a crisis in identity seems most exclusively their own.

Already in this portrayal, black and other minority males are deleted; and we can see that even the white female is not centrally displayed; perhaps this is why those white college females who were present at the gathering were stereotyped as necessarily pariah "Jewish females" (Gitlin, 1993). But where is the white pain? Mailer (1968: 284) continues:

> The sons and daughters of that urban middle class, forever alienated in childhood from all the good simple funky nitty-gritty American joys of the working class like winning a truly dangerous fist fight at the age of eight or getting sex before fourteen, dead drunk by sixteen, whipped half to death by your father, making it in rumbles with a proud street gang, living at war with the educational system, knowing how to snicker at the employer from one side of the mouth, riding a bike with no hands, entering the Golden Gloves, doing a hitch in the Navy, or a stretch in the stockade, and with it all, their sense of *elan*, of morale, for buddies are the manna of the working class: there is a God-given cynical indifference to school, morality, and job. The working class is loyal to friends, not ideas. No wonder the Army bothered them not a bit.

Here Mailer locates the irony of white pain—its class basis. To be sure, he is splitting hairs and neglecting the concrete, existential wretchedness of poor whites for the sake of an overgeneralized and romanticized portrait of white masculinity. But this itself is part of the construction of *the ideal* that white males are encouraged to pursue in the search for true manhood. And the essential tension of this peculiar implied trade-off accompanying the presence or absence of "class" may be denied but it is there to be seen by all, yielding an ironic racial pain:

> But the working class bothered the sons of the middle class with their easy confident virility and that physical courage with which they seemed to be born—there was a fear and a profound respect in every middle class son for his idea of that most virile ruthless indifferent working class which would eventually exterminate them as easily as they exterminated gooks. (Mailer, 1968: 285)

This is a powerful suggestion, but it is not a new one. Yet something special is being uttered by Mailer here—and put on display at the Pentagon demonstration: minorities and women are being "treated" to the humiliation of the middle-class white male. This is a powerful indictment—one that quietly contributes to the perception of the minority rejection of the white male as "top dog" (by forgetting one's place). Racialized gender power inheres in Mailer's suggestion that the truer, more critical "birthright" is physical courage, something "unnatural" to the middle class.

Physical strength and the willingness to work hard, to sacrifice for a possibly unattainable "American Dream" have long been acknowledged as features of working-class identity (Sennett & Cobb, 1972). Yet the "American

Dream" propels most working-class white males to become middle-class white males (Catano, 2001). So, their masculine "birthright" notwithstanding, they are caught in a painful place, one doubly racialized because of their failure to be fully "the man" (white) and the increasing encroachment on their idealized goal by multiculturalism, affirmative action, and women's rights. The rise of the new "angry white male," according to Michael Kimmel (2013), is largely about this class tension, but women figure significantly in the racialized pain—white pain—as well.

Mailer also sees the gendered pain.[28] Race, ethnicity, and gender are fused with class in an eerie way, as he associates the now-historic beating of females by working-class boys while the middle-class "boyfriends" watched like "wimps":

> The brutality by every eyewitness account was not insignificant, and was made doubly unattractive by its legalistic apparatus. The line of soldiers would stamp forward until they reached the seated demonstrators, then they would kick forward with their toes until the demonstrators were sitting on their feet (or legally speaking, now interfering with the soldiers). Then the Marshals would leap between their legs again and pull the demonstrator out of the line; he or she would then be beaten and taken away. It was a quiet rapt scene with muted curses, a spill in the dark of the most heated biles of the hottest patriotic hearts—to the Marshals and the soldiers, the enemy was finally there before them, all that Jew female legalistic stew of corruptions which would dirty the name of the nation and revile the grave of soldiers like themselves back in Vietnam, yes, the beatings went on, one by one generally of women, more women than men. (Mailer, 1968: 306)

Beyond all of the above, however, is the matter of pain—racialized pain. It is messy. It is also complicated. We can see this in the emerging and as yet unfinished narrative of Sergeant Bowe Bergdahl, the recently released Afghan hostage. Within the strong criticism of President Obama for exchanging Bergdahl for five Afghan "bad guys," there is the subtle and nuanced matter of what a real American man—the white male soldier—must be like in order to gain a *Saving Private Ryan* type rescue. As Secretary of Defense Chuck Hagel wrote:

> The options available to us to recover Sergeant Bergdahl were few, and far from perfect. But they often are in wartime, and especially in a complicated war like we have been fighting in Afghanistan for 13 years. Wars are messy and full of imperfect choices. I saw this firsthand during my service in Vietnam in 1968, when we sent home nearly 17,000 of our war dead in one year. And I see it today as Secretary of Defense. A few of you on this committee have experienced war and seen it up close.

> There is always suffering in war—not glory. War is always about human beings—not machines. War is a dirty business. And we don't like to deal with those realities ... but realities they are.
>
> Those of us charged with protecting the national security interests of this country are called upon every day to make hard, imperfect, and, sometimes, unpleasant choices based on the best information we have and within the limits of our laws—and always based on America's interests. War, every part of war, like prisoner exchanges, is not some abstraction or theoretical exercise. The hard choices and options don't fit neatly into clearly defined instructions in "how to" manuals. All of these decisions are part of the brutal, imperfect realities we deal with in war. (*Voice of America*, 2014)

Secretary Hagel's comments barely conceal a clash of stereotypes: what is a white man? What is a soldier? For some there will be a question raised here: aren't we just talking about a single soldier—any soldier—and what he seems to have failed to do? Perhaps. But if he were Arab, African American, Asian American, or even a graduate of West Point or Annapolis, would the response be the same? Perhaps. But this is a working-class, home-schooled white boy, whose father wears a ponytail, from a Midwest town in Idaho. Can a racialized society accept the idea that he (unlike the college boys Mailer stereotypes) recoils from war, spurred by a conscience that abhors the destructiveness of the invaders over the sacred loyalty to his comrades that defines both the soldier and white male? To be sure, Sergeant Bergdahl is no Sergeant York or Audie Murphy, war heroes from the hills of Appalachia who most 20th-century males, including John Wayne, wanted to measure up to. But he is a man, his vulnerability notwithstanding. And this is his pain—and the pain of those who rely on his *persona* for correct behavior. We may here recall Norman Mailer's litmus test: *The working class [white soldier] is loyal to friends, not ideas.*

White pain, like all racial pain, is defined partly in terms of the dialectic of betrayal, the clash between self-other interests and commitments (Gresson, 1982). This is a persistent possibility for all who are raised in a self-focused culture rather than one wholly or largely defined by the group. In Chapter 1, I cited Susanne Langer in this context; she saw the "ethnic imbalance" as essentially a complication created by this dialectical tension. Among whites, it has been an often cited but underexamined and underpublicized tension. Recent work on the resurgence of "white trash" imagery in the mass media threatens to change this tradition. Michael Wray (2013) writes:

> White trash. For many, the name evokes images of trailer parks, meth labs, beat-up Camaros on cinder blocks, and poor rural folks with too many kids and not enough

government cheese. It's a put-down, the name given to those whites who don't make it, either because they're too lazy or too stupid. Or maybe it's because something's wrong with their inbred genes. Whatever the reason, it's their own damn fault they live like that.

On the other hand, there are plenty of people now willing to wear "white trash" as a badge of honor. Much as African American youth turned the despised word nigger into an expression of pride and solidarity (usually as the abbreviated nigga) or the way that LGBT activists have reclaimed queer, some white people now identify as "white trash" to signal rebelliousness and cultural difference—their refusal of a bland, mainstream white society that oppresses and stifles.

White trash has always been a source of "spoiled identity" for a white majority that distanced itself from its self-defined self. This pained both the oppressors and the oppressed. Betrayal was embedded in this gesture of identity disavowal. It has been an ongoing source of white tension; it has also been one of the many fissures that enable white participation in social justice activism. More than one white has been thrust into identification with the other because of "white duplicity." To be sure, racial duplicity is bigger than whites; this is also why various minorities are sometimes able to disengage themselves from proscribed racial loyalties (Gresson, 1995).

From this view, anyone who has first accepted membership in an identity, then learns its limits by betrayal, is free to re-betray, or assume the role of "ironist." As sociologist Richard Brown (1987: 210) understood: "To see someone as the victim of irony is to see that person, relative to oneself, as submerged in unreflective absolutism." The ironist is one who understands the limits of absolutism, certitude, or inflexibility in defining irrevocable categories. As ironist, one explodes the terms of certitude—whites are so superior to non-whites that it is impossible for a white to marry or mate with one—by doing precisely what has been denied is possible: mate and marry a "lower" being. Or, yet again, one might exploit a reality show like *Here Comes Honey Boo Boo* to stick it in the face of a scandalized polite society.[29]

Conclusion: Cultural Pain as Racial Pain

Feelings of insecurity, confusion, uncertainty, and inadequacy are all examples of cultural pain. The history of slavery, racism, and segregation, added to today's conflicting expectations and pressure of being a minority and African American, all combine to create cultural pain.

– Peter Bell (Bell & Peterson, 1992)

In a self-help manual for recovering addicts, Peter Bell defined "cultural pain" as a range of emotions—confusion, anger, ambivalence, inadequacy, and uncertainty—that come from trying to please two conflicting cultural value systems: white and black. Bell's understanding of cultural pain might be better called "black pain" for as he observes: "As African Americans, we have experiences and feelings that most white people have never had. Three of these are color consciousness, cultural pain, and cultural boundaries" (1993: 13).[30] David B. Morris partly agrees with Bell; he wrote in *The Culture of Pain*: "Pain, after all, exists only as we perceive it. Shut down the mind and pain too stops. Change the mind (powerfully enough) and it may well be that pain too changes" (1991: 4).

But Morris would not agree that whites, or other nonblacks, are unlikely to experience cultural pain. In fact, Morris (1991: 39) offers an interesting racial illustration of the cultural (social) assumptions or values that influence or shape the experience of pain:

> Consider for a moment the institution of slavery. The ancient world had a saying that a man loses half his soul the day he becomes a slave. In America, where black slaves were regarded as merely, and by law, a form of property, the white, racist mentality that made a slave system possible included, as a crucial provision, the belief that slaves were incapable of human feelings and desires. It thus became a paradoxical article of faith among slaveholders that slaves did not feel pain.

Morris is here highlighting the fact that historical context partly influences how the perception and sensation of pain are received, or recognized. Further, he is pointing to the idea that cognition—thought—serves as an overlay to the meaning and significance of pain. Thus, when the young student from the University of Virginia asked if blacks and other minorities feel "racial pain," she was contextualizing the idea of "white pain" as something that stands out from among other forms of racialized pain. Her question was cogent in several ways. One of the most important is that her question invited a consideration of the relation of diverse "racialized" pains. How do they overlap, how do they differ? The moral and political significance of the implied question is appreciated, perhaps, in the following exchange from the tape recording of Don Sterling and his girlfriend:

> DS: It's the world! You go to Israel, the blacks are just treated like dogs.
> V: So do you have to treat them like that too?
> DS: The white Jews, there's white Jews and black Jews, do you understand?
> V: And are the black Jews less than the white Jews?

DS: A hundred percent, fifty, a hundred percent.
V: And is that right?
DS: It isn't a question—we don't evaluate what's right and wrong, we live in a society. We live in a culture. We have to live within that culture.
V: But shouldn't we take a stand against what's wrong? And be the change and the difference?
DS: I don't want to change the culture, because I can't. It's too big and too [unknown].
V: But you can change yourself.
DS: I don't want to change. If my girl can't do what I want, I don't want the girl. I'll find a girl that will do what I want! Believe me. I thought you were that girl—because I tried to do what you want. But you're not that girl. (TMZ Sports, 2014)

The reference to Israel and white and black Jews is perhaps uncomfortable, but it does highlight the complexity and complicated nature of the dance of agency and racial pain. In 2013, Yityish Aynaw was crowned as Israel's first black Miss Israel. But as one critic, Ruby Hamad (2014), observed,

In February, 21-year-old Yityish Aynaw became the first black Miss Israel. Born in Ethiopia, Aynaw was orphaned at the age of 12 and her maternal grandparents, already settled in Israel, sent for her and her younger brother. The rest, as they say, is history. Or it would be, if Israel wasn't still grappling with its own history of discrimination against black Ethiopian Jews since the first planeload were flown into Israel more than three decades ago.

To be sure, Israel struggles with race like all societies. And it is noteworthy that the elevation of a black Jew to the position of "Miss Israel" has been a quiet event in the United States. Still, the nation seems to be moving forward, and Sterling's reference to Israeli racism was intended only to make a point about culture and power in relation to racial pain.

Sterling is correct to emphasize the power of culture, and his girlfriend is also correct to note the agency of the individual. Hence, we see one aspect of racial pain in cultural context. But there is a subtle message embedded in Sterling's comment that must be surfaced: what cultural work does the image of "blacks treated like dogs" perform? In *African Americans and the Culture of Pain*, Debra Walker King (2008: 21) introduces a metaphor, *Blackpain*, that "exists outside of time. In fact, it is time—mythic time—and a memorial to the wounds and traumas some Americans wish to deny and discard."

King argues Blackpain is a weapon that American culture has created; moreover, this weapon consists of ideas, images, and practices that deceive whites about their own pain as well as that of others, notably blacks. David Smith (2004), author of *Why We Lie*, argues that self-deception is a form of lying that we use, in part, to fool ourselves so that we may fool or lie to (or about) others. From this view, Blackpain is self-deception. But it is a self-deception that touches the entire culture. And not just around race matters, although race is a special site for such cultural self-deception. This point was seen recently, after the Newtown, Connecticut, massacre, when President Barack Obama tried to use the "bully pulpit" to get legislation passed to curb gun violence: he failed; despite the image of young white babies killed in that idyllic Connecticut town, the NRA and gun lobby silenced a nation that says it wants better gun control and protection. The point is that we don't really want it; we lack motivation to act, until gun violence hurts us directly. Why? In part, we are insulated from really seeing the pain and destruction by the media and other sources.

The complexity I am trying to convey here is perhaps clearer in this example of racial pain and self-deception that involves Baltimore Ravens' football star Ray Rice. Rice recently gained infamy because of a video of him pulling his unconscious girlfriend (soon-to-be wife) from an elevator. Jonathan Zimmerman (2014) carries the ball in this particular critique:

> So let's imagine that Baltimore Ravens running back Ray Rice didn't strike a woman, knocking her out cold. Instead, suppose that he warned her against consorting with racial minorities and urged her not to bring them to his games.
>
> That's what Los Angeles Clippers owner Donald Sterling told a female friend in a recorded conversation, of course, which earned him a lifetime ban from the National Basketball Association. By contrast, Rice received just a two-game suspension from pro football commissioner Roger Goodell after the release of a video that showed Rice pulling his seemingly unconscious fiancée from a hotel elevator.
>
> Rice issued an eloquent apology at a press conference Thursday, calling his behavior "inexcusable." But what's equally inexcusable is the way Rice's team –and many of his fans— have embraced him. In America, apparently, it's worse to insult a body of people than it is to inflict bodily harm on a flesh-and-blood human being.

Zimmerman's point is well made, up to a degree. It's not a matter of which action is more serious: both are serious and should be treated as such. But consider what is at stake when we begin to address domestic violence head on: it involves taking on notions of manhood, masculinity, and, not surprisingly, race and class at foundational levels. In addition, flesh-and-blood human beings—bodies in pain, especially black female bodies—are not nearly as "real" or *embarrassing* as Don Sterling getting caught on an audiotape saying public unutterables.

But Zimmerman's reference to "a body of people" goes to the heart of cultural pain as racial pain: he makes Debra Walker King's point about *Blackpain* as a vehicle for escaping the profound cultural crime/dishonesty of black people's pain. In this case, Zimmerman does not recognize or consider the expression "body of people" actually includes Rice's wife (and Rice as well—his dastardliness notwithstanding). The tragedy here is not only that the individual victim(s) of domestic violence remains devalued, but that a "body of people" also continues to be under-experienced as *human*.

"There is no such thing as an illegal human being." Congressman John Lewis (2014) uttered these words on the eve of the GOP House vote to send 58,000 undocumented kids back to various Central American countries. His point was that actions taken to insulate one from complications—refugees—may resolve one's felt interests or rights, but to name or define people into some essentially "non-human" does not achieve its end *and* maintain one's own insistence that Americans are "exceptional."

Similarly, insulation from pain's consequences achieved through walling it off from oneself carries both risks and "bad" outcomes. It is precisely the fear or experience of joining the ranks of others who have been marginalized and become victims of cultural/racial pain that animates much contemporary white pain and anger. In the next chapter, I introduce a young white male, Matt Heimbach, very much aware of the racial pain of nonwhites and equally concerned with the idea that whites too are caught up in racialized pain. His reflection on the question of white pain is a fitting conclusion to this chapter and prelude to the next: "Is what happened to Native Americans horrible? Yeah. But that's what's happening now to whites in this country."

Part Two

WHITE PAIN AND THE DANCE OF AGENCY

... It [social justice activism] has failed to soothe the resistant "racial pain" for whites, who feel stereotyped into a collective condition of unique, and perhaps ineradicable, guilt.

– John Hatch (2006b: 258)

Identity is a construct, a fiction, but it is a deeply embedded, remarkably persistent, and necessary fiction. Sometimes people prefer to die rather than to relinquish their identity. Race is another fiction, preserved in this country because the arbitrary division between white and black helps to maintain white privilege. The fictions of race intersect with the constructions of identity to create the sincere fictions of the white self. These sincere fictions, incorporated on the level of object relations and therefore largely unconscious, sustain a white ego ideal and preserve the notion of the black as the "other," preventing us from recognizing the brutal reality of the racial oppression on which American society has always been based and from recognizing our own internalized racist notions. Until we confront the psychological underpinnings of racism and expose the sincere fictions of the white self, the only changes in American race relations will continue to be superficial.

– Hernán Vera & Andrew Gordon (No date)

· 3 ·

NARCISSISM AND WHITE PAIN

The White Male and the Masculinity Crisis—Again

> Humiliation is so injurious to the psyche, so threatening to the self, that it must be healed. When that sense of self is gendered, it is masculinity that must be restored. Anger and rage are the translation of that humiliation into the potential for action. And anger can mobilize the self to retrieve and restore the individual's sense of masculinity through any means possible, including violence.
>
> – Michael Kimmel (2013: 75–76)

> Is what happened to Native Americans horrible? Yeah. But that's what's happening now to whites in this country….
> … Some places in the United States they're slaughtering white Americans by the hundreds. Genocide doesn't have to be with guns and tanks and bombs.
>
> – Matt Heimbach (ABC News, 2014)

Prologue

Years ago, a student in my multiculturalism course suggested using a segment of the film *Higher Learning* (1994) to induce her peers to see racial equality as both right and necessary for American society. Aware of the complexities of her proposed pedagogical strategy, I suggested that some might not see the film's concluding message from her perspective, that is, a call to a nonracist, multicultural society founded on equality and mutual respect. The Monday following our initial conversation, she returned to my office. Showing both amazement and concern, she shared with me how her boyfriend, a white male non-education major, "proved" my point: "He watched the movie with me over the weekend. He said the movie made him want to be a white supremacist; he said the message was that whites ought to rule."

His position was surprising to her. But his attitude seems precisely what Robert H. Bork argues in his *Slouching Towards Gomorrah: Modern Liberalism and American Decline*:

> Multiculturalism is a lie, or rather a series of lies: the lie that European-American culture is uniquely oppressive; the lie that culture has been formed to preserve the dominance of heterosexual white males; and the lie that other cultures are equal to the culture of the West. What needs to be said is that no other culture in the history of the World has offered the individual as much freedom, as much opportunity to advance; no other culture has permitted homosexuals, non-whites, and women to play ever-increasing roles in the economy.... What needs to be said is that American culture is Eurocentric, and it must remain Eurocentric or collapse into meaninglessness. (1996: 311)

Although these are not the precise words of my student's boyfriend, they convey his understanding of the movie *Higher Learning*: to be a white supremacist is desirable. Nor is this attitude isolated to just a few disgruntled individuals. Increasingly, in both scholarly and popular literature, as well as in other media, attention is being given to young white males who share this attitude (Kimmel, 2013).

What is this attitude? In the epigraph, Matt Heimbach, a 22-year-old, middle-class college graduate, illustrates it: *life is not fair—the Native American got screwed and so will the white man if he surrenders his privileges, his competitive edge.* Featured on a 2014 ABC television special on the rising numbers of white hate groups in the United States, this young man was interviewed because he, like the young male introduced earlier, feels that the way things are currently developing—immigration activism, "militant Islam," gay and lesbian civil rights, Jewish "existence,"[31] and black thugism—represent genocide to the white race. Thus, while expressed as a personal rather than collective position, this young man is echoing Bork's "manifesto": *What needs to be said is that American culture is Eurocentric, and it must remain Eurocentric or collapse into meaninglessness.*

From this view, both white men's and the United States' identity are under siege from various sources, some domestic, and some international.[32] On the domestic front, many point to the changing status of the "middle class"—especially its losses in income, wealth, and a piece of the "American Dream." The rise of the Tea Party, especially, signifies this perceived identity injury. Racially, some see the rise of "Others"—notably, Hispanics and Asians—as an identity threat.[33] Of course, Barack Obama symbolizes these threats domestically and is often employed as a shorthand signifier of them. Through efforts to render him both an illegitimate and ineffectual president, moreover, it has been easier for some of his critics to portray President Obama as the *intimate* foreign enemy. Thus, he allegedly tears at the national fabric from within as the Chinese continue to "peck" away at the fragged national identity from without through theft of intellectual property. And more recently, Putin's reassertion of lost Soviet prestige (identity) through agitation in Europe and the Middle East has reaffirmed a growing dread of national decline under the administration of Barack Obama.

This feeling of a white race under siege is not a new idea; previous generations have expressed similar fears. But there is a new urgency to this recurring theme, as expressed in a testimonial blurb to Jared Taylor's (2011) *White Identity*:

> [This is] the work of an insightful, well-tempered, and above all, demandingly honest mind. *White Identity* is especially timely as the white population of America comes under intensifying demographic, political, cultural, and economic pressure from both within and without. Jared Taylor deserves our deep gratitude for declaring that whites must find a way to stand up for themselves in a world in which they are becoming a shrinking minority, even in their own once white-majority countries.

Written by J. Philippe Rushton, Department of Psychology, University of Western Ontario, this assessment of the book by Jared Taylor reveals the scope and depth of the passion currently characterizing one take on the white discourse on racial injustice. It is all the more noteworthy because this testimonial comes from Canada, a nation with its own complicated diversity issues. But then, Canada too shares in a Eurocentric tradition. The confluence of visions between, say, Bork and others advocates of this tradition is aided by a particular understanding of multiculturalism: "That multiculturalism is essentially an attack on America, the European-American culture, and the white race, with special emphasis on white males, may be seen from the curriculum it favors" (Bork, 1996: 304).

The young man mentioned above understood the "attack" implicit in multiculturalism as such when he responded that *Higher Learning* made him want to be a white supremacist. His attitude seems consonant with Gregory Rochlin's (1973) assertion that "wounds to the ego" stimulate aggression. We have been watching the emergence, consolidation, and execution of this aggression for the past 30 years in American race relations (Gresson, 1995). From individual expressions of racial rage on social media to the all-too-frequent instances of white police killing young black males, we are witnessing aggression in response to "wounds" to the racial identity of many whites. We have yet to adequately conceptualize the emotional underpinning of this aggression. Toward redressing this neglect, in this chapter and the next two, I revisit the multiculturalism discourse and its related issues—diversity, preferential privilege, and racial chauvinism—from a perspective I call "white pain."

White Pain: A Peculiar Racial Pain

Focusing on whiteness as a subject matter can be tricky. Perhaps Michael W. Apple put it as well as anyone in the foreword to *White Reign*:

> Having Whites focus on whiteness can have contradictory effects, ones of which we need to be well aware. It can enable people to acknowledge differential power and the raced nature of everyone—and this is all to the good. Yet it also can... run the risk of lapsing into the possessive individualism that is so powerful in this society. That is, such a process can serve the chilling function of simply saying "but enough about you, let me tell you about me." Unless we are very careful and reflexive, it can still wind up privileging the white, middle-class woman's or man's need for self-display. (1998: xi)

Michael Apple speaks a profound truth: the white person's need for self-display in relation to nonwhite persons is a constructed yet interstitial need. It is constructed by the specific values that Caucasians have evolved over the centuries in relation to other segments of humanity; it is interstitial because the need has been woven into the cultural character (Kovel, 1970). Nonetheless, this is a need that few whites readily recognize until they have been denied self-display. Let me be clear: whites do not hold a monopoly on this need; it is rooted in the biology of humans and finds expression in what Sigmund Freud called "primary narcissism." The point here is that race, ethnicity, class, and gender are major organizers for those who believe they are entitled to self-display.

I recall my most moving encounter with this propensity. In 1980, I was on tour in Africa for a month with 50 other Americans—half of them white, half black—from across the United States. This was a special, privileged group of world travelers; still, we were largely average Americans. All kinds of characters could be found among the group. But one thing stood out within a few days: attitudes toward the various encounters we had as we crisscrossed the African continent differed greatly from a racial perspective. The greatest difference was the whites' inability to adjust to being "not special." They had the unique difficulty of being told by black Africans where to go, what to do, and so forth. In addition, perhaps for the first time in their lives, these 25 "majority-group members" had to live—eat, sleep, socialize—with 25 "minority-group members" in countries dominated largely by people they defined as "minority-group members." By the trip's end, most of the whites were noticeably depressed, frustrated, and angry. This trip had been nothing like their little jaunts down to the West Indies or South America, places noted for catering to American tourists. Only recently have I understood that their pain might be given a name, white pain.

White pain is a form of racial pain. Because racial pain is typically related to the underdog, who has less social power, we often miss its presence among more privileged racial groups in the United States. But it's real. White pain is linked to a "white identity." Both terms allude to another idea: "whiteness." Whiteness—much like "maleness"—is a complex idea. I use the term to describe feelings that many whites report as a result of others' views of them. This is particularly true for privileged white men. (It is virtually impossible to talk about white pain as an identity marker without shifting to the white male, a shift that indicates the centrality of white men to any discourse in our Eurocentric society. This point is taken up in a later section.) For instance, in *White Men, Women and Minorities in the Changing Work Force*, Anthony Ipsaro writes the following:

> Women comprise the majority of the United States population and nearly half of the U.S. labor force. Immigrants and other minorities are expected to constitute a fifth of the labor force in another ten years. Today's interpretation of our founding documents promises equal access to the resources and wealth of this country. Yet White males continue to dominate leadership positions in America, in the corporate workplace, military, government, schools, churches, and the media. Women and minorities are asking, "Is this fair?" And White males are squirming. Their anxiety comes not because White men think they are the bad guys, but because others are treating them as though they are the bad guys: their partners, their children, women and minority co-workers, and younger men. (1997: 1)

Talk about white male pain is not new. At several important points in this country's history, white males have felt under siege or abandoned because of their race (Roediger, 1991). Notably, in the past, less privileged white males were called on to relinquish part of their racial privilege in order to include minorities, especially black males, in their unions and other labor-related fraternities and markets. Today, according to Ipsaro, the role of government initiatives on behalf of women and minorities appears especially troublesome; this affirmative action is "confusing" for white men.

White male "confusion," Ipsaro believes, is due to their observing "women and minorities wave the equal opportunity banner and use gender, color, and difference to gain monetary advantages and power positions. He watches these same women and minorities support cultural institutions (e.g., churches) and societal norms (the man as protector) that practice discrimination and oppression. This is confusing" (1997: 2). It is the pain generated by "confusion," contradiction—in himself as well as others—that may partially blind the white male to the continuing racial, gender, and class disparities and injustices in this country. Two other forces are operating as pedagogical cues in shaping this pain into specific discourses and convictions: (1) the role of the media and other societal institutions in promoting specific representations of white males versus the "other" and (2) personal biographies of "unreciprocated" compassion.

During the past several decades, many thousands of white males have become victims of economic recession. As thousands of blue-collar jobs and many middle-level, white-collar positions have been eliminated, these men have awakened to the realities racial minorities have long endured: a shrinking space for personal growth and advancement. One effect of this trend has been the decrease in the number of white males enrolling in and completing college. As a consequence, some white males are feeling the loss of privileges traditionally available to them. Simultaneously, they are bombarded with media images and liberation conversations in which they are identified as the oppressors of African Americans, women, and others. It is in such a context that we must understand and address the widespread malaise attributed to many white males, both on university campuses and at various sites celebrating white supremacy. For too many of these men, the past and its relation to the present are unclear, and they respond with a "disavowal of deviance" or reject being identified with the representation of white males as oppressors. Instead, they offer a discourse of white male victimhood.

The perception of a new, invidious oppression of white males has led to some fascinating judicial results. Besides the landmark cases reversing affirmative action in California and Texas, the courts have affirmed the presence of unfairness to whites. For instance, in the *Chronicle of Higher Education*, Katherine S. Mangan wrote:

> Three white law professors who claimed they were discriminated against by administrators at the historically black Texas Southern University have won a round in court. A federal jury awarded $169,000 in back pay and damages to the professors, Eugene Harrington, Thomas Kleven, and Martin Levy. The professors apparently received about $4000 less than their black colleagues with comparable experience.... The university is expected to appeal. "This is obviously a time when white males feel threatened, and it's something that African Americans are going to have to deal with," Mr. Douglas [a school official] said. (February 3, 1995: A18)

This is a powerful statement: *white males feel threatened*. Threat pertains to emotion. Emotion has always underlain race relations. Early scholars in sociology like Robert Park (1928) understood this very well and tried to account for this reality in their theories of racial assimilation and accommodation. In the above passage, there is clear reference to the changing plight of white males, symbolically, if not substantively; and therefore "African Americans are going to have to deal" with it.

This is an ironic though true statement. It invites a question: Must blacks accommodate whites by surrendering their liberation initiatives, or merely accept a legal and political system that has, and continues in many ways, to dismantle minority advancement? Must they love whites even though whites may not love them? The nation has long had to deal with this paradox; and it has only partially done so, and too often by accommodating the dominant group. Recent scholarship on "Angry White Men" points to this fact (Kimmel, 2013). Some of the current, ongoing changes in social and public policy are also suggestive of this adjustment, albeit at an institutional level. Recent judicial decisions by an "activist" Republican-leaning Supreme Court are cases in point: the *Washington Post*'s Robert Barnes (2013) reported, "A divided Supreme Court on Tuesday invalidated a crucial component of the landmark Voting Rights Act of 1965, ruling that Congress has not taken into account the nation's racial progress when singling out certain states for federal oversight. The vote was 5 to 4, with Chief Justice John G. Roberts Jr. and the other conservative members of the court in the majority."

Many will perhaps read the Supreme Court decision in the above case, as well as recent decisions regarding birth control and abortion, as singular, nonpartisan, nonracial matters. But these actions may also be read as the cumulative consequence of efforts to recover the "paradise lost" imagined by Max Rafferty in 1970. Recall the Civil Rights Act was a core change in the United States' relationship to its minorities and the poor. This legislation, part of the so-called Great Society, spearheaded the 1964 domestic social reform agenda of President Lyndon Baines Johnson. Poverty and racial injustice were the foci of the Great Society initiatives. There are those who believe that the initiatives were a partial success, but others believe that they were not only a failure but that they contributed to the weakening of the nation and damaged the national identity. Multiculturalism was seen by many as the "birth child" of Civil Rights activism and other social reform initiatives occurring during this period. Writing on Lyndon B. Johnson and American identity, Dolph Briscoe Jr. (2006: 22–23) recalls:

> Johnson knew that he must assure Americans that he was capable of leading their country through a dangerous and uncertain time. He would have to gain the trust of his fellow citizens, many of whom knew little about the new president. Americans looked to the president of the United States as a critical representative of their nation's identity. LBJ decided that he would adhere, to the best of his efforts in his administration, to a theme of continuity from the presidency of John F. Kennedy. He hoped this ideal would assuage fears about both the stability of the country and its identity.

But the rise of Black Nationalism and white resistance to the dream of a diverse American identity challenged Johnson and contributed to his despair of achieving the Great Society (Briscoe, 2006; McKee, 2010). Rather, as some have argued, Johnson's vision contributed to a rugged individualism (libertarian streak) that has contributed to the current "American discontent" (Sandel, 1996). Whatever the broader merits of this argument, it is clear that a strong libertarian impulse has captured the popular American imagination (Blanks, 2014), and it is within this broader context that we may understand the emerging complicated national response to race and other social reform initiatives.[34] In particular, white male identity has been especially compromised by the seeming simultaneous (and in their imagination, related) arrival of a weakened international reputation and the first black president.

Some intuited aspects of this complicated identity response to 1960s-era social reform. In *The Armies of the Night*, Norman Mailer (1968: 285) imagined the confrontation in 1967 between students, women, blacks, and liberals on one side, and the government, represented by young, white, working-class guardsmen, on the other side, in this way:

> It is safe to say that the beginning of this confrontation has not been without terror on each side. The demonstrators, all too conscious of what they consider the profound turpitude of the American military might in Asia, are prepared (or altogether unprepared) for any conceivable brutality here. On their side, the troops have listened for years to small-town legends about the venality, criminality, filth, corruption, perversion, addiction, and unbridled appetites of that mysterious group of city Americans referred to first as hipsters, then beatniks, then hippies; now hearing they are linked with the insidious infiltrators of America's psychic life, the Reds! The troops do not know whether to expect a hairy kiss on their lips or a bomb between their knees. Each side is coming face to face with its own conception of the devil!

I feel these lines are among the most profound statements made by Mailer in this novel, which, as I mentioned earlier, won both a National Book Award and the Pulitzer Prize. Of course, the work itself was a racial statement, a white male grappling with race, gender, and identity. And it is not happenstance that he hit upon *class* to give texture to his own and others' racial pain:

> Let us give the literal picture. At this early stage, before the demonstrators were to sit down, a close-packed line of MPs with clubs, backed by another line of soldiers, was supported further by separate U.S. Marshals a few feet behind them, arrayed like linebackers—it could not have been unself-conscious. In other places of tension and at other times, soldiers were to advance with rifles, with sheathed bayonets, with tear gas, but this had not happened yet on this front where the line of standing demonstrators was composed of a mix of SDS-Contingent with a greater number of unattached young demonstrators caught in the suction of the action. Posed against the lines of soldiers, already some historic flowers[35] were being placed insouciantly, insolently, and tenderly in gun barrels by boys and girls.

Norman Mailer was closing in on an earlier iteration of the white male crisis that Michael Kimmel has seen to underpin the rise of the angry white male. Here, however, it was the 1960s-era liberal whites who stood on the frontline, shielding and validating blacks and other minorities from a simple declaration of rioter, savage, ingrate. The moment was critical, I suspect, in several ways, not the least is the shame and fear forced upon the working-class white male (soldier):

> Standing against them, the demonstrators were not only sons of the middle class of course, but sons who had departed the middle class, they were rebels and radicals and

young revolutionaries; yet they were unbloodied, they felt secretly weak, they did not know if they were the simple equal, man for man, of these soldiers, and so when this vanguard confronted soldiers now, and were able to stare them in the eye, they were, in effect, saying silently, "I will steal your élan, and your brawn, and the very animal of your charm because I am morally right and you are wrong and the balance of existence is such that the meat of your life is now attached to my spirit, I am stealing your balls!" A great exaltation arose among the demonstrators in that first hour. Surrounded on the plaza and on the stairs, they could have no idea of what would happen next, they could be beaten, arrested, buried in a stampede, most of them were on the mouth of their first cannon, yet for each minute they survived, sixty seconds of existential gold was theirs. Minutes passed, an hour went by— these troops were more afraid of them than they were afraid of the troops! Great glory. They began to cheer. Those who were not in the first row yelled insults, taunted the soldiers, derided them—the demonstrators in the front looked into the soldiers' eyes, smiled, tried to make conversation. "Hey, soldier, you think I'm a freak. Why am I against the war in Vietnam? Cause it's wrong. You're not defending America against Communism, you're just giving your officers a job."

The loss of the soldier as the idealized white male was a powerful symbolic loss of white identity.[36] In Chapter 4, I take up this matter more fully. Here I want only to anticipate that discussion with the observation that the current white male anger that Kimmel and others speak about was there in 1967, and Mailer saw it. Noted critic Alfred Kazin's review of *The Armies of the Night* also saw the layered issues and the anxieties they carried:

"Armies of the Night" is a poorer title that [sic] the one Mailer gave to the portion of the book that appeared in the March issue of *Harper's*—"The Steps of the Pentagon"; but it does light up his main subject—the intellectuals, the students, the Negroes, the academic liberals and the marching women who personify the American opposition. From first to last, this book is about that opposition, its political and human awkwardness; that is why the book that seems too full of Mailer himself is really about Mailer's deepest political anxieties. Things are coming to a crisis, but the forces of protest symbolically assembled before the Pentagon seem to him limited in everything except courage. (It was women particularly who, as the weekend drew to a close, were beaten by the guards.) (Kazin, 1968)

This may read like so much ancient history, words and images thrown together in a strange if not altogether alien and awkward manner. Perhaps, but to those of us who were there, directly and indirectly, these are haunting though vaguely important images. This past is relevant to white talk about "blacks not letting slavery and a racist past go," like that of Brent Zuercher, in Chapter 1, who could not fully apprehend why he hated blacks as a group or how he would let go of his anger at them. This past moment is also related to Kimmel's (2013) astute assertion that gender—white women—is pivotal, like class, to contemporary white male anger. Moreover, it is in this particular part of the past—the radical sixties—that we may gain a window onto the fusion of "atonement" and the ongoing discourse of white vulnerability and victimhood in a multicultural world.

Atonement and the Discourse of White Victims

The 1960s were notably characterized by agitation among various subgroups seeking greater equality: blacks, women, students, the elderly, gays and lesbians, and so forth. The mobilization for liberation, moreover, was simultaneous and often connected with disagreement with U.S. foreign policy in Vietnam and other parts of the world. Symbolically, at least, one prominent object of this social upheaval was the white male. Indeed, much of the recent attention to the "white male as victim" is a result of decades of ideological and rhetoric accusation blaming white males for oppressing everyone else. Before the Iranian crisis in 1979, moreover, black political activism (the 1968 Olympics, Vietnam, Black Panthers, Black Muslims), feminist activism ("bra burning," creation of NOW, and Ms. magazine), and middle-class youth rebellion (student antiwar movement, hippie counterculture) had succeeded in establishing a cultural alternative to the era's dominant cultural pronouncements. The eventual losses in Vietnam, the return of American soldiers unheralded, and Watergate joined these other forces to suggest a dual and deadly belief: neither American foreign policy nor the American soldier were inviolate.

The white male situation was eerily reminiscent of *Alice in Wonderland*:

> "I'm sure those are not the right words," said poor Alice, and her eyes filled with tears again as she went on, "I must be Mabel after all, and I shall have to go and live in that poky little house, and have next to no toys to play with, and oh! ever so many lessons to learn! No, I've made up my mind about it; if I'm Mabel, I'll stay down here! It'll be no use their putting their heads down and saying 'Come up again, dear!' I shall only look up and say 'Who am I then? Tell me that first, and then, if I like being that person, I'll come up: if not, I'll stay down here till I'm somebody else'—but, oh dear!" cried Alice, with a sudden burst of tears, "I do wish they *would* put their heads down! I am so *very* tired of being all alone here." (Carroll, 1984: 11)

Here, Alice was struggling with the effects of eating the mushrooms that changed her size and affected her senses, including her ability to recite poems.

In this soliloquy, she both revises her self-identity (I'm Mabel) and imagines her interaction with the people—her family and significant others—outside of the hole.

In a peculiar way, the white soldier's anxieties and plight in the 1960s and 1970s were the same as Alice's (some might even see the plight of white policemen in black communities in a similar light). Within this context, moreover, arose a plethora of folk outside the hole who rushed to reassure white males that they were okay; and others, notably blacks and others, were the abnormal ones. Notably, as early as the 1970s, "white rights" advocates (Lynch, 1989; 1997) suggested talking more about their perceived injustices. The consequences could be seen, among other places, on the internet, where James Novak (1995) wrote "Why White Men Are Voting Republican: It's About Far More Than the Economy." In this feature article published in *Backlash*, produced by Shameless Men Press, Novak argued: "White men will be joined by many minority men because the issues that have made white men angry are the same issues that affect minority men in a similar if not the same way." This piece identified more than 70 infractions against men— things that presumably enrage all men—including:

65. Men resent that women and minorities are "affirmative actioned" into jobs, promotions, and graduate and professional school openings even when they are less competent than white men who are applying for the same positions.
66. Men resent that those same classes are often excused for their failure to perform adequately in their new "affirmative actioned" positions.
67. Men further resent the same classes above calling white males "racists," "sexist," or some other kind of "ists" for pointing out that white men are smart enough to recognize that a person without adequate skills or experience has failed.

Above, Novak conflates diverse groupings of males into a single category, "men." But the insinuation that all men share the same resentment toward "women and minorities" fails to persuade. Perhaps Novak too feels this, for he concludes, in an ironic deletion of minority men:

> White males are angered by indiscriminate and subjective judgments not based on identifiable rules but the whim of the female players. White males are expressing their anger, and expressing it in a socially acceptable way. They overwhelmingly voted for traditional and mostly white male Republicans in 1994. I expect that they

will vote in even higher percentages for traditional white male Republicans in 1996. If my predictions are even close to correct, Ellen Goodman and lots of strident feminists should be feeling "anxiety." But they need not get too anxious. White males wrote and passed every significant piece of civil rights and progressive legislation in America.

The years since 1995 have proved to be more complex than Novak could imagine: the controversial election of 2000 and the attacks of September 11, 2001, frame a different vision than he could have imagined. Still, in 2002, the internet carried ironically parallel visions. For instance, one site, Vanguard News Network.com (2002), reported the alleged outrage of a white woman responding to the racial turmoil in Cincinnati, Ohio. Entitled "An Angry White Female," it begins:

> Excuse me for being a "racist," but it seems like there have recently been a large number of racially motivated gang attacks against innocent White folks driving by or walking in the vicinity of black gatherings. Is it just my imagination? Am I tainted by the racist propaganda I read on the Internet? The reason I ask this is because when a black mob attack occurs, other blacks join in or cheer the attackers on (Yeah—get Whitey!). They attack the police when they try to protect the innocent citizen. What am I supposed to think, as a White woman, when I hear of or witness these things? Am I supposed to beat myself and demand more "diversity"? Am I supposed to look at the victim as a sacrificial lamb and justify it because the blacks feel they have been wronged by society?
>
> The most recent mob attack was in Cincinnati, following a "peaceful" protest against the shooting of an allegedly unarmed black man wanted on 14 warrants who ran from police and was fatally shot. The police were probably in the wrong. But the violence started right before the politicians began discussing the issue at a forum. The blacks didn't want this discussed, they wanted to loot and burn stores and attack innocent White people who happened to be in the area. What was strange was that the White-skinned leftists who usually incite such acts were nowhere to be seen. Perhaps they knew White people were going to be pulled from their cars and beaten by groups of black men. Maybe they knew White women were going to be beaten until blood ran down their faces?
>
> Rest assured, these White-skinned leftists are all over the Internet trying to defend such acts. One day, the tables may be turned, and if I have any say, the White-skinned leftists will be the first to answer to the Angry White Female.

From this alternative agency now propounded by many whites, we see that atonement has a dual pedagogical significance: to exonerate and educate. In this sense, healing is already embedded in the expression of "righteous indignation." Often we don't understand difference as a right to be, a press/ pursuit of self-interests, dreams, and aspirations. The fear of being stereotyped— made the same, rigidified into sameness, non-different—underpins much white male pain.[37] Again, I turn to one of the scholars praising Jared Taylor's *White Identity: Race Consciousness in the 21st Century*:

> In this brilliant and wide-ranging survey of the relevant science and history, Jared Taylor shows that racial consciousness is intrinsic[38] and that efforts to remake human nature are doomed to fail. He shows that in modern America, people of all races prefer the company of people of their own race; that racial diversity is more often a source of conflict than of strength; and that multiculturalism is changing the United States profoundly and to the detriment of most white people.

Written by Dr. Raymond Wolters, Keith Professor of History at the University of Delaware, this statement is but an echo of a sentiment that has seemingly gained in visibility and potency during the past three decades. Evidence for this statement is perhaps best seen in the discourse regarding the young, working, and middle-class white male student. Various early discussions of white male victimhood as a result of affirmative action policies by courts and bureaucrats have coalesced as the metaphor of the alienated white male.

White Pain and the Alienated White Male

What is alienation? Alienation has been given a variety of definitions, mostly by sociologists. It has come to be defined as helplessness, uneasiness, normlessness, and meaninglessness (see Gresson, 1982). Thus it is perhaps understandable that many would say that alienation is a feeling of strangeness with something—person, place, or thing—with which one ought to be "at home." For whites, notably white men, it may be clear how multiculturalism and affirmative action of any sort might bring them to the threshold of alienation. In 1989, Frederick R. Lynch, a sociologist, reported the results of his survey of white males. Entitling his study *Invisible Victims: White Males and the Crisis of Affirmative Action*, Lynch provides one of the most comprehensive discussions to date of what I call white pain.

> "What can we do?" sighed a nervous Midwestern Democratic party official when asked about Stanley Greenberg's findings of anti-quota feelings among whites. "White

males between the ages of twenty-eight and forty seem to think they're locked out. What are we going to do?" (1989: 179)

Such remarks capture the relational character of white pain. They also reflect the powerful role social critics, including scholars like Lynch, assume in the construction of the discourse against affirmative action. Identifying affirmative action as the villain, scholars like Lynch sometimes go beyond description to prophecy and prescription.

> This drive to reshape American society is colliding with the serious tensions produced by affirmative action. Even more serious conflict may lie ahead. As always, the young are less restrained by tradition and convention.... They are less willing to become a new generation of invisible victims. (172–173)

Today, Lynch's implied prophecy nears fulfillment: everywhere affirmative action gestures have fallen off, even as the backlash against "forced diversity and equity" continues against a largely hollow rhetoric of diversity. And the current "drive to reshape American society" has brought the nation to the greatest levels of economic inequality and social malaise since the 1920s; the rich are getting richer, the poor are getting poorer, and racial tensions sharper. Identifying white youth as the heirs of a "generation of invisible victims," Lynch continued his vision of the forthcoming—the present—conflict in an ironic description reminiscent of the Tea Party:

> Unfortunately, some anger against affirmative action may have surfaced in the form of ugly expressions of racism. There is racism among the young just as there is among their elders. But sociologists and journalists should not be so quick to label all objections to affirmative action as racist. (Lynch, 1989: 177, 181)

From this view, the historic election of an African American to the presidency of the United States exacerbated rather than alleviated "the ugly expression of racism." Many around the world hailed the "maturation" of the country, symbolized by Barack Obama, as racial progress. But for others, it was an omen. More than racial dominance was under siege: identity itself was being threatened. Understanding this threat, years before the election of a black president, Howard Winant wrote:

> Not only blacks (and other racially-identified minorities), but also whites, now experience a division in their racial identities. On the one hand, whites inherit the legacy of white supremacy, from which they continue to benefit. But on the other hand,

they are subject to the moral and political challenges posed to that inheritance by the partial but real successes of the black movement (and affiliated movements). These movements... deeply affected whites as well as blacks, exposing and denouncing often unconscious beliefs in white supremacy, and demanding new and more respectful forms of behavior in relation to nonwhites... (1997: 41)

Because of the limited success of the Civil Rights and other liberation movements of the 1960s, many have under-appreciated just how monumental an impact these movements did have on the stereotypic white racist psyche. But something critical occurred during the radical sixties, as Max Rafferty understood when he called for the recovery of "paradise." Extrapolating from W.E.B. Du Bois, Winant names this "white racial dualism:"

> Obviously they [the movements] did not destroy the deep structures of white privilege, but they did make counterclaims on behalf of the racially excluded and subordinated. As a result, white identities have been displaced and refigured: they are now contradictory, as well as confused and anxiety ridden, to an unprecedented extent. It is this situation, which can be described as white racial dualism. (1997: 41)

"Racial dualism" is not a new experience for whites, even though contemporary times have brought forth its reemergence, perhaps on a larger scale. We need only consider Thomas Jefferson, the gifted American president. Both his personal life—a long-term affair with a mulatto slave woman, Sally Hemings—and his famous reflection, *Notes on the State of Virginia* (1781–1782), reveal a man torn by conflictive and contradictory identities. He clings to both racist and libertarian value systems. He denies black humanity even as he participates in and co-creates it. And at the end, he left behind both "white" and "black" descendants. This is a personal genealogy, but it is collective as well. The very contradictions and confusions lived out by his progeny further remind us that "white dualism" is a longstanding reality of a racist society. And within this very contradiction, denial and regression continue to compromise the transformative possibilities of the nation. The behavior Winant identifies as dualistic may not be a new phenomenon, created by a rupture in a unified, holistic, white self-image and identity. Still this behavior does have an important relationship to what seems to be a critical contemporary identity crisis among white men. This behavior is too often hastily identified as "backlash," yet as quickly glossed as "inevitable." What is less often realized is the psychological or developmental significance of this behavior. Within the recent upsurge in discussions of "angry white males," we can discern aspects of this psychological challenge and locate some of the important ways it informs emerging race and gender relations.

Manhood and "Angry White Males"

> White working-class men represent a position of privilege at the same time they represent the loss of such privilege. It is this simultaneous moment of privilege and loss that we excavate when we turn our attention to the production of white masculinity. It is their whiteness and maleness, which privileges them. But it is also in this space of historical privilege that they begin to confront the realities of loss. (Weis, Proweller, & Centrie, 1997: 210–211)

The class feature of America's atonement may be underexamined in a society committed to denying its classism.[39] I have not directly announced and unpacked the significance to the "angry white male" metaphor on the intersection of class, race, and gender. I say metaphor because ultimately, class notwithstanding, the term applies to "white man." But scholars and researchers, especially feminists and those concerned with gender studies, have increasingly honed in on the impact of changing material conditions on white male identity. For example, I noted earlier that during the Million Man March, many white males asked black males if they were atoning for their wrongs toward white men. How does one make sense of this? Easily, if we understand that whiteness, particularly white male identity, is largely defined by its relation to others, like women, blacks, new immigrants, and gays.

White pain, the organizing concept of this book, pertains to loss. It signals the loss of the axis around which so much of white identity has been constructed in the United States (Roediger, 1991; Slotkin, 1973). During the period of slavery, for example, working white men were encouraged to accept slavery as God's will and told that menial work was antithetical to the meaning of being white. And to be male has meant that one is not only unlike the bestial black male (Bederman, 1995), but also that being a (white) man is the negation of being a woman (Lyman, 1981).

The changing world has gradually chipped away at this sense of self. Even before de-industrialization in the United States, we had evidence of this white male pain. In Europe after World War I, for instance, men returning from the battlefields found women working in jobs and occupying social spaces once reserved for men. Much of the poetry and writing created during this postwar era reflected their grief, confusion, and anger. The last 30 years or so of American social history have rehearsed precisely this pain, although in different forms and in response to localized intrusions into white male dominance. In particular, scholars such as Stanley Aronowitz, Henry Giroux, Lois Weis, Michelle Fine, Joe Kincheloe, and Shirley Steinberg have addressed white male angst and anger in terms of its implications for a diverse democratic project. Gail Bederman concludes in her brilliant study of gender and race between 1880 and 1917:

> First, the history of manhood and "civilization" suggests that contemporary difficulties facing poor and working-class men of color in the United States may have a cultural basis, in addition to their widely recognized economic and social basis. Whiteness has long been an intrinsic component of middle-class ideologies of manhood. This may well complicate many men's ability to gain the status of "men" in our patriarchal society. In other words, for men, just as for women, gender can complicate and exacerbate the cultural forces leading to racism.
>
> My major point is simpler, less tentative, and should by now be self-evident. This study suggests that neither sexism nor racism will be rooted out unless both sexism and racism are rooted out together. Male dominance and white supremacy have a strong historical connection. (1995: 239)

Jack Johnson was the first African American world heavyweight-boxing champion. I highlight him because his fate, relative anonymity, reminds us what a problematic racial attitude can lead to. Johnson was a "bad actor": he taunted white opponents and chose white female mates whom he sometimes battered. The time was the turn of the 20th century. The championship fight was fought on July 4, 1910. Johnson knocked out Jim Jeffries, who had retired undefeated six years earlier and returned to regain the title from Johnson, who had won it by knocking out Tommy Burns. Noting the white male effort to assert his primacy during this period, Bederman maintains: "Johnson was equally insistent upon his masculine right to wield a man's power and authority. He treated minor brushes with the law—his many speeding tickets and automobile violations—contemptuously, as mere inconveniences which he was man enough to ignore" (1995: 9).

This is a critical scene that Bederman constructs: at the very time white males are being forced to transform the terms of "manhood," a black man strikes out, claiming his own share of physical and political privilege. (Doesn't the arrival of and backlash against Barack Obama as the first black president seem to rehearse the plight of Jackson as the first black heavyweight champion of the world?) Jackson does this in a deriding manner; he taunts the myths of white male supremacy, even equates white with yellow (read as cowardice). Bederman explains the resulting emotional challenge and its class significance thus:

> As immigrants wrested political control from middle-class men in one city after another, a very real basis of urban middle-class men's manhood received both symbolic

and material blows. Immigrant men's efforts to control urban politics were, in a very real sense, contests of manhood—contests which the immigrants frequently won.

> Faced with the unthinkable—a black man had been crowned the most powerful man in the world!—interest in pugilism rebounded. The white press clamored for Jeffries to return to the ring. (1995: 13)

Given the current domination of boxing and most other "manly" sports by men of color, some might find the above description strange or even ridiculous. With the possible exception of the quarterback position in the National Football League, there seems to be no great white-male fear of confusing the control of the political arena with "contests of manhood." But Jack Johnson was living in a very different time. Bederman clarifies:

> Ever since 1899, when Jeffries first won the heavyweight championship, he had refused to fight any Negro challengers. Jack Johnson first challenged him as early as 1903. Jeffries replied, "When there are no white men left to fight, I will quit the business.... I am determined not to take a chance of losing the championship to a Negro." Ever since 1882, when John L. Sullivan had won the title, no white heavyweight champion had fought a black challenger, even though black and white heavyweights had previously competed freely. (1995: 1)

Jeffries's return to fighting began what came to be called the saga of the "Great White Hope." This term refers to the observation that some have longed for and sought to promote the arrival of a white male who can challenge the gradual movement toward non-white male dominance of various "manly" sports like boxing, basketball, and football. But Jeffries's loss resulted in a form of intimidation that even today we do not adequately address. The destruction of prosperous black communities in Florida and Oklahoma during the early 1900s is an example of white frustration, anger, and violence directed at black achievement. These examples were the mere tip of an iceberg:

> The ensuing violence showed what a bitter pill that was for many white American men to swallow. Race riots broke out in every Southern state, as well as in Illinois, Missouri, New York, Ohio, Pennsylvania, Colorado, and the District of Columbia.... Even the United States Congress reacted to the implicit aspersions Johnson's victory cast on white manhood.... Within three weeks, a bill suppressing fight films had passed both houses and was soon signed into law. (Bederman, 1995: 2–3)

The role of Congress in carrying out policies aimed at protecting white manhood, both symbolic and substantive, is a reminder of the ongoing role of legal and political institutions in managing race relations. The 2013 Supreme Court decision regarding the 1965 Voting Rights Act and state legislatures' voter registration policies are current illustrations of this traditional practice. While these political moves can be seen as responses to the changing demography and its implications for national and state elections, they also parallel the upsurge in white male violence against young black males who, like Jack Johnson, are often seen as a threat to white manhood. Likewise, Bederman argued that the excessive response to Jack Johnson's victory was due to an important development:

> Between 1890 and 1917, as white middle-class men actively worked to reinforce male power, their race became a factor which was crucial to their gender.... During these years, a variety of social and cultural factors encouraged white middle-class men to develop new explanations of why they, as men, ought to wield power and authority. In this context, we can see that Johnson's championship, as well as his self-consciously flamboyant, sexual public persona, was an intolerable—and intentional—challenge to white America's widespread beliefs that male power stemmed from white supremacy. Jack Johnson's racial and sexual challenges so upset the ideology of middle-class manhood that both the white press and the United States government were willing to take extraordinary measures in order to completely and utterly annihilate him. (1995: 5)

Today, very few people remember Jackson. Indeed, some histories of boxing never mention him as the first African American heavyweight. Yet Jackson, whom Muhammad Ali identified as his "spiritual father," was apparently multilingual and cosmopolitan, an anomaly in his time. Moreover, his insistence on his dominance as a man signaled a crisis for white manhood because race, along with economics and gender relations, participated in the construction of white manhood.

One idea argued by Bederman above is especially cogent to current mores in American identity politics: "white America has a widespread belief that male power stems from white supremacy." How does the election of a black man as president impact this belief to the degree that it is true today? Granting the tremendous advancements in racial and gender relations in the past several decades, if white racial dominance is pivotal to white male, and by extension, national identity and power, what jeopardy must Barack Obama represent?

Earlier, I indicated how current international crises have been partially framed in terms of Obama's deficiency of Alpha-male energy/leadership proclivities in interactions with Russian president Vladimir Putin or Israeli prime minister Benjamin Netanyahu. But to the immediate question, I suggest that it is quite disquieting—and a source of racial pain—for the nation to feel unsure of the competency of the president.[40] As argued in Chapter 2, all are spoiled by racialized identities, albeit in different ways. In this case, African Americans, for example, may struggle with shame at the first black president's apparent humiliation by a political party and some citizens' demonstration that he cannot act without their support even if many, many whites and minorities have elected him. They cannot, ultimately, make him "white" and therefore able to do the things that previous presidents seemingly did.[41]

This is a very critical point, but not one to belabor since my focus here is essentially the spoilage associated with Barack Obama for a racialized society whose ideal man/national image is a "white supremacist." By "white supremacist," I mean only to indicate someone who feels and enjoys an historical entitlement to be at the head of the table, and someone for whom everyone recognizes this "entitlement." What is implicit in the various rebuffs Obama has endured—from Arizona's governor Jane Brewer sticking her finger in his face on the airport tarmac, to Israel's Netanyahu's lecturing him on "the facts," to Russian leader Putin's dismissive body language during their meeting—is his "nonentitlement" to the position.[42] Some point to the "nonentitlement" accusations directed at former president George W. Bush because of the controversial 2000 election as a parallel undercutting any special treatment of Obama. There is, to be sure, a parallel to be made; and there is also a well-recognized, if not acknowledged, difference. This difference marks Obama's racialized impotence—his *racialized emasculation*.[43] And his implied impotence ultimately reflects painfully on both traditional black impotence and traditional white power. Thus, Obama, by virtue of his elevation to the presidency, "spoiled" it. He became a source of white pain. And all of the positive, supportive white people in the United States cannot undo this spoilage or pain for those whose personal/national identities demanded more: a white man. From this perspective, white male identity, in particular, has been spoiled. This is seen, for instance, in the recent upsurge of public discourse around blackface. Popularly associated with social life on the college campus, the resurgence of this persistent racial "mytheme" is very instructive on the connection between white pain and the perceived spoilage by black males.

Blackface and Racial Pain

Just months after 9/11, when the country was "united," a scandal hit the presses: "Frats suspended for racially offensive costumes" (Black Issues, 2001):

> Two Auburn University fraternities were suspended earlier this month because members dressed in Ku Klux Klan robes and blackface—one with a noose around his neck—during a Halloween party. Delta Sigma Phi and Beta Theta Pi fraternities, both with mostly White members, are being investigated for violating Auburn's discrimination and harassment rules.... In another photo, fraternity members are wearing blackface, wigs and shirts with the letters of Omega Psi Phi, one of four predominately Black fraternities at Auburn. None of the students have been publicly identified.

Days earlier, on Monday, November 12, 2001, in a piece entitled "Auburn Frat Boys Dumped for Race Incident," William C. Singleton III (www.blackplanet.com) wrote: "In another photo, a Confederate flag hangs behind a member in blackface and Afro wigs." This was not a new event in academia. In 1968, *The Temple University News* (March 27, 1968: 3) reported that Tau Epsilon Phi brothers presented a blackface show at their group sing. And from *The Emory Wheel* (Emory University, April 14, 2000), Jada L. Barksdale responded to the use of blackface by Kappa Alpha:

> One issue that I think that the administration as well as the student body needs to recognize is that this incident is only one in a long list of insensitive, racist acts committed by members of the KA fraternity. I understand that they are acts of individuals, but since no effort has been made by the fraternity to publicly punish or even restrict the behavior of these individuals, then I think that it is only fair that the entire fraternity be sanctioned.

Nor was the Auburn incident an isolated one in 2001. In an article entitled "Miss. Students Expelled from Frat," the Associated Press reported:

> Two University of Mississippi students have been expelled from their fraternity after an Internet photograph showed one dressed as a police officer holding a gun to the head of the second, who was in blackface. Similar steps were taken in Alabama by two Auburn University fraternities whose members also were photographed at parties in blackface—one with a noose around his neck, others wearing Ku Klux Klan robes.

Blackface is a symbolic cultural creation or artifact. It has a special meaning to a society that has used race and gender to construct a dominant understanding of white masculinity and manhood. Recent decades have seen an increased emphasis on the different meanings of masculinity and how these impact male identity and development (Kimmel & Messner, 2001). A major aspect of scholarship on manhood and the "masculinity crisis" attending various social, political, and cultural changes has been the recognition that race and gender help to define what it traditionally means to be a dominant white male heterosexual (Bederman, 1995; Horrocks, 1994, 1995; Ipsaro, 1997; Kimmel, 2013).

In "Media Blackface: 'Racial Profiling' in News Reporting," Mikal Muharrar (1998) observed: "Examples of issues defined in blackface and subjected to a racial profile include the black drug abuser and drug dealer, the threatening and invasive black criminal, the black welfare cheat and queen, and the undeserving black affirmative action recipient." What is this resurgence of blackface all about? Perhaps the answer is hidden in the apologies for blackface. In what seemed like days, the judiciary rushed to defend the fraternity men. The judge insisted that they be reinstated because of a First Amendment right. This is uncannily reminiscent of the U.S. Supreme Court's snatching George W. Bush from the fire in 2000. Some saw the irony. Shawn Ryan of the *Birmingham Post-Herald* reported: "It happened with the frat boys at Auburn. It happened a couple of years ago when Atlanta Braves pitcher John Rocker shot off his mouth. People said Rocker was being denied his First Amendment rights when he basically denigrated every ethnic" (November 26, 2001).

There are many ways of understanding this situation. These rationales point to the "underside" of a white male identity crisis. The question of white identity in the current millennium is important here, as some scholars have appreciated. Joe L. Kincheloe went to the heart of the matter:

> The white identity crisis is real and cannot simply be dismissed as the angst of the privileged. While it is in part such an angst, it is also a manifestation of the complexity of identity as class and gender intersect with race/ethnicity, an expression of the emptiness of the postmodern condition, and an exhibition of the failure of modernist humanism to respond to the globalism engulfing it....
>
> The pain of the perception of a new psychological disprivilege within an old privilege gnaws at contemporary white people.... The new disprivilege emerges from the increasingly valued concept of difference and Whites' lack of it. (1999: 163, 177)

Kincheloe was accurate in this assessment: *difference* has currency in today's world. He also touches on a deeper facet of white alienation: the pain of "psychological disprivilege." Michael Kimmel (2013), nearly a decade and a half later, named it "aggrieved entitlement." However named, the loss is real. It is personal and subjective. It is, nonetheless, confused and contradictory, thus leading to a perverse recovery motive and method: the "ugly-ing" and dehumanization of the other. This is the deeper sense of blackface. It is a form of cannibalism, in the sense of gaining power (visibility) through consuming one's victim. It involves assuming, at times, aspects of the identity of the stereotyped other in an effort of self-creation that ultimately exposes the poverty of one's own overvalued and inflated sense of self.[44] An example is the white middle-class adoption of some of the more self-playing aspects of hip-hop culture (Gresson, 1995), even the highly confusing practice of wearing one's pants low enough to expose the underwear.[45] In short, blackface is about both anxious aggression and recovery.

A parallel argument is made in the concluding chapter of *Angry White Men: American Masculinity at the End of an Era*, where Michael Kimmel writes:

> Reclaiming the country,…is a bit abstract; white men also seek to reclaim their manhood…. Reclaiming masculinity is more than a process; it's a statement—to yourself, to other men, to the world. Manhood is nothing if it is not validated by others; it is a "homosocial" performance. Of course, getting a girl is a sure sign that you're successful as a man (2013: 264–265).

Social Recognition. This is at the heart of blackface. *I am somebody because I can disdainfully "inhabit" the body of a fictional, devalued other.* I want to emphasize this point because of the apparent "inability" of certain whites to resist using this historical prop of the minstrel to enhance "whiteness." As I write this page in March 2014, the internet carries several stories of ongoing blackface incidents, complete with bloggers siding with or against the blackface impersonators. What is perhaps most significant to note is the structure of the blackface performance itself. In particular, the contemporary blackface episode often prominently involves the use of a white woman. (We saw this earlier with the incident at Auburn University, where sorority girls were dressed as Playboy bunnies.) She stands as the "prize," "the protected one." But she is more: *she is social recognition.*

The role white women may assume in aiding white masculine self-enhancement has been long observed by scholars (Bederman, 1995; Blee, 1991; Frankenberg, 1993; Kimmel, 2013). Of course, more recent times has seen some white women summarily accused of victimizing white manhood through their feminism even as they are recruited to "reaffirm white male entitlement" (Kimmel, 2013). What is perhaps less fully examined is white women's anger and share in the pursuit of a viable white identity in the multicultural world where blacks and other traditional minorities have projected themselves.

From this perspective, the white woman in blackface can be something more: *self-advocate*. This was powerfully depicted in an October 2013 blackface incident. A young white female, her brother, and another white friend used blackface to rehearse the Trayvon Martin/George Zimmerman tragedy: a "provocative" female wearing a male hat askew stands between two men in blackface: one male wears a blood-stained hoodie, the other wears a sweater reading "neighborhood watch" and points his fingers gunlike to the temple of the other male.[46] The young woman in this particular blackface incident apparently shares concerns attributed earlier to white men. As one news source reported:

> Caitlin Cimeno, who posted the picture on her Instagram account, once berated a black girl on social media who wore a "Black Girls Rock" T-shirt. Under the photo, Cimeno wrote "First of all, sorry but mommy lied to you and secondly, if I was wearing a short that said 'white girls rock' I would be stared at and called a racist cracker." (Shaw, 2013)

Ms. Cimeno's so-called berating of the black female undercuts a larger concern: white pride and white identity may not easily co-exist beside others'—particularly minorities'—self-affirmations. Some white women have been "invited" or chosen to not only define themselves through racialized performances like blackface, but also through gendered ritual performances like the Yellow Ribbon movements of 1979 and 1991 (see Chapter 4). But in all of these instances, the underlying focus is how to recover what has been lost. And in all these instances, the white male has surfaced as the "real" victim: *the "ironic" stereotype*.

White Male Identity as Stereotype

> *Wassup, Dr. Gresson—the maverick? Just seeing how things are going. This semester is pretty tough or maybe it's the professors. I was talking the other day about my field experience with my class and I used the word shit.... My professor told me to watch my language—can you believe that? Anyway, I don't think that my teachers enjoy my comic relief like you did last semester—do I stop being myself? Write me back if you get the chance.*

I got this email message some years back from one of my former students, Mark. I really like this young man, and I think he likes me as well. Actually, I find him remarkably similar to myself, and many of the young African

American males I have known over the years: bright, assertive, and kind-hearted, but sometimes vulgar and abrasive. But most of all, he wants to be "himself." What distinguishes this young man from these black youth and me is his racial-ethnic identity: lower-middle-class Irish Philadelphian. Because of his racial identity, Mark's question is both painful and paradoxical. It is painful because it reflects the struggle he has gone through trying to be both his father's beloved son and express himself as he feels himself to be. His question is a bit paradoxical at the same time because he will not have to change himself: rather, without changing himself, he can—and did—change his plight by changing his major from education to human development. As a young white male with great potential, he will not have to make the major changes in self he feels pressured to do. This is because the main adjustment he is being asked to make is learning to raise his class identity by better managing the language *codes* used by different social groups (Bernstein, 1971). That is, the academic environment he has chosen asks that he minimize or drastically curtail his free expression of behavior associated with being "white trash." But the inner tension he expresses reminds me of mourning. I call the process "dwelling in the surrender" and take it up more fully in Chapter 6. But what is the relevance of this mourning to white male identity?[47]

I have described elsewhere (Gresson, 1995) how many white males have felt like the real victims of oppression and generally have appropriated some aspects of oppression discourse to publicize their pain. We might point to the "woman as nigger" and "white power" slogans of previous generations. Lott and others remind us as well of a longer history of white male identification with "the Negro" in a group setting. It is important to understand that in many life circumstances white males may participate in this form of group identification. Whether fraternity men or "boys on bikes" or "rednecks in the wood," a shared reading of "blackness" enables them to locate themselves as white. In short, blackface has resurfaced in 21st-century America and signals a new point in the ongoing crisis in white male *and* female identities.[48] This crisis is both symbolic and substantive. It is symbolic because the cultural ideas of racial domination have been undermined by vast global changes. It is substantive for very much the same reason. The two dimensions are intertwined, and their joint presence both exposes and exacerbates the traditional "entitlement" of whiteness. For instance, consider how this dialectic might express itself in discussing the evolving "public" identities of Asian Americans. In his essay "Up Identity Creek," Jeff Chang (1998)) announced:

> If overeducated Asian American men—myself included—spent the eighties whining about being portrayed in the media as effeminate geeks, and bemoaning the loss of "our women" to white dudes, we are straight hoo-banging in the nineties. Now we can watch Jet Li kicking white ass on the big screen. We win all the DJ contests. We roll in the flyest Acuras and we run Silicon Valley. Cellular phone companies want our money because we've come a long way, baby.

This is powerful moment of "Asian-American self-display."[49] But the passage points to something else as well: the ubiquity of male rage and anger—and the experience of racial pain. Moreover, this aspect of self-display is dually ironic when placed alongside the stereotypically victimized Asian male and his co-stereotyped white male "oppressor." Thus, in April 2007, the nation was traumatized yet again with young male violence—rage and anger turned outward in a particularly if not exclusively American way: Seung-Hui Cho killed 32 people at Virginia Tech before committing suicide.

This event, involving a so-called model minority, revealed the depth of racialized and gendered pain. Implying that Asian Americans overcome whatever racism comes their way, the "model minority" myth denies subjectivity to the Asian American. Still, evidence of bullying and humiliation, implicit in the bravado passage above, reveals a deeper, more pervasive truth: *racial pain can lead to violence among other than white males*, even if such racialized violence is typically only associated with race if it is not committed by the white male (Kimmel, 2013: 85).

But even violence of this order does not necessarily touch the stereotyped white male's entitlement to cultural artifacts, like guns, that constitute individual and group identity. This was most powerfully seen when a young white male killed 20 children and six adults—all white—in Newtown, Connecticut. Again, the killer is depersonalized with a "mental illness" label and the "gun lobby" hastens to defend a peculiar complicity: the confluence of economic and cultural identity interests. The substantive dimension of the identity crisis is politico-economic and based in the "immorality" characteristic of capitalism. Capitalism, its apologists notwithstanding, simultaneously exploits racial difference *and* rejects it for profit. Capitalism loves no one. The fusion of the two dimensions—symbolic and substantive—of white identity crisis is illustrated in the Enron scandal of 2001 and the financial crisis of 2008: privileged white males (the ones also recognized as deserving of their privilege by the meritocracy myth) sacrificed millions, including middle-class white Americans (Reed & Chowkwanyun, 2012) for their own gain. The erosion of confidence in white economic institutions exposed millions of whites to a fate shared with minorities and other underprivileged people.[50] It is in such a context that people traditionally become vulnerable to various forms of fascist backlash behavior. The earlier discussed resurgence of blackface is a case in point.

But there is something even more powerful that has been taking place among many white males: a realignment that has aggressive features but is ultimately aimed at establishing a *terra firma*. For example, writing a decade after my initial impression, Michael Kimmel (2013: 276–277) concludes in a section on "What's Right About Being White,"

> The American White power movement is filled with guys over whom history is rolling. It's a steamroller, and it is unstoppable. Theirs is an anguished wail, the scream of a hatecord lyric, the venomous hatred of others who are in the same boat, scratching and clawing their way for their stake in the American Dream.... And underneath it all is the seething resentment of a lower middle class that finds itself utterly disenfranchised, dispossessed of their entitlement, threatened by new competition.

Here Kimmel offers a capsule assessment of the plight of the white male—classed, raced, and gendered. What he designates as "aggrieved entitlement" is the racial contract that underpins "white identity." What supposedly sets apart the person identified as "white" from *and* above non-whites—nationally, we speak of this as "American exceptionalism"—is a genius that has generated all the best things in the world. People may buy into this myth to varying degrees, but those who get left at the bottom ultimately experience betrayal. Ultimately, being "white" is supposed to mean "not being a victim" at the bottom of the food chain with the "barbarians."

In *The Hidden Injuries of Class*, Richard Sennett and Jonathan Cobb (1972: 31) wrote: "Isn't betrayal the inevitable result when you try to endow your life with a moral purpose greater than your own life?" They were particularly focused, in this question, on the sacrifices white working-class families, especially the men, brought into American capitalist society on the behalf of their families and, implicitly, their ideals of themselves. But as Sennett and Cobb found in their interviews with white South Boston residents in the early 1970s, the world was changing, and whites who had partly defined themselves in a particular way, often unkindly for nonwhites, found their efforts unappreciated: among other things, their children got educated, expanded their horizons, and enlarged their values and views (including race and integration), thereby leaving behind their parents. As a result, their current understanding of "white identity" was essentially under siege, even betrayed. Thus, Sennett and Cobb's question was ultimately a profoundly existential one: if your subjective, concrete self is also equivalent to the nation writ large, if as an individual you are "your people," "your race," "your country," don't you run the risk of disappointment at some point?

This is precisely a part of the problem today: white identity has been so uniformly linked to "American identity" as "whiteness" that disappointment has been the bitter fruit. Perhaps this is nowhere more evident than in the current international crises exposing the United States' "irrelevancy." And the symbolic head of this weakness, President Barack Obama, is a man whose own traditional racial identity—black—signifies a cruel irony. This "man who has 'failed' to lead the world" is "weak" because he must be for those who feel diminished by his occupying the White House, and yet, his "weakness" becomes their "weakness" for he represents them until 2016. (Of course, it must be said, as well, that the national weakness existed prior to choosing Obama as president; and there are those, like myself, who feel that only a desperate nation could bring itself to select a minority as its "savior."[51])

Conclusion: "Existential" White as Non-Spoiled Identity

Nancy Scheper-Hughes (2001) writes,

> However, "white" is a large and amorphous identity peg in the US and allows for multiple escape hatches and exceptions: white, but lesbian, white but Marxist, white but feminist, white but Spanish speaking, white but... um, dyslexic. The way to soften and to de-stigmatize "whiteness" in America today is by disqualification and the addition of a mediating (and previously stigmatized) counter-identity. This allows one to join the more socially acceptable ranks of the formerly nearly despised, victimized, and oppressed "communities of suffering" (Williams, 1994) that is broadly defined to include women, gays, and the disabled as well as racial/ethnic categories.

There is merit here, but there is also a problem: whites who want to be "existentially" white, free of the stigma sticking to "whiteness." Escape into a previous victim category is thus achieved through a rhetorical reversal (Gresson, 1995), switching, or reversing labels: the oppressed is now the oppressor; the oppressor now the oppressed. Making the murdered black males the aggressors is illustrative of this approach to identity "non-spoiling." In the next chapters we examine other dynamics of this non-spoiling. I call this process "white pain and the dance of agency."

John Foster (2013: 42) cites several instances of young white males that illustrate this struggle with perceived injustice from the media directed at white men. One young man depicts the complicated emotions, beliefs, and values pressing on him existentially in this way:

> Whenever I hear someone always pushing in, saying 'oh, it's the white man's fault, white man's fault,' like I don't know, that really gets annoying after a while 'cause …you know, I never really did anything, like I said my family never owned slaves or anything, you know I was never really [involved in]… racial tension or anything … you know, goin' crazy … runnin' around black neighborhoods, settin' stuff on fire, but, you know, [I] always hear about how me as a white person, I'm keeping black America down, but … you know, I almost think they're doin' it to themselves.

By naming the range of racist practices he has resisted, denounced, or otherwise avoided, this young man affirms his subjectivity: an innocent white man. Moreover, he not only disavows a racist investment in black plight, he seems posed to situate it squarely in the shoulders of blacks themselves. Herein is the basis for a sense of both racial hurt and injustice. Here we see a context for white pain as more than personal pain; "white pain" becomes a metaphor for the accumulated perceptions of racial innocence defiled: spoiled.

Moreover, this spoilage is reflected in the ongoing pain so many are currently enduring as we await, *painfully*, the conclusion of Obama's presidency. I don't know what historians will say of the great experiment; perhaps nothing more than first came the black, then the female. But the collective spoiled identity marking South Africa also marks us, those who support *and* undermine President Obama. But we must recognize that, on one plane at least, Obama is a metaphor for a racialized imagination, conscience, and struggle toward righteousness. And in his apparent and real failings, he brings us face to face with racial pain. Nowhere perhaps is this more understandably apparent than around his role as "commander in chief."[52]

Identity, especially national or group identities, are forged from both historical events and myths. The soldier, the white soldier, has long dominated the American imagination as the Alpha Male, the ultimate expression of righteousness, courage, sacrifice, and pure innocence. Even though we, as a nation, have continually failed to fulfill our commitment to the soldier, we have continued to push to the fore an image of nationhood and manhood intricately linked to the soldier. Beginning with Bill Clinton, then George W. Bush, and finally Barack Obama, the insistence that the president, the "commander in chief," be a war veteran was abandoned. But the election of a black "commander in chief" also shattered the image of a "manly man," one prepared to send the nation to war to affirm America's primacy, its status as the one and only, chosen by God, superpower. Thus, the election of a black man as president, especially one lacking the military pedigree of, say, Colin Powell, was implicitly an assault on American manhood, and a source of white pain.

In assuming this role, President Obama symbolically became "the Man," the father, the "white man." To assume this role is, of course, one aspect of contemporary white pain for those who resist this implicit fusion of white and black identities. But a larger aspect pertains to the role of the United States as the only superpower, and its apparent inability to influence the Middle East, Russia, or even Europe. Of course, everyone understands the dependence of the world on oil and the resulting vulnerability this creates for those with bombs and sanctions but lack of will to use them. Enter Obama. Conservative journalist David Brooks uttered the painful "truth":

> Basically since Yalta we've had an assumption that borders are basically going to be borders and once that comes into question if in Ukraine or in Crimea or anywhere else, then all over the world all bets are off. And let's face it, Obama, whether deservedly or not, does have a—I'll say it crudely—a manhood problem in the Middle East. Is he tough enough to stand up to somebody like Assad or somebody like Putin? I think a lot of the rap is unfair but certainly in the Middle East there is an assumption that he's not tough enough. (Armbruster, 2014)

The focus on President Barack Obama's decisions in Syria, Ukraine, and other places as a manhood issue is more than incidental. The need for a cowboy-president persona like Ronald Reagan/John Wayne is a part of the issue. We have always viewed America as the strongest—and there is no way we can easily accept anything else, like Putin in Russia and Assad in Syria, that contradicts this. And, to be sure, Obama as a Democrat is expected to have an uphill fight challenging the persona of militarily weak Democrats. But there is something more here.

> NBC's Chuck Todd agreed. "By the way, internally they [American officials] fear this you know it's not just Corker saying it, questioning whether the president is being alpha-male," he said. "That's essentially saying 'he's not alpha-dog. His rhetoric isn't tough enough.'" (Armbruster, 2014)

In the persona of President Barack Obama is contained both the "audacity of hope" and the plight of the wretched. *He symbolizes racial pain and its discontents.* And, as the quote from Sigmund Freud's *Civilization and Its Discontents* (epigraph to Part One) observes, it is part of the human condition to do both good and evil. With respect to race matters, this view invites us to address the issues of aggression in the defense of ego (self) and the self-other deceptions that index our racialized pain.

White identity is clearly more than a stereotyped this or that. It is certainly more than "racist" or "chauvinist" or "true believer." And it is precisely being stereotyped as this or that that offends many, especially young whites, today. Yet, it is precisely the combined agency of individuals insisting upon an existential assessment ("I am me; judge me for my own behavior") and the larger society or culture ("the institutional order") that pulls everyone into America's "Atonement." After all, this peculiar atonement activity is ultimately the renewal of the vision and presence of "innocent whiteness"—in a time when so many seek to dismantle it. In the next chapter, I focus on racial pain and atonement activities in schools and universities—the academy.

· 4 ·

WHITE STUDIES AND RACIAL PAIN IN THE ACADEMY

The Plight of the Neo-Liberal Agenda in the Existential Moment

Do not plague me with this "whiteness" business, you Hegelian robber.
– Personal communication from Rob Haskell (1994)

We are then able to understand that the vicissitudes of every life, just as emotional disorders, invariably engage our narcissism. And the recovery from injuries to it demands the services of aggression.
Gregory Rochlin (1973: 22)

Prologue: The Problem of "Whiteness"

Early during the preparation of this book, I received the opening epigraph in email from my closest friend and adopted brother, Robert Haskell, in response to an article I had written on the racial themes in the movie *Forrest Gump* (1994). The allusion to Hegel comes from a passage I first shared with him 20 years earlier when we both were doctoral students at Penn State University. I had found this remark in the preface to *The Concept of Irony* by Søren Kierkegaard. Kierkegaard, the father of existentialism, supposedly uttered it to the members of his master's thesis committee in 19th-century Denmark.

Rob and I both felt the sentiment deeply because of our constant battles with "the establishment." Over the years, we often repeated these words to each other about members of the establishment whom we felt were harassing us about some academic or public matter. We had never before said this to each other, though; this was a first. I did not feel overly bothered by the comment because we regularly chided each other about something. Our friendship, moreover, was far too strong to be undermined by such an incident. I mention it here because I think it illustrates the complexity of contemporary discourses on whiteness and the racial pain associated with it.

By associating me with the Kierkegaard incident, I believe Rob was alerting me personally to the painful aspects of whiteness talk. That is, "whiteness" represented something more than just pointing out racism to him. Rob felt "white pain" whenever he experienced unfair (in his mind) accusations of racism *and* those instances when, as my friend, he saw me endure racism. This is an important point, by the way: throughout nearly 40 years of friendship, Rob often was my "guardian angel." That is, he was necessarily touched and affected by instances of racism that he lived with me. This is the inevitable existential moment of shared reality of people who care for or love each other. Thus, when a banker who had just approved Rob for a loan, denied me a bank loan (even though I earned more than Rob and had a better credit rating), Rob asked for and received the money for me. And when the banker asked why he wanted the additional money, Rob retorted, "You know why I want it and whom I want it for."[53]

Rob had been my "white champion," against both white racism and black chauvinism over the years; he certainly understood the psychodynamics and sociology of racism. These facts lead me to the question, why does the notion of "whiteness" infuriate so many and lead otherwise progressive, fair, white scholars to identify it as yet another instance of "political correctness"? In part, the answer is that whiteness has come to be a source of study, an object of "the gaze." In addition, my talking about *Forrest Gump* as "the call back to whiteness" was related to one of the important developments of the past few decades: the critique of "whiteness" as a way of "dismantling white privilege" (Rodriguez & Villaverde, 2000). The initiative to challenge white privilege pertains, ultimately, to white pain. It is this relationship that I examine in this chapter.

The Nature of "Whiteness" and Its Tensions

The problem of "self-display" goes beyond the hurt feelings of a group of white tourists in an "unfriendly colored nation," as I described in the previous chapter.

It pertains to the idea of "whiteness" and the traditional privileges associated with it. But what is this "whiteness" business, to paraphrase my friend, Rob? "Whiteness" is a fairly new concept or idea in certain circles, namely, parts of academia that deal with analyzing power in America. Since most economic, military, communicational, political, and cultural power is dominated by persons and groups identified as "white," it now is common to speak of "whiteness." Of course, the control of most public or collective power (versus personal or individual power) has always rested with white Americans. What has made this concept so important is that many in the United States and elsewhere have realized the importance of naming this power. Most people do not regularly come into contact with either the word "whiteness" or the people who care to use it in their presence. The word per se is important only to a very small collection of scholars and political activists. My friend Rob, now passed, belonged to this group. But this man differed from most other white academics I have personally known with respect to matters racial. For one thing, he had included personal reflections on racial matters in some of his scholarly writings. A brief examination of his thoughts, many contained in his quasi-autobiography, *Adult-Child Research and Experience* (Haskell, 1993), is helpful to us in gaining a partial understanding of the whiteness issue and the matter of white pain.

"Whiteness": A Personal and Professional Legacy Examined

When I asked Rob about his email message to me, he expressed a number of concerns regarding the notion of "whiteness." For him, the notion:

- Seemed to identify white men as evil incarnate;
- Suggested whiteness is essential to white men;
- Ignored power as the real focus of liberation and oppression discourse;
- Ignored the interchangeability of race and gender when describing the destructiveness of power;
- Failed to be clearly identified as a "metaphor" rather than "something real";
- Promoted the continuance and intensification of racist conflict in the United States and elsewhere.

Rob was an extraordinary human being; a decent, courageous, and compassionate person. I loved him. We were friends and colleagues for nearly 40 years before he passed in 2010. We had lived and traveled together, both in the United States and Europe. He had seen me in good and bad moments, as I had him. Furthermore, he gave much thought to being "white" and expressed some of his reflections in an important book on the professional and personal significance of alcoholism. For instance, he wrote:

> Neither was I socialized into identifying with a heritage; I could not therefore understand people who identified with their social origins. When I went in the Army, I heard people talk and joke about various ethnic minorities. This, too, I thought made no sense. Were they not people just like me? What does where your grandparents were born have to do with the person standing before me?
>
> While working on my master's degree, I was required to take a course on race relations. The seminar was composed of about 15 students. Some were "Mexican," some were "Jews," some were "Italian," some were Black, and some were "American Indian." They all discussed their ethnic heritage and said how proud they were to be what they thought they were. I boldly told them that they made no sense. It was clear that I had insulted them. I did not mean to; I was just trying to figure it out. When asked what ethnic group I belonged to, I told them I did not belong to any group. They then asked what national origin I was. I said I was born in Portland, Maine. Okay, then, they said, so you do identify with being an American. I said "no" I did not. They asked if I considered myself a Mainer. I said I could somewhat identify with that.
>
> I knew what they wanted to hear. I told them my grandmother had once mentioned that I was Irish, English, and a "wee bit" of Scotch. They asked if I was proud of it. I responded by saying they might as well ask me if was proud of being a human from the planet called Earth. I completed the seminar without emotionally understanding what it was all about. (Haskell, 1993: 105–106)

Rob attributed his lack of "emotional understanding" to his personal biography rather than his racial privilege. Hence, the subtitle of his book is "Personal and Professional Legacies of a Dysfunctional Co-dependent Family." In this way Haskell explained his refusal to acknowledge difference as a personal matter of identity. But I see his capacity to insist—without major consequence—that race and ethnicity did not matter as *racial power*. Indeed, Haskell partially reveals the deep psychological character of whiteness when he describes his own growth beyond the provincialism inherent in much racial liberalism:

> Years later while teaching in Harrisburg, Pennsylvania, I interviewed Aaron, a candidate for a position on the faculty. He had black skin (actually it was brown). There was considerable prejudice, as well as "liberal" acceptance of Aaron. He was

a brilliant fellow. I thought of Aaron as simply a man who, by virtue of accident of birth, happened to have black skin, so that if he would wash it off, he and I would be the same. It was only years later that I realized that my "color blindness" was a kind of prejudice, too: People are different because of their experience of growing up in a different culture. For some 18 years now, Aaron and I have been brothers. Aaron is also an ACOA [adult child of an alcoholic]. (Haskell, 1993: 105)

In recent years, the "color-blind" argument has been recognized as a form of racial misrepresentation if not outright racism. Haskell saw it as such earlier than many social critics and "liberal" whites because he could observe daily how I personally endured and fought with racial pain. By naming me his *brother*—and we were—Haskell was assuming a "shared fate" with me. To be sure, he could and did enjoy privileges as a white male academic that I could not; and there were occasions when he asserted privileges for me as only a white male could (sometimes) for a beloved friend who was marginalized by society, as when he secured a bank loan for me.

But there is yet another aspect to Haskell's psychology that partially accounted for his capacity to move beyond the dominant group pressures to racialize in negative ways. In his autobiography we read:

> Many of my feelings, thoughts, values, beliefs, and behaviors have been marginal to the society in which I live just as it would be if I now went to live with Eskimos. When a person lives psychologically outside of his culture to a considerable degree for a sufficient period of time, and being told that he should be like everyone else, he begins to question his own sanity; he must be crazy. I had these feelings as a child. I made a vow I would not go crazy. There were times when I thought I was going crazy. During those times, I would beat my fist against the wall, breathe deeply, sing to myself, rock furiously in a rocking chair radio up loud and concentrate on each word. I was, in fact, having what is called a panic attack. ACOAs may have more than their share of these. (1993: 103–104)

Haskell understood the privilege aspect of his position. He introduced both a personal and a racial confession: his disassociation from the group-constructed and group-enforced mandates of racial identification. Because of this refusal to buy into whiteness, Rob experienced periods of panic; however, unlike most persons so stricken, his anxiety was caused by never being told that standing alone was okay. This emotional isolation reveals the irony in his behavior: making a choice that could be made effectively only if he remained invested in "whiteness" as a positive identity. That is, naming himself a "man" rather than a "white man"—even though he "acted" like a white male and enjoyed (even seized) many of the prerogatives of the white male.

In the earlier passage, Haskell revealed his limited appreciation of the racial dimension of an otherwise nonracial identity. Perhaps a bit of this attitude persisted in his outrage at my *Forrest Gump* essay. If he had no investment in whiteness, perhaps he would not have felt as much of the sting. I don't identify this quality as racist per se; it is an orientation that can appear even if one rejects the brutality of racism. Rob, for example, showed this while we were graduate students at Penn State University in the mid-1970s. The occasion was the day after a young (white) male had opened fire on an unsuspecting public on the campus of the University of Texas. We were walking past Pattee, the graduate library, and talking about some shared racist experience (over 20 years Rob and I had shared more than a few such incidents) when he said, "Aaron, if I were a black man, I would get on top of Pattee with a rifle and open fire on the public too." I replied, "You sound just like a white man."

For years, Rob did not understand my meaning, despite his knowledge that events similar to those he was describing were, at that point in time, primarily committed by white males. Beyond the statistical story, I was trying to share with Rob a fact— true for the time—about racial position: role-identified, random destructiveness due to personal pain is something one largely learns. It is often facilitated by a sense of entitlement. Not everyone who feels entitled or otherwise stigmatized commits the act, but rarely does someone outside the entitled group commit certain kinds of destructiveness. This is why until recently women rarely killed men, or blacks killed whites just because they were angry at the world. To be sure, today we recognize a more pervasive attitude of "entitlement" that seems to infect the society as a whole, and in ways that intersects race, gender, class, sexuality.

In addition, and this traditionally has been a source of black male pain, whatever their circumstances and fantasies, most minorities have understood in the very marrow of their bones the folly of expressing their racial pain by means of random retaliation. During the height of the black power movement in the 1960s, historians Rudwick and Meier wrote the following:

> It would appear that both in the World War I period, and today—and indeed during the ante-bellum era and at other times when manifestations of violence came to the fore—there has been a strong element of fantasy in Negro discussion and efforts concerning violent retaliation. The Black Muslims talk of violence, but the talk seems to function as a psychological safety valve; by preaching separation, they in effect accommodate to the American social order and place racial warfare off in the future when Allah in his time will destroy whites and usher in an era of black

domination.... Du Bois and others who have spoken of the inevitability of racial warfare and Negro victory in such a struggle were engaging in wishful prophesies. And Negroes have been nothing if not realistic. The patterns of Negro behavior in riots demonstrate this. In earlier times, as already indicated, those who brought guns in anticipation of the day when self-defense would be necessary usually did not retaliate. And Negro attacks on whites occurred mainly in the early stages of the riots before the full extent of anger and power and sadism of the white mobs became evident. (1969: 412, 417)

Elliott Rudwick and August Meier are discussing here the rhetorical aspect of racial rhetoric, notably black threats toward whites. In this passage, they also identify a major component of the enduring racial shame and pain that blacks, particularly black men, feel: the fear of physical, social, and economic retaliation by white men. This racial pain and knowledge partly underlay my inability to do anything more than fantasize about hurting masses of whites, even though, in theory, I am certainly as capable as Rob was to imagine the wholesale slaughter of others in retaliation for my perceived racial pain.

This is an important point. Whites seem to believe that minorities want to retaliate against them with catastrophic consequences. For instance, an entry in my diary from September 3, 1990, reads as follows:

Today I asked the students their response to the *Time* article, "Beyond the Melting Pot" [April 9, 1990: 28–30]. I was struck by the strong "fear" this essay caused for a few of the students: the observation that America is increasingly a multiracial and multicultural society; and that white Americans are becoming a demographic minority, seems to elicit fears of retaliation. One young woman said: "I didn't like the article because it seems to say that we are going to get paid back for what we did to blacks, Indians, and other minorities in the past. I don't think that I should be penalized for what happened in the past." I tried to reassure her and the others who might share her feelings. I said the black psychiatrist, Frantz Fanon, found [1968] that the dreams of mentally fatigued French soldiers in Algiers [Africa] often reflected a parallel concern: they often dreamed that they were being overwhelmed by hordes of blacks and destroyed in the manner western movies portrayed Native American massacres of white settlers. But these were just fantasies and fears: formerly oppressed people of color have rarely retaliated with kind toward their oppressors. Some students seemed consoled by my words. However, I could tell that most of the class did not understand the reason for fear a few had shown—not because minorities were as benign as I inferred, but because they can't even conceive of a society in which whites are not everywhere and in charge of everything.

Despite the historical insistence that "the other" is less than fully human, whites conceal a belief that the very humanness of "the other" must be defended against. Although various animalistic images—monkey, baboon, gorilla—have been conjured up to define "the other," what is feared is the expression of the full humanity of "the other." The duplicity implicit in white racial history strangles whites when racial matters surface, and the inability to confront this duplicity leads to the contradictory visions that permit some to claim the superiority of "whiteness" (Bork, 1996; Kirk, 1993) and others to insist that equality and justice permeate the land (D'Souza, 1995).

The irony is the peculiar conversation, or emotional logic, that underpins this duplicitous discourse. On the one hand, it is characterized by denial, but on the other, by despair. The denial is that racism and oppression are alive, and so whites are innocent. When incontrovertible evidence is shown, denial gives way to despair, a fear that these tendencies can never be overcome. But there are times and ways for rehearsing this racial inheritance, as Rob indicated in his autobiography. Sometimes when talking with Rob, I would push his button by seemingly essentializing white evil and destructiveness. This was not my intention; words sometimes are "bad" vehicles because they say both what we mean and more. Over time, I came to see that many whites can tolerate the particular, situational, historical destructiveness that whites have perpetrated as a part of whiteness only if it is clear that (1) they personally are disengaged from such "white evil" and (2) that "white evil" itself is a variant of human evil, no worse than that in Asian or African history.

Personally, I have been able to grant the first part of the "demand": individual whites are no worse than individual blacks, yellows, greens, or whatever. The second part is more difficult—historical circumstances being different—and requires a more qualified response.[54] I have often used the example of male/female battering to explain my reservation or qualification: While it may be true that women hit men as much as men hit women, as some argue, it is not true that the physical and societal consequences for female batterers are, collectively, the same as those for male batterers. Men are typically larger and stronger than women; moreover, society is organized to allow men unequal power to hurt, suppress, and intimidate women. Likewise, human destructiveness and oppression in bygone times may have been as vicious, systematic, and unrelenting as that associated with recent Western civilization. Still, it cannot match the destructive power unleashed on the world in the 20th century alone. The ideology identifying white European culture as the world's best and God's chosen (Bork, 1996; Kirk, 1993; Slotkin, 1973) argues that it has contributed unique gifts to the world. There is much truth in this belief, but there is much untruth as well. In particular, this ideology has often debunked alternative realities. It is chauvinistic; it is arrogant; and it is defined in opposition to "the other": homosexuals, women, and nonwhites.

As one consequence, millions of white youth committed to a democratic ideal are compromised when introduced to a multicultural discourse. This is seen by the relative elision of "white ethnicity" through the creation of whiteness as a racial identity. In a class assignment, a young white male of Irish, German, French, and Spanish background wrote, "I feel somewhat cheated from not being able to learn anything about my mother's side of the family and their cultural heritage. A large part of this may be that their family has been in this country since before the Revolution so they feel completely American." This young man continued his autobiographical reflection:

> One experience that I do not enjoy is that it seems like when I look into my heritage over the last couple of hundred years I feel a sense of shame. I feel this because unfortunately the Europeans feel superior to all other races and have done many awful things to a lot of different ethnic groups. This has caused me much grief because I enjoy history and different cultures and do not understand how we could feel this way and do the things that we did. This leads to one of the values that I hold that I do not want to but feel has been ingrained into me throughout the years of my life and the generations before. This value is the value of supremacy, or thinking that I am better than everyone else. I do not like having this but can see it at different points in my life. This value is key to understanding a lot of what the people with my ethnicity do.

Understanding the inability and undesirability of "erasing" everything white, some scholars sensitive to the dilemma of a new generation of white youth call for clarifying the "good and bad of whiteness" (Giroux, 1998; Kincheloe, Steinberg, Rodriguez, & Chennault, 1998; Rodriguez & Villaverde, 2000). These scholars differ from those who believe whiteness to be so perverse that it must be scrapped. But what is it precisely that these "recovery school of whiteness" scholars want to salvage? What can be identified that is good, admirable, and prideful?

I have come to see that these questions are especially important in classrooms trying to transform the limiting, undemocratic, and inhumane aspects of whiteness. In the multiculturalism teacher-education classroom, for example, I have tried to help my students access this transformative agenda through the use of autobiographical exercises. The following excerpt is from the essay of a bright, self-assured young woman. Pay particular attention to her effort to balance the things she is proud of—the things that she has identified with and internalized as parts of her own identity—with her ever-changing awareness of social oppression:

> I was raised under the principle that hard work will ultimately lead to success. My Irish-American paternal grandfather grew up in the coal regions of Pennsylvania during the worst of the Great Depression and my Dutch-English maternal grandfather lived on a farm in Indiana. Both came from humble beginnings and worked hard for every penny that they made. My father was raised by his schoolteacher parents in a modest home in Pennsylvania, working both after school and on the weekends. He graduated from Villanova and began working at an entry-level job at du Pont. His good work ethic and sharp people skills allowed him to advance on the corporate ladder.... Success is not solely measured by accumulation of wealth, but rather by happiness. I can see now why my parents are both very successful. They have not only achieved economic security, but have enjoyed raising three terrific children over the past 25 years. Instilled in my brothers and myself are the family values of hard work and ambition. For example, in the first grade, I was labeled and stigmatized with dyslexia. Rather than let my learning disability get the best of me, I worked extra hard to catch up to my peers. By the third grade, I was on reading level and by the 6th grade I was above reading level.
>
> I understand that by being "white" my family has always had social privilege. After serving in World War II, it was a lot easier for my grandfathers to get jobs than their "colored" counterparts. In addition, it was a lot easier for my father to get into college and then land a job in corporate America than it was for minorities at the time. To reframe this, in times of adversity, one could always count on their "whiteness" to help them out. That still holds true.
>
> My ethnicity could be characterized as "white" upper middle class. Since almost everyone in this country considers themselves to be middle class, then that might not narrow that down too much! Furthermore, I use the term "white" for lack of any better [word] to use. I do not regard my race in everyday life and understand that there is no absolute American "white-ness."... I have financial stability, a good education, and a traditional white nuclear family. I am empowered in all areas but one—I am still only a woman.
>
> Being aware of my ethnicity has allowed me to be conscious of racial and ethnic prejudices in our society. For example, I went to racially and ethnically diverse public schools growing up. I saw that the "white" students had better teachers and more money was spent on them. I am not ignorant of the social injustices in our school systems. I noticed that "black" students were always expected to be very athletic and not very academically oriented. White students were expected to perform better academically.

This young woman helps put flesh on the essential meaning of whiteness in its distinctiveness. At base, *whiteness pertains to privilege codified in terms of a color code and working to increase and retain power as symbol and substance.* From this view, much of white existence is no better or worse than any other. Moreover, while it may not be "Christian," "Democratic," or "just," the use of whatever means necessary to attain and retain power does not differentiate whites from others. Thus the transformation of American society does not solely pertain to changing or modifying whiteness. Still, it does require some changes among whites concurrent with other social changes (Butin, 2001).

What I am suggesting is that the fusion of white identity with power over several centuries and the continual renewing of this fusion through racism are the conditions that must be changed. It is the resistance to these twin tensions, in part, that causes white pain. A recent study (Foster, 2013: 60) on white discourse on race found that ambivalence is a central feature of how whites position themselves on race matters:

> This ambivalence allows whites to naturalize white or Anglo American culture, thereby allowing white supremacy to exist unabated and thrive.... Separated from the reality of multiracial and multicultural America, whites have the luxury of forming a kind of "dysconsciousness...." Because of white privilege, whites are able to shrug off concerns of white racism and forget about the gross inequities existing within their philosophies and the contradictions occurring throughout their repertoires on racial issues. This is a crucial process in the rationalization of the white racial frame, which reaffirms the entire process. Reinforcing white racism could be an unintended consequence of the ambivalence, while the manifest function is the management of one's face during a conversation. Still the rationalization of the racialized social system takes place.

I felt this tension in the preceding passage, and I sometimes felt it in my relations with my friend Robert. It is important to understand that others, including minorities, share this chauvinistic proclivity. It is inevitable, I suspect, that racial and ethnic identities convey a commingling of positive and negative elements. For instance, a young Jewish student completing the same exercise and clearly alert to the complex historical representation of Jews in "the Gentile world" accessed his ethnicity in the following manner:

> Judaism has also taught me the value of continuing the Jewish tradition. Judaism is a minority religion and as the rate of inter-marriage increases, the Jewish population is decreasing. Being Jewish is an important aspect of my life, and I want to share this with my children. For me, spreading the wisdom of Judaism, its teachings and its traditions with future generations, is something I feel very strongly about. In hundreds of years, I want Judaism to be alive and growing.... I have accepted many other values from Judaism...the importance of all humankind, the equality of all people, the capacity of all people to improve themselves, the importance of sharing and giving to

the less fortunate, and the freedom of choice and responsibility for one's actions. I use these teachings and ideals of Judaism in my everyday decisions and actions.

These reflections are complex, as they imply and conceal broad historical and political strokes and invite a diversity of perspectives and passions. For that reason, many see the academy as the wrong site for stimulating diversity discourses. Using the rubrics of "academic integrity" and "scientific neutrality," the depth of the white pain propelling much of "human science" remains understated and underexamined. The complexity here may be seen in the response to whiteness studies.

The Paradox of Whiteness Studies: The Teaching of Alienation

One of the unavoidable consequences of social change activism is the possibility that those seeking social justice for the oppressed may participate in oppression. This is an ancient idea, certainly traceable to biblical passages such as "Let he who is without sin cast the first stone" and classical references such as "Physician, heal thyself." The topic of whiteness studies illustrates this very well. A blog on Slate's website (1997) declared, "White Is a Color Too" and contained the following:

> A front-page article in the *Wall Street Journal* last month certified that "whiteness studies" has arrived. The burgeoning academic field—informed by both thoughtful race theory and liberal Caucasian guilt—has already spawned hundreds of acolytes; more than 70 books (according to the Center for the Study of White American Culture Inc.'s Web site; sub-specialties such as white trash, suburban resentment, and male ethnography; and a national conference held at the University of California this April 9, 1997). Among the field's primary objectives is exposing the privileges that come with being white in order to make them go away. The *Minnesota review's* [sic] current issue is titled "White Issue." This fall, *Transition*, a Harvard-based journal of global culture, will publish its own white issue, in which nonwhite scholars will weigh in on whiteness.

This is an exciting extract; it also is a powerful indictment of whiteness studies. First, it reports a negative article from the *Wall Street Journal*, and second, it rehearses and expands that negativity. The forcefulness of the negativity is achieved by putting down the Ivory Tower. By emphasizing the academy's cultural climate—as reflected in the ideas of subspecialties, elite institutions, academic journals, and so forth—it succeeds in reaffirming the Us/Them difference. This approach trivializes the field, whose goal is to expose "the privileges that come with being white in order to make them go away." How ironic, the passage seems to laugh, that whites—who are presumably privileged academics—dare undertake the task of exposing themselves as whites as a means of de-privileging themselves. Yes, it is a laugh—and so Harvard gets over on Minnesota by permitting nonwhite scholars to get in on the white bashing.

This depiction of so-called whiteness studies has been presented to the public in a way that fuels an already deep-seated sense of racial victimization. Consider the following letter to the editor of *The Chronicle of Higher Education*, entitled "Taking Pride in Being White":

> Seldom have I read such bias and distortion in a respectable publication as that reported in the article "Lifting the Veil from Whiteness: Growing Body of Scholarship Challenges a Racial Norm" (September 8). I do research on prejudice and know it when I see it. I favor fair treatment for all races, ethnic groups, etc. This fairness has to include whites as well as others. If *The Chronicle* article correctly reports their views, the scholars all seem hostile to whites and white identity. The only one who is clearly out front in his prejudice is Noel Ignatiev, the Harvard University lecturer who edits a journal called *Race Traitor*, with the motto of "Treason to whiteness is loyalty to humanity." The other scholars seem to be serving the same purpose, but with a false facade of objectivity. It is bad enough that whites are the victims of a quota system called affirmative action, which causes them (especially white males) to be discriminated against, to work (as I have in the past) for an incompetent supervisor, etc. Now you have academics putting them down. And there is an irony to all this. The irony is that of all the races and ethnic groups, whites have a record that is extremely good. The intellectual contributions of whites throughout history are impressive, and they have a low crime rate as well. The crime rate among blacks is very high, as is the amount of illegitimate births, which is now reported as 68 per cent of all black births. H.I.V. and AIDS are growing among blacks and Hispanics, while they are leveling off or declining among whites.
>
> We should want to keep the positive aspects of white culture, while of course getting rid of the negative aspects. More people should be proud of being white, given the great achievements of whites. Yet due to change in the immigration laws, it is quite possible that early in the 21st century, whites will become a minority in the U.S. This can be changed if the immigration laws are changed, but it will not be changed if we have more and more propaganda against whites.
>
> A few years ago I would not have imagined writing a letter such as this one. I felt the main problems were discrimination against blacks, Hispanics, women, etc. But it is clear that it has become all right to discriminate against whites, and people have to start speaking up and taking a stand. Most whites have little racial identity as whites. It is time that changed. As the article makes clear, whites are under attack for being white, despite their valuable contributions to civilization. (October 20, 1995: B3)

For me, the power of this passage is the pain it gives off. This man, a professor of psychology at a state university in the South, believes himself to be a fair, decent, and racially knowledgeable professional. Furthermore, he clearly has had personal experiences with unfairness based on "preferential privileges." Most of us can identify with him in this regard. We have known unfairness and we know ourselves to be largely fair, decent human beings. It is precisely this narrative power that makes this passage so much more powerful than the whiteness studies scholarship it critiques. As I showed in the previous section, whiteness studies fail to satisfactorily convince most people, especially those who are unsympathetic, that they have something meaningful to share. On the contrary, whiteness studies increasingly serve the interests of racists, widening the racial division so deeply embedded in American culture. They do so because despite their goodwill and sound scholarship, whiteness studies are characterized by duplicity. What do I mean by this statement? Certainly, whiteness scholars are largely sensitive, decent, and courageous. I mean that, contrary to their intention, whiteness studies enable whites to disavow racial privilege even as they assert, as whites did nearly two decades ago, the need for white power. Hence, this writer can say: "The irony is that of all the races and ethnic groups, whites have a record that is extremely good." This seemingly necessary position thus converges with more racially chauvinistic positions such as that of Russell Kirk (1993) who stated unabashedly in *America's British Culture* that whites are the superior race and ought to be on the top. Such positions also show convergence with more widely publicized commentaries such as Herrnstein and Murray's *The Bell Curve* (1994). Because of the efforts of recovery scholarship like this, contemporary whites are able to claim a racist ancestry without being characterized as racist; hence the preceding passage tells us that nonwhites are the really bad characters. Whites do not have to face their unique history of racist savagery and its unprecedented qualities, and so lynching and other forms of human destructiveness have been kept away from the image of white = civilized (Bederman, 1995).

Racial misery and decay are deep inside white culture, but control of the public representations of pain and pathos can fool even whites: A while back, a white neighbor and I were talking about black self-hate. He indicated that he had read about this phenomenon years earlier but had never really encountered the phenomenon in his all-white world. I noted that whites had their own self-hate dynamics, pointing out that the neighbors living down the hill from us in the trailer camp are called "white trash" and "trailer trash" by other whites, both working-class and middle-class whites. He was momentarily dazed and gradually smiled and softly admitted, "Yeah, I guess you're right.... I never saw it like that before."

What collective unconscious tendencies account for this blindness or myopia? How does it play itself out in teacher education and the challenges facing white teachers in diverse settings? I believe an important and useful clue is given in this brief autobiographical reflection, written by one of my students:

> I've been fortunate to have lived a fairly diverse life up this point. I was born in Washington, D.C., while my father was attending Howard Medical School. He once told me that at the time (the early 60s), students who weren't either Black or Jewish were the minorities on campus.... My family moved around a lot until I was almost six years old. We went from Washington to an area of San Diego known as Spanish Harlem to the Bronx in New York. In all of these neighborhoods, we were the only White family. Even when we lived outside of Philadelphia, we were the only non-Italian family. Until we moved to Aspen Hill (a community slightly north of Rockville, MD), I'd never seen people with blonde hair or light skin other than my sister, my mother and myself. When a Black family moved into our neighborhood, my parents had to explain why my sister's best friend never came out if we were playing with Desmond. I was nine years old, and this was the first time I'd ever experienced prejudice. Elementary school was filled with kids who looked just like me and I had now become aware of that fact. I started to understand the derogatory comments that relatives on my mom's side of the family (from "down South" in Virginia) sometimes made. My father's family, predominately Baltimore Jews, was even worst [sic] because they denied what they were doing.

One theme in this passage is the collusive nature of racial identity construction: one has to grow into one's identity through specific experiences. And in a world with contradictory messages about racial equality and the like, we see repeated instances of this problem even in the most liberal, decent families. To more fully appreciate the character of white pain in the academy, I now share a particularly though not singularly painful experience in my own academic life.

A Failed Multicultural Education Textbook: Whiteness, Gatekeepers, and the Academy

In 1993, I was asked to write a multicultural education textbook. The idea was to produce a volume that would be both marketable and groundbreaking. To be marketable, the book would address the traditional topics in foundations of education in a manner currently absent from most introductory textbooks. On March 2, 1993, I wrote to my publisher: "By helping students to contextualize their own experiences as citizens in terms of the evolving Teacher Reform crisis we can enhance both their learning and their future teaching. It is precisely this contribution to their education that Foundations has been struggling with for the past two decades." The publisher was pleased that I had chosen a narrative format emphasizing the interplay of autobiographical voice among diverse speakers. In his return letter, I sensed both excitement and expectation: "My cursory examination of an hour or so makes me very hopeful about the prospects for what you are attempting; you certainly argue convincingly for a book of this kind, at this time" (March 10, 1993). I was feeling fairly proud of myself at this point; I was particularly excited that my publisher felt positive about my narrative style. My elation was short-lived, however. His letter of July 23, 1993, began thus:

> I am generally pleased by the response of our reviewers. It seems to me that the storytelling aspect of the manuscript is going well, many of the pedagogical learning aids are useful and attractive, reviewers generally think you write well, and they applaud the book's multi-cultural emphasis. There are, however, one or two things we need to work out before I think I can offer you a contract. These issues are related, and they touch on the strong presence in this book of the author's own voice and own experiences, particularly touching on race issues. Although multiculturalism is one of the book's main virtues, three or four reviewers indicate that you have dealt with race too much, too strongly, or too polemically for the book to find a wide national readership. Because what you have written is clearly in places very personal, it is hard for me to tell you exactly how to cut back the discussions that most worry reviewers. I would say the discussion of the circumstances surrounding your birth is the sort of thing that reviewers found too personal, perhaps too loosely connected to a discussion of education in general, and too "hot" to suit a text with broad commercial aspirations.

The "groundbreaking" aspect of the textbook was to be achieved by having a working-class, minority author, and I had hoped to establish my "pedigree" by "writing myself into the text." Accordingly, I had tried to illustrate the power of narrative by telling the story of my birth: I was the first African American baby born in Norfolk (Virginia) General Hospital in 1947. My mother had gone into labor and was rushed to this white hospital by the paramedics who feared for her—and my—life. The hospital staff first rushed to admit her, then stopped—they had never delivered a black baby at this hospital. So my mother remained in the hallway until her physician, a Jewish refugee from

Hungary, came and threatened to bring murder charges against the hospital staff if my mother or I died.

I had told this story partly to indicate why I felt a strong identification with Jews and how heroic many whites were even during pre-1960s America. I had also told the story as a way of clarifying the importance of "indigenous" storytellers. I had not counted on the strong antipathy that the story stimulated in my white reviewers. My publisher was correct; even reviewers favorable to the book complained:

> I think that the author initially raises several thoughtful points regarding minorities, especially Blacks, in our society. He must be careful, not to allow this to degrade into defensiveness. We cannot continue to blame the White race for past travesties. It is time to move forward with such thinking and to speak from equality, not to simply continue to blame the White race for all shortcomings of our society. I have no problem with the author's writing style. I do have a problem [with his] attempting to use this book as a platform for White race bashing. Clothing that purpose in a foundations text is wrong. It surfaces in both chapters and is inappropriate.

This reviewer's words were especially painful because he liked my work. Clearly, I had failed to say what I wanted to say in an unproblematic way. But I did not immediately see what I had done wrong. Perhaps because so much had changed since the pre–Civil Rights era, I no longer had a sixth sense about these matters. In fact, it took some time for me to understand how telling the story of my birth, sui generis, *subjectively* constituted "blame of the white race for all human shortcomings." True, I did contextualize my birth in the racial relations dominant in 1940s Virginia. What this reviewer's comments told me was that any attempt to speak outside the designated discourse caused white pain. Hence I am now expected to "speak from equality" and avoid putting whites on the "defensive."

Another reviewer, from the University of Wyoming, labeled me a "social reconstructionist" and declared:

> The bitterness in the author's autobiography is understandable but his admittance that his life as a teacher is inextricably tied to his unhappy past would make it almost impossible for him to be objective as an author and a teacher.... Resistance as a result of guilt feelings on the part of White students is counter-productive to the creation of empathy. A genuine feeling of care for all children is a necessity for the teacher of today and tomorrow.... Students are not to be blamed for wrongs they have not committed.

Equating good or effective teaching with the absence of painful remembrances or present oppressiveness is very telling in this passage. Presumably, my "bitterness" places me outside of the mainstream realities from which "healthy" and "effective" teachers are chosen. It is a well-established principle of power relations (Wilden, 1988) that the more powerful persons often are better able than the less powerful persons to use language to support their claim to the "moral high ground" precisely because power remains at their disposal. In this case, this reviewer had power over me because ultimately most reviewers, authors, publishers, and education consumers share more features with him than with me. Thus, even as he "laments" the conditions that may have contributed to my "bitterness," he is able to label me both "tainted" and "flawed"—and hence unsuitable for teaching. For him, my experiences, passion, commitment, and, yes, cognitive competence are liabilities rather than assets. He—and this remains a dominant feature of contemporary whiteness/Americanist apologetics—actually believes that he and other members of the dominant social order are "non-tainted" and "objective." In addition, it seems to me that implicit in my reviewer's comments is a belief that somehow I can or should become so "value neutral" that I do my students a service by not placing before them competing realities and inviting them to choose, thereby "making it ideological" rather than "academic." This "request" or "logic of dominance" means leaving aside my own reality. Accordingly, my own knowledge and experience—the presumed basis for an alternative professional voice—are transformed into merely a difference of skin color. From a critical perspective, however, by separating students (and others) from the social world they inhabit and help construct, this reviewer continues in that tradition of teacher education that treats evil, destructiveness, and the like as reifications, that is, as independent entities constructed outside reality and more powerful than the people giving them reality. Still, a critical view can often fail to console someone marginalized even as he seeks to "do the right thing." I was devastated by these critiques.

But what had I expected? I had expected criticism of specific weaknesses in my writing style, mastery of the literature, and even my reasoning. I had not, interestingly, expected a personal assault. This is because, I must confess, I had been prepared to soften my views and knowledge in order to enter the big time. I had even been shrewd enough to ask the publisher to confer with me before sending the material out to reviewers in order to gain a better feel for them as my audience. He had written in response, "I will honor your request and I will look through it myself and chat with you about it before sending it to reviewers" (March 10, 1993). But he didn't—and the gatekeepers of official knowledge were not fooled. They saw that I wanted to reach the young, white leaders of tomorrow, to challenge them to not merely assume equality reigns but to accept the contemporary consequences of past acts of wrongdoing and to see how such a past persists even into the present. The gatekeepers said no!

It may be interesting to note that the loss of agency I reported experiencing in the preface began during this period of preliminary work on the textbook. Only later did my book on recovery fall on hard times. Indeed, as I write this, I am forced to wonder whether the removal of *The Recovery of Race in America* from the publisher's list didn't merely finish a process begun much earlier. Whatever the source of my sense of loss, the various reviewers' comments served to confuse, disorient, and ultimately anger me. Anger could come only later because so much of the destructiveness came through the partial praise for my effort. For instance, one anonymous reviewer praised the work as a novel:

> If I were using this textbook, I would add my own personal experiences as well as those in my class. I would also enjoy spending some time in class to discuss "narrative power." Nevertheless, *I do believe that some students would not have the level of maturity required to get beyond the fact that there may be an attempt to indoctrinate them in what they may perceive as fostering "political correctness."* Furthermore, when compared to traditional textbooks in foundations, it is extremely rare to find an author who writes from a personal perspective with the same degree of passion, if any passion at all. I must admit, however, that I read Chapter 1 as I would read a novel. My interest level was extremely high. (Italics added)

The ambivalence of this reviewer is perhaps more accurately read as ambiguity: he was less torn between two attitudes or emotions than alert to the presence of a strong tradition disdaining—even denouncing—passion in scholarly work. Nor is this a racial matter in the most simplistic understanding of "racial." I recall vividly that decades earlier, my department head at Brandeis University, asked me, in exasperation, why I closed my first book, *The Dialectics of Betrayal* (1982), with a plea for—and admission of participation in—scholarship wedded to passionate commitment. This man was a black African, albeit one most vulnerable to the influence of colonialist values and standards.

Still, while committed to passionate scholarship, I was true to the assimilation impulse in many American minorities, trying to shift my cultural lens or perspectives to be accepted, to be mainstreamed. Hence, when the next publisher—who had already given me a contract and cash advance—asked me to prepare new chapters for another review, I shamelessly and thoroughly erased all traces of "blackness" from the manuscript. I was so effective that one reviewer even identified me as "an experienced White male academic with a vast knowledge of minorities." He went on to ask, "Is that important for me as a reader to know?"

I later shared with my white female editor—again to my shame—my observation regarding this shift in perceptible voice in the text. In response, she wrote, "I agree with your sense of the reviews regarding the African-American issue that arose in the proposal stage. My sense is that it is no longer an issue. As long as you are not perceived as a 'dead, White male' (!) we're probably somewhere in the ballpark on this" (April 10, 1995).

I understand that she was trying to be cute or humorous. But she failed, and so did the partnership. I had gone far in trying to enter the mainstream, to win acceptance to the club. To do so, however, I would have to change, negate, and suppress my real story, my real self. I somewhat redeemed myself intellectually and morally, if not financially, through the publication of *The Recovery of Race in America* in 1995, when much of this textbook discussion was occurring, and later through my withdrawal from this particular textbook project. Still, for several years after this experience, I occasionally looked through the reviewers' comments and lamented my ability to "deliver the goods" that might have catapulted me into national prominence and won me other lucrative writing contracts. But my greater lament is that my white colleagues all too often have little or no faith in young white youth and their capacity to grow beyond the duplicity, deceit, and dishonesty of their forebears. To wit, I recall that one reviewer wrote cynically:

> While encouraging moral reflection about, for example, societal injustice authors need, it seems to me, to take special care their own judgments and values are subjected to critical review. I do not think this is the case in these two chapters either by the choices of content or by the writing itself.... The student essays do not show the quality of thought for inclusion in a text.... I immediately thought here's a case of the student giving the instructor what he wants to hear.

I am certainly aware that people may say what they think a more powerful person wants to hear. Indeed, this has been an essential part of my racial inheritance: saying what "The Man" wants to hear regarding himself and his goodness in a world suffused with pain generated by his non-goodness. But I believe that very few white students are so frightened by the few minorities in power positions that they systematically succumb to brown nosing. Still, this critique raised for me some questions regarding the role of the minority multicultural educator, especially in a predominately white classroom.

Over the years when I have reflected on these comments, I am repeatedly struck by a dual irony: (1) a black man might be so positioned in the academy as to merit a serious response from the gatekeepers, and (2) much pain and fear underlay their comments. The latter fact was especially powerful, since neither my writing ability nor my reasoning powers—traditional points of attack against minorities in academia—were cited as problematic. Beyond this, I was struck by a common clue to the crisis produced by a radical educator like myself for these and presumably other educators and majority-group students. Any critique of contemporary racial practices feels like a personal attack on the very character of the white individual and an attempt to dismantle everything known as self and valued as important to the collectivity.

Two things stood out for me especially in the preceding comments. First was the idea that white students "turn off" and refuse to receive communications that fail to represent "positive racial relations." Second was the intimation that racial passion born of racial oppression, such as my autobiography conveyed, precludes one from being an effective teacher of majority-group students. Having taught for more than 30 years at several predominately white institutions and practiced psychotherapy for nearly as many years with majority-group members, I reject both these suggestions. White students do not necessarily turn off when exposed to less than positive stories about racial relations. Nor do one's racial wounds necessarily disqualify one as an effective educator. Still, both suggestions do contain elements of fact and wisdom. And it is within the painful experiences of minority students in academia that we can often see the limits and possibilities of blaming the victims of oppression for both their victimization and their resistance to it.

Wide Wounds: Terrorism and Critical Thought

> If suffering is the lived experience that corresponds to the concept of alienation, a psychology of suffering would have to understand guilt, anxiety, depression, or hysteria as suppressed social relations. (Lyman, 1981: 58)

The refusal to talk about Vietnam and to deal with its excesses, like the refusal to consider what precedes terrorism, invites mythology—an "axis of evil"—and so the opportunity for critique is thus killed, silenced. I will take up an observation made by Kincheloe and Staley in 1983 on the rise of anticritical thought in schools on the Vietnam era. First, I anticipate that discussion with a further reflection on the matter of a democratic, anti-oppressive pedagogy.

One critical flaw in the insistence that the democratic teacher cannot act against oppressive attitudes and actions in the classroom—if they are presented as subjective understandings and individual opinions—is that it results too often in precisely the kinds of judicial decisions now being presented as First Amendment rights, even though they are blatant acts of racism. Consider the case of the Auburn University students who not only were reinstated after their expulsion by university officials but who also now have a multimillion-dollar lawsuit against the university for interfering with their right to carry out racist actions at the university and have them placed on the internet.

This attitude, interestingly, relieves resistant students from having even to entertain the alternative voices and curricula of non-oppression. For instance, today I received two interesting emails. One was from the dean of the Commonwealth College thanking my campus executive officer and everyone for successfully hosting President George W. Bush's visit to our campus to speak on urban education. The other email came later, from a former student. For me, the two emails suggest two separate cultures and worlds that seemingly never meet nor mesh, yet remain linked in a *dance of agency*. But to understand what I am trying to say, it is perhaps helpful to know that I might have met President Bush had I not been in New Orleans at a conference on education. To have met a living president, whatever my politics, would have been something indeed. But this is precisely the problem. I have great problems with the structure and operation of many institutions and actors in our society, including presidents. So to surrender my strong political concerns in a display of starry-eyed loyalty and hero worship would indeed have been difficult for me. But I know I would have been like putty in front of President Bush. So I was not disappointed in not meeting him despite my institutional pride that he chose to speak at Penn State.

To appreciate more fully the irony and profundity of my ambivalence, you might benefit from reading the other email I received that day (it was sent to me two days after Bush's visit). I include it here in full:

> This is Ninat and Daisy [pseudonyms for these African American females] and we just wanted to tell you about what happened in our Children's Literature class, get that!!! Greta [a young, white female transfer student from the main campus] decides to tell our teacher that this program [Urban Education] is ineffective and our Fall semester with you was a waste of time. Ninat and I could have killed her and we let the whole class know that it was on them if they got nothing out of that education.

I let them know that just as they had more expectations of you, you had many more expectations of them and that they missed the ball for the most part. Ninat came to your defense immediately, stating that she learned a lot and this is the best way for her to learn. Liz [a middle-aged white mother and wife] was pissed, quiet in her seat. She did blurt out by asking if Greta had read any of the books that you assigned. Of course she said yes, but she doesn't even come to class this semester. Ninat and I really just want to let you know that we "got it" and that you had a great impact on our intentions as teachers. We could afford to learn much more! from you and hoped that you would teach a class that is unassigned in the upcoming Fall. I now understand that this may not be a good idea. I am up to my neck in anger with them and I just plan to ride the next semester out. We would be sitting here for days writing if we told you about everything that has been going on. Some of our classmates hate you and that is painful to accept. Now they hate us too, so we stand together and that's cool. I would give nothing to be amongst those idiots!!!!!!!!! I just feel sorry for the children that they may one day teach. Your teaching was reflective of the power that our children need; sublime and understanding. Thanks again and we'll talk to you soon. We want to find some time for us to meet, maybe this summer in Philly or up here, whatever. Let Ninat know by e-mailing her back. I can't seem to get mine to work.

What is so ironic and significant to me—receiving this e-mail from these two beautiful, brilliant, and committed young sisters—is that their angry email arrived just days after Bush's historic visit to our campus. These two black women felt racial pain. The two white women also feel racial pain. What are the odds that Bush addressed this pain or the relation of teacher education to the educational changes he hoped to inspire and introduce? I am certain that the conversations with Bush were sanitized and thereby promoted a vision of non-responsibility for the urban educational plight that he came to address. In short, "innocence" is the dominant understanding of why so much despair and destructive energy surround the urban educational context.

I admit that my teaching is politicized. Roland Barthes (1972) calls "mythology" a kind of "depoliticized speech" because it fragments meanings by distorting and manipulating language so that everybody wins, and nothing really challenging occurs because the emotionally charged material is neutralized. Although one senses that something important may be happening, one detects a subtext beneath the words. Although I resist it, I regard such teaching and scholarship as relevant to the new resistance to the "posts" perspective on anti-oppression.

It is not surprising, however, that even before the academy adopted an official, scholarly position on this perspective, society struggled with ways of silencing the new voice of the voiceless (Gresson, 1995). A remarkably telling illustration of the structure—Molefi Asante and Deborah Atwater (1986) termed this the "rhetorical condition"—of minority-led discussions about anti-oppressive education and cohabitation was presented by Derrick Alridge. Alridge studied with me at Penn State University in the mid-1990s. Vigorously courted by several major institutions, he returned to his home in the South where he joined the University of Georgia. Often during his first years of teaching, he would share stories with me and compare notes on our respective teaching experiences. Like me, he began collecting student responses to his pedagogy because of their unique historical and instructive multicultural insights. In 2001, he published a chapter in which he recounts his early years of teaching:

> Teaching is another area of scholarship and knowledge dissemination where black scholars face the issue of the silencing of black voice. I recall a few incidents dealing with my "black" perspective and voice while teaching my first social foundations of education course at a predominately white institution. The class was about 99 percent white. In teaching the course, I relied heavily on my own worldview as a black man growing up in the American south. I also used my black voice in discussions related to our topics of educational history and policy. While I received good evaluations from the class in terms of my knowledge of the subject matter and organization of the class, I was somewhat surprised at the students' response to my being "too black" or black-focused in the dissemination of the information. I later realized that no matter how objective I thought I was, many of the students still received my lectures as too black and felt that I was blaming them as individuals for the educational inequities of blacks in the United States. (Alridge, 2001: 197)

It has been said that in many ways reality mimics fiction; it also may be said that the same applies to the academy and the "real world." Alridge's experience is reminiscent of my own as a black man whose entrance into the latter half of the 20th century found me no longer blatantly subordinate to whites but nonetheless subjected daily to blatant racist assaults and perennial paranoia with respect to white intentions toward me. Hence the peculiar double bind that Alridge and I share as black male academics is the call to teach as black men with the simultaneous insistence that we be "raceless."

The point is bigger than academia: what did Condoleezza Rice or Colin Powell, as blacks, bring to the Bush administration that is informed by a racist heritage? If nothing is gained racially by their presence other than their presence, then it is true, as my former student and close friend Susan Mason declared in 2000: "Multiculturalism is Dead! Now everyone gets to sing… it's just that everyone will have to sing the same song."

Why, it might be asked, must multiculturalism die? Why, moreover, must civil rights reforms writ large be reversed and "paradise regained"? There have been many answers to these questions. Ultimately, they seem to converge on a common explanation. As two scholars wrote:

> Identity is a construct, a fiction, but it is a deeply embedded, remarkably persistent, and necessary fiction. Sometimes people prefer to die rather than to relinquish their identity. Race is another fiction, preserved in this country because the arbitrary division between white and black helps to maintain white privilege. The fictions of race intersect with the constructions of identity to create the sincere fictions of the white self. These sincere fictions, incorporated on the level of object relations and therefore largely unconscious, sustain a white ego ideal and preserve the notion of the black as the "other," preventing us from recognizing the brutal reality of the racial oppression on which American society has always been based and from recognizing our own internalized racist notions. Until we confront the psychological underpinnings of racism and expose the sincere fictions of the white self, the only changes in American race relations will continue to be superficial. (Vera & Gordon, 2003:30)

Confrontation of the psychological underpinnings of oppression is an ongoing human struggle with a precise, urgent quality in a democracy. This is true not only of the United States. Today Israel has re-entered the Gaza Strip in search of Hamas terrorists: there we see played out in real time the struggle around identity and existential survival; and no one, partisan perspectives notwithstanding, is unaware of the agonizing death grip grasping at all sides. While perhaps not as graphic, the everyday struggle around racialized identities and personal integrity is nonetheless profound and engaging in daily life in the United States. Indeed, at this very moment national guardsmen have been called to Ferguson, Missouri, where local citizens—mostly black but others as well—have waged nearly two weeks of protest against police brutality. (I will return to this situation in the postscript.)

Conclusion: A Voice From the Past

I have not resolved a good part of the paradox of the minority educator. I revisit it each semester when I struggle with what is implicit in so thoroughly de-racing myself that I am perceived as "an experienced White male academic with a good knowledge of minorities." What does it take to be an effective minority teacher educator in the multicultural classroom? Too little attention has been given to this question, and I return to it in Chapter 6. There I take up the recent focus on the oppressive potential of anti-oppressive education. Here I would like to anticipate that discussion with an affirmation: the democratic educator must indeed bite the bullet, so to speak; this includes, at times, pursuing truth with a long view—saying things to students, even things that they find challenging, that one understands to be "true." In this one takes, or rather, accepts the risk that one may violate the democratic ideal.

Such an attitude means, at times, that one must go for years without validation. One may also, in a hostile academy, find oneself marginalized and subject to criticism from those protected by and supportive of that oppression interstitial to the academy. Still, I do find occasional validation, such as this email from a former student that I received just weeks before the publication of the first edition of *America's Atonement*:

> My name is Dave and I graduated from Brandeis in 1983. If you remember me then you are even brighter than I thought you were. I just wanted to let you know that I often think of you as the events of this world compel me to remember you and your teachings. I often joke with my brother, who also had you as a professor, that you missed your calling to make "big bucks" with the "Dialectics of Betrayal Part II—the Anita Hill and Clarence Thomas Story" or "Dialectics of Betrayal Part III—the Johnny Cochrane and Christopher Dardon Story." You "coulda" been some big shot on *Geraldo*. But I guess you'll just have to remain an outstanding professor. You were a real maverick at Brandeis; I liked your style. Lastly, *Dialectics of Betrayal* was a real "pain in the ass read" driving me to the dictionary every other sentence to look up all these fifty dollar words that you told us you were compelled to use in order to be accepted by the academic elites. It took me a couple of years thereafter to fully understand your thesis and as a result I have a better depth of understanding of many racial issues in this country. I hope you enjoyed my thoughts—you're great at what you do. Goodbye and God Bless, Dave

This young man—he must be nearly fifty! Gad, that makes me an ancient—was apparently one of the students I taught at Brandeis University in the early 1980s. It is truly awesome that he should reconnect with me in 2002. I only vaguely recall him or his brother. And it seems that he has not kept up with my career since 1983 or the books that I have written since then. Of course, that doesn't really matter to him or me. I can only presume that he was reaching out for his own fading youth and trying to connect to the past and gain some control over the chaotic times we now endure in America.

I, too, am searching for control, however short-lived or illusionary. What this young man's words and the other commentaries I receive from time to time offer is a soothing validation of a life lived at the margins. Ironically, the book that Dave spoke of, *The Dialectics of Betrayal*, is very instructive in a certain, bizarre way. Although it never won any awards or sold anything like the numbers that *The Recovery of Race in America* did, it remained in print for 18 years! Why? Perhaps because it dealt solely with minority pain; it was an okay book. White pain was not emphasized. Yet both pains are real and in need of soothing.

If we understand that the racial critique of whiteness promotes white pain as well as racial understanding, then perhaps we can begin to see that *the mediation of white pain* is a major initiative of the recent cultural wars that academics so often write about. In the next chapter, I turn to the question of mediation as a way of getting closer to an understanding of contemporary shifts in the multiculturalism discourse.

· 5 ·

MEDIATING WHITE PAIN

Ritual Recovery, Yellow Ribbons, and Patriotic Wars

The war in Vietnam threatened to tear our society apart. And the political and philosophical disagreements that animated each side continue to some extent. It has been said that these memorials reflect a hunger for healing. Well, I don't know if perfect healing ever occurs, but I know that sometimes when a bone is broken, if it knits together well, it will in the end be stronger than if it had not been broken. I believe that in the decade since Vietnam the healing has begun. And I hope that before my days as Commander in Chief are over the process will be complete.

– Ronald Reagan (1984: 1825–1826)

The final lesson of Vietnam is that no great nation can long afford to be sundered by a memory.

– George H. W. Bush (1989 inaugural address)

Through narrative and ritual, reconciliation vicariously walks humans through a broken world on a quest to reassert wholeness and moral order in the midst of the brokenness and the loss of shared moral ground…

– John Hatch (2006a: 7)

Introduction: Self-Examination Versus Group Healing

The various equality movements of the 1960s and 1970s were a partial reason for the rise of multiculturalism and diversity initiatives in the United States. Intricately connected to these domestic movements, the Vietnam War symbolized the nation's struggle with its own creed and promise of democratic inclusion and godliness. Multiculturalism and diversity demands were the forbidden fruits of this struggle. And as we have seen in the previous chapters, these initiatives brought with them considerable pain for many whites, even as other whites provided both leadership and other forms of support for these initiatives. In the 1980s, healing the wounds of this struggle—Vietnam, Black Power, the antiwar movement, and the feminist movement—was critical. In 1983, Joe Kincheloe and George Staley wrote in a special to *USA Today*, "Only a decade after the Vietnam debacle, public schools are once again equating critical inquiry into the formulation of American foreign policy with anti-Americanism" (1983: 30). The refusal to look too deeply beneath the surface is a common human trait, and despite its greatness, American democracy does not necessarily challenge this human propensity. For this reason, the "critical inquiry" that Kincheloe and Staley correctly encouraged actually flew in the face of the national objective described by Ronald Reagan and George Bush: healing the cultural, social, and political split associated with Vietnam and the social activism of the 1960s.

President Ronald Reagan understood this very well, and on November 11, 1984, when Frederick Hart's bronze statue of the three infantrymen was unveiled and dedicated, he spoke the words opening this chapter. This memorial was a mediating force. *Mediation* is defined as standing in between, acting as a connection between two otherwise separate, conflicting entities, ideas, or circumstances. Hart's memorial was offered as a compromise to those who felt that Maya Lin's memorial, The Wall, failed to promote healing for many Americans, especially those who felt we had failed to win the war because of weak leadership and the subversion of the antiwar movement.

Kincheloe, Staley, Reagan, and Bush bring us face to face with a complex matter: how do we balance our ideals and the pragmatics of social life? This is a perennial issue for a democratic society. Indeed, since the Vietnam–Gulf War period, 1972 to 1992, we have begun and continue to wage a "war on terrorism" that revisits the dynamic tensions of these earlier times. I will return to this connection later in the chapter. First, however, I offer one perspective on the manner in which white pain has been mediated in our society. In particular, I try to answer the question, "How does the white male, separated from the community through his hegemonic or collusive elevation to dominance, find his way back to at-oneness with the group?" This question is critical to understanding how power dynamics interface the diversity discourse reopened during the so-called radical 1960s, the period lamented by Max Rafferty and others like him.

One way of beginning this discussion is to return to the white male voice. To a considerable degree, white males are correct when they take a stand against the white male bashing that portrays them as the initiators and sole perpetuators of white male dominance in society. This observation both highlights the subjective reality of individual white males and exposes the collusion of others in constructing society. Anthony Ipsaro noted that white males become powerful because of society's collusion:

> But let me tell you a secret: Most men in most cultures have no sense of their power! They have remarkable power. Since that power is inherited through cultural gender expectations rather than earned, it is an invisible mantle. Although each male has his own brand of masculinity, all men share a relationship that fosters an alliance of domination and subordination. This is achieved through practices that exclude and include, exploit and reward, intimidate and reaffirm. The entire cultural system supports, reaffirms, and colludes with white males to keep them in power. Yet, most white males do not think of themselves as belonging to a powerful, elite group until others label them that way. (1997: 14)

The weak and strong together construct power. Others have said much the same thing: Dorothy Dinnerstein in *The Mermaid and the Minotaur* (1976) and Frantz Fanon in *Black Skin, White Masks* (1976) described how women, Jews, and blacks colluded with Euro-American racism to perpetuate white male domination. Mary Daly also brilliantly described the hegemonic drama with respect to gender:

> The Myth Masters are able to penetrate their victims' minds/imaginations only by seeing to it that their deceptive myths are acted out over and over again in performances that draw the participants into emotional complicity. Such reenactment trains both victims and victimizers to perform uncritically their preordained roles. Thus the psyches of the performers are conditioned so that they become carriers and perpetrators of patriarchal myths. In giving the myth reality by acting it out, the participants become re- producers and "living proof" of the deceptive myths. (1978: 102)

In the prologue to Chapter 6, a graduate student describes the white females in her women's studies class as afraid to challenge the white males. Perhaps this was the case, but female intentional cooperation or collusion in such incidents is an alternative reading of the situation. This is partly so because they, too, have an identity-investment in "whiteness." Kathleen M. Blee, in *Women of the Klan* (1991), discloses white women's investment in the Ku Klux Klan as central to their racial and gender identities. Ruth Frankenberg, in *White Women, Race Matters: The Social Construction of Whiteness* (1993:1), used interviews to depict "white women's lives as sites for both the reproduction of racism and challenges to it." Together, these works recognize and record specific ways in which white women can contribute to the continuation of white male power even as they resist it. This process was evident in the rise and ritualization of the so-called Yellow Ribbon Movement to mediate white male pain.

The Yellow Ribbon Movement and the Mediation of White Pain

> Yellow ribbons were used widely during the Iranian hostage crisis, but the practice was first adopted to welcome the returning prisoners from Vietnam, inspired by the 1973 love song by Tony Orlando and Dawn, "Tie a Yellow Ribbon round the Ole Oak Tree," about a returning convict.
>
> – Gerald Parsons (1991: 11)

In November 1979, Muslim revolutionaries seized the U.S. embassy in Tehran, Iran, and took 52 Americans hostage to symbolize the initiation of political and religious war on the "imperialist infidel" America. The president, Jimmy Carter, a Democrat from the South, was perceived as too weak and accommodating to tackle this aggression in the same way as would, say, Theodore Roosevelt, hero of American imperialism in the 1890s. When he was elected in 1976, Carter symbolized the redemption of the South, its recovery from the economic exile imposed as a result of losing the Civil War. But by 1979, Carter's failure to obtain the hostages' release symbolized America's failure in Vietnam: the failure of God's chosen country to vanquish a weaker, "evil" enemy (DeSousa, 1984; Hill, 1984). It was this Iranian crisis that led to the first national ritualization of the Yellow Ribbon Movement. Penne Laingen, wife of one of the American diplomat hostages, made a huge bow from several feet of yellow vinyl upholstery material and tied it around an oak tree in the front yard of her home in Bethesda, Maryland. In a seminal essay on the evolution of the yellow ribbon as an American folk icon, Gerald Parsons, of the Library of Congress's American Folklife Center, recalled:

> On the CBS broadcast of January 28, [1979] Penelope Laingen... was shown outside of her home.... "It just came to me," she said, "to give people something to do, rather than throw dog food at Iranians." I said, "Why don't they tie a yellow ribbon around an old oak tree? That's how it started." (1981: 9)

Over the next decade, the yellow ribbon periodically appeared at sites of American shame and defeat, notably when American military men were killed. Various authors have emphasized the heterogeneous motives of Americans with respect to the yellow ribbon symbol and the tension and conflicting meanings it encoded. Still, beneath this disruptiveness lurked the common recognition that the yellow ribbon emotionalism was emanating from precise sources and directed toward a precise mission. Penne Laingen fused a personal pain and need with a collective pain and myth. To say that the movement began with her gesture is inaccurate, but her gesture did become a collective motive and mission.

Like many women, Penne Laingen enacted the ritual encoded in the song. In so doing, she gave life to a myth, a desire. For many, perhaps most, Americans, her gesture, like that of the unnamed woman in the song, was cathartic and touched something deep within them. Although we did not know the history of the song's beginning, we probably associated it with Vietnam veterans. Some women made the connection right away. In March 1992, the American Folklife Center received a handwritten letter, which reads as follows:

> The July 15, 1991 issue of the *Library of Congress Bulletin* contained an article that implied that the Folklife [Center] believes that yellow ribbons were first used to welcome home prisoners during the Iran hostage crisis. However, I recall hearing on "Casey Kasem's American Top Forty," a nationally syndicated radio program, that yellow ribbons were used to welcome home some Vietnam POWs. According to Mr. Kasem, several people who had done this told the singing group Tony Orlando and Dawn about it during a concert of the group's.

Fig. 2. Sheet music cover for the 1972 hit song that became the pedagogical narrative for America's "Atonement" as ritualized in the Yellow Ribbon Movement.

The yellow ribbon song was published in 1972, and Tony Orlando and Dawn's recording of it was released in 1973 (fig. 2). Thus began the public oration of the plea from Vietnam and shortly thereafter began the public ritual of yellow ribboning. But to present this chronology of events as a natural unfolding begs the issue: how did such actions become the basis for the recovery of the American soldier as sacred icon? To answer this question we must consider the place of guilt and shame in the lives of Americans generally, and men and women respectively, since the start of the Vietnam War in 1965.

Vietnam was not only America's greatest military failure but also America's most unpopular war. Furthermore, the traditional ambivalence of women, particularly mothers, about their sons going off to war surfaced as a gender problem. Although a smaller part of the larger antiwar sentiment, the gender resistance to America's military presence in Vietnam was the most painful part of the domestic crisis of that time. Perhaps this was because so many sub-issues were linked to the gender crisis, all of which found resonance in the word "rape." This word struck at the heart of the American male/soldier's self-concept. Indeed, one of the recurring themes of Vietnam-era literature and film was the rape scene. We see the important connection of rape to women's role as antiwar demonstrators in Larry Heinemann's Vietnam-focused novel *Paco's Story*. The following quotation depicts a veteran's fantasy revenge on a college female, a symbol of feminism and the suffragist yellow-ribbon tradition:

> Been waiting for one of those mouthy, snappy-looking little girlies from some rinky-dink college to waltz up and say... "You one of them vet'rans, ain'cha? Killed all them mothers and babies. Raped all them women, di'n'cha"... "I ain't putting out for you, buster...." Okay by me, girlie.... 'cause I got seventeen different kinds of social diseases.... And when this happens—this conversation with this here girlie—I'm gonna grab her up by the collar of her sailor suit..., slap her around a couple times, flip her a goddamned dime... and say, "Here, Sweet Chips, give me a ring in a couple of years when you grow up." (Heinemann, 1986:156)

A number of works, largely fictional, addressed the role of women during the Vietnam War (Jeffords, 1989;1994). A recurring theme in much of this literature has been the failure of women to provide support in the form of an unconditional acceptance of war and male behavior in war. From the perspective argued by feminists like Mary Daly, on the one hand, unconditional acceptance of male aggression such as displayed in war is an act of female complicity. On the other hand, the refusal to accept war as necessary and inevitable might well represent the kind of nonsupport displayed by antiwar demonstrators. If such apparent nonsupport is allegorized in the female and if it truly generates the kind of fictional and actual misogyny depicted earlier, might women not share a parallel negative self-regard? Indeed, evidence from both World Wars I and II suggests women often accept responsibility for the entire society for failing to show support and remain faithful to military men. According to some scholars, women have been made to feel responsible for both the start and loss of war (Gilbert, 1989). Female guilt and traditional atonement rituals— grieving and mourning—converged in the Yellow Ribbon Movements of 1979 and 1991 to become a male recovery ritual. Many women felt guilt for the antiwar movement. Some of the women who became Vietnam nurses entered the war because of such guilt feelings. Similar sentiments, in part, stimulated the Yellow Ribbon Movement of 1991.

The Gulf War of 1991

In August 1990, Iraq invaded Kuwait. America quickly responded, identifying the invasion as an act of aggression against both a peaceful country and the world. America then guided the United Nations in establishing an international war offensive, with President George H. Bush's administration orchestrating the nation's and Congress's compliance with the U.N. mandate. The United States declared war on Saddam Hussein, and by May 1991, Iraq had been bombed into submission.

People magazine began its commemorative issue on the victory in Iraq with the following reflection:

> When it started last August, Iraq had the fourth largest army in the world, and the United States was said to have little stomach for war. When it was over, seven months later, Saddam Hussein's military machine was no longer an international threat, and the United States had purged itself of the ghost of Vietnam.... Wrapped in a yellow ribbon, this package [special issue] contains the unforgettable stories of the heroes (and, yes, a few of the villains) of the short, sharp war that helped a country feel good about itself again. (1992: 44)

To "feel good about itself again," America went to war. This idea was not the common rationale for the war in the days and months before victory had been achieved. Many people believed that the war was truly about Iraqi aggression and its threat to the world's economic and military stability. Some observers felt that the United States' need for oil underlay the decision to declare war on Iraq. But by the war's end many understood the redemptive motive, whatever its economic and political underpinnings: the nation's need to feel good about itself again. From this view, the Gulf War helped complete the meaning of the Vietnam War, particularly the reunion of the Vietnam veterans with other Americans. (The "war on terrorism" and current occupation of Iraq by American forces have again raised the specter of doubt regarding motive and method.)

This convergence of past and present—failure in Vietnam and apparent victory in the Persian Gulf—was an orchestrated redemptive drama. It did not just happen; it evolved over a decade or more. The war in the Gulf was itself a fulfillment of the psychological needs of the American people as much as it was a political need of the government. The yellow ribbon was a vehicle, albeit a source of ambivalence, for this healing to be acted out. The ribbon was everywhere, on trees, fences, car antennas, light poles, and doors of houses, barns, and churches. Although these rituals signaled that the yellow ribbon pertained to more than tradition building, even in 1992 the redemptive significance of the yellow ribbon ritual was under-expressed. War, the traditional American ritual of regeneration, was not yet acknowledged as a recovery activity, nor was the ribbon identified as a redemptive icon:

> The war with Iraq was a specific social context that raised deeply disturbing questions that were addressed through this folk art. The assemblages also dealt with other cultural and social contradictions: opposition to war versus support of the troops; loyalty to country versus abhorrence of war. The flags and yellow ribbons addressed these issues, allowing for some personal expression through the manipulation of the symbols. The ratio of yellow ribbons to flag-related icons, the placement of the symbols, and the use of the printed signs all helped to specify one's position on these issues. (Santino, 1992: 31)

In this passage, Santino raises several important points. First, for most Americans, support of the troops was not equal to support of war; it couldn't be otherwise for a country that had failed to heal the deep wounds associated with Vietnam. (Before the Gulf War, the nation had been characterized as having no stomach for fighting because of the memory of Vietnam.) Second, the ambiguity of the yellow ribbon allowed for the personalized narratives that Santino mentions. Third, the personalizing of narratives regarding war in visual form not only represented a potential repeat of Vietnam—sending multiple messages to the enemy—but also heralded the replacement of a single metanarrative of war (traditionally symbolized by the American flag) with many competing and sometimes conflicting personal narratives of commitment and discontent.

The underexamined aspect of the war at home was the effort to shape public understanding and values regarding the war. In 2003, notably, the country, having found its way back to Iraq, tried to weave a believable narrative of redemption through the discourse of an "axis of evil." Of course, the drama in the Middle East, including Israel's refusal to submit to a visit by the United Nations to areas in which it has perhaps committed atrocities, muted the American rationale for invading Iraq. What is important here is not who is wrong or right. My concern is to show the persistence of domestic-international issues that find the notion of American interests intermeshed with racial and national identity-based struggles around the world.

The complex issues embedded in what seems to be a policy matter pertain to the ways in which "American (white) identity" is both constructed and positioned vis-à-vis others at home and around the world. Although I will not develop the discussion here, it is worth noting that returning Vietnam veterans connected much of their self-soldier identity to images of John Wayne and the range of racial and national values with which he was associated. For instance, Mark Gerzon (1982: 109) observed, "The Reagan administration represented an energetic attempt to return to the 'John Wayne thing.' It hoped that young men would once again idolize the Soldier."

But if one part of the white male's identity pain as a soldier and a man derives from a militaristic or aggressive sublayer, another part derives from a romantic sublayer. In fact, it is here as well that we must examine why both aggression toward blacks and the embrace of the white bunny female occurred in the website representations of the Auburn University frat men (Norman, 2001). As discussed in Chapter 3, Gail Bederman (1995) argued that sexism and racism are intermeshed; similarly, Weis, Proweller, & Centrie (1997) found working-class male identity development relies heavily on depicting the black male as the dangerous sexual aggressor of white females as part of his own wooing of white females. The Auburn frat men's fusing of blackface and Playboy bunny seems to fulfill both Bederman and Weis's arguments. This fusion also points to the paradoxical nature of romance as ideology and narrative, and its relation to the lessening of white male pain. This fusion as well reveals the inevitable fusing of white identity with American identity. (This linking of American identity with whiteness in a proprietary manner partly explains the repeated observation of a racial divide between white and black on various issues including the declaration of war against Iraq.) Like blackface, romancing yellow is a racial ritual that supports the lessening of white pain.

Romancing Yellow and Lessening White Pain

Romance is a complicated matter in our society because romance is about idealism, hope, and "good feelings." We usually imagine a boy and a girl in love when we think of romance, as this image of a couple speaks to the ways that our society privileges or holds as natural, correct, and inevitable the coming together of male and female to create a family, clan, tribe, community, and even a nation. There is another side to the idea of romance, which is that it often conjures up images of betrayal, with somebody getting hurt by loving the wrong person or loving too deeply, that is, by being too romantic.

Who is romantic and who gets hurt can vary, as we know from books, movies, and personal experience, although the female is typically chosen as the one hurt by romance (Radaway, 1987). According to the romance as a story form or genre, boy meets girl, they fall in love, boy hurts girl, girl loses boy, boy is enlightened, and boy returns to girl, who finds love and marriage. Whatever the different attitudes toward this particular scenario, it is familiar and part of the way we separate male and female and understand the differences between the genders. To be sure, we humans create the meanings of these differences—as well as the differences themselves in many situations. Still, we largely accept, celebrate, and recreate these differences.

Women are called on to render this service as mothers, wives, sweethearts, and sisters. This is an aspect of romance, present in much military art, announcing, "We support our troops!" Patriotism and gender are romantically linked to military action in this manner. Gaye Jacobson, credited with beginning the Yellow Ribbon Movement of 1991, explained it this way:

> Patriotism had been missing from our lives ever since Vietnam. And, by God, we thought if we could do anything to do about it, we would. The yellow ribbon signifies waiting for someone you love to come home. I saw it as the one symbol people would look at and understand. (Cited in Santino, 1992: 44)

Jacobson's movement repeated the one began in 1979 by Camilla LaSpada, founder of "No Greater Love." Writing in the 1970s, LaSpada revisited the narratives of both Gail McGruder and Penne Laingen when she drew the clear romantic underpinnings of the military scene:

> Historically, the use of ribbons or "colors" appears in many contexts. Medieval knights wore their ladies' colors as a sign of remembrance. American Civil War women were the first to tie ribbons (often yellow) to trees to signify their hopeful wait for the return of their men. Later, cavalry units adopted a yellow stripe down the sides of their trousers, to set them apart from other services. (Personal communication, 1992)

The white female leadership in this ritualization of patriotism has been underexamined but is pervasive in media about the yellow ribbon. There is evidence that independent individuals and groups began carrying out the ritual shortly after the song became popular. I view this as the localization of the ritual. By "nationalization," I mean the adoption or appropriation of the ritual by the mass media and a network of myth producers. For example, Camilla LaSpada raised funds from various businesses in order to produce a massive number of yellow ribbon buttons that were then distributed nationwide. Both LaSpada and Jacobson felt that the yellow ribbon solved a crisis of identity.

Other women also attempted to mediate the fusion of patriotism and soldier with American foreign policy and aggression:

> During the Second War, we always had a flag in the window or on the door. Then during this conflict war and all, they were putting up the yellow ones. I got tired of seeing yellow ribbons on the trees and posts.... I used the red, white and blue. I went to the florist and told her that I wanted a large red, white and blue bow and then I hung it with this wreath that was already done in yellow.

I interviewed this speaker in 1991. At that time, she was a 70-year-old widow who lived alone with her dog in a small rural region of Pennsylvania. She supplemented a small fixed income with part-time work at a neighborhood food co-op. For her, the Yellow Ribbon Movement was reminiscent of World War II: she had a brother who served in that war and she recalls that gold stars were placed in the windows of homes where a son or daughter had been killed in combat. For her, too, the Vietnam era was one of conflict, conflict left unresolved by the presence of so much yellow. Media interpreters, however, often missed this subjective underpinning to yellow ribboning.

The failure of the media interpreters went far beyond oversimplifying the meaning of the yellow ribbons by actively constructing the preferred meanings. The war in the Gulf was not the only war waged during the winter of 1991. A "civil war" was also being waged on the home front:

> Sybil Roberts, whose nephew is in the Persian Gulf, was so angered by anti-war protesters at her door carrying petitions that she wrapped the columns on the porch of her Houston row-house with yellow satin, buried the facade under 14 giant yellow bows, and planted a sign in her lawn that read, "We support our troops" on [one] side and "Down with protesting" on the other. (*New York Times*, February 4, 1991, A16)

Few seemed to want to see the yellow ribbon as the redemptive ritual it was—an act of purgation and cleansing—yet the redemptive theme found its way into the war rhetoric: a *New York Times* editorial described tying the ribbon around trees as "no frivolity, but pleas, prayers, and hopes made visible" (*New York Times*, February 4, 1991, A16). For example, the article about

Sybil Roberts went on to observe that antiwar supporters also claim the yellow ribbon, that the cueing or compelling image is that of Sybil and her sign declaring protest as unpatriotic. For instance, the passage begins "whose nephew is in the Persian Gulf," a clause that serves to explain her behavior. The word *nephew* is one of many relational or familial concepts and images used during the Gulf War. This word signals the operation of a complex semiotic system. Here I want to indicate only how the media, wittingly and unwittingly, influenced the structure and meanings of the messages sent about the yellow ribbon through a complex and comprehensive cueing campaign.

Other segments of society also participate in the cueing process. The Washington officials who controlled the placement of monuments in that city are a case in point. Recall that Maya Lin's memorial was a source of controversy leading to the commission of the Hart memorial. The most recent and complete representation of the combined forefronting of the image and the ideology of American romance is the Women's Vietnam Memorial.

Before examining this instance of mediation, however, I shall turn briefly to the cinema's recovery role in the mediation of white male pain. The cinema has had a major collusive role in using the romance motif of white pain. The 1990s hit movie *Forrest Gump* is perhaps the most notable illustration of this form of collusion.

Recovery Cinema Mediates White Pain: The Case of Forrest Gump

> The sap is rising in America, and his name is Forrest Gump.... In this country, there's nothing harder to argue with than success, and to nearly everyone's surprise, Forrest Gump, has become a success... but few things need to be challenged more fiercely than this gentle, defiantly peculiar account of an idiot's pilgrim's progress through decades of American country.
>
> Stiff as a pole with his hair cut military short and his shirt buttoned up to his Adam's apple, Forrest Gump has become the pop-culture hero of the 90s. He's emerged as an Everyman symbol of all things to all people, moving from movie reviews to the op-ed pages, where essayists and critics have compared him to everyone from Huck Finn to "Harvey's" Elwood P. Dowd. (Hinson, 1994: G 1,1)

Students of ritualism have found that rituals that facilitate "nonbloody" conflict resolutions often build on disruption and conflict (Beers, 1992; Nieburg, 1973; Werbner, 1989). In pursuing *Forrest Gump* as a mediation of white pain, I propose a parallel argument: both explicit constructions in the movie itself and the resulting public discourse are part of the white mediation of the pain associated with the radical 1960s. That is, not only is white recovery encoded as a preferred racist/sexist narrative in the movie, but also the audience, reviewer, and critic may help concretize the preferred understanding, despite the possibility of diverse audience receptions and readings.

Since the early 1970s there has been an upsurge of "gendered conflict" in popular movies (Hedley, 1994) and racialization of violence in the cinema (Giroux, 1995). I have called this rhetorical strategy a "rhetorical reversal" (Gresson, 1995). Because it helps clarify the cultural work of films such as *Forrest Gump*, let me briefly define and illustrate the rhetorical reversal before proceeding further with my analysis of this film.

Reversal is a pivotal tactic with a most interesting logic. It pertains to the power to name, define, and negotiate reality. In the 1960s, blacks engaged in such behavior around the notion of "black." Before the 1960s, this word held largely negative connotation for most American blacks, but by seizing and embracing the word "black" and investing it with positive value, blacks engaged in a most significant form of reversal. One of the major reflections of the power shift, at least, symbolically redefined meanings according to their own interests. It is, for instance, now a part of Black folklore that Kwuame Ture (Stokely Carmichael) told the white press, "Black Power means whatever we say it means."

Blacks have assumed a different oppositional style in recent decades, focusing increasingly upon elaborating the nature and liberational role of Black literary and cultural theory and criticism. Instead, white women have increasingly assumed the vanguard challenge of white male appropriational tactics. The struggle for "self" control has been essential to this challenge of the canon. For example, "making reversals" is a major feminist strategy (Gresson, 1995).

Five interrelated dynamics seem closely associated with rhetorical reversal:

1. the experience of a personally debilitating loss of one's share in a collective hegemony, whether deserved or not;
2. a public—first personal, then collective—effort to recover the pragmatic and moral losses;
3. a gradual convergence of the public and private actions and analyses;
4. their dual justification and legitimation by various factions within society through negation of the previously reigning rhetorical situation; and
5. the gradual emergence of a reconciliatory, more inclusive formative image, purged of the former negativity of the lost moral context.

Both the oppressor and oppressed may participate in this recovery rhetoric tactic; thus, either out-group members or members of the oppressed group may direct reversals at the oppressed. The relative differences in history and real differences in power, however, ultimately make such rhetorical arguments less than persuasive.

In *Forrest Gump* we see the rhetorical reversal reach new heights of pedagogic destructiveness as it reteaches a generation the old ideas of racial positionality and distorts the history of mid-20th-century cultural politics. A film review in the *Detroit News & Free Press* (February 18, 1995: C7) describes the movie thus:

> The film views the social tumult of the 60s and 70s through the innocent eyes of Forrest, a slow lad who nevertheless understands right from wrong and leads a charmed life. Forrest... falls in love with Jenny, a beautiful girl who decides to pursue a worldly life of hippie protesting, unbridled sex and drug addiction.
>
> Their morals and behavior have different consequences. Forrest becomes a sports star, survives the Vietnam War unscathed and becomes a rich entrepreneur. Jenny wanders away from an abusive home to an abusive Berkeley boyfriend to prostitution, eventually contracting AIDS....

Few things are that straightforward, however, and the review continues:

> What *Pulp Fiction* and *Forrest Gump* represent is an Academy Awards contest between conflicting views of art. *Pulp* is the modern notion that art must shock and attack, which become ends in themselves. *Gump* returns to the idea that real art rediscovers virtuous truths that inspire people to do the right thing.
>
> The public has already cast its ballot for *Gump*, but we will have to wait until March 27 to see if the Academy feels likewise.

By constructing Forrest Gump as an innocent white male, one with less than normal intelligence, the mythmakers have found a means of mediating white pain. The white man who has no idea of evil, no active or conscious intent to hurt "others," cannot be held accountable for the way things happen. If racism, natural disasters, and sexism abound, so be it. In the midst of these horrible natural and manmade events, there remains a white man wholly innocent, wholly vulnerable, and wholly open to the world and its contingencies. Movies like *Pulp Fiction* and *Forrest Gump* reject the portrayal of the United States as racist, sexist, and classist, and both rely on a shared narrative of American redemption and regeneration through violence (Slotkin, 1973).

Henry Giroux summarized the implications of movies, notably *Pulp Fiction*, that racialize violence:

> Instead of focusing on how larger social injustices and failed policies, especially those at the root of America's system of inequality, contribute to a culture of violence that is a tragedy for all youth, the dominant media transformed the growing incidence of youth violence into a focus on black-on-black fratricide.... Such racially coded discourse serves to mobilize white fears and legitimize "drastic measures" in social policy in the name of crime reform.... Moreover, the discourse of race and violence provides a sense of social distance and moral privilege that places dominant white society outside of the web of violence and social responsibility. (1995: 333–334)

By neglecting this dimension of the racialized discourse of both *Pulp Fiction* and *Forrest Gump*, the aforesaid review juxtaposes false opposites and suggests that the decision to be made by the awards committee is somehow apocalyptic, a decision for either good or evil. In this way, the review participates in the white recovery project, for it suggests that *Gump*—both the movie and the character—stands on a moral high ground that abrogates its share in the misrepresentation of reality.

Related to this misreading is another, that the public is a monolithic whole, consciously determining the inherent moral value and worth of a cinematic creation by its vote at the box office. And yet there is something to be learned from the tone and turn of this review: the critics themselves are part of the fuel propelling the recovery project forward. This is so because of the way the critics responded to *Gump*: its transparency invites a critique that will itself become an opportunity for critique. Consider, for example, Hinson's criticism of the film:

> The strange thing here is that people who normally consider themselves too sophisticated for such a banal "feel good" message are being suckered by the picture's savvy packaging and swallowing it whole. They don't seem to notice—or don't care—that Gump doesn't direct his life in the way that most characters do and has no real motives or drives or psychology. When Gump asks Jenny to marry him, declaring, "I'm not a smart man, but I know what love is," they're happy to believe him even though there's nothing in the movie to suggest his statement. (1994: G1)

I agree with Hinson here, but I question whether we are ever that sophisticated, especially in regard to cherished values and redemptive ritualization. During this phase, resistance is little expected or tolerated, and those who do resist are eventually punished by whatever means available. Hinson's comments state the "truth," and yet it is precisely this "truth" that, once uttered, becomes neutralized again and again as movie critics gloss the "truth." This "truth," in the eyes of an increasingly cynical public, becomes more evidence of "political correctness gone amok."

Instead of yielding to this murderous ideological frenzy of the left, radicals, and minorities, "reasonable" people see the world through the eyes of *Gump*. This applies even to astute critics. Gene Siskel, for instance, explained:

> Our Flick of the Week is *Forrest Gump*, which begins as yet another case of a Hollywood star doing an Oscar turn playing a mentally disturbed character (*Charly, Rain Man*) but surprisingly turns into a marvelous, whimsical epic of contemporary America. That's because Forrest Gump (Tom Hanks) is more vehicle than person in this film, a vehicle that drives us through the last 40 years of American history. (1994: B4)

Recognizing that Forrest is a vehicle does not seem to alert Siskel to ask what precisely Tom Hanks is a vehicle for: what's the tenor? The emphasis on "whiteness" (and "blackness") in the first several minutes of the movies goes unexamined. Siskel is not alone, however, in his oblivion to the racial recovery encoded in the story. Thus Peter Travers, of *Rolling Stone*, says:

> *Forrest Gump* is a movie heartbreaker of oddball wit and startling grace. There's talk of another Oscar for Tom Hanks, who is unforgettable as the sweet-natured, shabbily treated simpleton of the title. The Academy is a sucker for honoring afflicted heroes. In Hollywood, it's always raining rain men....
>
> Zemeckis [author/director of the film] doesn't fall into the trap of using Forrest as an arrested development. He knows the limits of a holy fool who can't understand the hypocrisy of postwar America that this picaresque epic so powerfully reveals. The peace-love pretensions of the 60s are skewed as neatly as the greed decades that follow. But there is something of Forrest that Zemeckis would like to see rub off on us: his capacity for hope. It's an ambitious goal in this age of rampant cynicism. Godspeed. (Travers, 1994: 99)

Film reviews like these invite us to participate in a sacred ritual in which the complexity and pain of the past several decades are cast off for an optimism that can obtain only if we participate in collective denial or, to use Russell Jacoby's term (1975), "social amnesia." Amnesia is a good term to introduce here because it traditionally has pertained to a psychological stratagem used by the mind to defend itself from painful memory or awareness. What many people have understood regarding America since the early 1970s is that it seems intent on forgetting: first Vietnam, then the liberation struggles of the 1960s, then the folly of using wars like the Gulf War to conceal economic recession and the pathos of "late capitalism."⁵⁵ Nonetheless, it has been equally as clear to many that just as the amnesiac cannot be forced back into awareness, some forces in American society resist honest self-examination and self-accusation.

One mechanism for managing this "loss of memory" is the rhetorical reversal (Gresson, 1995). One of its most powerful expressions has been the attack against "political correctness." By insisting that efforts to regulate immoral, unjust, and destructive beliefs and behaviors are themselves flawed, and by encoding this stance as a righteous campaign against "political correctness," a diversity of actors have come forth as a "Give-Me-a Break" bloc. This pluralistic power bloc, heterogeneous in many ways, nonetheless shares the belief that being correct can become a bore and irritant. It is against this backdrop that the more critical film reviews may be read as assisting the recovery project, for this project is aided most often by situated support than that grounded in compliance with a comprehensive ideology. When applied to the case of negative film criticism of *Forrest Gump*, we can see the silencing power of the rhetorical reversal as "anti-PC" discourse. For example, given such a discursive climate, the following criticism, while cogent, seems both uninformed and anticlimactic:

> Now Forrest is hardly the first idiot hero to ride through a fiction, bodies dropping all around him.... Gump, however, refuses to suggest its idiot might be mistaken—he must come out a winner.... And America is cheering. Much as it cheered Ronald Reagan, who,... is the real proto-Gump. Reagan too was relentlessly upbeat. Reagan too was extraordinarily lucky. And his luck, like Gump's, was often built on the backs of people who suffered off-screen. Forrest had bankrupt shrimpers, martyred Vietnam buddies, and his wife, whose death was remarkably demure, considering her ailment. Reagan scored points off America's poor; somehow managed to cloak himself in heroism while apologizing for a needless screw-up that killed 241 U.S. servicemen in Beirut; and avoided tarnishing his reputation for optimism by spending too much time on AIDS. (Van Biema, 1994: 82)

Nor did several others seem to find a listening ear:

> I can't see how people with low I.Q.s or those who love them are in anyway comforted by all this hogwash. I can easily see how such people might be offended by its smug unreality. (Kauffmann, 1994: 28–89)

> This movie is so insistently heartwarming that it chilled me to the marrow. There are no moral crosswinds here, not a breath of doubt or unease to ruffle the Gump image... at once mazy and tight-assed, it foists upon us the myth that we can know better, and do better, by being dumb. (Lane, 1994: 79)

Michael Apple (1993), among others, has pointed to the failure of liberal and left critics to understand the sensibilities of the contemporary public. These reviews seem to bear him out, and their tone of moral righteousness is precisely the quality the right employs in turning the public against the left: "Don't Ram It Down Our Throats!"

Yet another leftist theme prompts even greater reactionary disdain. Consider the acidly cogent review by Amy Taubin:

> As you might have expected, I'm grumpy about *Gump*. This is, after all, *The Village Voice*. Like Kilroy before us, we were there at all those zeitgeist moments so we can tell for a fact that Forrest was not.... I can't write off the historical revisionism as an F/X spoof. The sight of Forrest picking up after that nice Negro girl on the steps of the University of Alabama pissed me off as much as Gene Hackman and William Dafoe's *Mississippi Burning*. White men: the past, present, and future are forever yours. (1994: 53)

Taubin is cogent in her tremendous rewriting of history embedded in this movie. She is also accurate in seeing the recovery of whiteness in the movie. As I described it, it was a "call back to whiteness."

Still, the allusion to "white men" works largely to convert the converted on each side. Likewise, in *Time*, Richard Corliss astutely pegged the film as a "male weepie," noting that "the only three movies of the past two decades to win both year's box-office crown and the Oscar for Best Picture— *Rocky*, *Kramer vs. Kramer*, and *Rain Man*—were canny, poignant fables of men in domestic crisis" (1994: 52–54).

These movies were about "white men," not just men, and the "domestic" crisis was less about domination by the females in their lives than the recovery of white male positionality in the popular imagination. These movies, like *Forrest Gump*, are a kind of romance—that is, they point to an idealized desire: the longing for something just beyond the immediate grasp, the concrete given. In each instance, a white man is re-united with his "before the fall" condition; and women and minorities are enlisted in the recovery. To see how the movie *Forrest Gump* joins the yellow ribbon ritual as a media ritual, we need only scratch the racial/sexual surface of the cellular representation of an America that never was.

Gender, Race, and Romance in *Forrest Gump*

From my reading, Gump—like many contemporary Americans—understands only what he wants to understand with respect to race matters. With the black female earlier and Bubba's momma later, Forrest silences their implicit representations of racial reality by not recognizing racial moment or tension. The scriptwriters operate through other vehicles as well. The audience, for example, is asked to recall the stereotypical Aunt Jemima as a remnant of the racist past in the "nonracist" present. Moreover, they try to deepen the image of Forrest as "racially pure" by fusing him with Bubba in front of the lieutenant, who is clearly elitist and implicitly "politically incorrect," if not racist, because he makes fun of Bubba's lips. Of course, it can be argued that many people seeing *Gump* have no racial memory of the allusions to blacks having thick lips, but this then raises the question of inclusion: why, then, refer to his lips as a site of humor or interest?

Race is not the only site used to re-inscribe an innocent white maleness. Consider Gump's female love object. Jenny is "guilty" of more than just promiscuity and ignoring Forrest's Vincentian devotion. She also is a coward, telling him as he leaves for Vietnam: "If you are ever in trouble, don't try to be brave, just run away." Presumably, this advice is intended to show her love for him and to recall that she was always telling him to run away from the bullies as a child. But her comments, given the failure to develop her character, mutes these nicer representations by emphasizing the idea that she, unlike Gump, has never grown up and recovered from the trauma of a painful childhood. Reviewers, too, struggled with the gender themes in *Gump*:

> He's a simple do-gooder with an I.Q. of 75 who lives by his doddering mama's (Sally Field) philosophy: "Life is a box of chocolates; you never know what you're gonna get." During the turbulent 1960s and 1970s, he worships his mixed-up childhood confidante (Robin Wright as an abused waif who samples all the antisocial vices of the time) while he himself becomes a college football star, a decorated Vietnam hero; a Ping-Pong champ; and a business tycoon. (Williamson, 1994: 40)

Although there has been some discussion of this dynamic in the feminist literature, few traditionally mainstream accounts take up the issue. Yet as is notably the case with *Forrest Gump*, Hollywood has been moving for some time toward disenchantment with the female or, as the reviewers call it, the passing of Hollywood's "Year of the Woman": "Forrest Gump's mother is so devoted to him that she sleeps with the local school principal to guarantee her son's 'mainstreaming.' Forrest's best friend Jenny is a similarly diminished woman... [although she finally]... bears a healthy and bright son and conveniently dies" (Ottenhoff, 1994: 860).

It is at this point in my analysis of *Forrest Gump* that we can perhaps best see how its dynamic unfolding fuses or converges with aspects of the yellow ribbon ritualism surrounding Vietnam. First, a brief comment on my teaching philosophy and pedagogy: I don't insist that my students agree with my interpretations or readings of texts. Some do, and some don't. But I do insist on considering alternative readings and not accepting that the academy and classroom are neutral sites transmitting neutral information and inviting "independent" thought and action. Interestingly, the relative impact of this alternative pedagogical effort can be seen in the response that this reading elicited in one graduate education student.

Paul H. was a 28-year-old white male completing his master's degree in education. He was married to a Mexican American woman and had one child. In addition, he had served in the Navy and taught in the Southwest. He planned on returning there when he had completed his work in math education. After returning from a visit to Washington, D.C., to see the various war memorials, he brought me several photographs he had taken. He had seen in our discussions of *Forrest Gump* a linkage to the Women's Vietnam Memorial. It was clear that his background and experiences significantly influenced his willingness to consider and explore the recovery perspective I had shared with his class.

What I had tried to help the class see was the way that gender is used to close in on and mediate the societal tensions emerging from multiculturalism and diversity enhancement activities. I had argued that the movie reflected a central feminist critique: the periodic need to reinscribe the patriarchy's dominance over females and other minorities requires that a particular imagery and ideology be forefronted (Daly, 1978; Modleski, 1991). Paul H. saw the memorial as a possible illustration of this view. After further exploration I discovered the memorial has a characteristic pose, what I have designated the "Pietà Embrace." I use this designation after Michelangelo's *Pietà* (ca. 1500) and the ideology of American romance. In the conclusion, I examine more fully this aspect of the interplay of gender, class, and recovery in the mediation of white male pain.

Conclusion: White Male Redemption and "The Maternal"

It's the moms of this nation—single, married, widowed—who really hold this country together. We're the mothers, we're the wives, we're the grandmothers, we're the big sisters, we're the little sisters, we're the daughters.
You know it's true, don't you?

– Ann Romney (2012)

Perhaps nowhere is the mediating maternal role better illustrated and institutionalized than in the military nurse (Fig. 3). I have called the pose in this artifact the Pietà Embrace, after Michelangelo's Pietà (Fig. 4). Together, these artistic creations convey both the persistence and power of certain images and

Fig. 3 A. Foringer's World War I Cross Poster, 1917.

Fig. 4 *The Pietà* by Michelangelo, 1498–1499.

ideas and the singular profundity of the maternal archetype. The yellow ribbon ritualism of women and American society joined the complex ideas generating the maternal archetype of Michelangelo. The various ideas, ideals and practices symbolized in their fusion, moreover, all have the quality of mediation.

The most recent and complete representation of the combined forefronting of the image and the ideology of American romance is the Vietnam Women's Memorial. (This memorial is used as the cover illustration for *America's Atonement*.) Dedicated in 1993, it shows three military nurses—a white, a black, and a Latino/Indian/Asian—mourning the death of a white male soldier. The white male soldier is held by the white female nurse; the black nurse looks heavenward; and the Latino/Indian/Asian nurse kneels on the ground gazing at the soldier's helmet.[56]

What a powerful memorial, but whatever its merits, this compromise monument is an unmistakable departure from the original concept, as Elizabeth M. Norman explains:

> In 1984, two former army nurses from Minnesota and Wisconsin proposed a monument honoring women who served in Vietnam. They founded the Vietnam Women's Memorial Project. The prototype statue, which they hope will eventually stand in Washington, D.C., is a woman dressed in combat fatigues; she has a stethoscope around her neck and bandage scissors sticking out of a pocket. (1990: 135)

This reworking of the public memory of Vietnam and its problematic status—especially among women who opposed the war as mothers and mates—is yet another instance of the recovery process and suggests still another way in which the relearning of race can be contested. Cultural studies have taught us the value of narrative: stories are critical to establishing subjectivity and, by the operation of empathy and remembrance, believability. Stories are rhetorically powerful tools. *Forrest Gump* illustrates this and more. When his friend Bubba dies, Gump tells us: "Bubba was my best good friend, and even I know that ain't something you can find right round the corner.... Bubba was gonna be a shrimping boat captain, instead he died right by that river in Vietnam."

How can you not love Forrest? I also lost black brothers in Vietnam, and I recall that they were drafted into war in numbers greater than their presence in the general population and that they have been perennially defamed and exploited by a harsh homeland. I like Forrest's story, but the men and women who stand behind his alleged idiocy offend me. They have him perform complex and profound social acts, eliciting in the process the compassion and complicity of those without a cultural memory of the contexts defining the events so nicely grafted onto the persona of Forrest Gump.

The racially coded recovery embedded in the ideology of romance serves to sever the white male persona from the rest of society—whether Kevin Costner in *Field of Dreams*; Mel Gibson in *Lethal Weapon*; Bruce Willis in *Die Hard*; Sean Connery in *Just Cause, Medicine Man*, and *Rising Star*; Patrick Swayze in *Ghost* and *To Wong Foo, Thanks for Everything! Julie Newmar*; or Tom Hanks in *Forrest Gump*—and having so severed him, excludes him from complicity in—and responsibility for—the social upheavals and crises characterizing the cultural landscape.[57]

The call back to whiteness encoded in these various movies must be understood as such, and the corruption of public mourning and compassion at the service of reactionary and undemocratic policies of containment must be recognized and challenged. By understanding "whiteness" as a curriculum and pedagogy, we move toward de-essentializing racist or sexist behavior by holding accountable the agents of racist schooling, including the media.

The portrayal of the Vietnam War in public schools (Kincheloe & Staley, 1983) was a powerful illustration of the nature of American patriotism and its intrusion into the curriculum and pedagogy of education. Moreover, Susan Jeffords (1989) argued that the continued popularity of Vietnam-related courses in the college curriculum pointed to the complex cultural work done by the representations of Vietnam as cultural product. In this chapter, I examined three interrelated ideas: gender, redemption impulses, and recovery representations. The gender issue has been the overriding concern.

A major concern of education reformers in the past several decades has been the exposure and elimination of practices that perpetuate unnecessary and unfair differences between males and females. One of the findings of the research on bias in the classroom is that female teachers who feel themselves above gender discrimination may also practice sex bias against females, those belonging to both minority and majority groups. For some people, this raises the question of how women can be taught to carry out practices that undermine women's liberation. Tania Modleski put the problem in this way: "We need to consider the extent to which male power is actually consolidated through cycles of crisis and resolution, whereby men ultimately deal with the threat of female power by incorporating it" (1991: 7).

For Modleski, women's activism on the behalf of gender equity threatens male domination in ways that lead men to undermine their efforts. Much research supports her argument (Daly, 1978; Jeffords, 1989; Melosh, 1991; Roszak & Roszak, 1969). One way this has been achieved is by getting women to turn their attention to taking care of or nurturing the men in their lives: husbands, fathers, sons, brothers. This tendency has been so effective and thorough in a society centered on the patriarchy that even oppressed groups parallel this model. For example, the late Audre Lorde characterized the necessity of black female self-love as due to an over-commitment to the oppressed black family: "In the light of what Black women sacrifice for their children and their men, this [call for self-compassion and self-love] is…much needed" (1979: 18). Rhetaugh Graves Dumas echoed her when she wrote: "I have felt the pangs of guilt evoked by those who would lead me to believe that to protect myself and promote my general welfare is to let my people down" (1980: 214).

Mediating white pain is not a simple task, nor is it unimportant or overstated. The mediators, moreover, often are women and assume salutary forms. Ann Romney understood this when she attempted to assist her husband's campaign for president in 2012. She attempted to appeal to the women voters by recognizing their mediating role. Others have recognized this role as well. Thus the primary website addressing the Vietnam Women's Memorial reported:

> Glenna Goodacre discovered the heart of a nation in the process of creating the Vietnam Women's Memorial. Seldom does an artist have the opportunity to be involved in an artwork that means so much to so many people. As Goodacre says, "To think my hands can shape the clay that heals the heart." She's rightly proud of a work that makes visible a memory while shaping the perception of that memory for future generations.

These words, by Susan Hallsten McGarry, are true. But they expose more than truth; they expose motive and mediation. We recognize in Goodacre's efforts precisely the kind of culture work Mary Daly argued that women pursue at the behest of the mythmakers. Thus, in confronting the lack of critical analysis that Kincheloe and Staley decried in 1983, we must again focus on the subjective value of certain actions beyond the question of "truth seeking" or "doing the right thing." Certainly, one persistent point implied in Gramsci's discourse on hegemony is the convergence of needs and interests between the dominators and the dominated. It is often here that the mediation of pain finds both a vehicle and a tenor for production. And it is here, as well, that such cultural work joins the broader military campaign to manage cultural, including, racial pain.

A Postscript: The Second Gulf War

The specter of Vietnam has been buried forever in the desert sands of the Arabian peninsula.

– President George Herbert Walker Bush, 1991

In 2003, the United States and its "coalition of the willing"—England, Australia, and Poland—invaded Iraq. Thus began the formal war to liberate Iraq from its leader, Saddam Hussein. The outcome of that war has yet to be determined despite the American declaration that the outcome—total victory—was all but achieved. History has revealed many sidebars to this war; and currently the nation seems poised on the brink of yet another civil war—this time, on President Barack Obama's watch. Whatever the outcome of the United States' presence in this part of the world, one cannot forget one critical sidebar: the American media's "embedment" in the war zone and, at times, their seeming complicity with the Bush administration.

The media has skirted the question of biased involvement but not completely. Peter Arnett, the veteran reporter for NBC and *National Geographic*, exposed this fine line reporters walk when he granted an interview to Iraqi television and expressed his belief that the United States had failed to achieve some of its objectives in the war. Many NBC reporters grieved for him even as they distanced themselves from the disgraced, disowned, and temporarily unemployed journalist.

There were other mediation tensions evident among the media covering the war and world opinions regarding the United States' ideal self-image. On one occasion, an MSNBC correspondent in Turkey held a live focus group with several Turks. This audience made it clear that they disliked Saddam but they did not think much of the United States either. Puzzled and flustered, the reporter asked, rhetorically, how could a non-Arab secular state hate us? The very question touches on one of the themes taken up in this chapter regarding the American self-image as honest, decent, democratic, noble savior of the free world.

At the conclusion of the session, the reporter observed what non-American media had been saying all along: people outside of the United States do not see the linkages between September 11, 2001, and the pain it caused our nation as the basis for invading Iraq. The reporter also observed that viewers ought to be concerned that what we see on television differs dramatically from what is seen in the rest of the world. Today, Al Jazeera America[58] is just one enterprise competing for the American viewing audience, seemingly in direct response to the perceived bias of traditional coverage of the world and marginalized groups.

This chapter began with a reflection: America is unwilling to examine its policies and practices. We have an image problem. This image problem is complex. This is not so much because America, like most nations, has both noble and ignoble interests. Rather, it is because we claim to stand above the rest—in the eyes of God and Man. Yet issues such as ruthless corporate capitalism, racism, and the like continue to plague the nation. For example, the first female casualty in the Iraqi war was a Native American mother. Her presence in Iraq on behalf of an oppressed people is uncanny given the continuing plight of Native Americans in this country. Perhaps even more telling is the fact that the first American prisoner of war from Iraq, Jessica Lynch, was a friend of this woman—and grieves her today even as she also tries to correct the military's misrepresentation of her heroics in Iraq (See Durante, 2013).

Contradictions like this are part of the reason that the U.S. "trails in the battle for world opinion" (*Atlanta Journal Constitution*, March 30, 2003, www. ajc.com) and has to wage a "war for hearts and minds." The confluence of domestic and international racial practices is illustrative. In particular, the perception that the United States invaded a "colored nation" fuses with the recognition that blacks, for instance, were less favorable toward the war than whites. An article in the *New York Times* (March 27, 2003: B15) on New Yorkers' war views, by Randy Kennedy and Diane Cardwell, is illustrative. Citing a poll where only 34 percent of blacks supported President Bush's presidency, these writers quoted a black nurse:

> "It's like Muhammad Ali said," she explained. "He said: 'Why should I fight? The Vietcong never did nothing to me.' Well, the Iraqis never did anything to me or mine. Why should we fight?"

Today we see that we still refuse to examine our foreign policy or the contradictions embedded in our ideologies of "American decency" and "democratic leadership" of humanity. We refuse to see what millions of others see when they look at us—this is the selfsame self-deception so characteristic of the slave-owners who truly believed that they were the saviors of the slaves (Genovese & Fox-Genovese, 2011). We also refuse to see ourselves as arrogant in our power. The rising tide of "Arab anger" expressed in the media confuses us because of this refusal. We seek to "understand" the "Arab mind" even as we reject knowledge about our own mind (Kincheloe & Steinberg, 2004).

The profound significance of this refusal is concealed in the words of the elder Bush after the first war in the Gulf region in 1991. Bush, mindful of the cultural crisis Vietnam constituted (Rowe & Berg, 1991), echoes the sentiments of those unwilling to learn from America's duplicity. Instead, we use war to "bury" our sins. The 2003 war in post-Saddam Iraq continued this style of crisis management. The embedding of the media helped manage the pain. Americans have been fed an almost surrealist set of war themes on MSNBC, FOX, and CNN. The future will decide how the world comes to view this practice in the scheme of things. Whatever that judgment we know that George W. Bush's chagrin toward the "nonpatriotic" and critical questions raised by the press corps reflects the very weakness Kincheloe and Staley observed in 1983.

In the next chapter, I explore the mediation process as it is expressed in the biographies and narratives of prospective teachers.

Part Three
THE PEDAGOGY OF HEALING

Dialectical irony implies a bondedness in which the ironist realizes her freedom only through unmasking the pretensions of her "victim," but in which the victim regains his subjectivity only through being ironized. To see someone as the victim of irony is to see that person, relative to oneself, as submerged in unreflective absolutism.

– Richard Brown (1987)

But know this: neither of their lives shall be in vain. The galvanizations of our communities must be continued beyond the tragedies. While we fight injustice, we will also hold ourselves to an appropriate level of intelligent advocacy. If they refuse to hear us, we will make them feel us. Some will mistake that last statement as being negatively provocative. But feeling us means feeling our pain; imagining our plight as parents of slain children. We will no longer be ignored. We will bond, continue our fights for justice, and make them remember our children in an appropriate light. I would hate to think that our lawmakers and leaders would need to lose a child before protecting the rest of them and making the necessary changes NOW…

– Sabrina Fulton (2014)

· 6 ·

MULTICULTURALISM AND SOCIAL JUSTICE

White Pain and the Search for a Non-Oppressive Cultural Turn

As a consequence of the "cultural turn," all social life must be seen as potentially political where politics is the contestation of relations of power.

– Kate Nash (2001: 77)

Affirmative action doesn't work? Really? I thought that is [sic] was a very effective way to give millions of low IQ Africans jobs and education that they otherwise would not possibly be qualified for. … So, what do they mean, "it doesn't work"? Depends on your point of view. As a means of weakening White society, and elevating our race enemies, I think it was extremely effective.

– Tanner Colby (2014)

Prologue

Some years back a former student called me for a consultation. After polite conversation, she began softly weeping. Eventually, after drying her eyes with tissues I had given her, she explained her tears in this way: "I'm sorry; I just had an unbelievable experience with racism." My first thought was that she had encountered an angry minority person striking out at a vulnerable white woman. But she quickly explained the reason for her distress with these words:

> I teach this course in women's studies. I have about 70 students, all white except for one black female. There are about 20 white males in the class, and it has been going really great until today. We were discussing "white privilege" and the white males took over. One declared that blacks are the privileged ones; he said that "black privilege" is the Negro College Fund. Another white male agreed, adding that the fact that he cannot freely walk through North Philadelphia is also "black privilege." All of the women seemed scared to challenge them.

A semester earlier, this woman had taken my graduate course on critical theory, gender, race, and representation. Despite doing well in that course, she told me that she now felt ill equipped to help her students and hoped that I might be able to suggest something that would help her convince them that the Negro College Fund and North Philadelphia were not truly instances of "black privilege."

The challenge faced by this young educator was a formidable one. We have already seen some of the barriers to introducing a democratic and critical pedagogy to those personally unfamiliar with the pervasive social oppressions in our society. In addition, the notion of white pain has alerted us to the potential assault implicit in an anti-oppressive agenda. More precisely, the individual identifying as "white" is not merely an established identity, someone else's finished product. Rather, she or he is an *agent, no doubt influenced by context but also acting against what is taken for granted or mandated*. This is one meaning of the "cultural turn." It is an important idea. Just today I heard this theme, listening to one political pundit from Pennsylvania, explaining how West Virginians and folk from Pennsylvania will respond to the Left's Senator Elizabeth Warren: according to this man, Chris Mathews, "culture" matters to people from these states (and others too).

As I listened to him, I saw the word "culture" applying equally to the two Florida policemen recently criticized for being members of the Ku Klux Klan and the young black males currently terrorizing the streets of certain parts of Chicago, Illinois. In all these instances, "culture" pertains to both values and beliefs and the precise ways that people have aligned themselves— through identities and interactions—with it. Thus, for some white males in Philadelphia, their own behaviors (including complicity) may escape reflective critique even as they accurately describe their felt experience that parts of that city are unavailable to them but okay for (some) blacks to travel. Similarly, some black males may feel racist aggression from policemen in the marrow of their bones but lack a meaningful connection to their own often brutal and destructive behavior to others.

Social justice as a goal must operate, in part, in this contradictory emotional space. That is, the individual and the collectivity are both acting all the time to make and remake the conditions that allow them to experience stability or normalcy, and they often act deceptively and contradictorily in the process. Further, "the normal" varies for individuals and collectivities. This is why social reform, social movements, and social justice pedagogy are complicated. As Kate Nash (2001: 86) observes, multiculturalism is also necessarily enmeshed in this emotional space of individual versus collective agency:

> Social movements challenge the idea of a single universal citizenship conceived of as the same set of rights for all citizens on the grounds that only those who conform to the norm of the white, heterosexual male head of household actually enjoy full citizenship rights in this sense. They contest what is 'normal', attempting to displace it as just one of a range of possibilities. In this respect, social movements challenge the idea of citizenship as consisting of individuals enjoying identical rights, put group rights on the agenda and imply a more open, pluralist model of society.

But identity threat and racial/white pain are very much implicated in any push toward a pluralist society. The blogger cited at the beginning of this chapter is to the point: it's perspectival. Within his emotional world, affirmative action is both unfair *and* working. How does one challenge this? How does one "reschool" this man to alternative "normals"?[59]

In this chapter, I focus on recent efforts to forward the social justice initiative within education while respecting the presence of white pain and the rights of those who may not readily identify with anti-oppressive perspectives and strategies. I thereby extend the earlier discussion of white pain in the academy by exploring its presence in the multiculturalism classroom. I begin with a brief statement of the assumptions giving rise to what came to be known as "multicultural teacher education."

The Rise and the Fall of Multiculturalism

During the decades leading up to the 20th century, a powerful struggle was underway to both define and defend the dominant ideas of who was American and what was his (not "her") rightful inheritance. Concepts such as "manifest destiny," the "Negro problem," the "Yellow Peril," "killing the Indian and making the man," the "woman problem," and "manly Christianity" were just a few of the ideas signaling an effort to convert many eyes into one vision and rigidify the established pecking order (Bederman, 1995). World War I and the New Deal era (which encompassed the Great Depression) stand as important events symbolizing, if not inviting, a silencing of the multicultural backgrounds and diverse interests among Americans (Melosh, 1991). War and economic and political ferment seemed to legitimize the suppression of difference and the insistence on universal suffrage. A myth—"the melting pot"—was the ideology used to explain this suppression of difference in life experiences and choices.

With the upsurge of the 1960s radicalism, these earlier tensions regarding race, gender, ethnicity, class, and sexuality regained national visibility and threatened the myth of a melting-pot society with a multicultural mandate. The insistence on a more equitable share in the American dream by those traditionally excluded resulted in a plethora of movements. Ideas such as the "War on Poverty" and the "Great Society" professed a "vision of possibility," a conviction that the United States was truly a participatory democracy and that the "scarce resources" of the richest nation on earth would be redistributed more equitably. The social changes and political discourse associated with black liberation or civil rights activity gradually widened to cover a wide range of real and perceived oppression of students, women, the young, the elderly, gays, and the physically handicapped.

This may be viewed as the rise of multiculturalism as a perspective or orientation. The idea of multicultural education grew out of this larger social context. Lois Weiner, for example, writes that multicultural teacher education took shape as African American educational issues were enlarged to include a diversity of minority groups:

> This growing concern that nonwhite, nonnative speakers of English were being educationally shortchanged enlarged the category of disadvantaged students. *The Thesaurus of ERIC Descriptors* introduced the term multicultural education in 1979, defining it as "education involving two or more ethnic groups and designed to help participants clarify their own ethnic identity and appreciate that of others, reduce prejudice and stereotyping, and promote cultural pluralism and equal participation."
>
> This orientation stood in stark contrast to the acculturation rhetoric that held all Americans were blended into a "melting pot" and thereby indistinguishable from all others in essential ways. Because of the threat this newer understanding held for many, the term "identity politics" came to signal the conflictive or combative aspects

of an orientation that discredited the truth or value of a monolithic "American identity." (1993: 38–39)

Writing from a minority-sensitive perspective, Louise White reflects the typical understanding of the challenge of multiculturalism for prospective teachers. Because teachers' attitudes, beliefs, and behaviors are typically shaped by their own environments, their impact on student achievement is through an

> unconscious reflex rooted in the teacher's own middle class background combined with training which consciously or unconsciously may not recognize the possibility of alternative cultural styles and cognitive modes. This combination results in a middle American ethnocentrism which is destructive to minority students, students from poor families, and any other student who deviates from the mythical norm espoused in teacher training institutions. (1973: 309)

Lois Weiner viewed the 1970s as the era of competency-based teacher education (CBTE) and multicultural teacher education, two strategies to improve teacher preparation for urban, minority education:

> A report issued jointly by two committees of AACTE, one on multicultural education, the other on CBTE, outlined their agreements. Teachers "need certain unique competencies in order to teach in culturally diverse situations," the editor noted. Another writer explained that "for most Blacks, bad teaching… is most often less a matter of a teacher's deficit in commonly practiced teaching skills than a matter of the reflection of a teacher's fundamentally negative feelings or expectations for Black children." Multicultural CBTE focused on the attitudes teachers needed, as opposed to cognitive skills, since the teacher's primary role was defined as the "facilitator of the acquisition of value systems consonant with a student's ethnic, cultural and linguistic background." (1993: 49)

The tremendous social demands for greater social justice for minorities and participation in the mainstream resulted in notions like "diversity" and "inclusion." Future generations of teachers also found as a part of their "inheritance" the expectation that they would be "multiculturalists." This expectation has persisted even as the social and political climate has recycled to the "right" with a corresponding shift in the dominant discourse of social justice (Chapman & Hobbel, 2010). It is in this newer discourse that the emergence of white pain is most apparent. It is also within this discourse that multiculturalism has been characterized as a potential oppressor and serves as an impetus for an alternative ideological stance: *the pursuit of social justice through an anti-oppressive educational strategy.*

White Pain and the "New" Anti-Oppression Discourse

Some years ago, the late Donald Willower, my mentor and colleague, gently chided me for insisting that race remained a major factor in society and education. He had been drawn to and influenced by the writings of the black conservative sociologist William Julius Wilson, author of the important book *The Declining Significance of Race* (1980). Wilson had gained prominence, but not without considerable debate and critique (see Gresson, 1982), for promoting the thesis that history and class, rather than race, accounted for the continuing societal inequities between whites and blacks in America. For Willower, this idea was persuasive, perhaps because it allowed us to continue working toward change without directly confronting racial or other non-class-based explanations for oppression and social inequality. Willower's preference to view and address our problems without confronting racism is perhaps visionary. There is considerable evidence that we are increasingly pursuing non-racial configurations of certain social injustices with correspondingly non-racist solutions and strategies for change. This newer orientation, broadly concerned with democratic education, emphasizes education for social justice (Darling-Hammond, French, & Garcia-Lopez, 2002; Dilg, 1999). Part of the importance of this emerging discussion is its insight into the pedagogy and psychology of healing. This can be seen in a debate facilitated by the American Educational Research Association on anti-oppression in education (Butin, 2001; Kumashiro, 2001, 2002).

The first essay was published in 2001 by Kevin K. Kumashiro, in which he argued for the pedagogical usefulness of the "posts" perspectives, that is, poststructualism, postmodernism, and postcolonialism. Perhaps the main contribution of this piece was its presence in *Educational Researcher*, for it eased the way for other scholars to share their own understandings of this somewhat marginalized or radical academic perspective. Dan W. Butin was one of the scholars who responded to Kumashiro. Butin (2001) understood Kumashiro's arguments on behalf of the "posts" perspectives as useful but problematic. His goal was to expose their limits and indicate how the perspective of Michel Foucault (1977, 1978) might overcome the danger of oppressive classroom learning and growth. Butin succinctly stated his central concern thus:

> The problem is that resistance has been conceptualized as something done only by those oppressed and oppression as something done only by educational practices

antithetical to anti-oppressive education. While Kumashiro acknowledges that anti-oppressive education may be "emotionally upsetting" (p. 8) and that we may actually "desire teaching and learning in ways that affirm... the silencing of other possible worlds" (p. 5), there is no discussion of the possibility that anti-oppressive education may itself be a pedagogy of silencing which is resisted by those in disagreement.... we must acknowledge that anti-oppressive education imposes itself upon students, from the texts to be read to the intellectual positions defended and attacked.

... anti-oppressive pedagogy does not admit the possibility that it too makes use of power in order to reject particular perspectives. I suggest that a "posts" perspective can. And in this admission lies a reformulation of teaching that provides an opportunity to fashion a less constrictive classroom practice. (Butin, 2001: 15)

Kumashiro, responding to Butin's essay in a companion reflection, chose a very "post" and powerful strategy: "As I read and reread Butin's commentary, I found myself attending to different aspects of the commentary and responding in different ways, depending on the lenses I used to read" (2002: 17).

But the strategy of multiple readings did not conceal the heart of Kumashiro's concern with Butin's apparent "resistance" to understanding what the "posts" perspective on power could yield:

There are several problems with this argument. "Posts" perspectives do not make it possible to say that a practice or perspective is "clearly" or "truly" anti-oppressive since they insist that all practices and perspectives are partial.... When reading Butin's commentary a second time, I felt concerned and found myself wanting to illuminate and problematize Butin's resistance to anti-oppressive education. Butin's discussion of an example from his own teaching experiences exemplifies the certainty and resignation that are commonplace among educators and that often hinder anti-oppressive change.... As an alternative, Butin argues that pedagogies informed by "posts" perspectives "construct situations within which students come to their own understanding of the issue in question," regardless of whether that understanding is something the teachers consider "oppressive" or not. (Kumashiro, 2002: 18)

Kumashiro highlights the notion of *resignation* but rushes on to cite Butin's other offenses. Kumashiro has correctly stated the value of "posts" terms such as "disruption," "resistance," and "tentativeness." His motive for a multiple reading, however, rehearses the very flaw in Butin that he exposes. He seems to know that one cannot continue to sit on the fence, or more precisely, that the insistence that one not "contaminate" science, including educational theory and pedagogy, is bogus. This very insistence is itself ideological and "contaminated." Thus his allusion to "resignation." There is a strategic loss, or resignation, that can accompany the failure to see that even democracy and "nonintrusion" (often called "interference") cannot be privileged by those who are struggling under the yoke of oppression. Discourse situated in the academy—vaguely insulated against the devastation of ruthless power—can afford to discuss matters under the rubric of "reason." People living under the oppressive yoke of a particular brand of democracy may not be able to grant its "greatness" above all else. The Iraqis suffering Coalition bombing in Baghdad come to mind in this regard: were we truly liberating or only killing them?

Kumashiro's arguments on behalf of the "posts" perspective triggers something akin to the response against "whiteness" studies: white pain and white retreat. Why? Butin illustrates the critical point: "Yet to presume that we can simply change to become less oppressive is to presume that our 'old' perspectives are just wrong and denies the contextual nature of how we come to believe what we do" (2002: 15).

Butin is trying to construct a classroom space, complete with possibilities and potentialities, that will "quicken" students' inner workings, yielding a "free thinker" who can do what she or he will. His conclusion is seductive if not persuasive:

> I hope that other classes, other situations, may further disabuse them of perspectives I deem objectionable. But this is irrelevant to my particular project. My project is to construct situations within which students come to their own understanding of the issue in question. Their understanding may be in direct opposition to my own perspective. Their understanding may be labeled oppressive. But that is the price I pay for conducting a "posts" classroom. Advocates of anti-oppressive education may balk at these suggestions. And well they should, for they offer only haphazard control over what the student will learn. But a pedagogy grounded on a "weak overcoming" is exactly one that embraces the partiality and unknowability of the teaching process. Constructing situations that force students to confront, resist, and resignify their identities and knowledges is what makes teaching an art form. One cannot know the end result, but I am not so sure that attempting to control it is a road better taken. (Butin, 2002: 16)

This takes us back to power and power relations and to what has already been constructed in the mainstream pedagogy and curricula: oppression. Kumashiro offers important corrections to specific points made by Butin, but his forcefulness seems muted in the face of what has been charged:

> By implication, a pedagogy informed by "posts" perspectives does not hope that students embrace or come closer to "the" anti-oppressive practice or perspective, nor does such a pedagogy need to resign itself to the fact that students might instead

embrace oppressive ones. Rather, it hopes that students question the effects of a variety of practices and perspectives, including the ones their teachers say are anti-oppressive. In particular, it teaches students to look beyond a variety of practices and perspectives, not to reject what they are taught, but to examine and experience ways that any practice or perspective can produce different knowledge, identities, relations, and so forth, sometimes oppressive ones, sometimes anti-oppressive ones, and sometimes both. (Kumashiro, 2002: 18)

Together, Butin and Kumashiro provide a vital service. They expose the complex challenges, indicating the limits and possibilities of the classroom teacher if certain logics of theory, policy, and practice predominate. They also highlight the implicit challenges of a psychopedagogy of healing that is responsive to white pain. But their analyses neglect one important dimension of this healing: the minority-based lessons of anti-oppressive education.

Anti-Oppressive Education—A Minority Perspective

Minority teachers in the classroom offer a critical alternative vision of anti-oppressive education. Butin and Kumashiro do not directly confront this dimension. In particular, white males typically receive much more deference and submissive student responses than women and minorities do (Schacht, 2000). While a white male may be rejected or resisted for presenting multiperspectival material, it seems to be minorities and women who most often find themselves challenged by, and challenging for, students who might resist anti-oppressive material (Lubiano, 2013). The conversation about "posts" perspectives has lacked sufficient recognition of these gender-, class-, and race-specific dynamics. This exclusion pertains most to the possibility of a detached exchange and construction of multiple learning sites. Indeed, I maintain that the very presence of a minority authority figure typically and routinely stimulates potentiality and possibility in challenging ways for most students, regardless of their background demographics. Let me illustrate.

Between April 13 and 23, 1993, a web-based discussion of male alienation in women's studies classes was held on WMST-L. A few excerpts provide a sense of the complexity mere attention to minority content may introduce:

> I have recently been approached by one of my students complaining that my course focuses entirely too much on women's issues. The course I am teaching is an Introductory Criminal Justice course. In the course description I mentioned that the focus of the course would be to critique the criminal justice system especially in

respect to gender and racial discrimination. I also mentioned on the first day of class that I would be teaching from a feminist perspective. This student argued that he is not getting the "basics" he needs for law school. The text book... covers the basics and is not from a feminist stance. This confrontation was very upsetting to me. I started questioning my teaching style only to discover that I have not focused on women's issues any more or less than racial issues and other extensions of the "basics." As I began talking to faculty I discovered that many professors who try to teach from a more inclusive perspective are attacked by their students—either directly, as I was, or through teacher course evaluations. I am relatively new to this list, so I don't know if this issue has been raised before, but I was wondering if anyone else has had similar experiences, and if anyone has suggestions about ways to teach from an inclusive perspective without alienating students—especially white males. Thanks (AGAIN!).

This writer was a female professor at Notre Dame. Her story stimulated dozens of email replies. One male response to her plea adds an interesting, perhaps predictable, dimension.

> My question for you is: have you quantified just how much time you spend on women's issues? I would guess that this student is perceiving a little as a lot. I have had similar experiences in teaching Introductory Statistics. In that class I have used word problems for including diversity. When I ask students to comment on the word problems there are always some who say "most of the problems deal with women's issues" or "too many deal with homosexual issues." In fact, a content analysis of the 300 word problems I use in a semester showed that about 1 in 6 deal with gender issues and less than 1% deal with sexual orientation.
>
> I think that one of the problems we will always face in including marginalized groups is the false perception that a little inclusion is a lot. Notice the phenomenon of last fall's elections. That was dubbed by the media the year of the woman. Yet when all is over there are still only 6% females within our U.S. Senate. While this may be a 3-fold increase it is still hardly more than a beginning.

This male respondent offered a powerful insight into the plight of the pro-democratic educator. But one may intuit a certain resignation in his comments, which rehearse that found in the Butin–Kumashiro debate. Another male seems to echo the concern I am raising:

> ... You've hit a very important nerve with your observation that being inclusive is seen by some as being narrow. One student commented on my evaluation that I am too pro-women. I considered this a victory, not a criticism. What pleased me is that the student did not say I was anti-men. I take pains to be fair and inclusive. I allow no gender bashing in my classes. Since men and women are accustomed to

having knowledge presented in the "neutral" male voice, they perceive the inclusion of women's voices as being a special interest and not the basics.

The challenge presented by "sensitivity to white males" and others who might resist anti-oppressive education is shown to be massive in these excerpts. Interestingly, the insights of multicultural educators are seen as helpful in healing the divide. Hence another respondent wrote:

> This is in reply to Patty O'Donnell's query about alienating male students in classes. I don't have any real answers to the question, but I would call everyone's attention to Patricia Williams' book *The Alchemy of Race and Rights*. In it, Williams describes many scenarios exactly like the one she described. Maybe it helps just to know it isn't you as the teacher that's the problem. What makes it even more relevant to Patty's situation is that Williams is a lawyer teaching in a law school. You might think about using it in the class; at least you might want to read it.

African Americans like Patricia Williams have, understandably, been at the forefront of sharing narratives of the unprecedented tensions created by their authority positions in the white academy. A major concern for others and myself has been the initial, ironic silence that white students frequently display, regardless of the content or position assumed by the minority educator. Gloria Ladson-Billings writes, "Student silence can be many things, but for those who are truly interested in pedagogy (particularly a pedagogy of difference), student silence can be deafening. It should not, however, be ignored" (1996: 85).

Ladson-Billings echoes and enlarges the sensitivity and insight minority educators and other democratic-oriented teachers bring to the multicultural classroom. Britzman and Pitt expand on the silence management theme she introduced:

> In our work, we learn from listening differently to the responses of our students, resisting our own impulse to self-mastery that seems to require us to view the students as in need of our correction. This orientation, we now believe, is the teacher educator's rush to application. Learning to listen to the structures that students display delays our own mastery. We do not know what will happen, but a great deal of our work concerns returning the student's question back to the student. The returned question has nothing to do with pleasing the teacher but, instead, may provide... more space for the student to consider her or his own conflicts in learning. (1996: 123)

By allowing "more space" for students to grapple with "resistance," multicultural educators reflect awareness of the painful nature of much learning and growth; they recognize the need to "dwell in" the teachable moment with their students. It is this "dwelling in," as the phenomenologist describes it, which serves as a bridge-support for the neophyte seeking to push beyond the safe borders of self-other understanding.

The commitment to anti-oppressive education, we see, has not suffered from a paucity of committed, non-oppressive teachers. Indeed, the liberatory ideas discussed by Kumashiro and Butin have been advanced by many earlier writers, including Ann Berlak:

> Changing, for members of dominant and subordinate groups who have internalized dominant stories, might not only mean coming to read experiences from the perspective of the oppressed. It may be possible to construct new stories that incorporate both (or several) stories into a single narrative where complementary versions that had previously been told and heard in isolation from one another are constructed into a single story in which the different versions match up. We would then be part of one another's stories—I would be part of your story as you are part of mine. Such stories would be tales of the painful effects of racisms that are, though to different degrees, experienced by all racial/ethnic groups, by both targets and perpetrators of racisms in Eurocentric and racist societies. Such stories, likely to be unfamiliar to both White peoples and peoples of color, would include narratives of White supremacy, but they would also frame racisms as community shared traumas that result in blindness, alienation, and deracination for us all. (1996: 100)

Implicit in Berlak's storytelling strategy is the notion of "shared fate" (Kirk, 1964). First introduced in the mixed-racial adoption studies of H. David Kirk, this concept refers to his observation that the more successful adoptive parents tended to be those who could acknowledge both their adoptive children's and their own "difference" rather than deny that either the child or they were defined partly by the adoptive condition. I have used the term more broadly to describe any condition where two or more people identify a sharedness (Gresson, 1995). Berlak's partial solution to the implicit oppressiveness of anti-oppressive education reflects the "shared fate" between the oppressor and the oppressed.[60]

The multicultural educators introduced in this section seem to share a common belief in the need for catharsis and the value of storytelling in the anti-oppressive classroom. Although storytelling does not address the full range of challenges facing democratic education in the non-oppressive classroom, it does introduce the opportunity for student growth in a less threatening environment. It also represents a step back from the insistence of guilt with respect to student participation in social oppression (read as oppressive monoculturalism). Further, it builds on accepted understandings of constructivism as a compelling description of the role of subjective reality in the processing and possible internalization of new information. In the next section, I describe my own effort to introduce storytelling and autobiography into the emotional work characterizing much anti-oppressive education.

Emotion Work in Multicultural Teacher Education

At SUNY-Albany, I taught cross-cultural clinical practice and family therapy techniques to working- and middle-class white females. At Penn State, my profession changed but my students are similar. Over the years, I have observed that much of the thinking characterizing a "liberal pedagogy" failed to deal with the existential realities of these students and the constructivist nature of the multicultural classroom. As a result, I have developed and implemented a series of courses that incorporate constructivist insights. I have been especially interested in how students understand their social positions and how they construct their narrative selves and relate them to the multiculturalism mission. Several ideas presented in the preceding sections underpin my curricular strategy. In addition, the approach I take has been informed by particular attention to the pedagogic implications of "social pain" and autobiographical work in the multicultural classroom. I turn now to a brief elaboration of this concept and how I have implemented it in my work.

Social Pain, Student Subjectivity, and Anti-Oppressive Education

> *What occurs to me is that such intellectual sparring, the very stuff of academic exchange, may be beside the point. For to ignore the emotional dimensions of this discussion, I think, is certainly to miss a good portion of what the argument may really be about: the emotional stake that these students have in their whiteness. But ignore it is precisely what pedagogical propriety will push us to do: circumvent the emotion and focus on reasonableness of argument. To do otherwise would seem to take us into an area that is off-limits—the realm of affect, which, as we all know, is present in the college classroom even as we avoid acknowledging it, almost as assiduously as we might avoid the mention of bodily functions.*
>
> – Wendy Ryden (2012: 117)

Social pain is pain—psychical, physical, spiritual—caused by social beliefs, values, or actions. It derives its meaning from society because most pain is ultimately mediated or understood through ideas, beliefs, and meanings that humans collectively construct. As I have defined it, racial pain is an aspect of social pain; likewise, white pain is a variant of racial pain. Multiculturalism as pedagogy "invites" specific "pain zones" for many white students. Some of the pain stimulated is inevitably linked to being "healthy." Audrey Thompson, writing on psychologically oriented whiteness theories, clarifies this point as follows:

> For psychological theorists of whiteness, a healthy white racial identity will not become possible until whites confront and accept their whiteness (abandoning colorblindness), acknowledge the privileges of whiteness, and take a consistently antiracist stance. The keys to developing a healthy white identity, then, are (1) developing an *awareness* of whiteness, including white privilege; and (2) acting in ways that make use of that knowledge to challenge personal and institutional racism. (1999: 2)

Pain is generally recognized as either healthy or unhealthy. As a signal to some incipient or latent danger, it is healthy, but as the signal of advanced disease, it is considered unhealthy. The questioning, resisting utterances of white students regarding multiculturalism issues and projects are, in this view, healthy.[61] A powerful illustration of this paradoxical situation is conveyed in this passage from Wahneema Lubiano (2013: 540) as she laments the challenge of generating empathy and critical thought in her Duke seminar on "Prison, the U.S., and the Citizen":

> This course has driven home for me in particular ways the inability of general public discussion—what my students are aware of in abundance but which they understand as "natural"—to accommodate elaborated and unelaborated discourses for cathected critical engagement, e.g., white supremacy and its connection to prison, the history of the U.S. state, and the idea of the citizen. If those of us who participate in teaching, research, and public intellectualism frequently take as our object of critique the limitations of the liberal bourgeois subject, we must also run up against the difficulty of moving our students from that hegemonic subjectivity to something more specifically critical.
>
> But this semester, I have run into another form of difficulty. Since there seems to be no location for even the much-derided liberal bourgeois subject to exist, the obstacle looms before me of helping to move my students from their internalization of the dominant narrative that explicitly and implicitly structures their active and passive acceptance of the massive carceral state, to a position of awareness: first, that they are living out such a state of affairs; and then, a realization that this state of affairs is in no way natural or inevitable; i.e., I nostalgically *long for* the simple presence of a liberal bourgeois subjectivity as a starting point in the classroom, as an on-ramp for empathetic transfer. I am forced, temporarily at least, to work toward generating that liberal bourgeois subject, in order to move my students past it.

Here, Professor Lubiano is describing the pedagogical plight of the critical educator. In particular, denial of individual responsibility or contemporary liability for presumably past (and therefore not currently operational) oppression fails to help in working beyond social pain. The efforts of multicultural teacher educators to track the stages or dimensions of these reactions to a transformative pedagogy may, accordingly, be translated as therapeutic actions or "social therapy."

The idea of social therapy has its roots in those areas of psychological treatment that appreciate the importance of connecting some forms of individually experienced social pain to the cultural or systems dimension of human functioning (Bowen, 1985; Lyman, 1981; Spindler & Spindler, 1994). Some correctives to white pain may be achieved by linking critical pedagogical ideas and therapeutic strategies. By critical pedagogical ideas, I mean largely instructional strategies aimed at transformation. By linking the "therapeutic" to critical pedagogy, I forefront loss, pain, and the healing implicit in a critical multiculturalism. But there is one sense in which anti-oppressive pedagogy may indeed be vulnerable to its characterization as oppressive: the assumption of "taintedness" by oppression may preclude the presence of "victory" over oppressive practices, or at the least, an openness to the gradual awakening to the inevitable presence of oppressive proclivities in us all. The so-called constructivist perspective in education has provided a partial corrective to this assumptive arrogance in its emphasis on the subjective role in the construction of knowledge and the understanding of new information. According to Ava McCall in her discussion of constructivist implications for teacher education:

> In order to heed Liston and Zeichner's advice to teacher educators to balance introducing social reconstructionist ideas to students with addressing their concerns as preservice teachers, we must know students better. We need to learn more about students' backgrounds and interests as well as develop a greater understanding of what contributes to their acceptance and resistance to feminist pedagogy and multicultural, social reconstructionist ideas. Even though the time needed to accomplish these goals might be significant, these efforts could become research studies and teaching improvement projects. (1994: 65)

It is perhaps ironic that the multicultural classroom could sometimes be less than democratic and less than edifying, especially when we consider how much thought and energy most multicultural teacher educators give to curriculum and instructional matters (Bollin & Finkel, 1995; Darling-Hammond et al., 2002). Still, we need to remind ourselves of the importance of engaging "students' experiences as central to teaching and learning. This means that teacher educators need to accept that the learner is an active participant in the construction of knowledge" (Kanpol & Brady, 1998: 11).

The recognition of student teacher constructions in the classroom is a critical yet too seldom emphasized challenge, especially with respect to multiculturalism. Realizing with Wortham and others the value of what I call *cognitive-emotional distance* from the material, in my classes I assign a term essay that allows for both autobiographical reflection and critique. An article by Linda Valli (1995) facilitates this initiative. In her article, Valli reports on a study of nine white preservice teachers placed in predominantly black urban, multicultural schools. Her intention had been to give these prospective teachers an experiential learning opportunity. I assign this article for two reasons. First, Valli's task or intervention engages the cognitive-affective domains of student teacher multicultural experience and thinking in a way that allows my students to more or less safely enter the discourse. Second, Valli provides one of the most sensitive and accessible discussions of certain contradictions in multicultural teacher education. Reflecting on the two contradictions with which her students repeatedly struggled in their multicultural education ("learning to be color blind" and "color conscious"), she advises:

> How can this analysis guide teacher educators in helping preservice students construct cross-cultural identities? The first and most obvious way is to show the limitations of the two mandates. The first reinforces stereotypes; the second imposes cultural domination. Only when they are viewed in dialectical relation do the mandates reveal the tensions and issues of race that new teachers must learn to handle. (Valli, 1995: 126)

In this formulation, Valli has made accessible for further intervention the contradictions of teacher education identified in earlier work, notably that of Mark Ginsburg (1988). Reporting on teacher education research at the University of Houston, Ginsburg identified many of the problematic aspects of prospective teacher beliefs cited by other scholars. As a partial corrective, he calls for the development of a "critical praxis" among prospective teachers. I have found his work provocative and especially valuable for graduate students. Undergraduates, however, often have difficulty seeing themselves in terms of these contradictions, as Bollin and Finkel (1995) report. Because of the way in which she conducted and describes her work, Valli seems to resonate better with my undergraduates, as they see themselves in her student teachers. A brief presentation of excerpts from several of their reflective essays may help illustrate the pedagogic value of subjective classroom exercises in the multicultural student teacher classroom.

Student Autobiography and Non-Alienated Pedagogy

To date, I have more than a thousand student reflections on Valli's work as it relates to their own student narratives. The results have been largely remarkable. Perhaps the most immediate value of the article as a pedagogical tool is to give students a chance to introduce themselves as "heterogeneous whites" with complex multicultural genealogies. Consider the following statement made by one of my students in his term essay/reflection on multiculturalism:

> Though I was not raised in a very diverse environment, the times that I grew up in, and the role models that I had, gave me a strong awareness and appreciation for the different ethnic groups that make up the larger world. I grew up in the State College area. My father was a professor of Philosophy and my mother was from an affluent Boston family. My mother's background help shape my perceptions of society with its enlightened Unitarian heritage.

This is an important comment. It not only invites whites to recall a history of liberal thinking and acting, but it also identifies contemporaries as situated in terms of the past. Without a vehicle for challenging the contradictions inherited by many students, this kind of sharing might have been truncated or silenced. While it is true that few of my students enter the class with this specific genealogy or pedigree, each enters with her or his own story and understanding regarding her or his diversity in the world. To challenge problematic positions is one thing, but first they must be heard. Already in the preceding passage, we recognize a "family memory" that often is underexamined in the multicultural classroom discourse: the perennial presence of "good white folk" even during times of "dirty racial business."

The young man just cited links his multiculturalist vision to a specific and unique biographical inheritance: his ancestors included a man who was both friendly to a famous abolitionist and himself set up a major charitable association in the northeast. Clearly, this could be read as yet another instance of a student giving the professor what he wants to hear. Recall this is precisely what one of my critics (Chapter 4) claimed my students were doing. But consider this: the student too may have an investment in seeing him or herself in a certain way. In fact, a major objective of anti-oppressive education is to allow "space" for enlargement of self-identity and self-ideal. The kind of student storytelling implicit in Berlak and others cited previously creates precisely this opportunity to change/construct biography.

This particular instance of a recollection of past glory actually exposes the dialectical nature of all knowledge construction; moreover, it illustrates recent understandings of the growth challenge to "whiteness":

> Rearticulating whiteness is an emergent project. We know the racism of our whiteness in part through recourse to particular methods of inquiry but in part also by our own resistances to change and by our temptations to see ourselves in particular racialized terms. A temptation for progressive whites is to not only be a good white but to be recognized as a good white. Identifying oneself as an anti-racist ally or aspiring to a final stage of moral white development, however, evades the problematic character of whiteness. In a racist society, whiteness is an inherently problematic position. (Thompson, 1999: 23)

Audrey Thompson has gone to the heart of the matter: there is a need to see oneself and be seen by others as "a good white person." Ultimately, for those committed to social justice, this need is critical if social pain is to be avoided. Beyond the offense against democracy implied in the notion of oppressive anti-oppressive education is another: the offense against an emerging self, one potentially moving toward enlargement. Interestingly, this very theme surfaces in the reflection of an African American male with a strong Afro-centric orientation, who uses the occasion to critique teacher educators generally:

> The problem... is that courses in which undergraduate education majors are prescribed—vestiges of one of our most recent revolutions in programs pertinent to the process of training future teachers—have not fulfilled the hope of bringing prospective teachers sociologically intimate to the growing minority-dominant society. Closer to the point, these courses were established in the wake of this country's drive toward multiculturalism, even cultural pluralism, yet, as the author concedes, it is widely believed that they have failed to sensitize students. In fact social stereotypes that were prevalent throughout her early upbringing—generalizations that members of her generation fought somewhat heartedly—are considered to be on the rise amongst generation x'ers. My concern is that teacher educators are engaging in multicultural efforts with little knowledge of beginning teachers' experiences in culturally diverse schools. Often, teachers try to incorporate multiculturalism into their curriculum without any knowledge of it themselves, which only leads to the encouragement of stereotypical attitudes and generalizations. Although multicultural education is a necessity in all classrooms today, if it is not incorporated appropriately, it could backfire and instead do more harm than good.

These thoughts remind us of the negativity that might accompany multicultural educational activity. What I have recognized from years of teaching cross-cultural, often emotional, material is the fact that I, a black male authority figure, create tension for my white students. I often mention this to them when explaining how minority students might feel with white teachers. For them, my presence becomes a source of "white identity crisis." I have referred previously (1997) to the task necessitated by this white identity crisis in multicultural education as "emotion work." What exactly is this pedagogical challenge? Perhaps one way of thinking about it is through review of an inquiry by Stanton Wortham (1994). Using techniques from linguistic anthropology, Wortham examined how something as simple as a classroom discussion using "participant examples" can affect one's teaching objectives:

> Discussion of an example sometimes leads classroom conversation off track. In such a case speakers do not get back to the topic that led them into the example. Instead, they move out from the example into a new topic—often inspired by the example.... Although the speakers may be overtly talking about the example, their characterizations of participants in the example can have implications for these same participants in the classroom conversation itself. When these implications become salient, the example can lead the classroom discussion off track. (1994: 1–2)

In this passage, Wortham's argument is reminiscent of earlier inquiry into the linguistic features of classroom material (see Haskell, 1987). But Wortham's inquiry extends the focus of earlier work in this area; in particular, he documents the progression of classroom interactions that, starting from a seemingly neutral position, degenerate into extraclassroom partisanship. It is here that we see the special significance of his findings for multicultural education: its skepticism of the efficacy of participant examples that promote extended classroom interaction.

Writing around the time of the applied research reports of several multicultural educators (see Bollin & Finkel, 1995; Valli, 1995), Wortham concludes in regard to "enacted participation": "If a teacher wanted students to experience certain interactional events and emotions... a participant example might help, if it encouraged students to lose control in the classroom interaction. But then the class would have to *step back* from this experience and reflect on it in light of the text" (1994: 171).

These last thoughts are important, as they speak to both the constructed nature of the curriculum and traditional classroom practice. In addition, they alert us to the undeniably deconstructionist character of radical curricula that insist that students confront the inherited or "official knowledge" (Spring, 1995). Furthermore, Wortham implicitly reminds us that we cannot escape the interplay of cognitive and affective content in certain kinds of pedagogical activity. Therefore, while his inquiry does not pertain precisely to multicultural education and discourse, it may be extrapolated to them in terms that may help us better understand some of the "backlash" themes identified in recent scholarship (Apple, 1993; Dziech, 1995).

Implicit in my African American student's critique, supplemented by Wortham's work, is the issue addressed briefly earlier: the threat multicultural inclusion per se constitutes in the classroom. For example, an Asian American student noted:

> Regardless of whether or not a teacher has moved beyond the color of a student, it is oftentimes impossible to make other students see their classmate for who they are and not for what race they represent. For example, I feel that in all of my classes, when any issue about Asians is the topic of discussion, most white students turn to look at me. To them, I represent my whole race and I am knowledgeable about everything that is Asian. Needless to say, this is far from the truth, yet I find that I am often in this position.

This student uses Valli's findings to talk about her classmates. As characteristic of most of my Asian students, she rarely spoke in class, although she performed well otherwise. Indeed, only once in 30 years have I had an Asian student challenge directly her white peers about whiteness and its privileges. I make this point not to imply something "essential" about Asian Americans; rather, I want to indicate how an observed tendency seems to be modified through autobiography when used as a nonthreatening invitation. Few whites or minorities are likely to have the background and perspective needed to succeed in multicultural situations. For most people, a complex developmental process is involved in gaining the maturity, competence, and other qualities associated with a transformative, multicultural challenge. But some do seem to recognize the hurdles. For example, consider a young man who was completing his student teaching in South Dakota at an American Indian school. In his paper, he wrote:

> A lot of students who become student teachers haven't for the most part, encountered any relations with inner-city black students or inner-city kids of all races. This situation would put a student teacher in a threatening situation, at least from their point of view. This would most likely be the case because they never were exposed to

black students or the environment they live in. Case in point, in my Art Education class this semester, I posed a question to my peers; "how many of you in this class would go into an inner-city school and teach?" One person out of twenty-four students raised their hand. I then asked why they wouldn't want to teach in an inner-city school. Their replies were, "I'd be afraid," "there is too much violence," and "the kids are too mean."

This young man is 28 years old, born and raised in Pittsburgh. He has three older brothers and one younger sister. He writes admiringly of his hardworking parents, of German, Irish, and Italian background:

> My parents both had to drop out of school before finishing high school. My father dropped out in the tenth grade to go and work for the family and tend to his mother. My mother dropped out of school in the ninth grade and her reasoning was because of her mother being ill. Both my mom and dad came from low-income situations. My dad's father was in the U.S. Army and his mother stayed home and took care of the three children. My mother's dad, well I am not too sure of, I don't know what he did or his background. He died when my mom was only five years old. Because of this my mother doesn't remember much of him. Her mother took care of her and her two brothers. My parents both had very rough childhoods but seemed to come off it OK.
>
> My father worked two jobs his entire life. My mother didn't start working until 1982. By that time all of the children were in school. My mother also worked two jobs and still does. My parents were and still are hard workers. They never had much for themselves because everything went to taking care of the five children and never had extra money for themselves. This was the main reason why our family didn't take many vacations.... My father passed away in May 1992 of a heart attack, he was forty-eight years old.

This story is familiar to many working-class white and minority families. I make this possibly challengeable point because Mike seems "very black" to me. In my vernacular community, this term means that he has the sensitivity from both knowing pain and interpreting it in a broad-based way that leaves his racial identity intact without withdrawing or escaping into the meager white privilege that accrues to whites for promoting their racial group. In short, Mike has that form of whiteness that constitutes the positive side of whiteness found in the writings that I have recently designated as the "recovery school of white studies" (Gresson, 2000: xi).

Mike's narrative is remarkably different from those offered by most of my white students. To be sure, they write about family trials, tribulations, and triumphs, and even about family values and honor. But few reveal intimacy with the raw brutalities of living near the "class line." Most of us are prepared to see a different picture of "whiteness." Another male, Todd, illustrates this:

> In second grade I won the citizenship award that my elementary school gave to the most outstanding citizen in each grade. I guess it actually meant the one who didn't get into trouble and the one who was generally nice to others. I guess that is what a citizen of our country is supposed to do and I certainly wanted to please my country. My parents were both at the assembly and I was so proud of myself. I guess that I have never lost that feeling.
>
> I was born in a centennial year of all coincidences and I was raised a good old American boy. I played baseball, sang in the Methodist church choir, and always watched fireworks on the fourth of July. I had no real sense of my family origins and I still don't. I know that my father's great grandparents were from Scotland and my mother descends from England, but this was far from important to me and, from what I could determine, to my family as well. As far as I know, I am solely an American and the rest of it doesn't much matter.
>
> My family was constructed as the model U.S. family. My parents raised their three children together in a middle-class suburb where we played in the backyard and walked to school. My father worked in a management position and my mother stayed home to take care of us kids. I can't remember a time when I didn't have almost everything that I wanted and I always had food on the table. I rarely think of myself as ever identifying with any ethnic group, although I guess that is not completely true. The most powerful portion of my identity that would define my ethnicity would have to be my religion. This played the biggest role in defining my values also. I was forced to go to church every Sunday along with Sunday school and the church choir. There were and are almost no ethnic minorities that attend my church. Yet I obtained Christian values from the church that strive towards equality for all, forgiveness of all and salvation for all that believe in Jesus and it is this set of beliefs with which I identify most.

This passage emphasizes the values that students often bring to the multicultural classroom. These values serve as cueing lenses, helping students simultaneously recognize and assimilate new, potentially damaging, information. Narratives like the preceding remind us of the contrast between these privileged lives and those of the vast majority of the minorities they will learn about in multicultural classrooms. Both privileged and poor whites, notably males, face a challenge in such classrooms. There is evidence, nonetheless, of transcendence among some of them. Transcendence requires, however, a reason and a vehicle for change within. Mike, introduced earlier, had gone into the military, served in Alaska, and known many lonely months during which he could think about life and his place in it. He once shared some of his journals written during this time in Alaska. A dominant theme was the painful sacrifices of his parents, notably his father who suffered and died during his absence from the mainland. Mike's encounter with multiculturalism was drastically different from that of most of his peers. As a result, his reflections often seemed elitist or superior with respect to his typically younger classmates:

> I am a junior here at Penn State and I have seen the bias and stereotypes that take place and play themselves out. Being from the inner-city of Pittsburgh, I can see the so-called "bad side" of what teachers perceive to be a bad thing in the inner-city schools (e.g. violence, drugs, fights, etc.). This is a false accusation. The inner city is no worse off than any suburban school. I am convinced that the problem isn't just black people, it is with teachers not knowing how to deal with or communicate with the students. In my opinion, this goes beyond race; it is ignorance and selfishness on behalf of the educator. Until educators understand how to deal with multicultural issues, they will be fighting the notion of racism and stereotyping until the day they either quit or retire.

Mike later married a middle-class woman whom he says marveled at his background and take on life. After he finished at Penn State, he acted on his multicultural understanding and commitment. He and his wife went to South Dakota to teach at a Native American school. Thus differences in background can affect both understanding and optimism. For example, listen to Jennifer:

> I am a white American female with strong beliefs that have been taught to me by my elders. My family origin is from Germany and Wales; however, I do not feel a close bond to these two countries. I have a very tight affiliation with the country I have known all my life, America. My loyalty to my country will assure that I will be the best teacher I can be to the future of our nation. Being from the city (Philadelphia), I have had a first-class look at some of the things that affect the children of the inner-city. Although I went to a suburban school, my dream is to educate children from the urban areas. These children are faced with horrific ordeals and settings. For instance, chains and bars on windows, unqualified staff, etc. I know that my parents raised someone with outstanding values that can help to "save" these children. I would not be happy teaching anywhere else but the city. I have alot [sic] to give. Although I am a white American, I want to teach African Americans. This may be because my father, who was superintendent and president of the PA School Board Association, has always told me "I can make a difference and I will."

> Looking ahead to two years from now when I will be looking to start my career as a high school educator, I can't help but think back to the third grade. I have many memories of coming home after school and retiring to the basement to teach my

stuffed animals on my small green chalkboard. I even remember begging my mother to bring home a grade book and a plan book so I could "officially enroll" all of my stuffed animals. My father, an intermediate school business teacher, and my mother, the intermediate school ninth-grade secretary, would come home every night and always discuss the latest school gossip at the dinner table. I guess I was conditioned to be an educator from the very start.

The key thing I want to emphasize here beyond the obvious influence of biography is the tone or quality of concern expressed by those students who do choose to face the social inequities of the multiculturalism mandate. Their voices are faint compared with those who choose the "safe" way; yet their voices are powerful because of the very privilege they enjoy. According to Angel, a junior,

> My future plans consist of student teaching in a Philadelphia inner city school, spending the next few years teaching disadvantaged children, and eventually holding a powerful position in society where I can improve education for those children....
>
> In elementary and junior high school our family was quite poor, though I never really [knew] this at the time. Later in life our family would change our social-economic status to upper-middle class. This has proven to be a critical point in my life as I have seen first hand how one is treated just on the basis of their apparent status.... I must quickly explain to you that I lived in Pennsylvania the first four years of elementary school. Here I was among all white students, but I was poor. Immediately I was placed in a remedial reading class, hence considered inferior. Then, in 4th grade, I moved to Florida where my school was half minorities and half white. After my experience of feeling less valued as other students in Penn, now in Florida I was privileged and saw others suffer because of my fortune. Coming from where I came I know this was wrong and could really empathize with minorities. I now wonder if I would have felt the same that I did if I had never seen that other side. What a scary world we live in. In these schools tracking was based on anything but ability. It was all a game, masterfully devised to keep the top on top and the bottom on bottom. What was considered an asset was having money, prestige and being white. I remember sitting in classrooms and knowing that what was happening to the students in the class wasn't fair. I think that was the first time I was ashamed of being white. If I misbehaved it was acceptable. If my work wasn't right it was re-examined. For some reason those teachers thought I was better than minorities. I was privileged. All of these experiences that have made my life what it is, have pushed me to become a seeker of justice, I decided to take my mother's advice and begin where a lot of professional instructors turn away—the inner-city. Where else is the fight for justice more important than in the lives of our children—our future? My influences have provided me with the right tools to be the kind of educator disadvantaged children need on their side. Everyone deserves a fair chance in life and I have the resources to help win that fight.

The understandings of these youth about themselves and others are both inspiring and instructive. In an earlier discussion, I challenged the idea of some of my critics that students are saying only what I want to hear, and I will not repeat my rebuttals. But I do want to restate my faith in the personal and professional integrity of these young people. I further believe that the so-called posts perspectives can be taught proactively yet non-oppressively.

Conclusion: Toward a Pedagogy of Transformative Mourning

Some years back, in my minorities and education class, several students led a discussion of Asian American experiences in the United States. I was particularly struck by one woman who shared her experience of emotional distress at learning about the horrible things done to Chinese Americans and Japanese Americans over the past hundred years. Because her presentation dealt with instructional aspects of teaching to or about Asian Americans, she was concerned with how to tell young white children about the Asian American past. She felt that children should not learn about this past because even she had had a hard time with the information, but she recognized that failure to teach it was part of the perpetuation of the injustice toward Asian Americans. Several class members joined in with recollections of the absence of any information about Asian Americans at various points in their education. A few noted that they were about to graduate and still had not learned about these things in social studies education and methods.

I was gratified that these students had researched the topic and that the class had been able to do some "emotion work" around it. Before this class—and with only three weeks left in the term—I had become more than a little despondent. Weekly, I watched the class of 60 struggling through the various presentations, anxiously awaiting the Thanksgiving break, and passing their enforced attendance at these presentations with "mental trips": reading the student newspaper, doing crossword puzzles, quietly chatting, and "sleepin' in class." But on this day, they came alive; they could understand the dialectical tension I so often reminded them that they had inherited. Something about this particular classmate's emotionality hit home. Their eyes largely conveyed "lights on; somebody's home," and I felt the students' engagement when I connected the class discussion of perceptions of Asian Americans to the current furor in Decatur, Illinois, and Cairo, Egypt. In Decatur, there was concern with Jesse Jackson's presence and advocacy on behalf of six black students who received two-year suspensions, from a white school administration, for fighting. In Cairo, officials and citizens were fearful that Americans would blame the entire nation if it were learned that a single Egyptian pilot was criminally responsible for the fatal airplane crash the previous week.

The sense of this student that her own "white pain" regarding Asian Americans cautioned her regarding the propriety of teaching this information to young children reminds us of the dual task we face in multicultural teacher education. We are trying to reach future generations by "re-teaching" the current generation. This is the ethical challenge we face. I personally experience it as more than a matter of ethics. For me, like the heroine in Tennessee Williams's *A Streetcar Named Desire*, I have long "counted on the kindness of strangers." I may or may not have the "professional license" to tell students about my racial vulnerability, my racial autobiography, or the like, since this fails to carry the "imprimatur" or "nihil obstat" of the academy's Magisterium (the "teaching church" operating out of the Vatican in Rome). But I have a commitment to black children and families who must also count on the kindness and justice of "good white folk" if we are to continue winning the battle against "evil," however understood.

I make clear to my students that their primary task is self-growth, self-enlargement. I can tell them this because I am, at 67, a part of the past that they study, a part of the "wretched other" that they seek to help, to deliver. And yet as a trained academic with two PhDs, I belong to the "cognitive elite" that Herrnstein and Murray (Gresson, 1996a) celebrate; thus I am "qualified" to "teach" in the academy even with my "marginalized" logic of inquiry. I tell them "my truth," having already defined it as a part of the dialectical inheritance they endure. What is this truth? What is important for them as prospective teachers is to gain some critical perspective through relating their own inherited strengths and social understanding to the multicultural condition.

When Max Rafferty denied the possibility of a future for multiculturalism, he certainly could not foresee a time when whites would feel alienated in places they had created and controlled. Still, the racial pain expressed by Rafferty seems similar to that expressed by the two young men convinced that certain organizations—the Negro College Fund—and geographical regions—North Philadelphia—are "black privilege." Because they constitute the dominant social grouping, their words and actions often conceal their underlying pain. For some, it may seem like an unnecessary waste of time and energy to dwell on the nature of and solution to this form of pain. After all, because whites continue to dominate the United States and much of the "civilized" world, it might be legitimately asked if they need "liberation fighters," especially minorities, to be their advocates.

I believe the answer to this query is yes and no. Along with a number of other scholars, activists, and humanists (Giroux, 1997; Ipsaro, 1997; Winant, 1997), I believe that contemporary whites occupy a unique historical position. Extrapolating from W. E. B. Du Bois's concept of "double consciousness," Howard Winant (1997) calls this "white dualism." I have previously viewed this social context and historical space as a transitional one in which emotional life is largely characterized by efforts to hold oneself together with ideas and beliefs—I call these "self-other metaphors"—that help one feel whole (1987, 1995). As it pertains to whites, this condition often leads them to feel like victims of a confused and brutal society. This quality, or "schizophrenic" tendency, is evident in the preceding illustrations. It also is pervasive in American society. Yet perhaps nowhere is it more evident than in the academy: universities, schools, and other learning-specific enterprises and institutions. It is in the academy that we see the battleground in microcosm: whites in pain, carrying on a symbolic and substantive war against the fictional enemy, diversity and affirmative action. But in the larger society there is evidence of the move to address white male anger and the attendant society-wide "aversive racism" now considered the new racism.[62] In the next chapter, I take a closer look as some of the themes and tensions attending the pursuit of racial healing.

· 7 ·

TOWARD A PSYCHOPEDAGOGY OF HEALING

Mourning and Mending Difference in the New Millennium

These sentiments are grounded in a fundamentally optimistic view of human history and character, a belief in our potential as a species to overcome through discourse the divisions and differences that separate us from our better natures, and from the spiritual and material coherence of beloved community. That potential, however, realized perhaps most powerfully in the possibility of racial reconciliation, remains elusive: indeed, the shift from traditional to modern or symbolic racism, from the rhetorics of redemption and reconciliation that destroyed the nation's first reconstruction and derailed its second, to the more subtle and insidious rhetorics of racial recovery, reversal and resistance, that have come to dominate public discourse on the subject of race, compels us to revisit the rhetoric of racism and rethink the politics of complicity.

– Mark Lawrence McPhail (2009: 2)

The legacy of racism in the United States is, among other things, a festering wound in the national ethos, born of the original cleavage between an abstract, universal rhetoric of individual rights and a concrete, particularistic rhetoric of collective (racial) exclusion from such rights, between the social contract enshrined in the Declaration of Independence and the Racial Contract insinuated into the Constitution and subsequent laws (written and unwritten).... To atone effectively for these hypocrisies and suture that wound, a dialogic rhetoric of reconciliation must simultaneously heal the divide between the personal and political—not conflating the two, but joining their distinct properties in a discursive alloy able to sustain the inherent tension between the discourse of individual rights and the rhetoric of collective reforms.

– John Hatch (2009b: 493–494)

Prologue: An Ability to Mourn, a Key to Healing

Some years back I spent a wonderful weekend with a white South African couple and a close friend. The friend had just returned from South Africa where she had been the guest of this middle-aged, upper-class couple who ran a psychology institute in one of the major cities. They had come to South Carolina as her guests. For me, this couple was a welcome relief from a painful encounter I had had many years earlier, in 1972, while on tour in Europe with several other white South Africans. I found this couple not only very decent and racially sensitive but also anxious to communicate to me the tremendous racial changes taking place in South Africa. The only difficult part of the visit was the pain I felt at their sense of historical guilt for the evils of apartheid and their current ambivalence toward the necessary but traumatic changes taking place in that country.

They accepted the need for some whites to be "destroyed" by the changes taking place, explaining to me, "if their positions and privileges are not taken away, there can be no change," adding "yet, we hurt for those who are chosen; they are our friends and have done nothing uniquely wrong. They, like us, have merely participated in and enjoyed the privileges that went with being white South Africans."

Throughout the weekend we spent together, we toured Charleston, ate in fine restaurants, shopped at the local markets, and talked about the costs of healing. My friend, a black woman, was dubious about the then-ongoing healing hearings in South Africa. She felt that the whites confessing past evils toward blacks were largely specious, and her white guests agreed. The couple's perspective on the truthfulness and contrition of white South Africans toward apartheid was insightful. They intuitively understood the peculiar problem that unrelinquished power poses for the psychology of healing. Indeed, their stance resonates fully with the ironic truthfulness in Bishop Tutu's confession with respect to the hearings: "Those people [white South Africans] have the capacity of destroying this land.... If there were not the possibility of amnesty, then the option of a military upheaval is a very real one" (Rosenberg, 1997: 86).

Bishop Tutu was uttering a pragmatic truth of both white power and possibility. His observation, moreover, hints at a constraint on "real reconciliation": the need to obtain contrition and compassion from a minority that still had the power to destroy the proceedings, to undermine the nonviolent and democratic transformation of South Africa.

It is, ultimately, because of this paradox of apology and power that both Mark McPhail and John Hatch present such painfully complicated if not totally pessimistic views on racial reconciliation in the opening epigraphs. Each of these scholar-activists has confronted repeatedly the challenge of constructing a vision of transformation sensitive to racial pain and its healing. At times, moreover, their visions have seemed to converge in a shared moment of hopefulness; and at others, they have diverged due to deeply felt frustrations at reconciliation. Their respective positions, moreover, seem to recapitulate that of Bishop Tutu: Can we achieve healing through individual and collective mourning?

The bishop's insight and stance calls for a special capacity, the ability to accept the vulnerability of the less powerful and to remain hopefully active in the pursuit of equity and justice. Like Mandela before him, Bishop Tutu has attained a kind of racial healing that comes only with psychologically working through this vulnerability. My South African friends, however, dwell in the pain of loss and the fear of change. It is difficult to yield to vulnerability under such conditions, and the escape back into power positions (whiteness) becomes especially tempting. In this chapter, I explore a variety of themes, often as meditations, pertinent to the psychology and pedagogy of healing. I begin with the notion of healing.

On the Nature and Psychology of Healing

What is healing? To heal means "to mend, restore, or make whole." The first two definitions of this word imply a prior state of unity or oneness. Healing here means solving the problems that led to the breakdown in relations—values, beliefs, caring—thereby enabling a sense of wholeness. The third definition of the concept of healing—making whole—does not necessarily imply a prior state of unity. It does, however, suggest movement toward unity. In each of these first two definitions of healing is the sense that the breakdown in relations occurred as a result of a violation of some form. Someone was injured.

As implied in these descriptions of healing, the injured and injuring parties are reunited when apology, atonement, and forgiveness have been worked through. While many situations calling for healing are simple and clear-cut, many others are not. Often, there already are socially prescribed procedures for bringing about healing; the involved persons need only commit themselves to asking for and granting forgiveness. Sometimes, however, the society itself lacks an understanding of, or commitment to, doing "the right things" needed to attain wholeness. This is especially true when unity never truly existed and/or restoration of the past cannot lead to wholeness. Consider the case of minorities in the United States. Inequality, discrimination, and oppression have been enduring forces in the history of this country. What passed for "wholeness" or "unity" was, in fact, a forced oneness: people and groups were locked into a pecking order (much like a caste system) and learned to participate with or relate to others according to prescribed rules and institutionalized systems of control, such as big business, government, and the criminal justice system. Under this arrangement, healing among non-equals is impossible. For healing to occur, one must be able to express one's feelings openly. Of course, this is not a "all or nothing" affair; some people do find ways and means of healing even under less than optimal conditions, and circumstances do change from time to time, thereby allowing degrees of healing. Nonetheless, whether partial or complete, ultimately healing must give birth to mutual respect and care and the shared vulnerability of equals.

This presents us with a pair of paradoxes. The first is the idea that one can violate what one has defined as essential to one's sense or understanding of self: a master violating a slave, a fisherman violating a fish, a cat violating a bird. In each of these examples, one identity is closely bound to the other in some critical way, a way seen as crucial to the existence of the other. What is paradoxical is that at various times and under differing conditions, humans have denied masters, fishermen, and cats access to these *defined* others. So slavery is abolished; fishermen are fined for taking too many fish; and cats chased away from the family's pet canary.

The second paradox is related to the first: the loss of identity accompanying a societal renegotiation of identity brings about a shared sense of violation, one for which both parties feel a need for justice, vindication, and renewal. I can illustrate this by returning to the prologue. There I described how my South African friends grieved for both the injustices of apartheid for black South Africans and the injustices endured by their fellow white South Africans who were chosen to be the "losers" or "sacrificial lambs" in order that some black South Africans could enter the "mainstream."

These two paradoxes of healing can be heard in the conversations of those caught in the throes of social changes such as racial and gender liberation. Unfortunately, too often they are not discussed and resolved. A closer examination of them can, nonetheless, illuminate the psychology of healing.

The Phenomenology of Healing

> Healing through narration and "opening up," involves an existential act of self-transcendence of an embodied person who organizes his/her experience in time.
>
> — A. L. Mirshara (1995: 180)

The term "phenomenology" has a special meaning in psychology and philosophy; in fact, it has many meanings (Wojnar & Swanson, 2007). I chose to use it here because I want to highlight the importance of one of the meanings central to this term in its various contexts: its focus, in this instance, on self-understanding and understanding of the community/society of healing-engaged persons. That is, how is healing experienced and/or described by those called on "to heal"? I precede my answer to this question with a brief story. Several years ago, during a group presentation by four white females, I "lost it." The scene was an all too familiar one: the assignment had been to make a presentation dealing with minority women's educational challenges. The four white females presenting this topic provided a good treatment of educational challenges faced by white women, but when asked about the absence of any discussion about black women or other minority women, they claimed they had no knowledge of them. Because this failure to cover the minority part of the assignment happened virtually every semester that I taught this course and their response was one frequently observed and critiqued in the critical race literature (Gresson, 1995; Hull, Scott, & Smith, 1982), I had taken great pains to ensure that they would not neglect the very groups the topic was designed to cover. So, when this group failed to deal with the topic as instructed, I lost it.

For me, their refusal was a form of violation: students have an obligation to cover the course material according to the rules of the teacher. Their refusal to do so was more than mere student neglect or even an individual decision to say no to the assignment. Their actions, for me, paralleled the arrogance of the "disenfranchised" oppressor. That is, even though these students were required to deal with nonwhite subjects—the focus of the course—they had exercised a privilege no longer available to them because of, yes, multiculturalism. In class, I dealt with this behavior. I criticized their particular behavior as a failure to follow instructions. I also related it to a habitual neglect of minority women by white females, citing one classic saying of black feminists that "all the blacks are men, all the women are white."

Later, the four women came to my office to apologize for failing to cover the topic. I also apologized for getting so emotional and further explained the reason for my passion. A few days later, two of the four returned to my office: they were upset. Upon reflection, they felt that I had singled them out by raising my objection in class rather than privately in my office. They agreed that they had been told what to cover and that they had failed to do so but still felt I had humiliated them. (For them, I, too, had committed a societal violation. This is an important matter for the issue of democratic education and is significant in the emergent discourse on anti-oppressive education. I return to this theme more fully in a later section of the chapter.) I asked them what they wanted me to do. They said I should apologize in front of the class. Given my values as a democratic, radical educator, I agreed. I would do so during the next class period. Both their request and my consent represented to me a mutually understood sense of shared vulnerability. They had initially cowered under the pressure of the teacher-student authoritarian relationship under which they had grown up and to which they largely subscribed as prospective educators. This was their vulnerability. But I teach from a position of relative equity about what is known and what is knowable. This epistemological radicalism on my part has informed both my scholarship (Gresson, 1977, 1978) and my pedagogy (Gresson, 1990, 1997). Moreover, my personal persuasiveness was largely due to a "post" perspective that acknowledged their "authority" as subjects despite their student status (1995). In addition, I claimed the right to tell them about my "minority perspective" as a fellow human being, and I challenged the dominant "official knowledge" (Spring, 1995) from this perspective that acknowledged the integrity of subjective experience even given the fact of so-called cumulative knowledge. Thus I too was vulnerable, and this is generally how I saw the situation.

Still, in preparing to address this matter in class, I found myself smiling at the situation: historically, a black man had few occasions to tell white females they needed to know anything about minority children; whatever whites chose to do or not to do was sanctioned by society. It was an accident of history—the radical social and cultural changes of the 1960s and since—that had placed us in this ironic *dance of agency*. Still, when I finally came before the class to address the situation, I had concluded that a mere apology would fail to honestly address "what did occur" or what I felt the situation merited in regards to an apology (Lazare, 2004). And so I linked my apology to a discussion of the difference between humiliation and humility. It seemed to me that in this case, humiliation was the result of these students feeling personally responsible for the broader racial situation. My failure, and it was definitely such, was permitting my own frustration as a victim of racism to overflow and negatively influence my position as the teacher. Ideally, I should have downplayed their failure to do what was asked of them during the class period and saved it for a private audience with them. In so doing, I perhaps would have fulfilled my own personal and pedagogical obligation. But reflecting on my failure and confronting my own preparedness to speak before the entire class, I was struck by these students' refusal to assume any public blame. Initially, they had said that I had not overstepped my bounds during the critique and that they understood my frustration. But later, for two of them at least, my actions had assumed the weight of an oppressive violation.[63] The conversation in my office did not resolve the problem; they were not healed. They did not feel right. They needed a particular transaction to take place in the classroom. Only then, perhaps, could they attain the necessary "transcendence" that allowed for healing.

This story reveals the "phenomenological" character of healing. Healing is a process that involves the feelings. As such, it has both physiological and cognitive dimensions. The physiological is the bodily aspect, the tightening of the jaws, the pounding of the head, the lump in the throat, the pain in the stomach, the compulsion to move toward or away from the other. We each had something at stake in the multiculturalism discourse and our bodies were physically involved in the exchange. To say "I lost it" is to admit a physical reaction—only later could I return to the episode more reflectively, putting on my professorial hat, so to speak. Still, for this bodily response to occur, however, one has to have a mediating lens, a way of understanding what things do and do not constitute a violation for one. This is the cognitive dimension. In this episode, both the white women and I were physiologically involved; we each shared a sense of violation at the global and the classroom levels; we each harbored a vision of the other as a "carrier of bad blood." The request for an apology exposed a hidden wound related to this bad blood between us. This "bad blood" is the cultural psychology of racism (Kovel, 1970) and sexism (Bederman, 1995) in the United States.

The request for an apology implies more. Some might say it is simply an insistence to be treated as "an individual" free of the stigma of "spoiled identity" (Goffman, 1963). Even though no one, except perhaps the powerful, can realistically imagine a place beyond the gaze of the other, there is another, thornier objection here: the request for an apology represents an attempt to renegotiate an identity's value even as one is advancing the privileges of that identity. The students and I both had something at stake: a belief/feeling that we were in the right. None of us involved could quite accept the full responsibility for the exchange even after admitting a level of "wrongdoing" or responsibility.

This episode suggests that healing pertains to both personal identity and subjective understanding of social justice. It is not a simple matter of the facts of the situation. Because this is so, healing occurs through a working back and forth between contrasting, sometimes contradictory, ideas of the facts and what is important. Healing is therefore a dialectical matter. Moreover, this quality of healing can be seen in the management of white pain as precursor to reconciliation.

Healing as a Dialectic: White Diversity Leadership as an Illustration

Healing is dialectical because it takes place in the presence of two powerful contradictions or uneasy tensions. First, there is the need to accept the experience of violation and a loss of something cherished. Second, whatever is recoverable can be only a partial recovery. The well-known expressions "suck it up" and "get over it," point to this aspect of healing as a compromised outcome at its best. Thus healing means confronting the original sacrifice (and loss) that led to the fractured wholeness that is now being "made whole" through yet another fracturing. This is why the language of, say, white racial recovery, generated notions like "reverse racism," "white male as victim of affirmative action," and "black racism." These speech events and experiences signal that healing is perhaps psychologically problematic from the start, especially when the original violation occurred in the service of identity formation. That is, to ask me to deny my "whiteness" as a condition of "equality" when my identity as "white" is predicated on my "superiority" is problematic. The request that one stops being a "man" of a certain kind so that another can be a "woman" in more liberating ways can be a difficult request to deliver: what kind of man can/ought one to become and can this be achieved by fiat? The two students who wanted me to apologize to them are but echoes of a more recent group, white males, making a parallel claim regarding "humiliation." Reporting on a diversity seminar by whites for whites, William Atkinson writes:

> If the goal of engaging white men in diversity is to succeed, the attitudes of white males will not be the only things that will need to change.... [One participant said]

"One of the most troublesome concerns I have is that, as we continue to do 'white men's work,' there is still much work for women and people of color to do on themselves and their beliefs about white men." (2001: 5)

Implicit in this insistence is the idea that white men are not what white men appear to be to the other. This repositioning of self in relation to other is a genuine response: it says, "I am in need of change, but so are others." The near absolute disconnect many white people now exhibit with respect to historical racism is suggested in this incipient conversation of female and minority "imperfection" and "violation" of white males. Nonetheless, the belief that women and minorities must act upon themselves reveals important clues to the dialectical nature of healing discourse and dynamics. This can be seen in recent efforts to include white men in the diversity leadership-training business. I want to examine further the report on this diversity leadership seminar as a way of clarifying the parameters of the dialectic.

White Diversity and Diversity Leadership

Recognition of white racism as a nonessential part of white identity allows for the very self-display that Michael Apple (1998) warns against. We see this everywhere, especially in affirmative action and diversity efforts. In a manner reminiscent of the "white power" slogans of the 1970s and 1980s, there has been increasing insistence on including whites in the equation of equity efforts. This is significant because whites do not generally perceive their racial benefits; rather, it is good societal management. It is likely that all societies that work well manage to move non-self-consciously from idea to actuality. Such is the case with whites in Western societies that have built up notions of individual and collective identity by devaluing "the other." It is in this context that the move toward white preeminence in diversity training can be best appreciated. Whites can now teach diversity, and they can participate—as peers if not as masters—in clarifying and conquering the barriers to greater democratic unity and inclusion in society and institutions.

This need to distance the white self from negativity is understandable, but it is also a condition for many whites to join the 21st-century diversity discourse. Consequently, white diversity is evolving from the insistence that racism is essentially dead in America. Buttressed by civil rights laws that sometimes work and a notably black presence within the American middle class, white diversity is an insistence on partnership with the "weaker" negotiating side of diversity initiatives.

William Atkinson is instructive here in his article about white men as full diversity partners. In particular, he reports on a consortium of three diversity consulting firms: EqualVoice in Minneapolis; Inclusivity Consulting Group in Portland, Oregon; and Integral Coaching and Consultation in Herndon, Virginia. The topics for these groups include the domination of the diversity coordinator position in most organizations by minority males or females. "It is rarely a white male." Why should it be?

> Michael Welp, a principal at EqualVoice, believes that for the diversity movement to reach the next level of effectiveness and change in organizations, white men must know a lot about diversity. "Most of what they know about diversity comes from women and people of color, which places a lot of pressure on these groups," he says. "White men need to learn how to engage each other, so that women and people of color don't have to do the whole job of educating us." (Atkinson, 2001: 1)

What does this mean? That white men don't now know how to engage with one another? What is at stake in minorities assuming the leadership of diversity leadership? What is the pressure on minorities for assuming this leadership role? The idea of full inclusion for white males in the new drama is important. Feeling left out from the access to work is symbolic:

> As a white male doing diversity work for 12 years, I noted early on that diversity managers were women or people of color 99 percent of the time. In fact, I found that I often was unable to get work in corporations because I was a white male. I'd always hear the question, "What do you know about diversity?" (Atkinson, 2001: 1)

Ironically, this consortium saw as one of its main tasks teaching white males that they are not merely individuals but part of a culture and a group. Robert Haskell, my close friend of nearly 40 years, certainly saw himself as an individual rather than as a group member. But in large measure, what allows this to happen is white power. The capacity to redesign the structure of diversity initiatives may simultaneously accomplish the tasks of the "enlightenment" and "re-containment" of minority momentum.

Recognizing the typical inability or refusal of white males to own racial privilege, workshop organizers like the above have several goals, including helping white men recognize their role in "the work" of diversity. "We want to eliminate the existing inequity of people thinking that women and people of color are the only ones who know about diversity, and therefore expecting them to teach everyone else," said Bill Proudman, president of Inclusivity Consulting Group. He continued, "We want to help white males see themselves and other white males as partners in 'the work'" (Atkinson, 2001: 3). Another goal is to create inclusive organizations. Thus Jo Ann Morris, a principal consultant with Integral Coaching and Consultation in Herndon, Virginia, reflected:

> The workshop's ultimate goal is to facilitate a strategic view of what it means to be an inclusive organization.... We look at what it means to have white men feel grounded enough and safe enough about what diversity is for them, individually and collectively, so that diversity is not just about everyone else except them.... (Atkinson, 2001: 3)

For decades, women and minorities were recognized as the victims of injustice and inequality and the logical leaders to train whites in general and white men in particular about the nature and process of diversity enhancement through affirmative action and other inclusive practices. This development enhanced both minority wealth and importance in the business world, thus yielding a dialectic: white men should also profit from the wisdom of inclusion, even though they dominate the social order in a manner that begets the initial inclusion mandate. (It is perhaps already clear that the discussion of anti-oppressive teaching as potentially oppressive overlaps with this logic.)

Healing thus requires a dual, almost simultaneous admission of loss. Society fails to deal adequately with the nature of the loss and the required "terms of re-endearment." It abandons individuals and collectivities to make subjective sense of its politics and policies but offers no consolation, no sense of justice. It is wholly pragmatic and unethical, yet it is infinitely moral, for its agenda is saving the collective-as-is. This is especially true in matters of social justice that have built up over centuries of mistrust, misdeeds, and mixed ideologies of who is blameworthy and who is righteous. Given this understanding of healing, we also may have a better grasp of the more psychological dynamics of healing as these have evolved around race and related matters.

Notes on the Psychology of Healing

> And we are fundamentally inclined to claim that the falsest judgments... are the most indispensable for us... that renouncing false judgments would mean renouncing life and a denial of life. To recognize untruth as a condition of life—that certainly means resisting accustomed value feelings in a dangerous way; and a philosophy that risks this would by that token alone place itself beyond good and evil. (Nietzsche, 1966: 12)

Although a philosopher by temperament and vocation, Nietzsche has been recognized by many as a premier psychologist. When I read these lines from his 1886 treatise *Beyond Good and Evil*, I became fixated on a particular vision or sensation: we are trapped, even though we must struggle to escape. Less mysteriously, these lines meant for me that the pursuit of truth, however defined, is a task only partly undertaken in our best interest. It may satisfy certain of our needs, but it will likely severely test others. Healing, guided or cautioned by this ambivalence toward knowing, pursues at least two psychological goals: mourning and mending.

Mourning: "Exorcising" the Loss

In *Passage to Ararat*, Michael Arlen "describes weeping and denial of the past as two ways of mourning the genocidal war of the Turks which destroyed the Armenians. This mourning cannot come to an end; the loss is too great to be learned from, or to be forgotten" (Lyman, 1981: 58). We have to hurt, to cry. Mourning implies a time or period of dwelling in pain. The educative outcome of this visit with the pain of loss is greater insight into and appreciation of what is actuality and necessity. Presumably, from here one is able to move forward: wounded, yes, but better for it.

The fear and uncertainty of what to do next may lead one to surrender to and enter a shared pursuit with the other.[64] This new, shared journey brings with it the possibility of genuine healing. But there may also be a positive—from some perspectives—adjustment in which appropriation of the desired loss or absence is pursued (see Bettelheim, 1962).

In the introduction to this chapter, I noted that white South Africans generally acknowledge that the black numerical majority and the resulting black South African leadership have put the whites living there on a very different growth trajectory than they are in the United States. This difference, moreover, amounts to a different felt need for and pursuit of healing than that recognized as a need in contemporary America. Thus, unable to find partial healing through a national recognition of racial wrongdoing, many African Americans display mourning behavior similar to that found by Arlen and the Armenians. For example, sometime back I was sitting in a black middle-class bar frequented by middle-aged African American men. One, a retired Baltimore policeman, was "bleeding," even though he had retired from the force well and alive. He expressed a hatred for the United States and called several of us "Uncle Toms" because we professed love for the country and accepted the idea that not all white people are evil. After the noise died down and he and I were able to talk more quietly, I saw the pain, the hurt beneath the bravado and hatred. He now lamented his participation on an inner-city police force that had exposed him to much abuse from both whites and blacks. He despaired over his own frustrated ambitions for promotion and success that had been damaged by his attempt to be "his own man" and a "human being" toward his fellow African Americans. He grieved openly about the ravages of racism in his professional life. And, when I was able to listen to his pain, affirm the injustice of his suffering, and the "screwed up human condition," he seemed a changed man. He exhaled. Then he thanked me and quietly left the bar. Somewhere from my subconscious, a thought appeared: somewhere I had recently read something linked to my bar experience. Later, I found the passage in Lyman's essay:

> But how is this reconciliation of the private and the historical achieved in one's own life? The tension between theory and practice becomes a chasm of alienation when private sorrows are suffered silently, unredeemed by collective reflection and response. Yet many contemporary voices speak out of this alienation. These voices are texts, fragments of memories from the unresolved past that cannot be mourned and eventually give way to peaceful recollection or determined action; that past haunts the present and the future will capitulate the past. (1981: 56)

The problem is psychological. The need is psychological, although the vehicle is ultimately political and the achievement social. This means that the "logic" or procedure for the desired change pertains to the mental and emotional worlds. Mourning is the expression of this logic. When it is successful, things fall into place. When it is unsuccessful, things are forced into *some place*. This is the very tricky business of healing. If the terms for healing are "unfair"—peace on my terms—then there may be a semblance of healing, but in Lyman's words, the "past haunts the present and the future will capitulate the past" (1981: 56).

We must understand that white pain, a form of mourning, has given way to a series of "determined actions" that I call recovery strategies. These actions have achieved a certain consolation for many whites, but at the expense of those who sense that some injustice has been perpetrated on them. The 2000 election symbolized this, and it will likely be decades before we can fully grasp this fact or realize that something on the order of the attack on September 11, 2001, had to occur to bring some form of healing to America.

This "healing," moreover is very much related to the tremendous "fall from grace" the Bush administration constituted and the nation's preparedness to rush a black man to the presidency (ahead of an acknowledged gifted candidate like Hillary Clinton). Moreover, the "national gerrymandering" of sentiment that allowed this "racial coup" has contributed, I believe, to the peculiar racialized narrative that will likely be an enduring part of the Obama legacy. It is not without merit, I feel, to suggest both that the nation has not become anything like a "post-racial" Shangri-La and that the rise of the Tea Party's ultra-Right rhetorics are expressions of a deeper wound than we can yet fully embrace. *Thus, for some people, mending, the other great pillar of healing, may yield "breakage" for others.*

Mending: "Plotting" a Recovery

Emerging from the break, mending pertains to those ideas, actions, and emotions that transform the separation, replacing disunity with unity, twoness with oneness. The dictionary is instructive here with its various definitions of mending: "repair," "amend," "correct errors," "improve," "reform," "heal." But the dictionary does not convey an idea of the sacred, although for humans this concept/vision is crucial to the attainment of "repairness."

Because it may be inequitable, mending is a dialectical unfolding. Viewed in this way, healing is perpetual; the end state is illusion. Only death can yield final mending. Pain and violence often accompany what seems to be a "nearly mended" situation because the terms of repair are not free of the violating formative ideas that caused the initial infraction. I mention again the controversy surrounding the proposed Firemen's Memorial in New York City. The need of some white men to challenge the proposed diverse firefighter icon reveals that healing draws on problematic values.

A picture of three white males hoisting the American flag is a healing image. A statue of white, black, and "colored" firemen hoisting the flag also is a healing image. Some would argue that a truly unified nation would have no difficulty in choosing one rather than the other. But this is the challenge: whose notions of mending images will make for a soothed soul? Norman O. Brown wrote:

> The external enemy is (part of) ourselves, projected; our own badness, banished. The only defense against an internal danger is to make it an external danger: then we can fight it; and are ready to fight it, since we have succeeded in deceiving ourselves into thinking it is no longer us. (1966: 162)

According to Brown, we are motivated to act aggressively, surgically, only when we have distanced the "bad," the "cancer," "the axis of evil," from ourselves. This is a core deception of ourselves—by ourselves (Smith, 2004). There is something familiar or "truthful" in the white male's query to the black male marching on Washington for a day of atonement: "Are you atoning for your crimes against me?" Whatever the flaws in this query and the thinking behind it, I sense wisdom of sorts; it is the sense that all are called to examine and change the conversation about inclusion. It is also the uttering of a profound fact: *seizing one's own human potential may undermine another's in ways that lead to the belief that atonement is required even though one has only acted to take back an original "birthright."*

The psychology and pedagogy of healing bring us face to face with ourselves. We are implicated in life; we take and we give. We eat to live, and in this act we sacrifice others. Under capitalism, in the type of democracy we have attained to date, the symbolic and substantive consumption of others is inevitable. We are, moreover, only partly motivated—and, even then, under duress—to be otherwise. Enron, Andersen, WorldCom, and Martha Stewart stand as only the tip of the iceberg of our guilt, greed, and destructive proclivity. We blanch at the losses perpetrated by Arthur Andersen and the Enron empire, yet we daily watch to see whether our own stocks—personal value—will suffer. And we pray for a quick, complete recovery of the Dow Jones, even after the massive meltdown of 2008 and the so-called jobless recovery that has left millions un- and underemployed.

Susanne Langer, cited in Chapter 1, wrote in her final, monumental work, *Mind: An Essay on Human Feeling*:

> The original motivation of sacrifice was, I believe, a sense of danger in the performance of an autonomous overt act that changed the agent's situation. Any such act, initiated by a single or multiple agent, is an exercise of mental power, and as such demonstrates the individuating activity of mind.... Something had been autonomously done; to restore the biological balance something would have to be yielded; and the readiest symbol of submission to the claim of the greater, ancestral life force is to give up some precious thing to it, i.e., to make sacrifice.... Sacrifice is par excellence the means of restoring the ethnic balance; and in this capacity it is never without a basic sense of loss and surrender. (1984: 133)

Langer's description is reminiscent of Dostoyevsky, Freud, Reich, and others who have struggled with the question of crime, guilt, and punishment with respect to the human condition. Recall the opening epigraph, Bishop Desmond

Tutu's concession to the power of the white South Africans is ironic, for to achieve healing, even to approach some semblance of reconciliation, he and the black majority must sacrifice to achieve "an ethnic balance." This requires of him and us both loss and surrender even in our victory. This is the paradoxical psychopedagogical wisdom of those who understand humanity's plight in terms of identity and power.

Reflections on Healing

In the remainder of this chapter, I offer several thoughts that invite reflection on the topic of healing. If healing is about both mourning and mending, then it requires conscious reflection on our thoughts and our actions.

Toward Healing: Anger, Silence, and Vulnerability

In 1981, I came across an article that made a great impact on my thinking about white anger. Peter Lyman, writing in *The Socialist Review*, examined the interface of silence, *ressentiment*, and the politics of anger. What struck me so deeply about this essay, in many ways ahead of its time, was the blending of so many critical notions from feminist, Marxist, and radical perspectives with regard to the plight of middle-class whites. He begins his essay with a passage from Adrienne Rich's *On Lies, Secrets, and Silence*:

> As I thrust my hand deeper into the swirl of this stream—history, nightmare, accountability—I feel the current angrier and more multiform than the surface shows. There is fury here, and terror, but there is also power, power not to be had without the terror and the fury. We need to go beyond rhetoric or evasion into that place in ourselves, to feel the force of all we have been trying—without success—to skim across. (1981:55)

In an endnote, Lyman explains the source and significance of this passage:

> This passage ends the essay..., which discusses the silence that isolates lesbians and black women, and the racism that divides them. It is a kind of therapeutic writing that recovers political power from the fragmentation and depression that is the result of suppressed and repressed anger, but in addition, it is a political writing that attempts to overcome the defects of anger and find a way from the self-righteousness of anger to a more general understanding of the structures that create it. (1981:72)

For me, the passage from Rich was powerful, but that from Lyman was even more so because he was moving beyond the issues that Rich identified specifically for the marginalized lesbian and black female to the white middle class. Focusing on Vietnam, Lyman reviews the poetry created by many of these veterans (remember, the year was 1980 and we had not reached a period where we could gloss over the painful sorrows and emotions).

> Guilty memories traumatize the present with anxiety as a form of self-punishment. And although guilt is part of the source of this poetry, it is more than a poetry of guilt; it is a political poetry.... The question of the meaning of the war in Vietnam for America has not been answered, and has been shifted from the polity to the soldier through a conspiracy of silence that transforms a political question into psychological symptom, a problem of veterans' benefits and "drug-related violence." (1981: 57)

Written more than two decades ago, Lyman's words remind us that glossing over the complex cultural and political challenges in our society leaves us vulnerable to being decentered, being untruthful. Consequently, so the Freudians tell us, the repressed conflicts seep out, uncalled and uncontrolled. To uncover what we have concealed, then, is essential to repairing the real damages rather than the fabricated ones that require considerable, though perhaps less courageous, remediation.

The Internet and Racial (Non) Healing

On Thursday, April 11, 2002, an email sent to me as a chain letter began with "Racism at Harvard Law."

> Dear Family and Friends,
> In recent weeks, members of the Black Law Students Association of Harvard Law School have been the targets of overt racial hostility. The tension began when a first year student published his class notes to the Internet: his notes refer to Black people using the term "nigs." When we requested that his notes be removed from the school's website, other students e-mailed in protest, defending their "right" to refer to Black people as "nigs," "niggers," and insisting that Black people, as a race, prove ourselves so that we won't be called "niggers." As individuals and as a group we have attempted to seek redress for our grievances from the administration. This process has ultimately proved unsatisfactory as offending professors have gone uncensored and the student perpetrators have gone unpunished. The situation has escalated because of the administration's lack of response. Students have dispersed flyers with anti-Semitic and anti-Black statements; professors have openly defended students that express their desire to use the n-word whenever referring to Black people. One professor

has even gone so far as to express to his class that Blacks have contributed nothing to Tort law. One student organization disrespectfully dismissed a young Black woman from its office believing her to be a member of the community seeking legal services. All the while, we have been trying to work through diplomatic, administrative means to resolve these situations but have been met with resistance from the administration and token apologies. We have resolved that we cannot accept this disrespect any longer. In light of the university's disrespect of us as a people we believe that a time for action has arrived. In the days to come, the Black Law Students of Harvard Law School will be taking affirmative action to seek redress for our grievances. We are composing a letter of our grievances and demands, contacting the national media, and planning public demonstrations in protest of the treatment we have experienced. We are being joined by La Alianza (Hispanic students of the law school) and the African Law Students Association. I ask that you would pray for me and for all of the students that are coming together in a statement of solidarity. I must confess to you that these events have taken a personal toll on me as well as my classmates. We are in need of your prayers and your support. If you are an alum of Harvard University, please contact me if you are able to lend a helping hand. We need the support of alumni in a big way. Most of all, please keep us in your prayers as the need for institutional change is tremendous and the time before exams is short. To be sure, the odds are stacked against us. Without a doubt, I know that God is with us in this time of trial. (1 Peter 1: 6). Until later, please take care and God bless.

Some years back, the Black Muslim leader Louis Farrakhan named the internet as a source of liberation against injustice and tyranny. Whether or not this will prove to be the case, the internet has clearly emerged as an important site for racial healing and hurting. The preceding email is an example. It invites some to join in a multiracial coalition against the persistence of racism; it may also incite those who might be named "racists" to further coalesce against a perceived threat.

Still, those sites that promote healing can be extremely instructive and inspirational. Consider the 1990s organization Healing Racism, Inc. Naming its mission the elimination of racism in the United States through grassroots community development, this site overviews a range of healing strategies. Its programs include "ally building" as a way to help healing. Franklin Sonn, South African ambassador to the United Nations, is quoted on the site as saying:

> And it's also impossible to go to healing without knowing the past, because the past is a funny thing. It comes up at the most awkward moments, when you least expect it, and then it disrupts the process of healing and reconciliation. But a very important point also to mention is that our government never expected this to be an easy process, never expected that the outcome would be pleasant. It was a painful process

to start off with, and it, therefore, took enormous courage for us as nation to face our past in the manner that it did. But,... it's out now, and now we can start with the healing process.

Once again we are reminded that healing must confront head on the perceived injustices. Even if these recollections are ultimately abandoned as "real," "reasonable," or "relevant" matters, their past reality and relevance must be accepted.

Bob Lupton (1995) told a powerful story illustrating this point in "The Great Racial Divide... An Opportunity for Healing," from *The Gospel and Our Culture*:

> Our black staff erupted in spontaneous applause and joyful cheers, our white staff sat in stunned silence.... The following morning when I arrived at the office my first phone call was from Albert Love, a black minister friend. After brief social exchanges, he went directly to the matter that prompted his call. It was the O.J. verdict. Knowing that most African-Americans could understand the justice in the jury's decision while many whites would see it as a miscarriage of justice, Albert wanted to prevent this difference of perspective from further fragmenting the community of faith. He sensitively affirmed any feelings that I might be experiencing that were different from his own.... How reconciling his sensitivity! I was aware that by this thoughtful act my need to generalize blame had been diminished.

Recall Mandela's historic healing gesture after his maltreatment. Albert, like Mandela, reached out beyond his own pain and woundedness to his wounded white friend. One may sense that the wounded majority-group person may feel a pain so great that the minority person must be the one to initiate sensitivity. When Mandela passed in 2013, conservative and progressive commentators alike expressed the universal significance of his role as wounded healer. This Christ-like image was especially clung to by white social critics like Joe Scarborough of MSNBC's "Morning Joe," who repeatedly spoke to Mandela's seemingly unshakable capacity for forgiving his oppressors. Notice here the equality we are implying: whites feel like victims, like minorities, and thus require care because they really do have relatively more power. This is a profound irony that I will return to in the final chapter. It rehearses earlier reflections on the dialectics of healing, the possibility that "fairness" as a logic has secondary importance to reestablishing a shared moment of "well-being." There are continual efforts to make healing work even when we do not readily encounter them. The range of initiatives, moreover, suggests that the initiative is serious. Thus we learn from the internet of educational healing efforts such as the Oaks Academy, which opened in Indianapolis in 1998 (StarNews.com, September 8, 1998), and is described as "a new school designed to bring racial reconciliation to the inner city."

In Pasadena, California, a church held a racial reconciliation weekend (June 22–23, 1996), facilitated by the Center for Healing of Racism in Houston. The Center's co-executive director, Barbara Hacker, explains:

> Racial reconciliation is not about making people feel guilty. It's not about making them feel responsible for something someone else did. It's not about stirring up the trouble of the past. It's about focusing on the future. It is about coming out of denial and acknowledging what happened. In our country horrible things happened. Slavery happened. Segregation happened. Racial discrimination happened, and it still happens.

The critical importance of these various initiatives and their dominating themes is their resonance with others mentioned elsewhere on internet sites dealing with healing:

> When we deny things or tell people who are experiencing pain and hurt that they are being too sensitive or that they shouldn't feel that way, or "I didn't do it," "I'm not racist," "I'm not prejudiced"—what we are doing is denying them their feelings, denying them their reality of what they have been experiencing.

Of course, this applies as well to the racist or the target of racism. There is a challenge—a dance of agency, as I have called it—in which individual subjectivities must be recognized, not coddled, condoned, but recognized. Again, Ms. Hacker:

> You don't have to approve or disapprove. You don't have to fix it. You just have to give people space to get it out. And once they've voiced it a healing takes place.... The job of the listener is to acknowledge that another has experienced pain. "I'm sorry you have experienced pain."

At Lamb and Lion Ministries (www.lamblion.com), Dennis Pollock writes the following in "Racism and the Church: Still a Need for Healing":

> Racism is a blight upon our nation. Not only the attitude of whites toward blacks, but blacks toward whites, Orientals toward Hispanics, and society in general toward Jews. Many conservative Christians are quick to denounce abortion and homosexuality, but are strangely silent on the issue of racism. It is almost as though racism has become a "conservatively correct" issue to overlook. (1996: 3)

The internet is full of hurt and healing. Marshall McLuhan declared in the mid-20th century "the medium is the message and the massage" and ushered in a new generation of thinking and writing on the power and promise of communications media and technology. The internet, too, is full of power and promise, an occasion for healing.

September 11 and the "New Humanity" Discourse

Another event arising from the trauma of September 11 was the National Conference for Community and Justice—Race, Ethnicity & Culture, shown on C-Span and hosted by Juan Williams, a journalist and commentator on National Public Radio and Fox News. A theme of this conference was "the new humanity." Many recognized in the violence and devastation of September 11 something beyond the moment. Motivated by different interests and concerns, the pursuit of a new humanity came from diverse thinkers and leaders. For example, among the speakers was the Nation of Islam leader Imam Deem Muhammad:

> We need to think deep into this thing... 9/11. Islam did not create that mind... the world created that mind.... America has a nature to go to the extremes.... [we need] a movement for community... we are in one room
>
> ... this earth is one earth... one community... a home for human beings.

Others also spoke of a "new human nature" for man. Reverend Daniel Coughlin, the chaplain of the U.S. House of Representatives, called for a "new look at human nature." Sharifa Alkhateeb, president of the Muslim Education Council, asked, "Whose idea of humanity shall reign? What is the middle point? What can go forth... benefit humanity... we may reach goals... but they won't be good ones." And Bishop Thomas Hoyt, president of the National Council of Churches, declared that we must seek "a willingness to die for humanity."

In these themes on the discourse of humanity, we sense that the pain associated with September 11 propelled many people to examine nonmilitary solutions. To be sure, the displays of might in Afghanistan and Iraq have soothed us to a degree. The specter of the World Trade Center and Pentagon in flames, while put deep into our preconscious, may find some solace in such actions. But there remains a sense that we must find alternative answers. The great challenge is looking into the other's pain and seeing our reflected narrative. This is a task we as yet largely reject. Whether expressed in terms of domestic racial relations and/or international relations, the challenge is much the same: vulnerable confrontation of the shared pain of human evil and destructiveness.

Apology and Reparations to Blacks, White Anger

> [Young white Americans] feel that there is nothing to forgive… they are afraid of what will come out.
>
> – Bishop Tutu

An online interview between Marianne Williamson, author of *Healing the soul of America*, and Mary Nurrie Stearns, editor of *Personal Transformation*, reveals this difficulty. When asked how the "cultural atonement" linked to America's slavery past could be achieved, Williamson observed:

> There are many ways such a ritual could be performed. If we wanted to do it, we could come up with a way. When Representative Tony Hall of Ohio submitted a bill in the House of Representatives suggesting that Congress apologize for slavery, there was such an outcry the bill didn't have a chance of going forward. Newt Gingrich called a congressional apology for slavery mere "emotional symbolism." He asked if it would teach one child to read. I say to you, it would, because it would remove some heavy blocks to our awareness of love. (INTERVIEW)

For a healing discourse to have a chance of working in the American dreamscape, it ultimately comes back to power and how one negotiates with specific individuals who comply with power's hegemonic hold, that is, the hold based on our personal and subjective surrender to the material goods and substantive freedoms we enjoy as "winners" in the American dreamscape.

Beyond this, one has to be able to overcome a certain disassociation. This greater barrier has a characteristic form: "I have done nothing to anybody—the past is not upon my head." This pervasive and passionate sentiment is uttered from the depths of the soul. From the mouths of those identified as heirs of the powerful and dominant, these words issue from persons determined to be fair, forthright, and productive citizens. Still, they trouble me. My concern is that these utterances will delay the transformative shifts we need if society is truly to become more democratic and righteous.

The late president of South Africa Nelson Mandela observed: "If the pain has often been unbearable and the revelations shocking to all of us, it is because they, indeed, bring us the beginnings of a common understanding of what happened and a steady restoration of the nation's humanity" (www.pbs.org, Online News Hour: Truth Commission, October 29, 1998). But contemporary Americans refuse to confront this past, rejecting healing and nurturing the restoration of racist sentiments. Consider the anti-apology efforts of David Horowitz as discussed at the CNN.com law center's open forum site by Anthony J. Sebok, professor of law at Brooklyn College and Findlaw columnist:

> Some compared Horowitz's effort to purchase advertising space in college newspapers for what was, in effect, a right-wing editorial with an earlier attempt by a Holocaust denier to purchase advertising space in college newspapers to publicize his extremely bizarre view that the Holocaust was a hoax.... Horowitz attempt[s] to set up a sort of balance sheet, to purportedly ascertain which groups benefited from slavery, and how. Horowitz contends that Africans (and other non-Europeans) participated in and benefited from living in the United States, rather than in Africa.

Horowitz reminds us that healing is problematic because emotion and intellect can be separated only when one does not feel an immediate personal threat. Years ago, when reflecting on the question of interminority group coalitions, I argued that we need images of the other and cooperative action that do not reduce our sensitivity to justice for all by falling victim to invidious distinctions and insensibilities (1977, 1978). But Horowitz has been revealed, exposed, by his willingness to undermine healing through his own reidentification with the "pigs" and "reactionary right" that he once fought against, thus enabling him to achieve a radical hero's status.

If there is no willingness to surrender to the pain of past transgressions, then healing will be perverted, for the aggrieved will be silenced, but live to speak and perhaps rise up again.

Israel, the War on Terror, and the Lesson of Shylock

In my youth, I recall reading somewhere that Shakespeare's tragic drama *The Merchant of Venice* was supposedly evidence that he was anti-Semitic. Personally, I read both Shakespeare and his Jewish character, Shylock, as powerful pedagogues for the pariahs of the world. Shakespeare, whether a real person or a composite of several, was indeed wise regarding the pariah, Shylock, if we see him as a composite of all humans, particularly racial and sexual minorities, who seek "justice" in the "domain of the unjust."

I recently shared my reading of *The Merchant of Venice* with an Israeli acquaintance. He immediately recognized and affirmed my reasoning. Citing the almost fatalistic role of Jews in human history, he declared that Jews had to be tough in order to balance (and here I recall Tevye, from the Broadway hit *Fiddler on the Roof*[65]) the contradictions of daily life. Agreeing with my reading of the pariah's paradox, he understood well the dangers and damage, psychic and physical, to one who accepts too deeply the healing terms of the powerful other.

In 2014, American minorities—African Americans, Asian Americans, Hispanic Americans, and so forth—share these dangers with the Israelis. The real advances invite and encourage us not only to forget the past but also to collude in the distortion of the present oppressive character of public life. The Israeli predicament with respect to healing is instructive here. Begin with the given: it is imperative that Israelis have both land and power in order to survive a mean world. How do they get them? They get them through the largesse of the Gentile world that has named Jews the pariah and exploited them politically for thousands of years. Like African Americans and others, Jews are invited to find acceptance by disidentifying with the other and preparing to survive through aggression with the other.

It is not that Arabs are nice, weak, or innocent. It's just that the Israelis have surrendered to hundreds of years of persecution and have accepted yet again—and certainly not unlike many others—the role of "middle minority." This term, common to the sociology of race relations and minorities, refers to those groups whose persecution by more powerful others is mediated and muted by hurting and oppressing others. The ironic significance of this role and its current currency is the recent observation that, since September 11, black oppression has diminished in the wake of increased Arab oppression in the United States. (Are blacks too, even at the near bottom, an emerging "middle minority"?)

My point is that Israeli (out)rage with Palestinian violence, however understood, resonates with U.S. foreign policy since September 11. The window of opportunity for Israeli activity created by America's "war on terrorism" and invasion of Iraq is transparent. But Israelis, like Shylock, are tragic heroes in the "Christian drama" in which anti-Semitism is forever lurking beneath the surface. For instance, consider U.N. Secretary General Kofi Annan. According to the *New York Times* (Wednesday, March 13, 2002, A9), he spoke out against Israel despite his strong support of her over the years:

> In the harshest language he has used since the present crisis began 17 months ago, Mr. Annan chastised the Israelis for the use of heavy weapons in civilian areas and called their occupation of Palestinian lands "illegal," demanding Israel's withdrawal.

The extreme vulnerability I speak of is perhaps most fully sensed when we read in the same article that:

> Some Israeli politicians harshly criticized the army for writing identification numbers on the forearms and foreheads of Palestinian prisoners. "It is totally unbearable for me," said Tommy Lapid, a member of Parliament and a survivor of the Nazi camps. "This is something that was done at Auschwitz." (A8)

This attack against Israel exposes the vulnerability of the underdog. It also tells us how the underdog, while colluding with power, can be recast in the role of villain by those in power. Hence, in a response to the Israeli claim that its actions paralleled the U.S. attack on Afghanistan, Richard A. Boucher, a spokesman for the State Department, said the administration respected Israel's "right of defense" but added, "We continue to be very troubled by Israeli Defense Force actions." He called it "imperative" that the army "exercises the utmost restraint and discipline to avoid further harm to civilians or worsening the humanitarian situation" (A8). Nor was the emergent anti-Israeli sentiment restricted to a single newspaper or writer. The *Baltimore Sun* noted that Israeli checkpoints were undermining Middle Eastern peace: "There have been well-documented incidents of harassment and lack of discipline. Pregnant women have been denied access to maternity wards, the sick from medical care, and mourners from funerals. Young men are arbitrarily taken and beaten and young women sexually harassed" (March 10, 2002, 5F). The point is that Israel behaved unwisely but possibly in the only way it could, given its "tracking." Thus, by April 2002, the media had begun reporting a rising tide of anti-Semitism in Europe. In vaguely disguised rhetoric, President Bush chastised Israel. In Europe, faint hints of a resurging anti-Semitism were taking center stage.

The above-cited examples are, for some, possibly overstating the case: Israel's ongoing vulnerability and entrapment in a racialized pain. The year in question above was 2002. Today is 2014. What has changed? Much, perhaps, has changed; and then again, maybe too little. Consider the present crisis between Israel and Hamas: teenagers—both Israeli and Arab—have been killed and missiles and bombs are once again flying back and forth across the skies, killing and threatening to kill innocent people on both sides. And how does this play out elsewhere? Well, according to one Paris news report, we get the following portrayal:

> From multiple expulsions in the medieval era to *L'Affaire Dreyfuss* and Vichy collaborationism, French Jews have every reason to be wary of antisemitism. And, sadly, despite the fact that 89 percent of French citizens this year reported having a favorable opinion of Jews, antisemitism appears to be on the rise in the Fifth Republic.
>
> But a violent incident that took place in Paris on Sunday widely described as antisemitic, using this narrative as the background, was actually a street fight between pro-Palestinian demonstrators and the Jewish Defense League; one that appears to have been started by the extremist latter in support of Israel's ongoing bombing campaign that has thus far claimed the lives of almost 200 Palestinians—80% of them civilians. (Knight, 2014)

These actions suggest that healing can be compromised when the rationale for violence used to achieve the upper hand can be easily turned back against one. This is an important point that goes far beyond Israeli-Palestinian dynamics: throughout American majority-minority group relations, minority violence as self-affirmation has been a source of increased majority group aggression (Gordon, 1975).

There is yet another nuance to this *dance*, as observed by Harvard scholar Orlando Patterson (1995: 27) on the occasion of the Million Man March:

> But, despite this imperative, a painful truth (one seemingly recognized by the participants in last week's march) emerges from the comparative sociology of group relations: except for those now-rare cases in which a minority constitutes the elite, the burden of racial and ethnic change always rests on a minority group. Although both whites and blacks have strong mutual interests in solving their racial problem, though the solution must eventually come from both, blacks must play the major role in achieving this objective—not only because they have more to gain from it but also because whites have far less to lose from doing nothing. It is blacks who must take the initiative, suffer the greater pain, define and offer the more creative solutions, persevere in the face of obstacles and paradoxical outcomes, insist that improvements are possible and maintain a climate of optimism concerning the eventual outcome. Or, to paraphrase Martin Luther King, it is they, and often they alone, who must keep the dream of a racially liberated America alive.

Of course, Israel operates like an "elite minority" but it is not wholly such. This remains its perennial tension as is shown by the ongoing internal debates regarding how to deal with the Palestinians and Ethiopian Jews. Like African

Americans, moreover, Israelis suffer under the gaze of powerful non-Jews. Thus, healing and reconciliation are ongoing, incomplete projects.

But the critical issue is, perhaps, the ongoing necessity to be "righteous"—watching out for both ally and enemy. In the case of Israel, for example, we need only consider that the recent uprisings and geopolitical crises in Ukraine, Egypt, France, the United Kingdom, Hungary, and elsewhere remind the world that scapegoats are a shameful curative for "ethnic imbalance" and racial pain. Thus, Moshe Cohen (2014) writes:

> Europe hasn't changed all that much, at least in regards to its feelings about Jews, according to Dr. Manfred Gerstenfeld, former head of the Jerusalem Center for Public Affairs. "They don't like to hear that," Gerstenfeld told a Haifa audience last week. "But it's clear that anti-Semitism is a part and parcel of the culture of Europe, not just historically, but currently."

The point is that Jews worldwide struggle for survival within national identity politics that preclude easy reconciliation. Hence, the prodding to be aggressive, unyielding, especially by neo-Conservative militarists and Christian fundamentalists in the United States, feeds a complicity narrative that often backfires on Jews (and other marginal minorities).

Moreover, the Israeli thrust or press for social justice toward, say, Palestinian minorities, has gone understated or supported, often, in defense of the flawed narrative that insists Jews are inextricably one with the "American culture." The important reconciliation work of Women in Black and other feminists in Israel is a case in point. Writing on feminism among Israeli and Palestinian activists, Giulia Daniele (2014) explains:

> Although the current mainstream literature and the associated political debate have both emphasised the boundaries existing among the ethno-national communities who live in the land of Palestine/Israel, the original meaning of 'inextricability' among Arabs and Jews, Palestinians and Israelis, as expressed by the leading intellectual Edward Said (1999), can still properly describe the most challenging pathway to be pursued. At the time of the first Aliyah…in the 1880s, close interrelations and shared initiatives between Arabs and Jews began to take place, and these have since continued, both at the theoretical level and in the form of practical activities on the ground, with women in particular being involved in these. Though such actions have included only small minorities of the populations, mutual cooperation, joint struggles and projects aimed at overcoming opposite narrative identities have emerged as one of the few alternatives with the potential to counter and to go beyond the increase of ethno-national exclusivist narratives in the region.

Nevertheless, the majority of these Palestinian-Israeli joint experiences have collapsed in the last decade, casting doubt on their real value and sparking controversy concerning their effect on the everyday lives of common people. Such unsuccessful outcomes have underlined the need to deconstruct not only the most dominant conceptions concerning nation-states and ethno-national narrative identities, but also their prospects of recognition and reconciliation in relation to the ongoing asymmetry between the 'occupier' and the 'occupied'.

Within this perspective on reconciliation is a powerful corrective—the renegotiation of "national narrative identities." Throughout our discussion of racial pain, in general, and white pain specifically, a parallel idea has been present though understated: as white men increasingly abandon seeing themselves as "entitled" by racial mandate, but bound by a shared plight and fate with other marginalized individuals and groups, they have a chance to "renegotiate" and "reintegrate" in a genuine and existentially believable way.

This argument is certainly at the heart of the analysis and solution offered in *Angry White Men* by Michael Kimmel (2013), a self-described middle-aged Jew from the Northeast. It seems to me that beyond the service Kimmel renders as a sociologist of masculinity issues is his existential embracing of the disinherited, entitled white American male. By mirroring his personal story as a liberal, academic white Jew with the "man in the street" (encountered during his research), Kimmel offers an alternatively hopeful vision of the new white American male. In a way his gesture parallels that of Frederick Lynch (1989): both highlight white male pain and invite white males to talk about it. But the critical difference lies in the courage to resist re-inscribing an "entitlement" narrative that mandates aggressive removal of the marginalized and oppressed. In this way, his actions seem to parallel those taken by Jewish and Palestinian feminists in the Middle East.

Rabbi Jonathan Sacks, chief rabbi of Britain and the Commonwealth, wrote in 2002 regarding anti-Semitism, notably the murder in Pakistan of the American journalist Daniel Pearl:

> He is shown being forced to kneel and confess that he and his parents are Jewish. His throat is then cut. Over his writhing body, a voice warns: "Americans and Jews should be ready to face a fate like Pearl." The struggle to break with being defined by one's otherness is pervasive. Then again, some Jews see anti-Semitism as part of Jewish identity. So did Jean-Paul Sartre, who claimed in his "Sur le question juif" that the only thing Jews had in common was that they were the victims of hate. It is not Jews who create anti-Semitism, he said, but anti-Semitism that creates Jews. I have fought that view all my adult life. It leads to the tortured psychology of Arthur

Koestler, who wrote: "Self-hatred is the Jews' patriotism," or Franz Kafka, who said: "What do I have in common with the Jews? I don't even have anything in common with myself." To me, Jewishness is about moral responsibility, not victimhood; about trust, not fear. Anti-Semitism is something that happens to Jews; it does not define who we are.

These are profound reflections and certainly a way of witnessing the healing that combats both pain and the descent into reactive or assertive aggression. For all marginalized and unjustly treated humans, even those once identified as "the oppressor," the challenging choice is to resist (re)definition into racialized nightmares that intensify inner rage and outward explosions.

Understanding the Cultural Psychology of Nonhealing

Healing, particularly that aimed at racial and other societal injustices, requires one to turn away from a cultural defense mechanism, one that has been socialized into the citizenry, one in which both victim and victimizer share in the construction of domination and the resulting need for healing—the return of "shared firstness" (Gresson, 1982).

What is needed is a massive, global change in the nature of the society. It is evident in the fact that the United States, having declared a "war on terrorism," has exposed the complexity of the ideas preceding and following the war campaign, for instance, in trying to establish a "coalition of aggrieved nations" and then insisting that the United States will act unilaterally when and if it needs to. This dualism says something not only about our society but also about our historical representation of aggressive action (Slotkin, 1973) and the ways that individuals are socialized into complicity with this system.

Notions like "axis of evil" fail even in the domestic situation in which parallel terrorisms exist. For example, we have largely forgotten Timothy McVeigh and the mentality that led seemingly decent young white men to kill in a manner similar to that of the September 11 attacks and to receive the support of domestic militia in a manner similar to that of some Arab communities after September 11.

Since the death of Timothy McVeigh, who bombed the federal building in Oklahoma in 1995, killing more than a hundred people, there have been numerous other occasions where young white men have killed as part of their pain and their racial anger. One of the most penetrating features in Michael

Kimmel's new book, *Angry White Men*, is his discussion—through discourse with white men—about how these acts of violence fit into the narrative of white pain and nonhealing. In a chapter titled "Angry White Boys," Kimmel reviews and reanalyzes much of the study and writing on school shootings. It is here that he locates a critical site of nonhealing:

> These are not just misguided "kids," or "youth," or "troubled teens"—they're boys. All of them. They are a group of boys, deeply aggrieved by a system that they may feel is cruel or demeaning. ... What transforms the aggrieved into mass murderers is also a sense of entitlement, a sense that using violence against others, making others hurt as you hurt, is fully justified. (2013: 75)

In all cases, these acts are horrifying, and all were committed by human beings convinced that their actions were righteous.[66] Such "axes of evil" are not isolated phenomena. The anti-abortion contingency, for instance, is notable here. Identified by former President Bill Clinton as perpetrators of "domestic terrorism," these groups, like the Army of God (see savethebabies.org), are all around us, and their thinking is instructive with respect to the psychopedagogy of healing. As anti-abortion activist Bob Lokey stated in a documentary on the movement, "There is a point at which your emotions can only take so much." The activists' thinking is cogent: "Stop abortion with a bullet, a bomb... you stop abortion on demand."[67]

I have just finished watching a 1999 terrorist movie *Arlington Road* starring Jeff Bridges and Tim Robbins. The terrorists win. They are white men and women and children seeking to live the American dream free of government interference. They believe themselves to be right, and they believe that terrorism is necessary in a war against evil. How are they different from those nations defined as an "axis of evil"? Does our willingness to resort to this invidious distinction reflect our inability to see or accept the linkage between them and us? If so, how can we hope to change them or ourselves? Can we, as a nation, insist that, say, blacks or Native Americans forget and forgive the atrocities visited upon them, yet refuse to embrace a similar "paradox of healing" toward external attackers?

"Training for Uncertainty" and Identity Politics

Thinking about my own life—my struggle for space to be me and to flourish as me—I confront the white male identity struggle as a fellow traveler. That is, I see matters of difference, development, and secure vulnerability as paramount. I will illustrate what I am feeling with a story. A few nights back, I stopped in my neighborhood bar. It was a rainy Sunday evening. The bar was nearly empty. I was sitting to the side, watching Tiger Woods win another match and editing this book. The bartender, a middle-aged lady, was chatting with two other patrons who were also her good friends. The conversation wandered here and there, about this and that. At one point, the women became very animated, talking about raising sons and daughters and being grandmothers. One woman began telling a story of how her youngest son, a 30-year-old bachelor who still lived at home with her and his father, had been scratched in the face by his girlfriend. She was very upset with this young woman and expressed a desire to let her know that "I have raised my sons to not touch a woman physically.... I don't expect a woman to hit him even though he is a grown man because I raised him to not ever hit a woman regardless of the reason."

There were many nuances in this particular conversation that I found intriguing. The one that struck me most—and clearly the one of greatest significance to these black mothers—was the particular vulnerability of their sons to women when trained to be nonaggressive or nonretaliatory toward women aggressors. These mothers seemed anxious because, as black women, they had insisted that their sons be different from most other men and not protect themselves against female abuse.

It is precisely this absence of "identity armor" that many white males I have spoken with describe when discussing women and nonwhite males. Specifically, they mention the isolation, the sense of being uncertain about where they fit. My friend Robert beautifully described just this emotionality in a passage from his semiautobiographical work, quoted earlier, in Chapter 4:

> When a person lives psychologically outside of his culture to a considerable degree for a sufficient period of time, and being told that he should be like everyone else, he begins to question his own sanity; he must be crazy. I had these feelings as a child. I made a vow I would not go crazy. There were times when I thought I was going crazy. During those times, I would beat my fist against the wall, breathe deeply, sing to myself, rock furiously in a rocking chair radio up loud and concentrate on each word. I was, in fact, having what is called a panic attack. ACOAs may have more than their share of these. (Haskell, 1993: 103–104)

Robert was here attributing his emotions to being an adult child of an alcoholic mother. These emotions are also often present in other situations, including those characterized by uncertainty of who one is vis-à-vis others, how one stands, and what one should or should not do or say. A student recently wrote in an autobiographical essay that her interactions with her estranged father were characterized by this same kind of uncertainty. Because her mother and father tell different stories of the family breakup, she asked,

> With my dad, I wonder if my brothers or I are ever really happy and comfortable… you have to beware what you say for fear you step on his toes by doing or saying something that even though it matters little to us, my dad finds a way to take offense.… We are always on edge around him, trying to be the angel kids that we are not.

The need for a secured vulnerability is critical to healthy existence. Some psychologists, especially those concerned with the development of healthy, autonomous individuals and citizens, have described this condition as "object constancy" (Blanck & Blanck, 1979). It is that point emotionally at which people do not come undone because of the disappointments or assaults to their ego that go with life. For example, a man loses his mate to another, grieves for while, then picks himself up and goes on; a woman loses a job and makes the necessary adjustments personally and professionally to find another position. To reach this point, people must have been raised to believe that they are okay even if they are not at the center of the universe, even if they are not always affirmed. This is an important theme in the emerging literature on whiteness. For example, Becky Thompson, associate professor at Simmons College, wrote for the *Boston Globe* in 1997: "What I've learned in 10 years of teaching about race identity is how to experience a much richer life than I was born into." She goes on to say that, increasingly, white Americans will be finding out that "you don't have to be the center of the universe to be part of the universe." (Yemma, 1997: A1)

What is important here is finding a balance between the propensities for self-display that Michael Apple attributes to whites and, far less likely but nonetheless deadly, for escape into destructive self-negation. Michelle Fine wrote several years ago:

> With the generosity of a Spencer Foundation grant, Lois Weis and I, with our graduate students, have been conducting interviews in Jersey City and Buffalo with white, African American, Latino, and Asian young adults—age twenty-one to twenty-nine—poor and working class. In one slice of this project we have collected oral histories from white working-class men, narrating, in part, their current economic plight. By listening to these "angry white men" one can hear how global flight of capital and the consequential labor-market scarcity has sharpened and prolonged racial identities,

> tensions, and sedimentation. While relative to their fathers these white working-class men have taken a disproportional hit under the macroeconomic policies of Reagan and Bush, the flight of capital out of the Northeast and out of the country, and the dismantling of blue collar unions, these men, when interviewed, lay blame for their economic woes squarely at the feet of African American males. (1997: 62)

Fine's observations are critical to our conversation because she locates loss of illusion as a source for pain among less-privileged white males. This is a real issue for anti-oppression activists, even though black males have long endured, and continue to endure, precisely this dislocation. It is, in part, this loss that many feel underlies much machismo and male self-destruction among certain classes of minority men.

An interesting alternative message issues from some white men: minorities should view them in a different way than they have previously. This is a call for the recognition of *white male heterogeneity* and *changeability*. An impasse is implicit in the insistence that women and minorities change, too. It is important to recognize that white males like those interviewed by Fine and her colleagues must have "functional" alternatives to the "privileges of whiteness" if change is to be successful. One aspect of an alternative identity is recognition by the other as a growing being. To be sure, there is a certain irony and immaturity in this need. Thompson (1999) has called this the need for whites to be recognized as "good people" for doing the right thing. She is correct, I believe, in suggesting that this expectation must be overcome. Still, some form of recognition by the other does seem to be essential. I can only return to the image of Mandela's donning the Afrikaner's football jersey, even though he had been the injured one. The gesture—turning the other cheek, going the extra mile—is necessary for healing among unequals, maybe even for equals. But it cannot be the final resolution to the power imbalance.

Conclusion

Apartheid was abolished in South Africa in the early 1990s. "White rule" was at an end. Blacks assumed a greater political and social primacy, and whites were induced to participate in a dance of guilt as part of a national drama of contrition and reconciliation. Around the country, nightly television programs portrayed whites soliloquizing on their complicity in the country's racist legacy and reign of tyranny. Mandela's government had inaugurated these public hearings in July 1995 as part of the National Unity and Reconciliation Act.

According to Bishop Desmond Tutu, head of the Truth and Reconciliation Commission, the practical justification for the Reconciliation Act was to protect the new multicultural democracy by appeasing powerful and well-armed whites. This unfolding story reminds us of both similarities and differences between South Africa and the United States. Mandela's South Africa, like Lincoln's country, had to find a way of replacing racist ideology and national policy and practice with a vision of suffrage for all. Each had to grapple with the democratic implications of one vote for one citizen, and both accomplished this end more or less.

But the United States is not South Africa on many dimensions. The meaning of race and its centrality to white American identity is one of these dimensions, which is central also to the meaning and operation of race in the contemporary and emergent discourse on diversity. This discourse ranges from traditional affirmative-action policy debates to diversity in the workplace and the more recent "racial profiling" of potential terrorists. Racial identity, especially for white males, is linked to both manhood and socioeconomic placement. Changes in both the understanding of masculinity (Bederman, 1995) and the political economic infrastructure threaten the dominant white male self-understanding. Moreover, the very structure of much multiculturalism activity has an aspect of character assassination that must be addressed differently now than in the past.

At present, South Africa is working through its dialectical heritage. In the United States, the various liberation efforts of the past three decades also have been churning along toward some form of stasis. But the South African and American struggles for racial equality are very different species of human struggle. In the United States, the concession to racial minorities was and remains an accommodation. It is because this adjustment was largely symbolic and involved verbal and visual strategies that compromised traditional white self-other understandings that recovery and atonement are necessary (Gresson, 1995). Unfortunately, there is a deep-rooted problem here. In his brilliant Regeneration through Violence, Richard Slotkin (1973) opens with an epigraph from D. H. Lawrence's *Studies in Classic American Literature*:

> But you have there the myth of the essential white America. All the other stuff, the love, the democracy, the floundering into lust, is a sort of by-play. The essential American soul is hard, isolate, stoic, and a killer. It has never yet melted.

There is much about this depiction that might be challenged, and rightly so. Chief among the challenges might be the fact that the country is becoming increasingly less white and more diverse. In addition, the classic discussion of black and white itself is becoming more problematic. Other groups have increased both their power and visibility and have revealed as well "the essential American soul." There is no doubt that the old ways of seeing Us/Them are changing, and the future complexion and composition of the country have yet to be clarified. But it is precisely this cultural and social change that calls forth a prior "American soul," one constituted through myths and histories that continue to be used in the struggle to retain some of the traditional image of a "white" self.

Recent discussions of white youth identification with hip-hop culture as well as the reemployment of blackface by white college students point to this struggle. As such identity fluxes play out on the societal landscape, we are reminded that this entire process has a strong history:

> The mythopoeic mode of reconciling historical paradoxes enables us to glory in this role, on the one hand, and to take the curse off our axe- and gun-work, on the other, by allowing us to identify with what is wounded or destroyed. In the captivity myth, the unfilial emigrant is reconciled with his family by identification with the suffering of the female captive and by his recognition that his masculine will to achieve in the wilderness world is the true cause of her suffering. But the vicarious suffering obtained through the captivity myth atones for the sin and permits the continuance of the emigrant's career. (Slotkin, 1973: 563)

Slotkin is describing here how the mythology of the American frontier enabled the "winning of the West." Significant in his description is the belief that sins can be atoned for through vicarious identification with the vulnerable and the vanquished. Some writers have described this process as cannibalism,[68] but it is perhaps best understood in the contemporary context by notions such as "white male as victim of affirmative action," "reverse racism," and "black racism." The rise of the notion of "white power" symbolizes this process of atonement and the convoluted logic underpinning these other metaphors. This term signals the nature of the "new racism," which is largely semiotic or sign based, employing the mass media to convey the "bullets" that "kill" imagination and intellect.

The second Iraq War of 2003 also echoed the phantasm of atonement-seeking described by Slotkin. The words attributed to Saddam Hussein on the eve of his destruction seem uncannily relevant: "They thought that they would be able to heal their wounds if they went against Baghdad." Should we be surprised that an evil tyrant recognizes a traditional modus operandi?

Have we not, at least in part, continued our conqueror's career in Iraq even as we claim sinlessness and atonement for past sins? If not, how do we explain the repeated insistence that the American flag be raised in Baghdad, or that the soldier who displayed the Stars and Stripes about the statue of Saddam Hussein confessed he was "just following orders"?

These questions have yet to be answered. But we are moved to ask them, and perhaps that best instructs us in the continuing dialectics of social pain and collective healing. Pedagogy of healing, whatever this may be, must be pursued with these questions and others in mind. We are wont to focus on material realities—land, homes, cars, money—and even psychosocial needs—self-worth, social recognition, but we must also reckon with another force: *self-deception*. The role of self-deception in our lives is a much-needed discussion. Philosopher David Livingston Smith (2004: 3), in *Why We Lie*, introduces the discussion in this way:

> Why did self-deception take root in the human mind? As we will see, the propensity for self-deception probably became part of our nature because it was so helpful to us in our dealings with one another. Not only does lying to oneself soothe many of the stresses of life, but, more importantly it also helps one lie to others. One of the most important insights of modern socio-biology is that self-deception is the handmaiden of deceit: in hiding the truth from ourselves, we are able to hide it more fully from others. Therefore, like deceit, self-deception lies at the core of our humanity. Far from being a sign of emotional disturbance, as both popular and psychiatric folklore suggest, it is probably vital for psychological equilibrium.

Social justice pedagogy within the contemporary American context must reckon with self-deception writ large: one defined by glaring and intensifying contradictions. This final reflection, then, confronts the place of self-deception in the human project, particularly as that project considers the pursuit of greater social justice as a precursor to global human survival. The recent emphasis on the "affective turn" in the cultural politics of everyday life (Ahmed, 2004; Ryden & Marshall, 2012) recognizes the increasing need to consider individual agency and intrapsychic dynamics in the discourse of social justice. This conceptual and strategic turn offers both promise and increased uncertainty for the psychopedagogy of healing. This, nonetheless, is a fairer, truer, and hopefully, more fruitful reorienting for cultural workers.

· 8 ·

POSTSCRIPT

Relational Justice and the Pedagogy of the Wounded Healer

The greatest cultural task of our age might be the investigation of the role of relational, not merely economic, justice, in contemporary society. And the greatest gap in our social science pertains to the denial of the psychological significance of retributive social dynamics.

– Boszormenyi-Nagy & Spark (1973: 74)

Social justice education begins with people's lived experience as the ground for developing a critical perspective and actions directed toward social change...coalitions bring together multiple ways of understanding the world and analyzing the oppressive structures within it...

– Adams & Bell (2007: 13–14)

As a young psychologist practicing family therapy in West Philadelphia's black communities in the 1980s, I stumbled upon the work of Ivan Boszormenyi-Nagy, Hungarian American psychiatrist and founder of Contextual Family Therapy. Working with lower-income minority families, I especially appreciated the value of his emphasis on mutual care and respect within the family for achieving healthy outcomes in treatment. So often, these families suffer from precisely this shortcoming: needing and demanding extraordinary trust, understanding, and support while being unable or unwilling to deliver the same. As a result, all family members frequently find themselves in a vicious cycle of betrayal. In this cycle of hurting and being hurt, such families resemble the racialized Americans we have met in the preceding chapters.

In calling for greater attention to *relational justice*, Boszormenyi-Nagy was thinking not only of troubled families, but society at large. More specifically, he was concerned that professional helpers, including social justice activists, address the emotional consequences of people—even those fermenting social injustice—feeling that their loyalties and sacrifices are unappreciated. When they feel this way, people often "slip" into getting even (Gresson, 1982). This is part of what Boszormenyi-Nagy meant by "retributive social dynamics." Although the term has a theological (atonement) connection, I want to emphasize its psychological dimension because social justice activists and social policymakers alike have too often neglected it. This neglect, moreover, has elements of societal self-deception. By societal self-deception I mean all those platitudes, policies, and practices American society has instituted to "combat" racism even as it denies the root causes and ongoing institutional supports for it at home and abroad. In this regard, one of the important lessons of post-apartheid South Africa was the realization that individual and national interests are not necessarily or precisely the same. Michael Ignatieff (1998: 169), reflecting on the limitations of the Truth and Reconciliation Commissions set up to address the white atrocities of the apartheid era, wrote: "We tend to vest our nations with conscience, identities and memories as if they were individuals. It is problematic enough to vest an individual with a single identity: our inner lives are like battlegrounds over which uneasy truces reign; the identity of a nation is additionally fissured by region, ethnicity, class and education."

The important lesson implicit in this observation is that the individual has her or his own complicated motivations, memories, and moralities. These may not, moreover, be the same as adopted by the nation-group to achieve a semblance of peace and justice. On the contrary, individuals may be additionally aggrieved by society's self-deceptions and feckless mandates to be just, fair, and inclusive. After all, everyone—including the super-rich and powerful oligarchs—can ultimately find a reason for self-protection against real and/or imagined injustices. Thus, for example, insistence that "white privilege" must be dismantled strikes too many, even some of the "socially oppressed," as peculiar. This is the reason that ultimately relational justice must be called upon to offset societal self-deception *and* retributive social dynamics.

The point is that culture largely bears the responsibility to sanction and teach serious, unequivocal mutual respect and care. People must trust and respond affirmatively to each other, both in families and within societies: to be for self *and* others.

Where there is a breakdown in this instinctual contract, there is dysfunction and disaster. We see this today, for example, among the Palestinians in Gaza and the Jews in Israel—or the Ukrainians sympathetic to the West and those identified with Russia. Closer to home, Ferguson, Missouri, painfully comes to mind.

Within these cases of conflict and violence, there lurks an *emotional* and *personal* motive of fairness or justice. Regardless of assigned blame for the violence or its reprisals, individuals and collectivities on all sides feel aggrieved. As it pertains to race matters, we have seen in the preceding chapters that the origins or destructiveness of racism notwithstanding, all racialized persons know shame, pain, and anger—and call for "retributive justice." Police are especially notable in this regard. Existentially, they always have had a dirty, complicated job: too little pay, minimal respect, and insufficient societal care for the good they do. Always and everywhere, I suspect, the police have had to seize their relational justice where, when, and how they can. Sometimes this has been noble, others, not so noble. Being caught, moreover, between the elites and the less fortunate (often they have come from the latter group), they are vulnerable to lived experiences that made them even less compassionate to the less fortunate than they might have been. For the wretched are human, and capable of doing the very things that will deepen their socially structured tensions with "authority." But this we largely know. The problem is that we act as if this is not sufficiently important to create a series of warring narratives of "good guy" and "bad guy." Moreover, we proceed in ways that seem to seek justice for all but actually exacerbate the problem. And it is within this context that we may see the exchanges around "good guy"/"bad guy" as what Boszormenyi-Nagy and Spark term "retributive social dynamics." In this postscript, I want to briefly reflect on a few of these relational dynamics for social justice teaching and learning. I start with a short reflection on a national crisis that began just as I was beginning this final chapter: the August 2014 racial crisis in Ferguson, Missouri.

Racial Pain in Ferguson, Missouri …and Beyond

In August 2014, the state of Missouri witnessed a convergence of societal self-deception and retributive dynamics: Ferguson, a small town that used to be predominantly white and is now largely black, with a history of racial tension, explodes when a white policeman kills an unarmed black youth. The community protests the death and apparent refusal to treat the victim and his family justly (however defined), and the town is thrust into chaos with some looting and related violence; the police, outfitted in military gear left over from the Iraqi War, try to enforce a curfew. Days of continued protest, accusation, and apologetics lead to a national and international spectacle. Notably and predictably, police are criticized for "over the top" reactions to black protest; police claim to protect themselves, releasing (allegedly at the press's request) a video of Michael Brown shoplifting minutes before his encounter with the policeman who shot him. Local, regional, and national government officials respond to the growing tension; and even President Obama chimes in. Representative John Lewis asks Obama to federalize the National Guard and protect people exercising their First Amendment rights; reporters too are arrested for "unlawful assembly." Attorney General Eric Holder and the Federal Bureau of Investigation journey to Ferguson days later, to assure the black citizens of a "fair and thorough" investigation. Slowly, the "wheels of justice," however understood and valued, again begin to turn and the prosecuting attorney promises a long, long process.

I write this description of events in Ferguson, Missouri, nearly six months after beginning this second edition, and a year since the dramatic trial of George Zimmerman for the killing of Trayvon Martin. The acquittal of George Zimmerman was quickly followed, it seems, by yet more killings of black youth: Jordan Davis was killed by Michael Dunn, Renisha McBride was killed by Theodore Wafer, and Michael Brown was killed by Darren Wilson. In all these cases, the youth were unarmed; and the white men were armed. And in each case, efforts were made by some to shield the killers from criticism or consequences and to demonize these young blacks as somehow worthy of death.

I begin this postscript with this litany of black youth killings because it points to the stubbornly resilient issue of America's "atonement". The apparent upsurge in the visibility of white-on-black youth murders is perhaps numbing. As I indicated in an earlier chapter, Robert Jay Lifton (1999) argued that psychological numbing was the consequence of events like the nuclear bombing of Hiroshima and Nagasaki. Perhaps the massive human destruction we witness daily, all thanks to high-tech mass media, has intensified this blunting of our sensitivities so we can barely feel the human carnage we witness. If this is so, then all those concerned with social justice must recalibrate the nature of the challenge and the means of achieving the desired ends.

One of the (mis)fortunes of living a long life is the frequent sense that one has been there before. For me, this sense of déjà vu takes me back to when I lived in Atlanta, Georgia: between 1979 and 1981, some 30 black youth, mostly males, were killed. Wayne Williams, a black male, was convicted of two of these murders. The others remain unsolved. Of course, conspiracy theories, mostly involving the KKK and the white-controlled criminal justice system, have dominated this somewhat ancient period. Still, I feel today, more than three decades later, much as I felt then: helpless and convinced that somehow these black babies were paying for something much bigger than bad parenting, poverty, or a random serial killer.

For one thing, there is the irony that, in moments like Ferguson, *everyone has a grievance; everyone sees his or her survival at stake*. Further, the seeds of mistrust and trauma are both historical and current in nature, which makes everything so crazy and undermines the well-meaning social justice activism of various individuals and groups. What's more, the almost surreal attack on the black (male) body in recent months seems, to me, to shout the crescendo of white pain that seems subjectively linked to the black body in pain.

For some time now, critical theorists and pedagogues have been pleading for greater attention to the affective component of social justice education. Recognizing the emotional and subjective experiences of millions of whites with respect to both multiculturalism and the perceived threats of a beyond-whiteness agenda, these activists have asked that we attend both the implicit epistemological and pragmatic teaching challenges. We must, in addition, understand the current lapse in repressed rage at racial change as expressed in the increased killings of blacks and increasing legislative attacks on women, minorities, and the poor writ large. A few thoughts are especially in order with respect to the metaphoric destruction of black male bodies.

Atonement and the Black Body in Pain

Honor your son and his life, not the circumstances of his alleged transgressions. I have always said that Trayvon was not perfect. But no one will ever convince me that my son deserved to be stalked and murdered. No one can convince you that Michael deserved to be executed.

– Letter From Trayvon Martin's mother, Sabrina Fulton, to Michael Brown's family (Fulton, 2014)

Racialized identities and interactions are shot through with a special pain that is born, in part, from having to affirm if not embrace "bad actions." "Bad actions" are, of course, socially defined and negotiated like most other things in society. The expression "boys will be boys" stands as a powerful illustration of this social and psychological fact. But "bad actions" have a special history and ongoing role in the tableau - like relation between white cop and black male. In each instance, socially defined "assumptions" shape the way each of these players sees his/her identity and the appropriate—safe—expression of personal agency. For example, as I watch the unfolding justice drama (again) around Darren Wilson's killing of Michael Brown, I am struck anew by the varying "bad actor" narratives that have arisen to enfold and exonerate each of these tragic figures. And I feel yet again that the justice drama has less to do with each of these victims and his real or alleged unjust aggression toward the other than with what society needs in order to avoid becoming the apocalyptic nightmare so often portrayed in Hollywood films. Because the "justice" society demands will vary from time to time and case to case; moreover, one is left asking what is to be learned that can be used as "difficult" but "approachable" knowledge?

I think one answer to this question is contained in the message from Sabrina Fulton, Trayvon Martin's mother, to the parents of Michael Brown: recognize the humanity of your son; he was not perfect, he could be a "bad actor;" *but he did not deserve to be a sacrificial lamb to a cowardly society*. When the "sacrificial lamb" is defamed, and the "slayer" is praised, this process exposes a perversity of society—not the heroism or villainy of the "lamb" and "slayer." It is perhaps correct that the "slayer" be judged "innocent" through the collective affirming of the "rightness" of his lethal actions. After all, it is doubly dangerous to suggest that he is also a "bad actor." Such an admission exposes the collective bond between a tainted (racist) society *and* the character of those whose identities are partly shaped by performing specific roles within it.

Difficult knowledge though it might be, most of us can certainly see, upon forced engagement with the facts, that the core relation between "white safety officer" and "black male danger" has been warped since the time of slavery. The manumission of slavery did not remove the essential tension in this relationship. Self-deception has allowed us all to deny this fact to varying degrees, but the police (both white and black) and their archenemy, the black male, existentially know a shared fear and shame. It is this shared fear and shame that social justice activists must increasingly engage.

In this context, "policeman" may blend in with "angry white men" and the "Tea Party," the most recent voices in the call for "white justice." And as vulgar, disingenuous, or distasteful as these expressions may appear to some critics and social justice activists, they represent the lived experiences of many, singularly and collectively. Those who have identified the black male body, in particular, as a site for expressions of "We're not going to take it anymore" will recognize, perhaps, that there is an eerie symbolism in the current wave of killings of young black men in broad daylight, without even the pretense of imminent *physical* danger to the white men involved. What is too rarely uttered is the fact that the danger is *psychic*. This orientation is, of course, the underlying argument of *America's Atonement*: "white pain" is the psychic pain that drives whites, especially men, to kill blacks, largely male. (Obviously, and not unimportantly, black pain is also why blacks kill blacks in such disproportionate numbers and radical Islamists kill Muslims so viciously; this, of course, is about self-hate, the theme of a forthcoming volume on post-racial society.) Stripped of all the rhetoric and counter-rhetoric, this is a ritual that often evades comment even as we pay lip service to its presence and evil. Still, it continues. Much like the ritual wife-battering associated with Super Bowl weekend, this stands like an alien but familiar presence. But it is not alien; and it is not unassailable. Still, this ritual evil must be first faced if it is to be transformed later.

In short, the killing of young black men, their possible crimes and existential danger notwithstanding, is an atoning activity. I felt this was true in Atlanta in the 1980s and I feel the same today about the seeming crescendo of racialized killings. Two of the most important indicators of this reading of the current series of murders are (1) the simultaneous black (out)rage, and (2) call for peace protest, understanding, and healing in the midst of ongoing white aggression. This dynamic—a perverse retribution justice—rehearses the already identified rhetorical interaction of black protest identified by Rudwick and Meier (1969). While this pattern has the partial effect of gaining white and international sympathy for the "wretched" blacks under siege, it also affirms the alternative white narrative of "blacks as animals" and allows for the added insult of treating blacks like militant extremists/terrorists by confronting them with military assault tanks and the like: this is because the black outrage so often seems turned back upon itself; and this leads white sympathizers like Brent Zuercher (Anderson & Zuercher, 2001) to wonder about the sanity of black folk.

To see the upsurge in white killings of blacks as atoning activity is to suggest that the achieved "justice" is a lull in the tension, but not a significant shift for the mutually aggrieved that continue to feel disrespected, devalued, and dismissed. It is significant that the Ferguson, Missouri, case brings together the particular configuration that it does: a largely poor, working-class black population in a previously working-class, predominately white town where the chief political figures and law enforcement personnel are white men. The social-emotional exchange in this county in Missouri is suggestive of a larger national predicament and plight. The presence and engagement of white social-justice seekers and white reporters at the site of the siege both give hope of positive change and expose the scope of the institutionalized injustice embedded in the personal narratives of the police chief, governor, and others who see events differently than most of the protesting blacks and their white and other non-black allies.

Sigmund Freud, as quoted in the opening epigraph to Part One, considered the problem of unprovoked violence as endemic to the species. For Freud, violence was something that must be faced, even though it is a part of our nature that we often use self-deception to deny or distance ourselves from it. It has long seemed to me that the avoidance of painful truths about racial pain and violence has underlain the slow progress toward a broader, deeper social justice. That the black body in pain is complicit in this slowness is a fairly recent theme, although the Jewish body in pain has certainly shown the long historical trajectory of this form of complicity. Indeed, Freud argued that Jews played a notable role in their own plight by assuming roles that Gentiles could later scapegoat. (Of course, Kurt Lewin also cogently understood that Jews, like many marginalized groups, sometimes bought into the idea that if they were "good enough," they could avert being mistreated; thus, he distinguished between "personal troubles" and "public issues" to help distinguish between psychological and sociological facts.) I mention this fact of "complicity" here not to "blame the victim" but to highlight the strategic importance of neutralizing this complicit role in the furtherance of social justice. That is, we must hasten to name complicity in race matters (McPhail, 1991) as a partial corrective to both the injustice of some "white blame" and the neglect of the *relational* challenge "white racial violence" poses for social justice seekers. Upon doing so, we still face a formidable challenge. A part of this challenge is placing social justice activism within the context of "narcissistic culture."

The "Me Generation" and Racialized Identities

Earlier today, I happened to catch a bit of a Dr. Phil show. The topic was the so-called Me Generation. The guest was Dr. Jean M. Twenge, a psychology professor and researcher, author of a recent study on narcissism in contemporary

American culture, *Generation Me: Why Today's Young Americans Are More Confident, Assertive, Entitled—and More Miserable Than Ever Before*. Dr. Phil often showcases guests who may scandalize and entertain, but they also frequently offer insights into us as a nation. In this instance, the show merely reminded me of what many have been stating for decades: the constant drift of the nation into a me-focused culture. Some argue we have always been me-focused; others identify the label with the baby boomers and their progeny.[69] Whatever the truth, there is clear evidence that the self-display, the sense of entitlement and "specialness" that characterizes so many today is intense, even tragic. From "selfies" to reality TV, and everything in between, we have been encouraged—and have encouraged in our turn—self-absorption. But there is an even more insidious aspect to this narcissism: the growing wealth inequality.

The growing global wealth inequality is driven, in part, by this narcissism, or emphasis on the self over the group. Susanne Langer's comments about the "ethnic imbalance" come to mind again. The move away from responsibility to the collectivity and the refocus on self-interests in a single-minded fashion underpin many social ills. The scope of the connection between this cultural narcissism and global inequality and poverty has been seen by men like Pope Francis, who recently shook up the global financial communities with his pronouncement on wealth inequality and the poor:

> Today, in concrete terms, an awareness of the dignity of each of our brothers and sisters whose life is sacred and inviolable from conception to natural death must lead us to share with complete freedom the goods which God's providence has placed in our hands, material goods but also intellectual and spiritual ones, and to give back generously and lavishly whatever we may have earlier unjustly refused to others. (Radio Vatican, 2014)

Future sustainable development goals must therefore be formulated and carried out with generosity and courage, so that they can have a real impact on the structural causes of poverty and hunger, attain more substantial results in protecting the environment, ensure dignified and productive labor for all, and provide appropriate protection for the family, which is an essential element in sustainable human and social development. Specifically, this involves challenging all forms of injustice and resisting the "economy of exclusion," the "throwaway culture" and the "culture of death" which nowadays sadly risk becoming passively accepted. (Radio Vatican, 2014)

But as profoundly human and urgent as his words are, the pope is laboring against the "trade winds" of primary narcissism and culturally constructed selfishness sustained by a societally produced desire for more and more for me. And this fact is not unrelated to "white pain" and racial suffering. In a very thoughtful opinion essay in an edition of *Time* magazine featuring essays on narcissism, former basketball great Kareem Abdul-Jabbar (2014) reflects:

> Will the recent rioting in Ferguson, Missouri, be a tipping point in the struggle against racial injustice, or will it be a minor footnote in some future grad student's thesis on Civil Unrest in the Early Twenty-First Century? ... Unless we want the Ferguson atrocity to also be swallowed and become nothing more than an intestinal irritant to history, we have to address the situation not just as another act of systemic racism, but as what else it is: class warfare. By focusing on just the racial aspect, the discussion becomes about whether Michael Brown's death—or that of the other three unarmed black men who were killed by police in the U.S. within that month—is about discrimination or about police justification. Then we'll argue about whether there isn't just as much black-against-white racism in the U.S. as there is white-against-black. (Yes, there is. But, in general, white-against-black economically impacts the future of the black community. Black-against-white has almost no measurable social impact.)....

This fist-shaking of everyone's racial agenda distracts America from the larger issue that the targets of police overreaction are based less on skin color and more on an even worse Ebola-level affliction: being poor. Of course, to many in America, being a person of color is synonymous with being poor, and being poor is synonymous with being a criminal. Ironically, this misperception is true even among the poor....

I'm not saying the protests in Ferguson aren't justified—they are. In fact, we need more protests across the country. Where's our Kent State? What will it take to mobilize 4 million students in peaceful protest? Because that's what it will take to evoke actual change.

The return to *class* as a critical, though under-appreciated, part of the racial tension in the United States and elsewhere brings our discussion of white pain, notably white male anger, full circle. As Michael Kimmel (2013) argued, white males are increasingly feeling left behind—but isn't this precisely what people are saying about blacks in the many "Fergusons" across the country? And does Kareem not seem an echo of Kimmel and others when he maintains whites should be joining with minorities to fight the system? Rand Paul's (2014) libertarianism seems pertinent here:

> The middle class has to join the poor and whites have to join African-Americans in mass demonstrations, in ousting corrupt politicians, in boycotting exploitative

businesses, in passing legislation that promotes economic equality and opportunity, and in punishing those who gamble with our financial future.

Otherwise, all we're going to get is what we got out of Ferguson: a bunch of politicians and celebrities expressing sympathy and outrage. If we don't have a specific agenda—a list of exactly what we want to change and how—we will be gathering over and over again beside the dead bodies of our murdered children, parents, and neighbors.

The plea for a "coalition of the willing" among vulnerable whites and minorities is suggestive. Of course, capitalists scoff at the idea; and most of us find our eyes glazing over with images of "totalitarian" despots and socialist scarcity—anathema to us selfies. Yet, even if we are not yet ready to turn in our capitalist cards, social justice activists must begin to re-inject white-black/minority alliances into their discourse against racial injustice. Joe Kincheloe (2006: 45) was one of the most persistent, self-committed advocates of this racial turn; in his essay on Southernification, he cogently called for an engaged interracialist moment in this way:

> Like Howard Dean—*but with more sensitivity to the emotional register* of references to the Confederate Flag—I do not want to "write off" the South as a regressive racial/cultural domain. If we are to be Southernified, the process should involve the development of a lived interracialism, an inclusive sense of community and its importance in everyday life, a collective racial consciousness based on a shared historical memory of the nation's blood and darkness, a racial redemption in which we all participate, an appreciation of the land and our collective cultivation of it, a recognition of the interracial contributions to the nation's most imaginative and innovative artistic production, and an understanding that one of the dominant socio-political impulses of our time, the recovery movement, is leading us down a path of inevitable ethical and political devastation. (Italics added.)

As was characteristic of Kincheloe's work, the essay, which this passage concludes, is full of critical and strategic insights. There is the possibility that one may miss the beautiful racial turn that the essay itself constituted: written in a pivotal yet often marginalized Africana studies journal, *Souls: A Critical Journal of Black Politics, Culture, and Society*, this article offered Kincheloe, a son of the South, a chance to articulate where we have arrived as a racialized nation in the first decade of the 21st century. He, like the late Dr. Manning Marable, founder of *Souls*, understood the place of the *psychical* in any collective, coalitional struggle. More precisely, in this work Kincheloe had begun to articulate what may be seen as an understanding of the "identity trauma" of whiteness in the "post" era.[70] He was beginning, especially in this essay and his 1999 piece on white pain, to articulate, with sensitivity *and* insistence, the identity shifts whites need to make if they are to resist the pull into racial recovery. One step toward this rhetorical and strategic turn is recognizing in ourselves the "wounded healer."

The Wounded Healer and Difficult Knowledge

Whether we try to enter a dislocated world, relate to a convulsive generation, or speak to a dying person, our service will not be perceived as authentic unless it come from a heart wounded by the suffering about which we speak.

— Henri J. M. Nouwen (1972)

The "wounded healer" is one whose pain, wounds, and endurance have enabled her or him to be authentic with those receiving counsel, consolation, and enlightenment. We may take it for granted that educators and social justice activists are attuned to their own woundedness and are able to *use self* in their teaching and activism. Still, it bears constant reminding and encouragement from fellow workers. Moreover, the nature of "difficult knowledge" (Britzman, 2000) makes it all the more critical to be a wounded healer. Yet, it is precisely in affirming our woundedness and identifying with *some* wounded others that we may threaten yet other wounded ones. Within the racial domain, this is evident every time President Barack Obama speaks on race: he is accused of being "divisive." Beneath the absurdity of this rhetoric is a perhaps unspeakable rage and pain of rejection and non-inclusion. This is why "difficult knowledge" has become an increasingly important aspect of the "affective turn" in social justice pedagogy.

We have a powerful example of the complicated, potentially reactionary operation of difficult knowledge, for example, as a result of the efforts of one wounded healer, Eric Holder. Ten days into the crisis in Ferguson, Missouri, Attorney General Eric Holder went to this town to assure the black citizens that he was going to ensure that a fair, thorough investigation would be carried out. He also wanted to connect with the racial pain felt by the citizens. To do this, he relied, in part, on his own racial pain, racial profiling and the police:

> The eyes of the nation and the world are watching Ferguson right now. The world is watching because the issues raised by the shooting of Michael Brown predate this incident. This is something that has a history to it and the history simmers beneath the surface in more communities than just Ferguson.

> We have seen a great deal of progress over the years. But we also see problems and these problems stem from mistrust and mutual suspicion.
>
> I just had the opportunity to sit down with some wonderful young people and to hear them talk about the mistrust they have at a young age. These are young people and already they are concerned about potential interactions they might have with the police.
>
> I understand that mistrust. I am the Attorney General of the United States. But I am also a black man. I can remember being stopped on the New Jersey turnpike on two occasions and accused of speeding. Pulled over.…"Let me search your car"… Go through the trunk of my car, look under the seats and all this kind of stuff. I remember how humiliating that was and how angry I was and the impact it had on me.
>
> I think about my time in Georgetown—a nice neighborhood of Washington—and I am running to a movie at about 8 o'clock at night. I am running with my cousin. Police car comes driving up, flashes his lights, yells "Where you going? Hold it!" I say "Whoa, I'm going to a movie." Now my cousin started mouthing off. I'm like, "This is not where we want to go. Keep quiet." I'm angry and upset. We negotiate the whole thing and we walk to our movie. At the time that he stopped me, I was a federal prosecutor. I wasn't a kid. I was a federal prosecutor. I worked at the United States Department of Justice. So I've confronted this myself. (Holder, 2014)

Speaking to students at St. Louis Community College—Florissant Valley on Wednesday, August 20, 2014, Holder was exposing his own vulnerability as a black man in the United States in the 21st century. His comments were consoling, especially for the blacks in pain in Ferguson. His reflections on racial experience, however, are (like those of President Barack Obama) also a source of painful and difficult knowledge. Stories of racial profiling and racial pain from the mouths of very prominent and powerful black males remind us all of the "real deal": our collective vulnerabilities to each other and the vicissitudes of life. Moreover, such narratives graphically expose the closeness of despair and hopelessness when one labors under oppressive social conditions.

White policemen and college students, as much as black attorney generals and presidents, share these feelings of hopelessness and vulnerability. Thus, wounded healers are needed for them as well as those identified as the classic victims of racial and other social oppression. Students in social justice classes, especially, are vulnerable to threatening or painful information, and must receive, in addition to empirical facts, affective experiences rooted in the self of the teacher/activist. I realized this fact, not for the first time, during my visit to the University of Virginia. When talking with the large group in Professor

Alridge's multiculturalism class in 2013, I had the occasion to engage a young white male. He was dressed in fatigues, a "good ole boy" cap and actually was dipping snuff. When I asked him his thoughts on the issue at hand, he looked me straight in the eyes and said with a smile: "You don't know who you're asking…" Holding his eye and smiling as well, I responded without hesitation: "Yes, I do; that's why I came to ask you what you thought."

We had connected; he and I both knew and felt it; I think much of the class did also. What he specifically thought or shared on the topic is secondary to the fact that he felt recognized and affirmed, in both his "identity" *and* his vulnerability. And he recognized my vulnerability too. This is not, of course, the totality of the social justice agenda or project. But it is very much an aspect that must and is receiving more attention. I gained a new appreciation of this fact when I met with the graduate students facilitating the small breakout sections of the class I spoke with at the University of Virginia. These young professionals were both bright and committed educators; in addition, they were sensitive and caring toward their undergraduates in the course. Still, several of them told stories of disengaged or sometimes resistant learners. They wanted so desperately to share their knowledge of social injustice and the changes needed to improve life for us all. But their work often involved the imparting of "difficult knowledge," which, according to Pitt and Britzman (2006: 379), "signifies both representations of social traumas in curriculum and the individual's encounter with them in pedagogy."

The challenge these social justice educators face is, in part, how to use "the self" in its very vulnerability to connect with the other in a way that allows for a shared encounter with the painful knowledge at hand. This is one of the emerging challenges of a critical pedagogy sensitive to the affective turn. You might ask, how does this look when trying to make sense of something like the difficult or painful knowledge—empirical and imagined—one might associate with the crisis in Ferguson, Missouri?

The Dialectics of "Bad Performance" and the Use of Self

Trayvon Martin's mother, Sabrina Fulton, may or may not have seen the video released by the Ferguson police, in which a young black male, allegedly Michael Brown, is shown stealing goods from a store and intimidating the noticeably smaller, possibly minority store manager. Still, her open letter to

Brown's parents suggested that she was all too alert to the attempt police were making to character assassinate the deceased youth; her words implied as much. But notice how she used herself, embracing and expose her own painful awareness that Trayvon was human, not perfect, not an angel. By her comments she also demonstrated the challenge we all face when confronted with the *dialectics of bad performance*. That is, people often commit actions that are far from perfect. But there are both instinctual and relational pressures to provide relief or "excuses" for bad behavior or actions. I mentioned in an earlier chapter that I frequently encounter this dynamic in my clinical practice: a parent is painfully aware of their child's bad behavior in school and may even have him/her in therapy for this reason—and yet hastens to offer excuses for why the teacher, school, or someone else was wrong (too). This type of conflict can be devastating for a child and the family, as well as a nightmare for others. Add to this familial dilemma the larger societal challenge that occurs when the "bad actor" is, say, the racialized white policeman or black male youth.

The dialectics of bad performance are real in the minds of people, especially when confronting painful knowledge. Consider one blogger's reaction to the perceived injustice of blaming white people, notably the police, for the destructiveness marking black existence:

> I know it's frustrating when annoying right wingers like myself always rain on the cop-hating, death-to-whitey parade to point out how black kids are, by and large, under attack from other black kids, and the black community is in a tragic state of self-destruction. But we wouldn't need to do that if the Mike Brown and Trayvon Martin kinds of incidents weren't immediately seized upon to prove a universal narrative of black victimhood. You want to simply discuss Mike Brown? Fine. Wait until the facts are in and the smoke has cleared (literally) and we can talk about Mike Brown. But liberals aren't interested in making this a narrow and specific conversation. They want to make Mike Brown into another casualty of White America's war on black teens. It's in response to that kind of nonsense that one must introduce a few other items for consideration. If this is to become a debate about the plight of black Americans (and I'm not the one who turned it into that) then the debate will be utterly useless if it doesn't begin and end with the sad reality that 70 percent of black kids are born to unwed mothers. Over 60 percent of black children grow up in homes without fathers. Black people are killed by other black people much more frequently than by cops. Black babies are murdered in the womb at such a pace that now, in cities like New York, a black child has a better chance at being aborted than born. (Walsh, 2014)

I have quoted this passage at length because it reads like a litany of the ongoing apology for racism and other social injustices. But it also contains some "true statements" that must be worked with rather than denied or ignored. To do the latter only strengthens the litany of counterpoints employed to further the dialectics of bad performances. For example, by "embracing" Mr. Walsh's litany, I was able to feel the perverse truth it contains: people can be driven to accept and perform what has been assigned them by society—even Mr. Walsh, or me. This is a well-known idea; but it is not necessarily appreciated in the pedagogical moment. This is why the emerging scholarship on social justice pedagogy, and its emphasis on the affective turn, must increasingly consider the place of compassion in its practices.

The late Catholic priest and professor of theology Henri J.M. Nouwen (1972: 41) saw *compassion* as the relational vehicle for achieving this end. In his meditations on the role of the *wounded healer*, he saw the need for helpers to transform themselves as a necessary aspect of teaching and achieving social justice:

> Through compassion it is possible to recognize that the craving for love that people feel resides also in our own hearts, that the cruelty the world knows all too well is also rooted in our own impulses. Through compassion we also sense our hope for forgiveness in our friends' eyes and our hatred in their bitter mouths. When they kill, we know that we could have done it; when they give life, we know that we can do the same. For a compassionate person nothing human is alien: no joy and no sorrow, no way of living and no way of dying.

Although his thoughts were shaped by a Christian context, the relational and pedagogical significance of this view of compassion bears remarkable similarity to emergent social justice pedagogies. In this attitude, Nouwen both anticipated and modeled qualities identified with cultural worker Paulo Freire, especially in his *Pedagogy of Hope* (1994), and the idea of the "Easter experience." Both perspectives emphasize the use of self to further social justice initiatives. In part, the use of self involves changing one's own attitudes and style of relating.

In my work with families, one observation has been and remains true: children see the duplicity and dishonesty within their families and communities. Sometimes these children grow up to resist these lessons of self-deception, and at other times, they adopt them. In most cases, they do a bit of both. It is for this reason, in part, that the "racialized other" in each of us stands in need of "atonement." But this fact does not negate the need for real, painful racial atonement by the perpetrators of individual and institutional racism. Compassion in the social justice educator is partly achieved through modeling vulnerability and partly through co-creating with the learner a hopeful alternative to the documented injustices with individual identities and institutional structures.

Human deception dwells within us all and permeates everyday life and social interaction. What is often neglected in daily interaction, including teaching, are the myriad injustices seen and absorbed by youth. What does the failure to change tell them and us? What does the belief in social justice and social change tell us and require of us? What actions are they pursuing in an attempt to engage their own dance of agency?[71]

Many have been asking what is "postracial" about 2014? There is considerable evidence in this revised edition of "*America's Atonement*", as well as other sources, to decry the very idea of "postracial." Yet, among the arguments that have been made for the present time as "postracial," I would add one more: we are living in an aggressively and non-apologetically *existential moment*: a time/place that is meaningful and vital *right now* to those who want to be agents, be active *and* effective. This is, I believe, the degree of truth to the idea of the "postracial." Of course, this has very little to do with racism—structural, individual, corporate, or global. It has everything to do with the "liberation" of the affective, the various forces that undergird our emotions, feelings, and ways of seeing ourselves in the world.

It is collusive to act as if self-deception is not actively affecting social justice generally and racial justice in particular. Pedagogies must struggle with these facts. The existential moment is the time/occasion/opportunity for creating new alliances, new consociates (Schutz, 1972). On the need to connect contemporary Jewish youth and diaspora challenges, Jon A. Levisohn (2012) has written:

> Most aspirationally, the pedagogy of peoplehood might cultivate a passion for a collective Jewish mission in the world. Coming to love that purpose, that ideal, and pursuing that purpose in the world, inevitably draws one into a relationship with others who share that purpose. Now, if it is true that individuals develop a sense of connection to and concern for a larger collectivity in the ways that I've described—through the practices of story, language, and love—then we should notice that peoplehood education does not conflict with other substantive, content-rich Jewish educational efforts but rather comfortably co-exists with them. The pedagogy of peoplehood may require a certain focus and intentionality but it is not fundamentally distinct in any way, and it is certainly not limited to face-to-face social interactions. So peoplehood is not a way to buy Jewish continuity on the cheap. We should not imagine that we can give students a quick injection of peoplehood through an encounter with other Jews, and then sit back and reap the benefits.

This attitude also parallels the dance of agency in *Letters Across the Divide*. As John Hatch (2009b) wrote, there was an important growth that occurred for the white partner in this discourse. But David Anderson and Brent Zuercher (2001) had to struggle together, bound by a certain religious faith and good will. They had to mirror compassion for each other. For example, it would require a good deal of emotion work for many African Americans to tolerate, and then transcend the following existential moment by Brent Zuercher (2001: 32):

> We have this idea in America today that black rage is an appropriate, tolerable response to the racism under which blacks have been victimized. I do not believe this idea is supportable with biblical teachings. I ask again, where are the black ministers preaching to the black congregations that resentment and rage, even though natural human responses, are sin? Do these ministers exist? The majority of black ministers I see are using their position and title as a means to fuel blacks' expression of their resentment and rage—this is a travesty and a severe violation of a minister's fiduciary duty of "shepherding the flock." God holds spiritual leaders accountable for the teaching and guidance they provide. I pity the minister that must answer to God for stirring up the emotions of resentment and rage within His people.

My immediate reaction to this passage, Christian background notwithstanding, is that it is not the minister who "stirs the emotions of resentment and rage" within me but the arrogance of the utterance that I must be asked yet again (recall Orlando Patterson in the previous chapter) to rise to the occasion of apparent white "aggrieved entitlement" such as Zuercher expresses. But, like David Anderson (2001: 37), after granting but reframing his friend's paradoxical casting of all blacks in a way that he chastens blacks for doing to whites, I would hopefully say, as he did: "If I were to base my opinion of whites on my negative experiences, I would never be a reconciler. I base my view of people in general on the fact that the awesome God of creation creates them and that it is His image they bear."

The pursuit of compassion is not the singular requirement of a critical social justice pedagogy, but it's an essential element in confronting the powerfulness of racial pain. It is perhaps inescapable, in the contemporary world, for identities and interactions to not produce racial pain—especially in the social justice-focused classroom. Still, it will be increasingly helpful for learners to be engaged with pedagogies in which learners feel engaged by teachers whose own woundedness is both familiar and engaging.

Aaron David Gresson III
Owings Mills, Maryland
September 6, 2014

NOTES

A Personal Preface

1. See *The Chronicle of Higher Education*, January 5, January 19, and April 26, 1996. These news features cover the charges against the University of Minnesota Press, the racial divide at the university presses, and the dismissal of charges against the director of the university press. Although Biodun Iginla, the Nigeria-born former senior editor, planned to file a civil suit against Ms. Lisa Freeman, the university, and the press, nothing was subsequently reported about this.

Introduction

2. In 2009, a white female blogger received what was voted the best Yahoo response to why whites weren't invited to the Million Man March: "It wasn't about white people? So now its okay then for us White people to have a White people million man march and black muslims [sic] won't mind that? What this was about was getting REVENGE from white rich people, and really all white Americans who aren't Muslims." This passage addresses both the felt unfairness of the March as well as its perceived mean-spiritedness.
3. See Parker and Barreto (2013) and Skocpol and Williamson (2012).
4. Actually, there has long been an appreciation of the shared damage of the master-slave dyad. See Stephen David Ross (1995).
5. The reference to sacrifice is a very important theme pertinent to the issue of class and white identity. In Sennett and Cobb (1972), it is argued that sacrifice is the experience that working-class whites embrace as a condition for pursuing the American Dream. Moreover, these authors argued that the experience of betrayal derives from seeing others—notably welfare recipients—gaining the rewards without enduring the humiliating sacrifices of the American socioeconomic contract. This young man, of course, is giving both a story of this sacrifice and its relation to his felt "entitlement" to "privilege."
6. See Aaron Lazare's (2004) discussion of the non-apology; also see John Hatch's (2006a) review of the book.
7. "Atonement" is required also for "betraying" the whiteness contract (whiteness as property right). That is, whites too must answer for, or be rewarded for, "acting white." Traditionally, we reserve the notion "acting white" for nonwhites whose behavior, in some socially acknowledged way, is "white." The negativity ascribed to the nonwhite individual is that

the behavior—something that can be mimicked—belongs to whites and should not be imitated. When whites are therefore "punished"—or called out by authority figures—for "acting white" (being "politically incorrect") they can feel betrayed. "Atonement," then, pertains to reaffirming the right to be white. In the extreme, this means the reaffirmation of the straight, white, working-class male. This type of atonement is manifest in several sites—and has been documented in scholarly work for the last several decades (Gresson, 1995). The significance of this "breached identity contract" is what leads Michael Kimmel (2013) to call the angry white male the sufferer of an "aggrieved entitlement."

8 Both "cultural turn" and "affective turn" are terms that refer to certain values, beliefs, and practices that are ongoing and evolving in society, but that have only slowly found their way into scholarly discussions of individual agency. In particular, "cultural turn" relates to the increasing awareness of an observation made by Sigmund Freud long ago to the effect that the individual is only partly socializable, that he or she remains able to see, experience, and act differently than social structure and dominant culture dictate (Becker, 1964).

9 This attitude is central to the misunderstanding of the nature of trauma or its ongoing effects in a context that both underplays the past and misrepresents the continuities of "past" bad behavior in the present. For a powerful discussion of this attitude and its implications, see Ahmed (2004).

10 A point needs to be made here regarding the style of writing on race matters where the author is painfully and profoundly aware of the gaze of the audience and thus constructs her/his narrative in a certain way. On this stylistic, Wendy Ryden (Ryden & Marshall, 2012: 29) writes:

> A similar strategy is enacted in my opening narration for this chapter when I tell the two childhood stories involving my father, where I lyrically focus on the setting of doomed romantic ruins (in anticipation of the white melancholia evinced by the later adolescent self) and confess the private painful truth of my white upbringing while assuring the reader with my feelings of shame and dislocation about my desire to break free from white patriarchal rules. I have positioned myself as an innocent child caught up in the racist/ sexist world of adults who must, in order to survive, make the tragic choice of joining the white order and then feel the shame and anger that would motivate me to break free. I further establish ethos with metatextual commentary, which shows a struggling consciousness trying to reconstruct a memory, and by presenting this child as a victim of patriarchy and a sympathetic member of the working class—indeed I even position the father and brother as victims of something beyond their control in that regard. That all of these things are true is beside the point—I am not accusing myself or anyone else of lying, posturing, hoaxing, or having bad intentions in the quest to interrogate whiteness. Instead I am pointing out that the need to confess is understandable as a generic construction and as the need to find an ordering narrative for what is often perceived and represented as trauma—a survivor's narrative to live by, one that involves the reconstitution of a palatable—and empowered—white subject, palatable to both the self and the society to which the self seeks entry. And I am

then asking how useful can such narratives be in combating racism when one of their primary functions necessarily produces a refocusing on the injured white self? And do they, however inadvertently, in their promotion of the rehabilitated white identity, dangerously contribute to the erroneous idea that we currently inhabit a postracial era merely haunted by the gothic whiteness of the past?

This is a powerful pedagogical query. Its ongoing significance is seen, for instance, in the evolving national discourse around Ferguson, Missouri, site of the killing of Michael Brown by policeman Darren Wilson in August 2014. A major issue in this drama was the apparent effort of the chief of police to shape a narrative that demonized the young black male and sanctified the officer who killed him. The question facing social justice and peace activists in this Missouri town is how to work with the emerging, competing narratives.

11 See Alan Mann (2005), who argues that the loss of meaningful concepts of sin and guilt in contemporary society results, in part, in the loss of a belief and experience of doing wrong to others. Moreover, in such a society, one can only be a victim. An interesting review of the book is available at www.opensourcetheology.net/node/1273.

12 Some researchers have found a significant, powerful case of cognitive dissonance in the race discourse of some young white students: a non-tolerance for racist attitudes and a firm commitment to racist institutional practices that maintain "white privilege" (Foster, 2013).

13 There is currently taking place a bizarrely similar drama among "crazed" Jihadists in Nigeria: young African females are being kidnapped and sold for mere pennies as part of a reign of terror by men who claim it is holy and righteous to refuse these youth and women access to education. What I am pointing to is the capacity to do remarkably violent and unjust things while claiming holiness. Of course, the Crusades remain a major exemplar of the duplicity of this type of thinking.

14 Two forces seem to undergird this inferiority complex: public criticism and the lack of resources to change the ascribed racialized identity, according to Maxwell. In this regard, Joe L. Kincheloe (2006: 42–43) wrote: "The South is a site of redemption forged by trauma and pain. The trauma and darkness of the South's racial history obviously has crushed hope and emancipatory impulses. Yet, in the midst of pain derived from such realities, resting at the core of the dialectic of place, emerges the possibility of grace of character gained via anguish and bereavement. The question quickly emerges from such an assertion: does historical liberation require trauma?"

15 The mental health implications of the financial crisis of 2008 as it relates to race matters are taken up in an international context by Meulink-Korf and Noorlander (2012: 159):

> How we reflect upon the world we experience is to a huge degree a matter of perception and definition. An immediate cause for the subject of this article is our perception of the consequences of the worldwide financial-economic crisis that started in 2008. This crisis, and the dominant economy behind it, leaves big debts for the generations to come. It is no wonder that there seems to be much, but vague, concern about 'the future'. Many people are worried about the claims of their work; will they be able to function well when they get older? For youth,

existence may become a matter of competition where they are constantly afraid of failure. 'Scapegoating' seems to be a release, to rid ourselves of our problems. In the short run, this seems effective (for the scapegoaters, not for the scapegoats). In the long run, this creates injustice and often violent revenge.

These are powerful reflections. In Chapter 8, I take up aspects of their argument. They also point out another issue about "natural allies": "One of the problems of globalization is the disconnectedness among people who should be allies by fate but aren't connected in actual solidarity" (2012: 160). How true! Of course, this is an ongoing matter: Marx thought the proletariat would overthrow its oppressors, yet it too often joined them even to its own peril. Yet, even today social commentators and critical scholars pose the question: why? For instance, Michael Kimmel (2013) argues that angry white men ought to be joining forces with minorities because their real oppressors are not the blacks and other minorities, but the corporations, Wall Street, etc.

16 "Tutu and Franklin: A Journey Towards Peace," PBS, February 9, 2001. See www.pbs.org/journeytopeace/thedoc/.
17 Much of the emerging literature on white race discourse ultimately struggles with this tendency. See Foster (2013).
18 See Charles Murray (2013).
19 See Alan Mann (2005).

Racial Pain in the 21st Century

20 Trauma is a technical term associated with the strong, often overpowering, negative emotional effects of violence of various types, including war, sexual abuse, and, increasingly among some clinicians like myself, the effects of racial and other forms of oppression. I am using the term here to include but go beyond Robert Jay Lifton's term "psychological numbing," described later in this chapter.
21 Morris (1991: 139) writes in *The Culture of Pain*:

> The faith was paradoxical because painful punishments served as a common means of discipline and control. Yet slaves might be beaten in the same spirit that horses were broken to the saddle or dogs trained. The slave felt enough pain to permit obedience but not enough pain to expose such methods (to the slaveholders who employed them) as inhuman. The belief thus persisted among white slave-owners and their apologists that blacks and whites lived in a very different relationship to pain. The pain of slaves was considered either wholly trivial or—however inconsistent the logic—richly deserved. Black pain, in the eyes of the white-run Southern culture, had in effect a minimal social existence. White pain, by contrast, cried out for relief.

A more recent perspective is found in research on racial empathy. Jason Silverstein (2013: 1) writes: "The racial empathy gap helps explain disparities in everything from pain management to the criminal justice system. But the problem isn't just that people disregard the pain of black people. It's somehow even worse. The problem is that the pain isn't even felt. An even more critical discussion of this empathy gap is argued in Andre Seewood (2014).

22 T.S. Eliot's best-known drama, based on the murder of the archbishop of Canterbury in 1170.

23 Some argue that Sojourner did not utter these words; rather, it is maintained that these are the sentiments of the white female narrator of Sojourner's speech. The point is nonetheless made: the oppressed person's sense of self and righteous insistence on personhood can be recognized by even a person from the dominant group.

24 This passage is from a *New York Daily News* article, with the headline: "Candidates at Republican primary debate for Idaho governor's race reveal bizarre views" and the caption: "'Blitzkrieg!' Politically incorrect biker gang leader Harley Brown stole the show at the GOP primary husting on Wednesday, revealing his plan to use 'the blood of Jesus' to take their land back from the feds. He also noted that 'taxes are a drag.' Retrieved from http://www.nydailynews.com/news/politics/republican-primary-candidates-idaho-governor-reveal-bizarre-views-article-1.1794585.

25 Deborah Britzman (2000) has paid particular attention to the affective aspect of learning and teaching. Her seminal efforts, in fact, have encouraged important pedagogical and social-justice-oriented reflection. Jessica Heybach-Vivirito (2012: 26), reflecting on the reactions of her student teachers to viewing pictures of American soldiers and their captives at Abu Ghraib, explains "difficult knowledge" in this way:

> When faced with difficult knowledge, many respond with anxieties, defensiveness, or a silent "putting up with" only to quickly discard all disequilibrium when the experience has ceased. In the case of teacher education, in particular, how often do authentic spaces exist to sort out this myriad of emotions that occur both in the content and the process of learning to teach? Britzman (2000) argues that teacher education has yet to "grapple with a theory of knowledge that can analyze fractures, profound social violence, decisions of disregard, and how from such devastations, psychological significance can be made" (p. 200). What happens to the teacher candidate who learns to see the world more honestly? The students in my classroom viewed images of war, torture, and social agony—they witnessed an alternative, critical, and difficult set of visuals. Not only did students witness the pain of the other, but the trauma of being witness to a history they did not recognize as their own.

Whether confronted with the slain babies in Newtown, the Palestinian casualties of Hamas-Israeli violence, the Jews in Auschwitz, or the lynched black men pictured with white picnickers, learning can be difficult and painful. And it can be resisted, resented, and reactionary. Multiculturalism, from this view, is an assault on the "innocent." "Reasoned" pedagogy is part of the assault and must be rethought in order to address the affective. More will be said about this as we proceed.

26 In this exchange, racial pain is evident across gender, class, and race. Interestingly, Dr. Phil titled this and related episodes as "spoiled and entitled." Although the two

episodes I saw focused on minority women and economic eagerness, the ideas of spoilage and entitlement are cogent markers for the issue of racial pain across diversities. It is not surprising, moreover, that "privileged" women and races feel disinherited when traditional minorities pursue a "piece of the action." For additional racial pain discourse, see a protracted discussion of this segment at a black blog site: http://www.topix.com/forum/afam/TF8373AAVVHTG2G3H. Also see Krystale E. Littlejohn (2012) on racial mixed dating.

27 There is considerable pain due to race mixing. As with most things, there are those who celebrate different ethnic groups mingling, dating, marrying, and socially engaging differences. Even then, we may see the underlying vulnerability to racial pain:

> When I started our blog Sweet Fine Day in 2008 to document the start of our new bakery business while raising our 2 young daughters in NYC, I didn't realize that what I was also documenting was the everyday life of our multiracial family. This was told through photographs and stories of the relationships that my children have with their grandparents, the food that we eat, some of the traditions that we celebrate and the questions my children were asking as they became older and more self-aware of racial identity. Readers always responded to these posts and wanted to read more. It inspired me to seek out other families to photograph so they too could tell their stories.
>
> It's a bit hard to imagine that up until 1967, interracial marriages were still illegal in some US states. Since then, the population of biracial children soared 300% in the 1970s and rose accordingly every decade. Multiracial Americans have become the fastest growing demographic group. According to the 2010 Census, more than 9 million Americans identified themselves as multiracial — a jump of 32% in 10 years.
>
> The Mixed Race Project is a glimpse inside the homes and lives of some of these multiracial families. I didn't want to focus on taking traditional portraits—there is certainly enough visual documentation on the beauty of mixed race people out there already — but I felt that portraying families in the context of their homes made a stronger impression of how we live. Mixed race families are, in fact, just like any other American family. While the stories of these particular urban families are just a very small survey and do not represent the experiences of all multiracial families, these photos are candid portraits of what Mixed Race America looks like today. (www.themixedrace-project.com/About-The-Project)

Within these words is a plea, an invitation, to connect. This is an added source of pain for anyone trying to escape already institutionalized images and emotions defining one as alien, strange, deviant. Technologies like the internet allow one to reach out for affirmation and possibly diminish the opportunities for or likelihood of rejection or accusation.

28 There is something powerful but unspoken here. It can and should be spoken because today there is an increased outcry against college rape (Berenson, 2014), Arab and African war rape, and Afghan brutality against women—and yes, the seeming never-ending violence

against women in American society by angry white men. This issue is partly addressed in Chapter 4.

29 Ashley F. Miller (2014) writes:

> My first realization that *Here Comes Honey Boo Boo* had become a complex discursive phenomenon came with the appearance of an image from the show in my social media feeds. In this animated image, June Shannon, the overweight matriarch of the show, careens down a water slide in her bathing suit with joy on her face. This image became popular on Tumblr, with hundreds of reblogs, and spread elsewhere online. Most of the previous discourse I had encountered around the show was negative and focused on how "trashy" the show was, but, in my social media feeds, people praised the show for fat acceptance of "real" bodies and embraced June's joy. There were still negative comments about the show but they were complicated by people claiming identity with her around one of the same signifiers, her weight, that was used to mock her and call her "white trash."

There has always been a "rebellious" feature to the notion of "white trash." The Confederate flag, the "Johnny Yuma" rebel character, even the Nazi swastika are symbols of this rebellious streak. This is why individual minority persons, say bikers, may wear a Nazi helmet or sport a Confederate flag. This sentiment is also why many see "white trash" as symbolic of racialized pain, and identify with, rather than, shy away from them.

The within-group tension associated with the show, and the term "white trash," moreover, points to the complicated origins and social uses of the term. Matt Wray (2013) clarifies:

> The term white trash dates back not to the 1950s but to the 1820s. It arises not in Mississippi or Alabama, but in and around Baltimore, Maryland. The best guess is that it was invented not by whites, but by African Americans (both free and enslaved) as a term of abuse—to disparage local poor whites. Some would have been newly arrived Irish immigrants, others semi-skilled workers drawn to jobs in the post-Revolution building boom. Still other trashy types may have been white servants, waged or indentured, working in the homes and estates of area elites. As it does today, the term registered contempt and disgust, and it suggests sharp hostilities between social groups essentially competing for the same resources—the same jobs, the same opportunities, and even the same marriage partners. ...
>
> But if white trash originated in African American slang, it was middle-class and elite whites who found the term most compelling and useful—and ultimately, this is the crowd that made it part of popular American speech. p. 1

Politics, it has been argued, makes for strange bedfellows. In this instance, poor oppressed blacks are aligned with middle-class whites to hurt poor whites, who, of course, align with other whites to oppress and hurt blacks and other minorities. Thus, racial pain is complicated, weaving in and out of varying identities.

30 I should state here that Bell's concern is to help recovering addicts; accordingly, the level of his analysis and sharpness of his concepts are of less immediate concern than speaking in a style that is accessible to his audience.

Narcissism and White Pain

31 It is important to note that Jews are perennially cast as both allies and enemies. Thus, even though currently Israel enjoys ambiguous support from the Religious Right, she also stands in jeopardy—the "killing of Christ." The great psychologist and Jewish émigré Kurt Lewin once noted how during the early 20th century, American populists groups attacked Jews simultaneously as capitalists and communists. Thus, in the present context, Jews remain an "other" that continue to be attacked as such despite Israel's identification as the precursor of Christianity. This strange alliance parallels, of course, the use of Catholicism as a precursor/supporter of anti-abortionist activism by the Right. Politics indeed makes for strange bedfellows. I take up this tension in the discussion of Israel in Chapter 6.
32 See Tobin Harshaw (2007); Blake Sifton (2010).
33 Justin Hayet (2014) focuses on the Jewish identity crisis and illustrates the scope of possible diaspora dynamics.
34 A most insightful blog discussion on this theme begins:

> Libertarians tend to think of freedom as either a means to an end of maximum utility—e.g., free markets produce the most wealth—or, in a more philosophical sense, in opposition to arbitrary authority—e.g., "Who are you to tell me what to do?" Both views fuel good arguments for less government and more personal autonomy. Yet neither separately, nor both taken together, address the impediments to freedom that have plagued the United States since its founding. Many of the oppressions America has foisted upon its citizens, particularly its black citizens, indeed came from government actors and agents. But a large number of offenses, from petty indignities to incidents of unspeakable violence, have been perpetrated by private individuals, or by government with full approval of its white citizens. I would venture that many, if not most libertarians—like the general American public—haven't come to terms with the widespread, systemic subversion of markets and democracy American racism wreaked on its most marginalized citizens. Consequently, libertarians have concentrated rather myopically on government reform as the sole function of libertarian social critique without taking full reckoning of what markets have failed to correct throughout American history. (Blanks, 2014)

It is worth noting here that libertarians have been frequently seen as less than sympathetic to the concrete issues of racism in American society. This attitude actually accords with the above description by Blanks. But during the recent, ongoing Ferguson, Missouri, racial crisis, none other than presidential hopeful Rand Paul gained national attention as the only Republican leader to speak out on the complicated plight of black males in relation to the criminal justice system:

> The shooting of 18-year-old Michael Brown is an awful tragedy that continues to send shockwaves through the community of Ferguson, Missouri and across the nation. If I had been told to get out of the street as a teenager, there would have been a distinct possibility that I might have smarted off. But, I wouldn't have expected to be shot. The outrage in Ferguson is understandable—though there is never an excuse for rioting or looting. There is a legitimate role for the police to keep the peace, but there should be a difference between a police response and a military response.
>
> The images and scenes we continue to see in Ferguson resemble war more than traditional police action. ...
>
> Given these developments, it is almost impossible for many Americans not to feel like their government is targeting them. Given the racial disparities in our criminal justice system, it is impossible for African-Americans not to feel like their government is particularly targeting them. This is part of the anguish we are seeing in the tragic events outside of St. Louis, Missouri. It is what the citizens of Ferguson feel when there is an unfortunate and heartbreaking shooting like the incident with Michael Brown.
>
> Anyone who thinks that race does not still, even if inadvertently, skew the application of criminal justice in this country is just not paying close enough attention. Our prisons are full of black and brown men and women who are serving inappropriately long and harsh sentences for non-violent mistakes in their youth. (Paul, 2014)

While it has been noted that this kind of talk might be seen as politically motivated, it nonetheless exposes the complicated nature of libertarian thinking.

35 Mailer is here referring to the use of yellow flowers—symbol of both suffragism and the peace movement in which suffragists like Alice Paul were involved. The Yellow Ribbon Movement taken up in Chapter 5 is, I argue, partly rooted in this critical moment described by Mailer.
36 John Hevelin (2008) wrote on Amazon.com's readers' blog:

> It takes a certain kind of man to beat a defenseless, nonviolent woman with a riot baton. America had caught of glimpse of this kind of man during the Civil Rights demonstrations in the 1950s and early 1960s, men willing to use dogs and fire hoses against Negro children, but this was still seen as an aberration of the segregationist, racist South. It would not be until the following year when these men would gain greater visibility at My Lai, raping and butchering innocent women and children. It was white, middle-class America's introduction to the fact that "our boys" could be less than heroes. Mailer speculates at length why so much of the violence was directed at women, but I don't think his explanations suffice. For men who opposed the draft, the support of sympathetic women was crucial. Faced with accusations of being

cowards and homosexuals, the love and compassion of activist women helped young men find the courage to resist induction and face prison and ostracism by society. (For an example, see the poster by Joan Baez and her sisters, "Girls Say Yes to Boys Who Say No".) Mailer says that soldiers at the Pentagon were "taunted" by hippie girls exposing their breasts, but he forgets about the "Summer of Love" and the counterculture affirmation of Life—the hippie girls weren't taunting the soldiers, they were trying to remind them that there is an alternative to violence and death. Make love, not war. And for other women, opposing the war and the draft was a statement of their independence of the patriarchy. And that night, violent men took their revenge on independent women.

37 This is occurring, however, even as many white males continue to rely on society's invitation to hate and demonize the other, particularly black males, in forging a cherished identity by stereotyping them (Fine, 1997; Kimmel, 2013).
38 The biology of racism, like the biology of self-deception, is both cogent and complicated. It is true that there is evidence that humans behave in ways that promote the construction of racist practices. But these tendencies, while human, are not uniformly or universally evolved. This is an important point, one that speaks to the reason some of us do not accept the argument that all forms of human aggression are essentially "morally equivalent." It is perhaps interesting that current American ideology refuses to morally equate Israeli aggression with Arab aggression, or traditional white racism as equivalent to contemporary "black thugism." This is not to say that there are not significant differences in some comparisons. Still, clearly, the power to define "moral equivalency" is a matter of cultural politics, greatly dependent upon *power*. Ironically, perhaps, self-deception seems to be more elemental for it seemingly accounts for the insistence by some to gerrymander agreement on what is and is not morally equivalent.
39 Interestingly, several recent sociologists have taken up the question of class among whites. Beyond the issue of class and white masculinity examined by Michael Kimmel (2013), Charles Castle (2007) has considered class and "white trash," and Armstrong and Hamilton (2013) examine the role of class and gender on the rise of "college sluts."
40 Here it is helpful to recall that President Lyndon Johnson stated that he chose a particular persona upon assuming the presidency in 1963 in order to soothe the anxieties of the nation after Kennedy's assassination. In important ways, the nation's readiness to permit a black man to assume the presidency signals a collective crisis—wars, global recession, and so on. Still, we must recall that the nation (if not the world) shared a historical "stain":

> Therefore, the female, in this order of things, breaks in upon the imagination with a forcefulness that marks both a denial and an "illegitimacy." Because of this peculiar American denial, the black American male embodies the only American community of males which has had the specific occasion to learn who the female is within itself, the infant child who bears the life against the could-be fateful gamble, against the odds of pulverization and murder, including her own. It is the heritage of the mother that the African-American male must regain as an aspect of his own personhood—the power of "yes" to the "female" within.

This different cultural text actually reconfigures, in historically ordained discourse, certain representational potentialities for African-Americans: 1) motherhood as female blood-rite is outraged, is denied, at the very same time that it becomes the founding term of a human and social enactment; 2) *a dual fatherhood is set in motion, comprised of the African father's banished name and body and the captor father's mocking presence*. In this play of paradox, only the female stands in the flesh, both mother and mother-dispossessed. This problematizing of gender places her, in my view, out of the traditional symbolics of female gender, and it is our task to make a place for this different social subject. In doing so, we are less interested in joining the ranks of gendered femaleness than gaining the insurgent ground as female social subject. Actually claiming the monstrosity (of a female with the potential to "name"), which her culture imposes in blindness, "Sapphire" might rewrite after all a radically different text for a female empowerment. (Spillers, 1987: 80; italics added).

I have quoted Hortense Spillers at length here because she powerfully frames aspects of the broad cultural discourse currently playing out around black male youth killings by white males. I highlighted the passage: *a dual fatherhood is set in motion, comprised of the African father's banished name and body and the captor father's mocking presence*. Who's your daddy?!! This is a question/statement most of us would prefer to downplay in daily intercourse; it's too painful and pregnant with possibilities. Yet, the black male has traditionally been denied the persona of "father of the nation," and this is precisely what President Obama embodies by virtue of the office. The image is not easy to ingest, especially for many Americans. The vulnerable white male, confronting a changing world order is thus "invited" to see his father figure in Barack Obama. Is this too much cultural work for the nation? Perhaps.

41 It is well worth noting that many of President Obama's conservative critics like to contrast his style of leadership (or lack thereof) to Ronald Reagan and Bill Clinton. Although race will not typically be raised in such moments, one cannot help sense the implicit message: he's black. Yet, it is equally clear that a "true" black Alpha male would not have been available for elevation to the presidency at this point in time. Ironically, both his biracial and African ancestries are pertinent qualifiers to his being a suitable candidate for the office.

42 Recently, in an interview for *The New Yorker* (Topaz, 2014), President Obama made this surprising (to the media pundits) comment: "I think that, for both Joe [Biden] and for Hillary [Clinton], they've already accomplished an awful lot in their lives.... The question is, do they, at this phase in their lives, want to go through the pretty undignifying process of running all over again." This comment may be read as a less-than-subtle statement of not only the campaign process, but also the humiliation that may attend life in the presidency. To the normal vulnerabilities of this office, another factor affecting President Obama has to do with the underexamined significance of a black man in the United States presidency. Racial gains notwithstanding, the *affective* factor must include attention to the place of the "black father" as (non) authority figure in American cultural life. As David Marriott (1998: 134–135) notes: "What could it mean to identify with a father who is socially degraded?" In this question, he partly confronts the emasculation embedded in the slavery experience and its relevance to "the present situation of thinking about the black family in terms of

trauma, mourning, and memory in America: namely, the epoch of slavery and its catastrophic effects on black kinship ties between mothers and daughters as well as between fathers and sons. Under slaveholding forms of white paternity, the black male was subject to a paternal law which effectively removed him from paternal rights and filial ties...."

Of course, the insistence that the past is the past—forget it!—is belied by both what we know of posttraumatic syndromes and the ongoing retraumatization daily life imposes on all socially oppressed persons, including whites, in American society. The injunction "things are better now" has a degree of truth and significance, but it fails to address so much more that needs to be said and done. Of course, from the Supreme Court to the person on the street, this degree of truth constitutes a whole—or as much of a whole as there is going to be. In the face of this, there can be expected the same "irrational behavior" as seen in Gaza where Hamas seems to be crazed. This is a familiar pattern, but one that we so often find must be meditated by self-deceiving discourses and performances.

43 Michael Rogin (1996) describes Jewish adoption of blackface historically as a vehicle for countering their group vulnerability; in this context, he also discusses authors familiar with Jewish and black emasculation. An especially powerful examination of black male emasculation is found in David Marriott's (1998) psychopolitical analysis of the "absent black father." Pertinent to the present analysis, Marriott notes the emotional consequence of a father whose authority is aborted by racist violence such as lynching:

> For the black boy, such racism intrudes in terms of an inequality of fathering, whose symptom is that of the black father's social and symbolic destitution, and whose trauma is the breach of black male narcissism by racialized cultural fantasy and white paternal ownership. In such quasi-foundational moments the black father is an object to be mourned and guiltily disavowed precisely because his destitution represents the son's own self-injury.... This means, in effect, that the black son (and daughter) is presented with a paternity unnameable as such and one mediated by the history of a white paternal injunction; the aporia of whose identification—"be like me and do not be like me"—becomes transformed into "be lynched and do not be lynched" (1998: 134).

44 This point has a special significance when we understand that not only, nor primarily, whites employed blackface. In a most revealing study, the Jewish presence in blackface has been shown in a manner both humanizing and sympathetic to a fuller understanding of the "middleman" minority role assumed by certain white ethnics and Asians:

> Slave owners like Jefferson—including his own father-in-law and nephew, and likely Jefferson himself—produced children whose condition followed that of their slave mothers. Claiming that it was the black desire for white that required the separation of the races, Jefferson inverted a white male desire for black. In his day, that desire took the forms of labor and sex, chattel slavery and miscegenation. As expressive performance—in the form of blackface minstrelsy—white possession of black would help produce a second, cultural, Declaration of Independence during the Age of Jackson.

> Nonetheless, there was always a contradiction between the logic of natural rights and white supremacy. Almost from the moment of its inception in the late nineteenth century, the immigrant Yiddish press began to protest against the denial of equality to African Americans. "POGROM IN PENNSYLVANIA" is the headline Alfred Kazin remembers above a 1920s *Jewish Daily Forward* report of a lynching. Lynchings and race riots, pogroms in the promised land, were, in the oft-repeated phrase, "a stain of shame on the American flag." Consciously invoking the Declaration of Independence, the phrase unknowingly reproached Jefferson for blaming the "stain" on victimized black bodies. Many Jews who were entering the melting pot had their own stain of shame, however—burnt cork—for by the turn of the twentieth century Jewish entertainers were the major blackface performers. And their stain is the link between Jefferson's Declaration and blackface Ted Danson's *Made in America*. Jews in the entertainment business—vaudeville, Tin Pan Alley, Hollywood—were creating mass culture for the immigrant, industrial age. (Rogin, 1996: 15)

The point is that blackface today rehearses an earlier period of identity fluidity in the United States, when diverse groups were finding their way, trying to become "American." Today, with a black president and an increasingly large and active minority voting bloc—one that helped elect a black president—there is renewed threat. And the language has become eerily reminiscent of the past: the recent influx of undocumented, parentless colored children from Central America at the southern borders, notably Texas, has led to Governor Rick Perry calling out the National Guard and declaring the nation under attack, invasion.

45 The complicated social underpinnings of this practice for diverse groups should be noted here; I have seen both "down and out" older urban blacks and whites do this as well as black females identifying as "butch." See Stephens and Phillips (2003); also an article on black lesbian identity at http://en.wikipedia.org/wiki/Butch_and_femme.

46 See www.blackyouthproject.com/2013/10/white-woman-who-posted-racist-halloween-picture-fired/.

47 Eric Lott presented a discussion some years back on "Why White Boys Sing the Blues: Lott Explores 'Racial Cross-Dressing.'" Although the presentation is cited, it precise content is no longer available. Here is the review as I presented it in the first edition:

> Eric Lott, Professor of English at U. Va., spoke to a packed hall at Swem last Thursday about "Racial Cross-Dressing and the Construction of American Whiteness." He treated antebellum minstrel shows, Elvis, Mick Jagger, Vanilla Ice and Lee Atwater as one continuous phenomenon, which is significant not as racism or exploitation, but rather for what it reveals about whites' notions of whiteness and blackness. To Lott, these "blackface" performances show a white male "fascination" with the color line, a self-conscious desire to assume a black identity temporarily. Lott described this sentiment as natural, not because white Americans somehow lack the earthy, casual virtues they attribute to blacks, but rather because they define certain painful and pleasurable experiences as black in

order to maintain an artificially "respectable" white self-image. Lott pointed out that minstrel shows began in the 1840s, when women's Victorian standards of morality were becoming increasingly powerful in white society. White males reacted, like Huck Finn, by seeking opportunities "to be Negroes together."

48 Indeed, the "identity crisis" is ongoing for all in society. And as implicit in the notion of "spoiled identity," all who share in this spoilage may be expected to be seen pushing against one or the other aspect of the devalued features.

49 Perhaps this will turn out to be the subjective meaning of "postracial": the possibility of the *other*'s racialized self-display as a symbolic swipe at the essentialized white man. This is a theme that has already gained currency in the so-called affective turn.

50 To be sure, whites largely recovered from the economic downturn in comparison with minorities. Still, the repeated violation of "entitled" whites exposes the nature of the game. Vocal and highly visible critics like Senator Elizabeth Warren largely fail to dent much of the counter-narrative—capitalism has done more for more people than anything else in human history—but this "failure" serves to stir up the anxieties and sense of helplessness that helps create the Tea Party and Occupy Wall Street.

51 This idea is not new. In October 2014, the first female head of the Secret Service was fired, partly because of the numerous failures attributed to the agency before and during her watch. Pundits did not miss the fact that she was only brought in to deal with a long-standing cultural issue in the Service after so many white men had failed. It might be also noted that she was chosen, it has been argued, over a black male—another minority—for "visual effect." This "glass cliff" effect is not accepted by some, however; see for example Allapundit (2014, October 2), "Fired Secret Service director's strategy for the agency: 'We need to be more like Disney World.'" Retrieved 10/8/14 from http://hotair.com/archives/2014/10/02/fired-secret-service-directors-strategy-for-the-agency-we-need-to-be-more-like-disney-world/

52 It is perhaps apparent that Obama's various labels—king, foreigner, Kenyan, savior who walks on water, and so forth—are related to this role. I believe that the repeated expressions of disappointment in Obama, running parallel to the mounting evidence of internal sabotage of his efforts by Congress, etc., point to the self-deception in our lives.

White Studies and Racial Pain in the Academy

53 This episode comes to mind today as Ferguson, Missouri, continues to reel from the result of an unarmed black male killed by a white policeman. In particular, I am reminded here of "white privilege" and how it plays out: Senator Rand Paul, for instance, noted that as a young man he might have talked back to the policeman who shot Michael Brown without fearing death for disrespect or talking back. Rob saw race matters much as Rand Paul in this instance; and I was the beneficiary. To be sure, there are and have always been many like Rob; the critical observation here is that "white privilege" creates the necessity for the "non-chosen" to count on the kindness and availability of "guardian angels."

54 The issue of moral equivalence is a complex one: who gets to say that things, good or bad, are of equal weight? Who gets to say that the U.S. support of Israel is morally superior to Iran's support of Syria? This is an ongoing dialectic, a difficult conundrum. The position I have taken here reflects my feeling and interpretation of my experience. I don't have to prove this to someone else's satisfaction when they are operating from a different set of experiences. I mention it here because one reviewer (Hatch, 2006b) of the first edition of *America's Atonement* felt I did not defend my reluctance to grant the moral equivalency many whites desire. I think the more important matter is the latent insistence/desire that people, say victims, have to "take it and like it." On the contrary, I may have to take it, but I don't have to like it or agree with it. This is true for all of us to a degree.

Mediating White Pain

55 By "late capitalism," I mean the current economic malaise and structural crises affecting the nation and the world; notably, the "jobless recovery" from the 2008 recession, and the widening income gap between the rich and the poor, and the increasingly large number of so-called middle-class people joining the ranks of the poor. This is an extension of the earlier meanings given to the term. See, for example, Fredric Jameson (1997).

56 It is noteworthy that my designation of this figure as representing Asian/Latina/Native women differs significantly from how others have emphasized it. According to Glenna Goodacre's official site:

> The kneeling figure has been called "the heart and soul" of the piece because so many vets see themselves in her. She stares at any [sic] empty helmet, her posture reflecting her despair, frustrations, and all the horrors of war. The soldier's face is half-covered by a bandage, creating an anonymous figure with which veterans can identify. Even though he is wounded, he will live. I want this to be a monument for the living (www.vietnamwomensmemorial.org/memorial.php).

57 It is important to note that recent cinema scholarship has identified an even more powerful expression of recovery cinema in the so-called magical Negro films. In a major study on this form of film, Matthew Hughey (2009: 543) writes:

> Recent research on African American media representations describes a trend of progressive, antiracist film production. Specifically, "magical negro" films (cinema highlighting lower-class, uneducated, and magical black characters who transform disheveled, uncultured, or broken white characters into competent people) have garnered both popular and critical acclaim.

To be sure, not everyone will share Hughey's reading of either the existence of such a film form or the range of films he includes in it: *The Matrix trilogy*, *The Green Mile, and The Legend of Badger*. Still, it seems suggestive that the recovery/redemption film form I identified seems to be continued in films that, Hughey argues:

... constitute "cinethetic racism"—a synthesis of overt manifestations of racial cooperation and egalitarianism with latent expressions of white normativity and anti-black stereotypes. "Magical Negro" films thus function to marginalize black agency, empower normalized and hegemonic forms of whiteness, and glorify powerful black characters so long as they are placed in racially subservient positions. The narratives of these films thereby subversively reaffirm the racial status quo and relations of domination by echoing the changing and mystified forms of contemporary racism rather than serving as evidence of racial progress or a decline in the significance of race.

58 According to Wikipedia, "Al Jazeera America (AJAM) is an American basic cable and satellite news television channel that is owned by the Qatar royal family's Al Jazeera Media Network. The channel, which was launched on August 20, 2013, directly competes with CNN, HLN, MSNBC, Fox News Channel...."

Multiculturalism and Social Justice

59 There are many ideas covered in this book that build on assumptions greatly contested by various scholars. I don't intend to engage these debates with the present audience. However, I do want to mention, when appropriate, some of the background thinking pertinent to my discussion. For instance, on the agency-social structure theme, Nash (2001: 79), writes on the cultural turn and the role of culture in the identities-interactions processes,

> Probably the most influential example of a theory based on the idea that culture is constitutive of social relations and identities is the structuration theory of Anthony Giddens. This is despite the fact that Giddens rarely uses the term 'culture' and never uses it in this general sense. His main concern is, of course, the relation between structure and agency. Drawing on ethnomethodology, he argues that social structures are reproduced in the everyday practices of social actors who are knowledgeable about the practices in which they are engaged. As Giddens sees it, while structures provide the resources for social action, they are only realized through the skilled interactions of social actors (Giddens, 1984). It is in so far as knowledge is seen as an aspect of culture that Giddens's theory of structuration is a theory of the cultural constitution of social relations and identities.

One important implication of this thinking is that social justice educators can continue to expect to encounter students who resist being forced to talk about "institutional racism" or to acknowledge that their own subjectivities are complicit with the ongoing renewal of oppression. I take up additional aspects of this issue in Chapters 7 and 8.

60 The classic discussion of master-slave has routinely inferred a shared fate, a complementary bond. This discussion focused largely on the fact that both master and slave lose some

portion of their humanity in the enslavement process. Later thinkers, such as Gramsci, seem to retain this complementary bond. Hence Gramsci defines "hegemony" as collusion between the more and less powerful around some shared investment, even though the less powerful are effectively enabling and abetting their own domination.

61 I suggested earlier that a certain degree of pain and loss are inevitable in a truly multicultural teacher education curriculum. Denial of this necessity is itself illustrative of the inevitable social pain (racial, gender, class) that accompanies growth. For example, black middle-class teachers in urban schools have been often observed to be ineffective with lower-class, urban black pupils (Anyon, 1995; Yeo 1997a, b). For them, as for white teachers, important social structural and institutional factors often underlie their failures (Shujaa, 1996; Weiner, 1993).

62 On aversive racism, see Gaertner and Dovidio (1986); Crisp and Turner, (2007); and Kovel (1970).

Toward a Psychopedagogy of Healing

63 Again, we see the dialectic at work. This surrender to and identification with the other has been called "identification with the aggressor" when undertaken by the less powerful in relation to the more powerful. Self-hate is a popular way of identifying this behavior that seems conciliatory (Gresson, 1982). The recent suggestion that whites calling for the elimination of "whiteness" are self-hating rather than "non-racist" is related to this "identification with the aggressor" theme. Thus we see that healing is dialectic and only partly fulfills the "wholeness" metaphor it implies.

64 The great "positivist, scientific" experiment, of which the academy is an example, has a fraudulent feature: it assumes that what goes on in the classroom has a motive different from that of public propaganda. But this is untrue when we try to implement a "human science" with both moral authority and technical competence. The "logic" of the classroom is an assumption that we can "air" our differences without damaging our selves. This also is not true. In Chapter 6, I discussed the work of Stanton Wortham (1994), who describes how the use of certain examples in the classroom can lead to extraclass partisanship. That is, what goes on in the classroom can deepen rather than loosen problematic perspectives and values. Of course, more recent work on pedagogies of anti-racism and non-oppression (Butin, 2001) pushes the point even further.

65 *Fiddler on the Roof* was a 1964 Broadway musical. It was based on Sholom Aleichem's short story "Tevye and His Daughters" and is set in 1905 in Anatevka, a small Jewish village in Russia. A dairyman, Tevye, is the central character as he attempts to manage a changing world, one in which his three daughters are making choices that challenge Jewish tradition. The term "fiddler on a roof" is a metaphor for Jews living in diaspora, seeking to balance the plight of a pariah people. Tevye says that life for the Jew is very much like a fiddler trying to keep his balance on a roof, and that this balancing act is possible only because of "tradition." He says: "Because of tradition, each Jew knows who he is and what God expects him to do."

66 In a review of Kimmel's book, Hanna Rosin (2013) notes:

Kimmel makes a convincing case that this shift has to do with a sense of aggrieved entitlement, showing how these boys spent a lot of time fending off insults to their masculinity from the "jockocracy" that ruled their schools. But Kimmel also strains a little too hard for a tidy sociological explanation, arguing mightily (and pointlessly) against the idea that these attackers were singularly deranged or psychotic. Like the suicide bombers he compares them to, one can be both uniquely psychologically vulnerable, a total outlier, and yet tuned in to a broader cultural trend.

Her point is cogent, but Kimmel needed to make the point for a specific reason: it gets to the uncomfortable link between psyche and society, the individual and the group. Traditionally, the term "sociopath" was used to describe disturbed behavior/thinking *shared* by a collectivity. The term "psychopath" was reserved for "isolated," presumably wholly individual psychopathology. Today, the terms are often used in mystifying ways that miss the fact that so much violent behavior in this country seems uniquely *tuned into* certain cultural values around privacy, First Amendment rights, and guns as essential parts of the "whole" person. Kimmel wants, correctly I feel, to forcefully short-circuit our temptation to engage in psychological reductionism, insisting that everything is psychological (read as an "outlier" event).

67 For an elaboration of Bob Lokey's perspective, see The History Commons website run by the Center for Grassroots Oversight ("CGO"). http://www.historycommons.org/entity.jsp?entity=bob_lokey_1.

68 For one of the most profound statements on this topic as it applies to contemporary society, see Sagan (1974).

Postscript

69 The Dr. Phil episode can be found at www.drphil.com/shows/show/1328. For a useful and balanced take on the new focus on narcissism, see Elspeth Reeve's (2013), "Every Every Every Generation Has Been the Me Me Me Generation." Reeve notes, for example,

> Millennials are the "ME ME ME GENERATION," writes Joel Stein for the cover of *Time* magazine, which is apparently a marked departure from the Baby Boomers, who were the plain old "Me Generation" (one me, no caps) and who created the "Me Decade" in the 1970s, and who coined the phrase, "But enough about me… what do you think about me?" in the 1980s when they were raising the next narcissists, Generation X. Sometimes you get the sense that these magazines' cultural writers have very little experience with the entire American culture, and prefer to make their grand analyses based on what people they know in the gentrified parts of cities like New York and Los Angeles were talking about at brunch last weekend. The type of young person that magazine writers come across most frequently are magazine interns. Because the media industry is high-status, but, at least early on, very low pay in a very expensive city, it attracts a lot of rich kids. Entitled,

arrogant, spoiled, preening — those are the alleged signature traits of Millennials, as diagnosed by countless magazine writers. Those traits curiously align perfectly with the signature traits of a rich kid. Have you seen your intern on Rich Kids of Instagram? If so, he or she is probably not the best guide to crafting the composite personality of a generation that fought three wars for you.

I have quoted this passage in order to assign a "flavor" to the class discourse that partly joins the race discourse as they converge in segments of the "me generation." In *The Armies of the Night*, Norman Mailer was similarly attuned to the confluence of social justice activism and the various segmentations of society, i.e., white, black, young, old, female, privileged, and poor.

70 Kincheloe was keenly alert to the psychological in the political, the subjective in the structural. He was, in fact, helpful in encouraging me, a clinical psychologist, to re-commit myself to the emerging field of critical psychology. For a useful essay on the issue of "identity trauma," see Derek Hook (2005).

71 The National Service movement in the U.S. is alive and strong. According to a 2007 *Time* magazine article, "A Time to Serve: The Case for National Service" by Rick Stengel, more than 61 million Americans dedicated 8.1 billion hours to volunteering in 2006, and the nation's volunteer rate has increased by more than 6 percentage points since 1989. Volunteer and civic engagement have not been at this level since the 1970s. Why are so many people volunteering? One explanation, according to the article, is that mostly young people in the U.S. believe that the government is broken. America's youth see a healthcare system that doesn't function, and an education system that fails to teach basic reading and writing skills. Also, since 9/11 many Americans have been motivated to do community service in the U.S. as hundreds of thousands have been deployed overseas to fight two wars. (Stengel, 2007)

REFERENCES

ABC News. (2013, January 16). 'I Call It Natural': What One White Separatist Claims Would Make a Better America. *ABC News Nightline.* http://abcnews.go.com/US/white-separatist-claims-make-america/story?id=21466004

Abdul-Jabbar, K. (2014). Opinion: The Coming Race War Won't Be About Race. *Time.* Retrieved 8/22/14, from http://time.com/3132635/ferguson-coming-race-war-class-warfare/

Adams, M., & Bell., L.A. (2007). *Teaching for Diversity and Social Justice.* New York: Routledge.

Adelekan, A. (2000). The Million Man March: Christian Appropriation and Transformation, *Koinonia* XII (1): 1–32.

Ahmed, S. 2004. *The Cultural Politics of Emotion.* New York: Routledge.

Allison, C.B. (1995). *Present and Past: Essays for Teachers in the History of Education.* New York: Peter Lang.

Allmendinger, B. (1992). *The Cowboy: Representations of Labor in an American Work Culture.* New York: Oxford University Press.

Alridge, D.P. (2001). Redefining and Refining Scholarship for the Academy: Standing on the Shoulders of Our Elders and Giving Credence to African-American Voice and Agency. In L. Jones (Ed.), *Retaining African Americans in Higher Education: Challenging Paradigms for Retaining Students, Faculty & Administrators.* Sterling, Va.: Stylus.

American Psychological Association. (2008). Children and Trauma. Retrieved 10/8/14 from http://www.apa.org/pi/families/resources/children-trauma-update.aspx

Anderson, D., & Zuercher, B. (2001). *Letters Across the Divide: Two Friends Explore Racism, Friendship, and Faith.* Grand Rapids, Mich.: Baker Books.

Ansell, A.E. (1997). *New Right New Racism: Race and Reaction in the United States and Britain*. New York: New York University.

Anyon, J. (1995, Fall). Race, Social Class, and Educational Reform in an Inner-City School. *Teachers College Record* 97: 69–94.

Apple, M.W. (1993). Constructing the "Other": Rightist Reconstruction of Common Sense. In C. McCarthy & W. Crichlow (Eds.), *Race Identity and Representation in Education*. New York: Routledge.

Apple, M.W. (1998). Foreword. In. J.L. Kincheloe et al. (Eds.), *White Reign: Deploying Whiteness in America*. New York: St. Martin's Press.

Armbruster, B. (2014, April 4). New York Times' David Brooks Says Obama Has 'A Manhood Problem in the Middle East.' *Think Progress*. Retrieved 9/14/14, from http://thinkprogress.org/world/2014/04/20/3428792/brooks-obama-manhood-problem-middle-east/

Armstrong, E.A., & Hamilton, L.T. (2013). *Paying for the Party: How College Maintains Inequality*. Cambridge, Mass.: Harvard University Press.

Aronowitz, S. (1992). *The Politics of Identity: Class, Culture, Social Movements*. New York: Routledge.

Asante, M. (1988). *Afrocentricity*. New Brunswick, N.J.: African World Press.

Asante, M.K., & Atwater, D. (1986, Spring). The Rhetorical Condition as Symbolic Structure in Discourse. *Communication Quarterly* 34: 170–177.

Associated Press. (2001, November 8). Miss. Students Expelled From Frat. Retrieved 9/24/14, from https://groups.yahoo.com/neo/groups/fraternalnews/conversations/topics/284?var=1

Atkinson, W. (2001, August 1). Bringing Diversity to White Men. *HR Magazine* 46(9). Retrieved 9/14/14, from http://www.shrm.org/publications/hrmagazine/editorialcontent/pages/0901atkinson.aspx

Bakhtin, M.M. (1986). *The Dialogic Imagination*. Austin: University of Texas Press.

Baldwin, D. 2005. Black Belts and Ivory Towers: The Place of Race in U.S. Social Thought, 1892–1948. In Boston College Editorial Collective (Ed.), *Culture, Power, and History: Studies in Critical Sociology* (pp. 309–364). Boston: Brill.

Banks, J.A. (Ed.). 1981. *Education in the 80s: Multiethnic Education*. Washington D.C.: National Education Association.

Banks, J.A., & Banks, C.A. (Eds.). (1989). *Multicultural Education: Issues and Perspectives*. Boston: Allyn & Bacon.

Barnes, R. (2013, June 25). Supreme Court Stops Use of Key Part of Voting Rights Act. Retrieved 9/14/14, from http://www.washingtonpost.com/politics/supreme-court-stops-use-of-key-part-of-voting-rights-act/2013/06/25/26888528-dda5-11e2-b197-f248b21f94c4_story.html

Barthes, R. (1972). *Mythologies*. Trans. Annette Lavers. London: Granada.

Becker, E. (1964). *The Birth and Death of Meaning: A Perspective in Psychiatry and Anthropology*. New York: Free Press of Glencoe.

Bederman, G. (1995). *Manliness and Civilization: A Cultural History of Gender and Race in the United States, 1880–1917*. Chicago: University of Chicago Press.

Beer, S.H. (1996). Ragged Individualism: A Review: *Democracy's Discontent: America in Search of a Public Philosophy*, by Michael J. Sandel. *The Wilson Quarterly* 20(3): 89–91.

Beers, W. (1992). *Women and Sacrifice: Male Narcissism and the Psychology of Religion*. Detroit: Wayne State University.

Bell, P., & Peterson, D. (1992). *Cultural Pain and African Americans: Unspoken Issues in Early Recovery*. Center City, Minn.: Hazelden.

Bell, T.H. (1986). Education Policy Development in the Reagan Administration. *Phi Delta Kappan* 67(3): 487–493.

Bennett, C.I. (1990). *Comprehensive Multicultural Education Theory and Practice*. Boston: Allyn & Bacon.

Berenson, T. (2014, June 27). 1 in 5: Debating the Most Controversial Sexual Assault Statistic. *Time*. Retrieved 9/21/14, from http://time.com/2934500/1-in-5%E2%80%82campus-sexual-assault-statistic/

Berger-Knorr, A.L. (1997). Unlearning Privilege: Gender, Race, and Class in Reading Methods. Ph.D. diss., Pennsylvania State University.

Berlak, A.C. (1990). Experiencing Teaching: Viewing and Re-viewing Education. Paper presented at the annual meeting of the American Education Research Association, Boston.

Berlak, A.C. (1996). Teaching Stories: Viewing a Cultural Diversity Course through the Lens of Narrative. *Theory into Practice* 35: 93–101.

Berliner, M.S., & Hull, G. (1996). Diversity and Multiculturalism. Marina del Rey, Calif.: Ayn Rand Institute/Center for the Advancement of Objectivism.

Bernstein, B. (1971). On the classification and framing of educational knowledge. In MFD Young (ed). *Knowledge and Control: New Directions for the Sociology of Education*. London: Collier Macmillan, 47–69.

Berrin, D. (2011, October 28). The Madoff Mea Culpas: Repenting Sins Not Your Own. Retrieved 9/14/2014, from http://www.jewishjournal.com/hollywoodjew/item/the_madoff_mea_culpas_repenting_sins_not_your_own_20111028

Bettelheim, B. (1962). *Symbolic Wounds: Puberty Rites and the Envious Male*. 2nd ed. New York: Collier.

Black Issues. (2001, November 22). Fraternities Suspended for Wearing Racially Offensive Costumes. *Diverse*. Retrieved 9/24/14, from http://diverseeducation.com/article/1768/

Blanck, G., & Blanck, R. (1979). *Ego Psychology II*. New York: Columbia University Press.

Blanks, J. (2014, June 27). Looking Back to Look Forward: Blacks, Liberty, and the State. Retrieved 9/14/14, from http://www.libertarianism.org/columns/looking-back-look-forward-blacks-liberty-state

Blee, K.M. (1991). *Women of the Klan: Racism and Gender in the 1920s*. Berkeley and Los Angeles: University of California Press.

Blum, D.E. (1991, May 29). Faculty Notes: White Male Professor Sues Black Women's College. *The Chronicle of Higher Education*, A12.

Bollin, G.G., & Finkel, J. (1995). White Racial Identity as a Barrier to Understanding Diversity: A Study of Preservice Teachers. *Equity & Excellence in Education* 28(1): 25–30.

Boothby, N. (2008). Political Violence and Development: An Ecological Approach to Children in War Zones. *Child and Adolescent Psychiatric Clinics of North America* 17(3): 497–514.

Boothby, N., Strang, A, & Wessells, M. (Eds). (2006). *A World Turned Upside Down: Social Ecologies of Children and War*. West Hartford, Conn.: Kumarian Press.

Bork, R.H. (1996). *Slouching Towards Gomorrah: Modern Liberalism and American Decline*. New York: Regan Books.

Boszormenyi-Nagy, I., & Spark, G.M. (1973). *Invisible Loyalties: Reciprocity in Intergenerational Family Therapy*. Oxford, England: Harper & Row.

Bowen, M. (1985). *Family Therapy in Clinical Practice*. New York: Jason Aronson.

Breen, M.D. (1965). Culture and Schizophrenia: A Study of Negro and Jewish Schizophrenics. Ph.D. diss., Brandeis University.

Briscoe, D. (2006). *He Was Ours: Lyndon Baines Johnson and American Identity*. Unpublished Masters, thesis Baylor University. Retrieved 8/18/14, from https://beardocs.baylor.edu.

Britzman, D.P. (1991). The Terrible Problem of Knowing Thyself: Toward a Post-Structural Account of Teacher Identity. *Journal of Curriculum Theorizing* 9: 22–46.

Britzman, D. (2000). If the Story Cannot End: Deferred Action, Ambivalence, and Difficult Knowledge. In R. I. Simon, S. Rosenberg, & C. Eppert (Eds.), *Between Hope and Despair: Pedagogy and the Remembrance of Historical Trauma* (pp. 27–58). Lanham, Md.: Rowman & Littlefield.

Britzman, D., & Pitt, A.J. (1996). Pedagogy and Transference: Casting the Past of Learning into the Presence of Teaching. *Theory into Practice* 35: 117–123.

Brown, N.O. (1966). *Love's Body*. New York: Vintage Books.

Brown, R.H. (1987). *A Poetic for Sociology: Toward a Logic of Discovery for the Human Sciences*. Chicago: University of Chicago Press.

Brundage, W.F., (Ed.). (2011). *Beyond Blackface: African Americans and the Creation of American Popular Culture, 1890–1930*. Chapel Hill: University of North Carolina Press.

Butin, D. (2001). If This Is Resistance I Would Hate to See Domination: Retrieving Foucault's Notion of Resistance within Educational Research. *Educational Studies* 32: 157–176.

Capehart, J. (2014). Rep. Mo Brooks Talks "War on Whites" as the GOP Loses the Battle for Votes. Retrieved 9/14/14 from http://www.washingtonpost.com/blogs/post-partisan/wp/2014/08/04/rep-mo-brooks-talks-war-on-whites-as-the-gop-loses-the-battle-for-votes/

Carboda, D.W. (Ed.). (1999). *Black Men on Race, Gender, and Sexuality: A Critical Reader*. New York: New York University Press.

Carby, H. (1993). Encoding White Resentment: Grand Canyon—A Narrative for Our Times. In C. McCarthy & W. Crichlow (Eds.), *Race Identity and Representation in Education* (pp. 236–247). New York: Routledge.

Carroll, L. (1984). *Alice's Adventures in Wonderland & Through the Looking-Glass*. New York: Bantam Classics.

Castle, C. (2007). 'White Trash' Identities, Media, and Popular Culture: Redefining White Hegemony in Contemporary American Culture. *Cultural Landscapes* 1.1: 3–33.

Catano, J.V. (2001). *Ragged Dicks: Masculinity, Steel, and the Rhetoric of the Self-Made Man*. Carbondale: Southern Illinois University Press.

Chang, J. (1998, December 15). Up Identity Creek. Retrieved 10/8/14 from http://colorlines.com/archives/1998/12/up_identity_creek.html

Chapman, D., Deans, B., & Nelson, C. (2003, March 30). War in the Gulf: Special Coverage: U.S. Trails in Battle for World Opinion. *Atlanta Journal-Constitution*.

Chapman, T.K., & Hobbel, N. (Eds). (2010). *Social Justice Pedagogy Across the Curriculum: The Practice of Freedom*. New York: Routledge.

Charles, J.C. (2013). *Abandoning the Black Hero: Sympathy and Privacy in the Postwar African American White-Life Novel*. New Brunswick, N.J.: Rutgers University Press.

Chennault, R.E. (1998). Race, Reagan, Education, and Cinema: Hollywood Films About Schools in the 1980s and 1990s. PhD diss., Pennsylvania State University.

Chennault, R.E. (2006). *Hollywood Films About Schools: Where Race, Politics, and Education Intersect*. New York: Palgrave.

Coates, T. (2008, August 7). White Racism White Resentment. Retrieved 9/15/14, http://www.theatlantic.com/entertainment/archive/2008/08/white-racism-vs-white-resentment/5593/

Cockburn, C. (2007). *From Where We Stand: War, Women's Activism and Feminist Analysis*. London: Zed Books.

Cohen, M. (2014). Expert Says Anti-Semitism 'Part and Parcel of European Culture'. Retrieved 10/9/14 from http://www.israelnationalnews.com/News/News.aspx/178788#.VDbY8uffJdA

Colby, T. (2014). The Massive Liberal Failure on Race. Part 2, Affirmative Action Doesn't Work. It Never Did. It's Time for a New Solution. Retrieved 9/15/2014 from http://www.slate.com/articles/life/history/features/2014/the_liberal_failure_on_race/affirmative_action_it_s_time_for_liberals_to_admit_it_isn_t_working.html

Constantinides, D. (2011). Redefining Ourselves: Navigating Life with a "Spoiled Identity." Damon Constantinides. Retrieved 9/15/14, from http://www.therapistdamon.com/2011/05/redefining-ourselves-navigating-spoiled-identities/

Cooper, B. (2014). The Politics of Black Women's Hair: Why It's Seen With Skepticism—and a Need to Discipline. Retrieved 9/15/14, from http://www.salon.com/2014/04/22/the_politics_of_my_black_hair_why_its_seen_with_skepticism_and_a_need_to_discipline/

Corliss, R. (1994, August 1.) The World According to Gump. *Time* 1:52–54.

Corti, C. (2002). Finding Myself in My Students: A Step Toward Transforming Social Dynamics in the Classroom. In L. Darling-Hammond, J. French, & S.P. Garcia-Lopez (Eds.), *Learning to Teach for Social Justice* (pp. 52–65). New York: Teachers College Press.

Crisp, R.J. & Turner, R.N. (2007). *Essential Social Psychology*. London: Sage.

Crosby, F.J. (1997). Confessions of an Affirmative Action Mama. In M. Fine, L. Weis, L.C. Powell, & L. Mun Wong (Eds.), *Off White: Readings on Race, Power, and Society* (pp. 179–186). New York: Routledge.

Cruz, R. (2014). A Racial Justice Bucket List for 2014. *Colorlines*. Retrieved 9/15/14 from http://colorlines.com/archives/2014/01/a_racial_justice_bucket_list_for_2014.html

Dalton, H.L. (1996). *Racial Healing: Confronting the Fear Between Blacks and Whites*. New York: Doubleday/Anchor.

Daly, M. (1978). *Gyn/Ecology: The Metaethics of Radical Feminism*. Boston: Beacon Press.

Daniele, G. (2014). Jerusalem Link Feminism between Palestine and Israel. Retrieved 10/10/14 from http://www.ingenere.it/en/articles/jerusalem-link-feminism-between-palestine-and-israel

Darling-Hammond, L., French, J., & Garcia-Lopez, S.P. (Eds.). (2002). *Learning to Teach for Social Justice*. New York: Teachers College Press.

DeSousa, M.A. (1984). Symbolic Action and Pretended Insight: The Ayatollah Khomeini in U.S. Editorial Cartoons. In M. J. Medhurst & T.W. Benson (Eds.), *Rhetorical Dimensions in Media: A Critical Casebook* (pp. 204–230). Dubuque, Iowa: Kendall/Hunt.

Dickar, M. (1999). Teaching in Our Underwear: The Liabilities of Whiteness in the Multi-Racial Classroom. *William and Mary College Researcher* 11: 1–22.

Dilg, M. (1999). *Race and Culture in the Classroom: Teaching and Learning Through Multicultural Education*. New York: Teachers College Press.

Dillard, C.B. (1996). Engaging Pedagogy: Writing and Reflecting in Multicultural Teacher Education. *Teaching Education* 8: 13–21.

Dinnerstein, D. (1976). *The Mermaid and the Minotaur: Sexual Arrangements and Human Malaise*. New York: HarperCollins.

Doane, J., & Hodges, D. (1987). *Nostalgia and Sexual Difference: The Resistance to Contemporary Feminism*. New York: Methuen.

Douglas, D. (2013, December 3). Why Are Black Women Punished for Having Natural Hair? Retrieved 9/15/14 from http://www.alternet.org/civil-liberties/stop-policing-my-hair-when-black-girls-shine-we-shine

Douglass, F. (1963). *Narrative of the Life of Frederick Douglass, an American Slave*. Garden City, N.Y.: Doubleday & Co.

Dr. Phil (2010). Spoiled and Entitled. Drphil.com. Retrieved 9/715/14, from http://www.drphil.com/shows/archive/?date=2010-11

D'Souza, D. (1995). *The End of Racism: Principles for a Multicultural Society*. New York: Free Press.

Dumas, R.G. (1980). Dilemmas of Black Females in Leadership. In L. Rodgers-Rose (Ed.), *The Black Woman* (pp. 203–215). Beverly Hills, Calif.: Sage.

Durante, T. (2013). Jessica Lynch: Former POW Reflects on Iraq War. Retrieved 9/15/14, from http://www.dailymail.co.uk/news/article-2302339/Jessica-Lynch-Former-POW-reflects-Iraq-War-10-years-rescue.html

Dyer, A. (2013). Million White Man March. Retrieved 9/15/14, from http://spirituwellness.wordpress.com/2013/10/16/million-white-man-march/

Dziech, B.W. (1995, January). Coping With the Alienation of White Male Students. *Chronicle of Higher Education*: B1–B2.

Ellsworth, E. (1989). Why Doesn't This Feel Empowering? Working Through the Repressive Myth of Critical Pedagogy. *Harvard Education Review* 59: 297–324.

Ellsworth, E. (2005). *Places of Learning: Media, Architecture, Pedagogy*. New York: Routledge.

Emmet, A.H. (2003). *Our Sisters' Promised Land: Women, Politics and Israeli-Palestinian Coexistence*. Ann Arbor: University of Michigan Press.

Enoch, M. (2014, January 26). Goyim Privilege? *The Right Stuff*. Retrieved 9/20/14, from http://therightstuff.biz/2014/01/26/goyim-privilege/

Faludi, S. (1992). *Backlash: The Undeclared War Against American Women.* New York: Anchor Books.

Fanon, F. (1967). *Black Skin, White Masks.* New York: Grove Press.

Fanon, F. (1968). *The Wretched of the Earth.* New York: Grove Press.

Feagin, J.R., & Hernán, V. 2001. *White Racism: The Basics.* (2nd ed.). New York: Routledge.

Fine, M. (1997). Witnessing White. In M. Fine, L. Weis, L.C. Powell, & L. Mun Wong (Eds.), *Off White: Readings on Race, Power, and Society* (pp. 57–65). New York: Routledge.

Fiske, J. (1994). *Media Matters: Everyday Culture and Political Change.* Minneapolis: University of Minnesota Press.

Fiske, J. (1993). *Power Plays, Power Works.* New York: Verso.

Fortgang, T. (2014, April 2). Checking My Privilege: Character as the Basis of Privilege. *The Princeton Tory.* Retrieved 9/20/14, from http://theprincetontory.com/main/checking-my-privilege-character-as-the-basis-of-privilege/

Foster, J.D. (2013). *White Race Discourse: Preserving Racial Privilege in a Post-Racial Society.* Lanham, Md.: Lexington Books.

Foster, P. (1990). *Policy and Practice in Multicultural and Anti-Racist Education.* London: Routledge.

Foucault, M. (1977). *Discipline and Punishment: The Birth of the Prison.* New York: Vintage Books.

Foucault, M. (1978). *The History of Sexuality. Vol. 1, An Introduction.* New York: Vintage Books.

Frankenberg, R. (1993). *White Women, Race Matters: The Social Construction of Whiteness.* Minneapolis: University of Minnesota Press.

Freire, P. 1970. *Pedagogy of the Oppressed.* Trans. M.B. Ramos. New York: Continuum.

Freire, P. (1994). *Pedagogy of Hope.* New York: Continuum.

Freire, P. et al. (Eds.). (1997). *Mentoring the Mentor: A Critical Dialogue with Paulo Freire.* New York: Peter Lang.

French, J. (2002). Idealism Meets Reality. In L. Darling-Hammond, J. French, & S.P. Garcia-Lopez (Eds.), *Learning to Teach for Social Justice* (pp. 59–70). New York: Teachers College Press.

Freud, S. (1930/1961). *Civilization and Its Discontents.* Trans. & ed., J. Strachey. New York: W.W. Norton.

Friedman, M. (2014, April). Here Comes a Lot of Judgment: Honey Boo Boo as a Site of Reclamation and Resistance. *The Journal of Popular Television* 2(1): 77–95.

Fulton, S. (2014). Read This Letter From Trayvon Martin's Mother to Michael Brown's Family. Retrieved 8/18/14, http://time.com/3136685/travyon-sybrina-fulton-ferguson/

Gaertner, S.L., & Dovidio, J.F. (1986). The aversive form of racism. In J. F. Dovidio & S. L. Gaertner, (Eds.), *Prejudice, discrimination, and racism* (pp. 61–89). Orlando, FL: Academic Press.

Gardner, H. (1993). *Multiple Intelligences.* New York: Basic Books.

Gardner, S., Dean, C., & McKaig, D. (1989). Responding to Difference in the Classroom: The Politics of Knowledge, Class, and Sexuality. *Sociology of Education* 62: 64–74.

Gaylin, W. (1984). *The Rage Within: Anger in Modern Life.* New York: Simon & Schuster.

Gee, J. (1992). *The Social Mind*. Westport, Conn.: Greenwood Press.

Genovese, E.D., & Fox-Genovese, E. (2011). *Fatal Self-Deception: Slaveholding Paternalism in the Old South*. Cambridge: Cambridge University Press.

George H.W. Bush Inaugural Addresses of the Presidents of the United States. Friday, January 20, 1989http://www.bartleby.com/124/pres63.html.

George-Kanentiio, D. (No date). What Is Atonement? Reflections on Atonement. Retrieved 9/15/2014, from http://reflectionsonatonement.com/atonement/what-is-atonement/

Gerzon, M. (1982). *A Choice of Heroes: The Changing Face of American Manhood*. Boston: Houghton Mifflin.

Gibbs, N. (1995). The EQ Factor: New Brain Research Suggests That Emotions, Not I.Q., May Be the True Measure of Human Intelligence. *Time* 146(1): 60–69.

Giddens, A. (1984). *The Constitution of Society: Outline of the Theory of Structuration*. Berkeley, CA: University of California Press.

Gilbert, S.M. (1989). Soldier's Heart: Literary Men, Literary Women, and the Great War. In E. Showalter (Ed.), *Speaking of Gender*. New York: Routledge.

Gilman, Robert. (1983/1996). 200 Years of Identity Crises: A Cultural History of American Moods and Self-images in 8 Big Steps. Retrieved 7/11/14, from http://www.context.org/iclib/ic03/gilman2/

Ginsburg, M.B. (1988). *Contradictions in Teacher Education and Society: A Critical Analysis*. New York: Falmer Press.

Giroux, H.A. (1995). Who Writes in a Cultural Studies Class: Or, Where Is the Pedagogy? In K. Fitts & A.W. France (Eds.), *Left Margins: Cultural Studies and Composition Pedagogy* (pp. 3–16). Albany: SUNY Press.

Giroux, H.A.. (1997). *Pedagogy and the Politics of Hope: Theory, Culture, and Schooling*. Boulder, Colo.: Westview Press.

Giroux, H.A. (1998). *Channel Surfing: Racism, the Media and the Destruction of Today's Youth*. New York: St. Martin's Press.

Gitlin, T. (1993/1987). *The Sixties: Years of Hope, Days of Rage*. New York: Bantam.

Goffman, E. (1959). *The Presentation of Self in Everyday Life*. New York: Bantam Books.

Goffman, E. (1963). *Stigma: Notes on the Management of Spoiled Identity*. Englewood Cliffs, N.J.: Prentice-Hall.

Goldberg, D.T. (Ed.). (1990). *Anatomy of Racism*. Minneapolis: University of Minnesota Press.

Goleman, D. (1995). *Emotional Intelligence*. New York: Bantam Books.

Goodman, J. (1988.) Constructing a Practical Philosophy of Teaching: A Study of Pre-service Teachers' Professional Perspectives. *Teaching and Teacher Education*, 4121–137.

Goodwin, L. (1997). Multicultural Stories: Preservice Teachers' Conceptions of and Responses to Issues of Diversity. *Urban Education* 32:117–145.

Gordon, M.M. (1975). Toward a General Theory of Racial and Ethnic Relations. In N. Glazer & D.P. Moynihan (Eds.), *Ethnicity: Theory and Experience* (pp. 84–110). Cambridge, Mass.: Harvard University Press.

Gore, J. (1993). *The Struggle for Pedagogies: Critical Feminist Discourses as Regimes of Truth*. New York: Routledge.

Grant, C. (1994). Best Practices in Teacher Preparation for Urban Schools: Lessons from the Multicultural Teacher Education Literature. *Action in Teacher Education* 16: 1–18.

Gresson, A.D. III. (1976). Non-negotiables and Academic Activist. *Black Sociologist* 5:4–6.

Gresson, A.D. III. (1977). Minority Epistemology and the Rhetoric of Creation. *Philosophy and Rhetoric* 10: 244–262.

Gresson, A.D. III. (1978). Phenomenology and the Rhetoric of Identification: A Neglected Dimension of Coalition Communication. *Communication Quarterly* 26:14–23.

Gresson, A.D. III. (1982). *The Dialectics of Betrayal: Sacrifice, Violation and the Oppressed.* Norwood, N.J.: Ablex.

Gresson, A.D. III. (1987). Transitional Metaphors and the Political Psychology of Identity Maintenance. In R. E. Haskell, (Ed.), *Cognition and Symbolic Structures: The Psychology of Metaphoric Transformations* (pp. 163–187). Norwood, N.J.: Ablex.

Gresson, A.D. III. (1989). Equity and Excellence Among Ethnic Groups: Toward the Transcendence of Self-Deception. In D. G. Carter & J.J. Harris III (Eds.), *Excellence and Equity—A Reassessment* (pp. 103–115). Bloomington: Indiana University Press.

Gresson, A.D. III. (1990). *Black Amnesia.* Baltimore: Transformation Books.

Gresson, A.D. III. (1995). *The Recovery of Race in America.* Minneapolis: University of Minnesota Press.

Gresson, A.D. III. (1996a). Coda: Relational Justice and the Cognitive Elite. In J. L. Kincheloe, S.R. Steinberg, & A.D. Gresson III (Eds.), *Measured Lies: The Bell Curve Examined* (pp. 433–440). New York: St. Martin's Press.

Gresson, A.D. III. (1996b). Postmodern America and the Multiculturalism Crisis: Reading Forrest Gump as the "Call Back to Whiteness." *Taboo* 2: 11–33.

Gresson, A.D. III. (1997). Identity, Class, and Teacher Education: The Persistence of "Class Effects" in the Classroom. *Review of Education/Pedagogy/Cultural Studies* 19: 348–356.

Gresson, A.D. III. (2000). Preface. In N. M. Rodriguez & L. Villaverde (Eds.), *Dismantling White Privilege: Pedagogy, Politics, and Whiteness.* New York: Peter Lang.

Gresson, A.D. III. (2008). *Race and Education Primer.* New York: Peter Lang.

Gussow, Adam. (2006). Where Is the Love? Racial Wounds, Racial Healing, and Blues Communities. *Southern Cultures* 12(4): 33–54.

Hacker, Barbara. (1996). http://centerhealingracism.org/notes-from-barbara-hackers-inspiring-journey-of-healing-racism/

Haines, H.W. (1986). What Kind of War? An Analysis of the Vietnam Veterans Memorial. *Critical Studies in Mass Communication* 3: 1–17.

Halim, A.A. (2012). The 21st Century Jim Crow. Retrieved 9/16/14, from http://chicagomonitor.com/2012/11/the-21st-century-jim-crow/

Halperin, M., & Heilemann, J. (2013). *Double Down: Game Change 2012.* New York: Penguin Books.

Hamad, R. (2014). The Hypocrisy of a Black Miss Israel. Retrieved 9/17/14, from http://www.dailylife.com.au/news-and-views/dl-opinion/the-hypocrisy-of-a-black-miss-israel-20130401-2h2qr.html

Hamber, B. & Wilson, R. (1999, January 27–29). Symbolic Closure Through Memory, Reparation and Revenge in Post-conflict Societies. Paper presented at the Traumatic Stress in South Africa Conference, Johannesburg, South Africa. Retrieved 7/7/14, from http://www.csvr.org.za/

Harper, H., & Cavenaugh, S. (1994). Lady Bountiful: The White Woman Teacher in Multicultural Education. *Women's Education* 11: 27–33.

Harris, J.D. (1986). The Rhetoric of the Vietnam Veterans Memorial: An Analysis of News Magazine and Network Television News Coverage. M.A. Thesis, Pennsylvania State University.

Harshaw, T. (2007). America's Identity Crisis. Retrieved 6/12/14, from http://opinionator.blogs.nytimes.com/

Haskell, R.E. (Ed.) (1987). *Cognition and Symbolic Structures: The Psychology of Metaphoric Transformations*. Norwood, N.J.: Ablex.

Haskell, R.E. (1993). *Adult-Child Research and Experience: Personal and Professional Legacies of a Dysfunctional, Co-Dependent Family*. Norwood, N.J.: Ablex.

Hatch, J.B. (2003). Reconciliation: Building a Bridge from Complicity to Coherence in the Rhetoric of Race Relations. *Rhetoric & Public Affairs* 6: 737–764.

Hatch, J.B. (2006a). On Apology: A Review. *Rhetoric & Public Affairs* 9(3): 524–528.

Hatch, J.B. (2006b). America's Atonement: Racial Pain, Recovery Rhetoric, and the Pedagogy of Healing: A Review. *Rhetoric & Public Affairs* 9(3): 528–531.

Hatch, J.B. (2009a). *Race and Reconciliation: Redressing Wounds of Injustice*. Lanham, Md.: Rowman & Littlefield.

Hatch, J.B. (2009b). Dialogic Rhetoric in *Letters Across the Divide*: A Dance of (Good) Faith Toward Racial Reconciliation. *Rhetoric & Public Affairs* 12(4): 485–532.

Hayet, J. (2014, April). A Lurking Identity Crisis Beneath Pollard Debate. *Jewish Times*. Retrieved 9/17/14, from http://jewishtimes.com/21997/a-lurking-identity-crisis-beneath-pollard-debate/#.VBmCN_ldWSo

Hedley, M. (1994, December 1). The Presentation of Gendered Conflict in Popular Movies: Affective Stereotypes, Cultural Sentiments, and Men's Motivations. *Sex Roles*: 721–740.

Heinemann, L. (1986). *Paco's Story*. New York: Farrar, Straus & Giroux.

Herf, J. (1987). *Reactionary Modernism: Technology, Culture, and Politics in Weimar and the Third Reich*. New York: Cambridge University Press.

Herrnstein, R.J., & Murray, C. (1994). *The Bell Curve*. New York: Simon & Schuster.

Hevelin, J. (2008). Read the History, Skip the Novel (I was There). Customer review of Norman Mailer's *The Armies of the Night*. Retrieved 9/17/14, from http://www.amazon.com/The-Armies-Night-History-Novel/product-reviews/0452272793/

Heybach-Vivirito, J. (2012). Learning to Feel What We See: Critical Aesthetics and "Difficult Knowledge" in an Age of War. *Critical Questions in Education* 3(1): 23–34. Retrieved 9/17/14, from http://education.missouristate.edu/assets/AcadEd/Critical_Questionsfinal.pdf

Hill, A. (1984). The Carter Campaign in Retrospect: Decoding the Cartoons. In M. J. Medhurst & T.W. Benson (Eds.), *Rhetorical Dimensions in Media: A Critical Casebook* (pp. 182–203). Dubuque, Iowa: Kendall/Hunt.

Hinson, H. (1994, August). Forrest Gump, Our National Folk Zero. *Washington Post* 14: G1. Retrieved 9/28/14, from http://www.washingtonpost.com/wp-srv/style/longterm/movies/review97/fforrestgump1.htm

Holder, E. (2014, August 20). Excerpts of Attorney General Eric Holder's Remarks at a Community College. Retrieved 9/17/14, from http://www.justice.gov/iso/opa/ag/speeches/2014/ag-speech-140820.html

Homans, P. (1989). *The Ability to Mourn: Disillusionment and the Social Origins of Psychoanalysis.* Chicago: University of Chicago Press.

Hook, D. (2005). *A Critical Psychology of the Postcolonial* [online]. London: LSE Research. Retrieved 9/17/14, from http://eprints.lse.ac.uk/950/1/Criticalpsychology.pdf

hooks, b. (1994). *Teaching to Transgress: Education as the Practice of Freedom.* New York: Routledge.

Horrocks, R. (1994). *Masculinity in Crisis: Myths, Fantasies and Realities.* New York: St. Martin's Press.

Horrocks, R. (1995). *Male Myths and Icons: Masculinity in Popular Culture.* New York: St. Martin's Press.

Howerton, K. (2014). White Privilege Doesn't Mean What You Think It Means. Retrieved 9/20/14, from http://www.huffingtonpost.com/kristen-howerton/white-privilege-doesnt-me_b_5296914.html

Hughey, M.W. (2009). Cinethetic Racism: White Redemption and Black Stereotypes in "Magical Negro" Films. *Social Problems* 56(3): 543–577.

Hull, G., Scott, P. & Smith, B. (1982). *All of the Women Are White, All of the Blacks Are Men, But Some of Us Are Brave: Black Women's Studies.* Old Westbury, N.Y.: Feminist Press.

Ignatieff, M. (1998). *The Warrior's Honor: Ethnic War and the Modern Conscience.* London: Chatto & Windus.

Ikard, D. (2013). *Blinded by the Whites: Why Race Still Matters in 21st-Century America.* Bloomington: Indiana University Press.

Ipsaro, A.J. (1997). *White Men, Women and Minorities in the Changing Work Force.* Denver, Colo.: Meridian Associates.

Isaacs, H.R. (1975). *Idols of the Tribe: Group Identity and Political Change.* New York: Harper & Row.

Jacoby, R. (1975). *Social Amnesia: A Critique of Contemporary Psychology from Adler to Laing.* Boston: Beacon Press.

Jaher, F.C. (1994). *A Scapegoat in the New Wilderness: The Origins and Rise of Anti-Semitism in America.* Chicago: University of Illinois Press.

Jameson, F. (1997). Culture and Finance Capitalism. *Critical Inquiry* 24: 246–265.

Jeffords, S. (1989). *The Remasculinization of America: Gender and the Vietnam War.* Bloomington: Indiana University Press.

Jeffords, S. (1994). *Hard Bodies: Hollywood Masculinity in the Reagan Era*. New Brunswick, N.J.: Rutgers University Press.

Jewel, K.S. (1993). *From Mammy to Miss America and Beyond: Images and the Shaping of U.S. Social Policy*. New York: Routledge.

Jurecic, A. (2012). *Illness as Narrative*. Pittsburgh: University of Pittsburgh Press.

Kadish, D.Y. (1991). *Politicizing Gender: Narrative Strategies in the Aftermath of the French Revolution*. New Brunswick, N.J.: Rutgers University Press.

Kanpol, B. (1997). Critical Pedagogy for Beginning Teachers: The Movement from Despair to Hope. *Journal of Critical Pedagogy*. Retrieved 9/3/14, from http://www.lib.umwestern.edu/pub/jcp/issueII-1/kanpol.html

Kanpol, B., & Brady, J. (1998). Teacher Education and the Multicultural Dilemma: A "Critical" Thinking Response. *Journal of Critical Pedagogy* 1: 1–17.

Katz, J. (2003). Advertising and the Construction of Violent White Masculinity: From Eminem to Clinique for Men. In G. Dine & J.M. Humez (Eds.), *Gender, Race, and Class in Media: A Text-Reader* (2nd ed.) (pp. 349–358). Thousand Oaks, Calif.: Sage.

Kauffmann, S. (1994, August 8). Different. *New Republic*: 28–29.

Kazin, A. (1968, May 8). The Trouble He's Seen. Review of *The Armies of the Night* by Norman Mailer. Retrieved 7/14/14, from http://www.nytimes.com/books/97/05/04/reviews/mailer-armies.html

Kellner, D. (1991). Reading Images Critically: Toward a Postmodern Pedagogy. In H. Giroux (Ed.), *Postmodernism, Feminism, and Cultural Politics: Redrawing Educational Boundaries* (pp. 60–82). Albany: State University of New York.

Kennedy, Randy, & Cardwell, Diane. (2003, March 27). "New Yorkers' Sharp Divisions Fall Roughly on Racial Lines," *New York Times*, B15.

Kilbourne, J. (2000). *Can't Buy My Love: How Advertising Changes the Way We Think and Feel*. New York: Simon & Schuster.

Kimmel, M.S. (2013). *Angry White Men: American Masculinity at the End of an Era*. New York: National Books.

Kimmel, M.S., & Messner, M.A. (Eds.). (2001). *Men's Lives* (5th ed.). Boston: Allyn & Bacon.

Kincheloe, J.L. (1999). The Struggle to Define and Reinvent Whiteness: A Pedagogical Analysis. *College Literature* 26: 162–195.

Kincheloe, J.L. (2006). The Southern Place and Racial Politics: Southernification, Romanticization, and the Recovery of White Supremacy. *Souls: A Critical Journal of Black Politics, Culture, and Society* 8(1): 27–46.

Kincheloe, J.L., & Staley, G. (1983, July). Vietnam to Central America: A Case of Educational Failure. *USA Today*: 30–32.

Kincheloe, J.L., & Steinberg, S.R. (1997). *Changing Multiculturalism*. Philadelphia: Open University Press.

Kincheloe, J.L., & Steinberg, S.R. (2000). Constructing a Pedagogy of Whiteness for Angry White Students. In N. M. Rodriguez & L. Villaverde (Eds.), *Dismantling White Privilege: Pedagogy, Politics, and Whiteness* (pp. 178–197). New York: Peter Lang.

Kincheloe, J.L., & Steinberg, S.R. (2004). *The Miseducation of the West: How Schools and the Media Distort Our Understanding of the Islamic world.* Westport, Conn.: Praeger.

Kincheloe, J.L., Steinberg, S.R., Rodriguez, N., & Chennault, R. (1998). *White Reign: Deploying Whiteness in America.* New York: St. Martin's Press.

King, D.W. (2008). *African Americans and the Culture of Pain.* Charlottesville: University of Virginia.

Kirk, H.D. (1964). *Shared Fate: A Theory of Adoption and Mental Health.* New York: Free Press.

Kirk, R. (1993). *America's British Culture.* New Brunswick, N.J.: Transaction.

Klumpp, J.F., & Holliman, T.A. (1979). Debunking the Resignation of Earl Butz: Sacrificing an Official Racist. *Quarterly Journal of Speech* 65: 1–11.

Knight, S. (2014, July 15). Violence Outside Paris Synagogue Falsely Attributed to Anti-Semitism. Retrieved July 16, 2014, from http://mondoweiss.net/2014/07/synagogue-attributed-semitism.html

Kovel, J. (1970). *White Racism: A Psychohistory.* New York: Vintage.

Kozol, J. (1991). *Savage Inequalities: Children in America's Schools.* New York: Harper Perennial.

Kumashiro, K.K. (2001). "Posts" Perspectives on Anti-oppressive Education in Social Studies, English, Mathematics, and Science Classrooms. *Educational Researcher* 30: 3–12.

Kumashiro, K.K. (2002, April). Three Readings of D. Butin's Commentary. Retrieved 9/3/14, from http:// www.AERA/net. 31

Lacy, M.G., & Ono, K.A. (Eds.). (2011). *Critical Rhetorics of Race.* New York: New York University Press.

Ladson-Billings, G. (1996). Silences as Weapons: Challenges of a Black Professor Teaching White Students. *Theory into Practice* 35: 79–85.

Laingen, L.B. (1992). *Yellow Ribbon: The Secret Journal of Bruce Laingen.* New York: Brassey's.

Lane, A. (1994, July 25). The current cinema. *The New Yorker,* p. 79.

Langer, S.K. (1984). *Mind: An Essay on Human Feeling.* Baltimore: Johns Hopkins University Press.

Lather, P. (1990). Staying Dumb? Student Resistance to Liberatory Curriculum. Paper presented at the annual meeting of the American Educational Research Association, Boston.

Lazare, A. (2004). *On Apology.* New York: Oxford University Press.

Levin, B. et al. (1989). *Who Built America? Working People and the Nation's Economy, Politics and Culture.* New York: Pantheon Books.

Levisohn, J.A. (2012, July 8). Pursuing the Pedagogy of Peoplehood: More than Mifgash. *Jewish Philanthropy.* Retrieved October 4, 2014, from http://ejewishphilanthropy.com/pursuing-the-pedagogy-of-peoplehood-more-than-mifgash/

Lewis, John. (2014, August 1). Speech on House Floor on Vote to Deport Dreamers. (Shown on MSNBC).

Lifton, R.J. (1999, November). Evil, the Self, and Survival: A Conversation. Retrieved 9/3/14, from http://globetrotter.berkeley.edu/people/Lifton/lifton-con3.html

Littlejohn, K.E. (2012). Racing "mixed race" in the 21st century. Retrieved 6/8/14, from http://gender.stanford.edu/news/2012/racing-%E2%80%9Cmixed-race%E2%80%9D-21st-century

Loewy, R.F. (2008, December 19). Bernard Madoff: Jewish Perspectives. Retrieved 6/29/14, from http://trymyrabbi.com/sermons/bernard-madoff-jewish-perspectives

Lorde, A. (1979). The Great American Disease. *The Black Scholar* 10: 16–20.

Lubiano, W. (2013). Affect and Rearticulating the Racial "Un-sayables." *Cultural Anthropology* 20(3): 540–543.

Lugg, C.A. (1996). *For God and Country: Conservatism and American School Policy*. New York: Peter Lang.

Lupton, B. (1995, December). A Time for Healing. *The Gospel and Our Culture* 7(4): 1–2. Retrieved 9/28/14, from http://www.gocn.org/files/074-newsletter.PDF#page=1

Lyman, P. (1981). The Politics of Anger: On Silence, Ressentiment, and Political Speech. *Socialist Review* 57: 55–74.

Lynch, F.R. (1989). *Invisible Victims: White Males and the Crisis of Affirmative Action*. Westport, Conn.: Greenwood Press.

Lynch, F. (1997). *The Diversity Machine: The Drive to Change the White Male Workplace*. New York: Free Press.

Macedo, D., & Steinberg, S. (Eds.) (2007). *Media Literacy: A Reader*. New York: Peter Lang.

Mailer, N. (1968). *The Armies of the Night: History as a Novel, The Novel as History*. New York: Plume/Penguin Books.

Mangan, K.S. (1995, February 3). *Chronicle of Higher Education*, A18

Mann, A. (2005). *Atonement for a "Sinless" Society: Engaging with an Emerging Culture (Faith in an Emerging Culture)*. Crown Hill, Milton Keynes: Paternoster.

Marable, M. (1980). *From the Grassroots: Social and Political Essays Toward Afro-American Liberation*. Boston: South End Press.

Marriott, D. (1998). Black Paternity and Social Spectatorship. In J. Campbell & J. Harbord, *Psycho-politics and Cultural Desire* (pp. 124–142). London: UCL Press.

Matt Heimbach (ABC News, 2014). http://abcnews.go.com/Nightline/video/young-racist-white-separatist-movements-rising-star-21579344

Mattingly, C. (2002). *Appropriate[ing] Dress: Women's Rhetorical Style in Nineteenth-Century America*. Carbondale: Southern Illinois University Press.

Maxwell, A. (2014). *The Indicted South: Public Criticism, Southern Inferiority, and the Politics of Whiteness*. Chapel Hill: University of North Carolina Press.

Mazurek, R. (1999). Freirean Pedagogy, Cultural Studies, and the Initiation of Students to Academic Discourse. In C. Pari & I. Shor, *Critical Literacy in Action: Writing Words, Changing Worlds* (pp. 208–322). New York: Boynton/Cook Heinemann.

McCall, A.L. (1994). Rejoicing and Despairing: Dealing with Feminist Pedagogy in Teacher Education. *Teaching Education* 6: 59–69.

McDonough, K. (2013, December 2). Three White College Students File Racial Discrimination Complaint Against Professor Over Lesson on Structural Racism. Retrieved 9/18/14 from http://www.salon.com/2013/12/02/three_white_college_students_file_racial_discrimination_complaint_against_professor_over_lesson_on_structural_racism/

McGarry, S.H. (1994, July). Editor's Perspective. *Southwest Art*: 56.

McIntosh, P. (1993). White Privilege: Unpacking the Invisible Knapsack. In V. Cyrus (Ed.), *Experiencing Race, Class, and Gender in the United States* (pp. 209–213). Mountain View, Calif.: Mayfield.

McIntyre, A. (1997). *Making Meaning of Whiteness: Exploring Racial Identity with White Teachers*. Albany: SUNY Press.

McKee, Guian. Editor. (2010). Presidential Recordings of Lyndon B. Johnson Digital Edition: the War on Poverty, 1964. (University of Virginia Press, Rotunda Electronic Imprint). Retrieved 10/10/14 from http://presidentialrecordings.rotunda.upress.virginia.edu/essays?series=WarOnPoverty.

McKee, J. (1993). *Sociology and the Race Problem: The Failure of a Perspective*. Urbana: University of Illinois Press.

McKenzie, Mia. (2014, February 3). 4 Ways to Push Back Against Your Privilege. Black Girl Dangerous. Retrieved 10/8/14 from http://www.blackgirldangerous.org/2014/02/4-ways-push-back-privilege/

McNabb, A. (2014, February 5). White-Presenting Black Girl Dangerously Self-Detonates. *The Right Stuff*. Retrieved 9/20/14, from http://therightstuff.biz/2014/02/05/white-presenting-black-girl-dangerously-self-detonates/

McNamara, R. (1995, April 23). The Final Briefing. *Pittsburgh Post-Gazette*: F1, 4.

McPhail, M.L. (1991). Complicity: The Theory of Negative Difference. *The Howard Journal of Communications* 3(1, 2): 1–13.

McPhail, M.L. (2004). A Question of Character: Re(-)Signing the Racial Contract. *Rhetoric & Public Affairs* 7: 391–405.

McPhail, M.L. (2009). The Politics of Complicity Revisited: Race, Rhetoric and the (Im)possibility of Reconciliation. *Rhetoric & Public Affairs* 12(1): 107–123.

McWilliams, C. (1948). *A Mask for Privilege: Anti-Semitism in America*. Boston: Little, Brown.

McWhorter, J. (2000). *Losing the Race: Self-sabotage in Black America*. New York: Free Press.

McWhorter, J. (2013, August 22). Don't Ignore Race in Christopher Lane's Murder. *Time*. Retrieved 9/17/14, from http://ideas.time.com/2013/08/22/viewpoint-dont-ignore-race-in-christopher-lanes-murder/

Melosh, B. (1991). *Engendering Culture: Manhood and Womanhood in New Deal Public Art and Theater*. Washington, D.C.: Smithsonian Institution Press.

Meulink-Korf, H., & Noorlander, W. (2012). Resourcing Trust in a Fragmenting World: The Social-Economic Dimension and Relational Ethics in the Track of Boszormenyi-Nagy. *European Journal of Mental Health* 7:157–183. Retrieved 7/30/14, from http://ejmh.eu/mellekletek/2012_2_157_Meulink_Noorlander.pdf

Miller, A.F. (2014). Introduction to Redneckaissance: Honey Boo Boo, Tumblr, and the Stereotype of Poor White Trash. Retrieved 6/12/14, from http://freethoughtblogs.com/ashleymiller/2014/05/13/redneckaissance-honey-boo-boo-tumblr-and-the-stereotype-of-poor-white-trash/#_ftn1

Mills, C.W. (1959). *The Sociological Imagination*. New York: Oxford University Press.

Mishara A. (1995). Narrative and psychotherapy—The phenomenology of healing. *American Journal of Psychotherapy* 49(2): 180–195.

Mitchell, K. (2014). How the Army Ostracized Me for My Own Hair. Retrieved 9/18/14, from http://thinkprogress.org/culture/2014/04/24/3429934/army-regulations-hair/

Modleski, T. (1991). *Feminism Without Women: Culture and Criticism in a "Postfeminist" Age.* New York: Routledge.

Morris, D.B. (1991). *The Culture of Pain.* Berkeley: University of California Press.

Muharrar, M. 1998, September 1). Media Blackface: "Racial Profiling" in News Reporting. *FAIR: Fairness and Accuracy in Reporting.* Retrieved 9/26/14, from http://fair.org/extra-online-articles/media-blackface/

Murray, C. (2013). *Coming Apart: The State of White America, 1960–2010.* New York: Crown.

Nakayama, T.K., & Krizek, R.L. (1995). Whiteness: A Strategic Rhetoric. *Quarterly Journal of Speech* 81: 291–309.

Nash, K. (2001). The "Cultural Turn" in Social Theory: Towards a Theory of Cultural Politics. *Sociology* 35(12): 77–92.

Nash, R.J. (1995). A Neo-Essentialist Diatribe Against American Education. *Journal of Teacher Education* 46: 150–155.

Nieburg, H.L. (1973). *Culture Storm: Politics and the Ritual Order.* New York: St. Martin's Press.

Nietzsche, F.W. (1966). *Beyond Good and Evil: Prelude to a Philosophy of the Future.* New York: Viking Press.

Niggermania.net. Nigger Jokes! Retrieved 4/24/2014, from http://niggermania.com/

Norman, E. (1990). *Women at War: The Story of Fifty Military Nurses Who Served in Vietnam.* Philadelphia: University of Pennsylvania Press.

Norman, T. (2001, November 1). No expiration date on stupidity at Ala., Miss. Colleges. *Post-Gazette.* Retrieved 9/28/14, from http://old.post-gazette.com/columnists/20011109tony1109p1.asp

Nouwen, H. (1972). *The Wounded Healer: Ministry in Contemporary Society.* New York: Doubleday.

Novak, J. (1995). Why White Men Are Voting Republican. Retrieved 3/28/14, from http://www.backlash.com/content/gender/votemale/novak.html

O'Malley, M. (No date). Subjectivity—What Is It? Retrieved 7/8/14, from http://theaporetic.com/?page_id=2184

Ottenhoff, J. (1994, September). Of Wolves and Men. *Christian Century:* 859–861.

Owens, J. (1999). Ending the Race Crisis in the 21st Century. Retrieved 7/21/14 from http://www.ourcivilisation.com/usa/

Paget, H. (2001). Sociology: After the Linguistic and Multicultural Turns. In B. R. Hare (Ed.), *2001: Race Odyssey: African Americans and Sociology* (pp. 77–96). Syracuse, N.Y.: Syracuse University Press.

Park, J. (No date). About the Mixed Race Project. Retrieved 9/21/14, from http://www.themixedrace-project.com/About-The-Project

Park, R.E. (1928). Human Migration and the Marginal Man. *American Journal of Sociology* 33: 881–893.

Parker, C.S., & Barreto, M.A. (2013). *Change They Can't Believe In: The Tea Party and Reactionary Politics in America.* Princeton, N.J.: Princeton University Press.

Parsons, G. (1981). Yellow Ribbons; Ties with Tradition. *Folklife Center News* 4(21): 9–12.

Parsons, G. 1991. How the Yellow Ribbon Became a National Folk Symbol. *Folklife Center News* 13(2): 9–11.

Patterson, O. (1997). *The Ordeal of Integration: Progress and Resentment in America's "Racial" Crisis*. New York: Basic Civitas.

Patterson, O. (1995). The Paradox of Integration. *The New Republic*: 24–27.

Paul, R. (2014, August). Rand Paul: We Must Demilitarize the Police. Retrieved 9/18/14, from http://time.com/3111474/rand-paul-ferguson-police/

Phelan, P., & Davidson, A.L. (1994). Looking Across Borders: Students' Investigations of Family, Peer, and School Worlds as Cultural Therapy. In G. D. Spindler & L. Spindler (Eds.), *Pathways to Cultural Awareness: Cultural Therapy with Teachers and Students* (pp. 35–59). Thousand Oaks, Calif.: Corwin Press.

Phelan, A.M., & McLaughlin, H.J. (1995). Educational Discourses, the Nature of the Child, and the Practice of New Teachers. *Journal of Teacher Education* 46: 165–174.

Pinderhughes, E. (1982). Black Genealogy: Self-Liberator and Therapeutic Tool. *Smith College Studies in Social Work* 52: 93–106.

Pitt, A., & Britzman, D. (2006). Speculations on Qualities of Difficult Knowledge in Teaching and Learning: An Experiment in Psychoanalytic Research. In Kenneth Tobin & Joe Kincheloe (Eds.), *Doing Educational Research: A Handbook* (pp. 379–97). Rotterdam: Sense Publishing.

Pollock, M. (2006). Everyday Antiracism in Education. Retrieved 9/19/14, from http://www.understandingrace.org/resources/pdf/rethinking/pollock.pdf

Powell, J.A. (2000). Whites Will Be Whites: The Failure to Interrogate Racial Privilege. *University of San Francisco Law Review* 34: 1–29.

Radaway, J. (1987). *Reading the Romance: Women, Patriarchy and Popular Literature*. London: Verso.

Radio Vatican. (2014, May 9). Pope to UN: Resist the Economy of Exclusion, Serve the Poor. Retrieved 9/19/14, from http://en.radiovaticana.va/storico/2014/05/09/pope_to_un_resist_the_economy_of_exclusion%2C_serve_the_poor/en1–797707

Rafferty, M.L. (1970). *Classroom Countdown: Education at the Crossroads*. New York: Hawthorn Books.

Rajendran, L.P., Walker, S., & Parnell, R. (2013, November). The Dialectic of Place and Passage of Time. *Kaleidoscope* 5(2): 132–145.

Reagan, R. (1984). *Weekly Complication of Presidential Documents. U.S. Office of Federal Register, National Archives and Records Service*, General Services Administration. Washington, D.C.: U.S. Government Printing Office.

Reed, I. (1999). Buck Passing: The Media, Black Men, O.J. and the Million Man March. Carboda, D.W. (Ed.). (1999). *Black Men on Race, Gender, and Sexuality: A Critical Reader* (pp. 46–53). New York: New York University Press.

Reed Jr., A., & Chowkwanyun, M. (2012). Race, Class, Crisis: The Discourse of Racial Disparity and Its Analytical Discontents. *The Socialist Register*. Retrieved 8/18/14, from http://ssc.wisc.edu/~chowkwanyun/ReedChowkwanyunSR.pdf

Reeve, E. (2013, May 9). Every Every Every Generation Has Been the Me Me Me Generation. *The Wire*. Retrieved 10/1/14, from http://www.thewire.com/national/2013/05/me-generation-time/65054/

Reft, R. (2012). Joy and Pain: What Jeremy Lin Tells Us about 21st Century American Race Relations. Retrieved 9/21/14, from http://tropicsofmeta.wordpress.com/2012/02/17/joy-and-pain-what-jeremy-lin-tells-us-about-21st-century-american-race-relations/

Rich, A. (1979). *On Lies, Secrets, and Silence: Selected Prose, 1966–1978*. New York: Norton.

Riddle, J. (2014, April 24). Meet the Poster child for "white privilege" – then have your mind blown. Retrieved 9/19/14, from http://youngcons.com/meet-the-poster-child-for-white-privilege-then-have-your-mind-blown/

Robbins, J.S. (2013, July 15). White on Black Murder: Who Really Is Killing Whom? Rare. Retrieved 9/20/14, from http://rare.us/story/white-on-black-murder-who-really-is-killing-whom/#JFbyTIu8UAggd2Yc.99

Robinson, B.B. (No date). "Crash" Causes Pain. Retrieved 7/16/2014, from https://www.nationalcenter.org/P21NVRobinsonCrash605.html

Rochlin, G. (1973). *Man's Aggression: The Defense of the Self*. Boston: Gambit.

Rochlin, G. (1980). *The Masculine Dilemma: A Psychology of Masculinity*. Boston: Little, Brown.

Rodriguez, F. (1983). *Education in a Multicultural Society*. Washington, D.C.: University Press of America.

Rodriguez, N.M., & Villaverde, L. (2000). *Dismantling White Privilege: Pedagogy, Politics, and Whiteness*. New York: Peter Lang.

Roediger, D. (1991). *The Wages of Whiteness: Race and the Making of the American Working Class*. New York: Verso.

Roediger, D. 1994. *Towards the Abolition of Whiteness*. New York: Verso.

Rogin, M. (1996). *Blackface, White Noise: Jewish Immigrants in the Hollywood Melting Pot*. Berkeley: University of California Press.

Romney, A. (2012, August 28). Transcript: Ann Romney's Convention Speech. Retrieved 9/19/14, from http://www.npr.org/2012/08/28/160216442/transcript-ann-romneys-convention-speech

Rosenberg, P. (1997). Underground Discourses: Exploring Whiteness in Teacher Education. In M. Fine, L. Weis, L.C. Powell, & L.M. Wong (Eds.), *Off White: Readings on Race, Power, and Society* (pp. 79–89). New York: Routledge.

Rosenberg, Tina. (1996, November 18). Recovering From Apartheid. *New Yorker*: 86–95.

Rosin, H. (2013, November 24). Even Madder Men: "Angry White Men," by Michael Kimmel. Retrieved 6/6/14, from http://www.nytimes.com/2013/11/24/books/review/angry-white-men-by-michael-kimmel.html?pagewanted=all&_r=0

Ross, S.D. (1995). *Plenishment in the Earth: An Ethic of Inclusion*. Albany: SUNY Press.

Rossing, J.P. (2014). Critical Race Humor in a Postracial Moment: Richard Pryor's Contemporary Parrhesia. *Howard Journal of Communications* 25(1): 16–33.

Roszak, B., & Roszak, T. (1969). *Masculine/Feminine Readings in Sexual Mythology and the Liberation of Women* (1st ed.). New York: Harper & Row.

Rothstein, S.W. (1994). *Schooling the Poor: A Social Inquiry into the American Educational Experience*. Westport, Conn.: Bergin & Garvey.

Rowe, J., & Berg, R. (Eds.) (1991). *The Vietnam War and American Culture*. New York: Columbia University Press.

Rudwick, E., & Meier, A. (1969). Negro Retaliatory Violence in the Twentieth Century. In A. Meier & E. Rudwick (Eds.), *The Making of Black America: Essays in Negro Life and History*, vol. 2. New York: Harper & Row.

Ryden, W., & Marshall, I. (2012). *Reading, Writing, and the Rhetorics of Whiteness*. New York: Routledge.

Sacks, J. (2002). Behind European Anti-Semitism. http://www.beliefnet.com/Faiths/Judaism/2002/05/Behind-European-Anti-Semitism.aspx?p=4#

Sagan, E. (1974). *Cannibalism: Human Aggression and Cultural Form*. New York: Harper & Row.

Salvio, P. (1994). What Can a Body Know? Re-figuring Pedagogic Intention into Teacher Education. *Journal of Teacher Education* 20: 283–289.

Sandel, M.J. (1996). *Democracy's Discontent: America in Search of a Public Philosophy*. Cambridge, Mass.: Harvard University Press.

Santino, J. (1992). Yellow Ribbons and Seasonal Flags: The Folk Assemblage of War. *Journal of American Folklore* 105: 19–33.

Sartre, J.P. (1956). *The Anti-Semite and Jew*. New York: Washington Square Publishers.

Schacht, S.P. (2000). Using a Feminist Pedagogy as a Male Teacher: The Possibilities of a Partial and Situated Perspective. *Radical Pedagogy* 2(2). Retrieved from http://radicalpeda-gogy.icaap.org

Scheper-Hughes, N. (2006). Mixed Feelings: The Recovery of Spoiled Identities in the New South Africa. In L. Romanucci-Ross, G.A. De Vos, & T. Tsuda (Eds.), *Ethnic Identity: Problems and Prospects for the Twenty-first Century* (pp. 346–374). Lanham, Md.: Rowman & Littlefield.

Scheper-Hughes, N. (2001, April/May). Mixed Feelings: The Recovery of Spoiled Identities in the New South Africa. *The Multiracial Activist*. Retrieved 9/19/14, from http://multiracial.com/site/content/view/442/27/

Schick, C. & St. Denis, V. (2005). Critical Autobiography in Integrative Anti-racist Pedagogy. In L. Biggs & P. Downe (Eds.), *Gendered Intersections: An Introduction to Women's and Gender Studies* (pp. 387–392). Halifax, NS: Fernwood.

Schutz, A. (1972). *The Phenomenology of the Social World*. Evanston, Ill.: Northwestern University Press.

Seewood, A. (2014). S&A 2013 Highlights: Why White People Don't Like Black Movies. Retrieved 8/15/14, from http://blogs.indiewire.com/shadowandact/why-white-people-dont-like-black-movies

Sennett, R., & Cobb, J. (1972). *The Hidden Injuries of Class*. New York: Vintage Books.

Shakespeare, W. *The Merchant of Venice*. Retrieved 9/4/14, from http://www.shakespeare-online.com/plays/merchant_3_1.html

Shaw, A.R. (2013). White Woman Who Posted Racist Trayvon Martin Photo Reportedly Fired From Her Job. *Rolling Out*. Retrieved 3/9/14 from http://rollingout.com/shame-on-you/white-woman-posted-racist-trayvon-martin-photo-fired-job-reportedly/#

Shor, I. (1996). *When Students Have Power: Negotiating Authority in a Critical Pedagogy*. Chicago: University of Chicago Press.

Shujaa, M.J. (Ed.). (1996). *Beyond Segregation: The Politics of Quality in African American Schooling*. Thousand Oaks, Calif.: Corwin Press.

Sifton, B. (2010, June 11). America's Identity Crisis. Retrieved 6/10/2014, from https://www.adbusters.org/magazine/90/americas-identity-crisis.html

Silverstein, J. (2013). I Don't Feel Your Pain. *Salon*, Retrieved 9/20/14, from http://www.slate.com/articles/health_and_science/science/2013/06/racial_empathy_gap_people_don_t_perceive_pain_in_other_races.html

Simon, R.I. (1991). *Learning Work: A Critical Pedagogy of Work Education*. New York: Bergin & Garvey.

Simon, R.I. (2001). *Divided We Stand: How Al Gore Beat George Bush and Lost the Presidency*. New York: Crown.

Singh, R. (1997). *The Farrakhan Phenomenon: Race, Reaction, and the Paranoid Style in American Politics*. Washington, D.C.: Georgetown University Press.

Siskel, G. (1994, July 8). "Forrest Gump" Upholds a Great American Tradition. *Chicago Tribune*: 7, B4.

Skocpol, T., & Williamson, V. (2012). *The Tea Party and the Remaking of Republican Conservatism*. New York: Oxford University Press.

Slade, A.F., Narro, A.J., & Buchanan, B.P. (Eds.). (2014). *Reality Television: Oddities of Culture*. Lanham, Md.: Lexington Books.

Slate. (1997, May 25). White Is a Color Too. Retrieved 9/27/14, from http://www.slate.com/articles/arts/egghead/1997/05/_2.html

Sleeter, C.E., & McLaren, P. (Eds.). (1995). *Multicultural Education, Critical Pedagogy, and the Politics of Difference*. Albany: SUNY Press.

Slotkin, R. (1973). *Regeneration Through Violence: The Mythology of the American Frontier, 1600–1860*. Middletown, Conn.: Wesleyan University Press.

Smith, D.L. (2004). *Why We Lie: The Evolutionary Roots of Deception and the Unconscious Mind*. New York: St. Martin's Press.

Smolkin, R. (2001, July 18). Harvard Study Finds Large Divide in Northeast U.S. School. Retrieved 9/20/14, from http://old.post-gazette.com/headlines/20010718race0718p2.asp

Sowell, T. (1994). *Inside American Education: Its Decline*. New York: Free Press.

Spillers, H. (1987, Summer). Mama's Baby, Papa's Maybe: An American Grammar Book. *Diacritics* 17(2): 65–81. Retrieved 9/24/14, from http://engl651-jackson.wikispaces.umb.edu/file/view/Spillers+-+Mama's+Baby.pdf

Spindler, G.D., & Spindler, L. (Eds.). (1994). *Pathways to Cultural Awareness: Cultural Therapy With Teachers and Students*. Thousand Oaks, Calif.: Corwin Press.

Spring, J. (1995). *The Intersection of Cultures: Multicultural Education in the United States*. New York: McGraw-Hill.

Stengel, R. (2007, August 30). A Time to Serve: The Case for National Service. *Time*. Retrieved October 3, 2014, from http://content.time.com/time/specials/2007/article/0,28804,1657256_1657317_1657570,00.html

Stephens, D.P., & Phillips, L.D. (2003) Freaks, gold diggers, divas and dykes: The socio-historical development of African American female adolescent scripts. *Sexuality and Culture*, 7, 3–47.
Sykes, H. (1995). Feminist Views on Radical Pedagogies: Dangerous Struggles. *Journal of Teacher Education* 46: 71–73.
Tan, C. (2011, July 28). Asian Women with White Men Suck? Retrieved 9/21/2014, from http://diaspora.chinasmack.com/2011/malaysia/christine-tan-asian-women-with-white-men-suck.html
Taubin, A. (1994, August 9). Two or Three Things: Plus Ça Change. *Village Voice*: p. 93.
Taylor, J. (2011). *White Identity: Race Consciousness in the 21st Century*. Oakton, Va.: New Century Foundation.
Taylor, L.K. (2011a). Feeling in Crisis: Vicissitudes of Response in Experiments with Global Justice Education. *Journal of the Canadian Association for Curriculum Studies* 9(1): 6–65.
Taylor, L.K. (2011b). Global Justice Education as a Pedagogy of Loss: Interrupting Frames of War. In H. Smits & R. Naqvi (Eds.), *Thinking About and Enacting Curriculum in Times of War*. Lanham, Md.: Rowman & Littlefield.
Thompson, A. (1999). Review of *Off White: Readings on Race, Power and Society*, M. Fine et al. (Eds.). *Education Review*. Retrieved 9/20/14, from http://www.edrev.info/reviews/rev76.htm
Tizard, B., & Phoenix, A. (1993). *Black, White, or Mixed Race: Race and Racism in the Lives of Young People of Mixed Parentage*. New York: Routledge.
TMZ Sports. (2014, April 27). Donald Sterling. New Audio Released: I Put Food on Black People's Tables. Retrieved 9/20/14 from, http://www.tmz.com/2014/04/27/donald-sterling-new-audio-released-clippers-black-people/
Topaz, J. (2014). Obama: 2016 Could Be "Undignifying." Retrieved 7/12/14, from http://www.politico.com/story/2014/07/obama-2016-new-yorker-joe-biden-profile-109168.html
Travers, P. (1994, July 14). Forrest Gump. *Rolling Stone*: 99.
Truthandaction.com. (2014, May 16). Operation American Spring: Ret. Colonel Creates March on Washington. Retrieved 9/20/14, from http://www.truthandaction.org/operation-american-spring-ret-colonel-creates-march-washington-may-16-2014/
Twenge, J.M., & Foster, J.D. (2008). Mapping the Scale of the Narcissism Epidemic: Increases in Narcissism 2002–2007 Within Ethnic Groups. *Journal of Research in Personality* 42: 1619–1622.
Tylee, C.M. (1990). *The Great War and Women's Consciousness: Images of Militarism and Womanhood in Women's Writings, 1914–1964*. Iowa City: University of Iowa Press.
Valades, J. et al. (1997). A Critical Case Study Approach to Questions of Identity and Racialized Mixed Heritage. *Journal of Critical Pedagogy* 1(1).
Valli, L. (1995). The Dilemma of Race: Learning To Be Color Blind and Color Conscious. *Journal of Teacher Education* 46: 120–129.
Van Biema, D. (1994, August 24). Forrest Gump Is Dumb. *Time*: 82.
Vanguard News Network.com. (2002). Angry White Female. "Black Mob, White Sob." Retrieved 3/28/14, from http://www.vanguardnewsnetwork.com/v1/index49.htm

Vera, H., & Gordon, A. (2003). *Screen Saviors: Hollywood Fictions of Whiteness*. Lanham, Md.: Rowman & Littlefield.

Vera, H., & Gordon, A. (No date). Sincere Fictions of the White Self in the American Cinema: The Divided White Self in Civil War Films. Retrieved 7/17/14, from http://www.clas.ufl.edu/users/agordon/white.htm

Voice of America. (2014, June 11) Testimony of US Secretary of Defense Hagel, House Armed Services Committee. Retrieved 6/14/2014, from http://www.voanews.com/content/secretary-of-defense-chuck-hagel-hearing-on-the-transfer-of-detainees-house-armed-services-committee/1934678.html

Waller, J. (1998). *Face to Face: The Changing State of Racism Across America*. New York: Plenum Press.

Walsh, M. (2014, August 11). Police Officers aren't the ones destroying the black community. Retrieved 9/20/14, from http://themattwalshblog.com/2014/08/11/police-officers-arent-the-ones-destroying-the-black-community/

Warped Network. Incredibly Offensive Jokes. Retrieved 1/24/14 from http://www.slightly-warped.com/

Weiner, L. (1993). *Preparing Teachers for Urban Schools: Lessons from Thirty Years of School Reform*. New York: Teachers College Press.

Weiner, L. (1995). Constructing the "Other": Discursive Renditions of White Working-Class Males in High School. In P. L. McLaren & J.M. Giarelli (Eds.), *Critical Theory and Educational Research* (pp. 203–222). Albany: SUNY Press.

Weis, L., Proweller, A. & Centrie, C. (1997). Re-examining "A Moment in History": Loss of Privilege Inside White Working-Class Masculinity in the 1990s. In M. Fine, L. Weis, L.C. Powell & L.M. Wong (Eds.), *Off White: Readings on Race, Power, Society* (pp. 210–228). New York: Routledge.

Werbner, R.P. (1989). *Ritual Passage, Sacred Journey: The Process and Organization of Religious Movement*. Washington, D.C.: Smithsonian Institution Press.

Wertsch, J.V. (1985). *Vygotsky and the Social Formation of Mind*. Cambridge, Mass.: Harvard University Press.

Wessells, M. (2006). *Child Soldiers: From Violence to Prevention*. Cambridge, Mass.: Harvard University Press.

Wessells, M. (2009). Do No Harm: Toward Contextually Appropriate Psychosocial Support in International Emergencies. *American Psychologist* 64: 842–854.

White, L.R. (1973). Effective Teachers for Inner-City Schools. *Journal of Negro Education* 42: 308–314.

Wielsch, D. (2013). Relational Justice. *Law and Contemporary Problems* 76: 191–211. Retrieved 7/7/14, from http://scholarship.law.duke.edu/lcp/vol76/iss2/13

Wilden, A. (1988). *System and Structure: Essays in Communication and Exchange* (2nd ed.). London: Tavistock.

Williams, T.M. (2008). *Black Pain: It Just Looks Like We're Not Hurting*. New York: Scribner.

Williamson, B. (1994, September 4). Forrest Gump. *Playboy*: 26.

Wilson, W.J. (1980). *The Declining Significance of Race: Blacks and Changing American Institutions* (2nd ed). Chicago: University of Chicago Press.

Winant, H. (1997). Behind Blue Eyes: Whiteness and Contemporary U.S. Racial Politics. *New Left Review* 225: 73–89.

Wojnar, D.M., & Swanson, K.M. (2007). Phenomenology: An Exploration. *Journal of Holistic Nursing* 25(3): 172–180.

Wortham, S. (1994). *Acting Out Participant Examples in the Classroom*. Philadelphia: J. Benjamins.

Wortham, S. (2001). *Narratives in Action: A Strategy for Research and Action*. New York: Teachers College Press.

Wray, M. (2013, June). White Trash: The Social Origins of a Stigma Type. Retrieved 9/20/14, from http://thesocietypages.org/specials/white-trash/

Wray, M., & Newitz, A. (Eds.) (1997). *White Trash: Race and Class in America*. New York: Routledge.

Wu, W.F. (1982). *Chinese Americans in American Fiction, 1850–1940*. Hamden, Conn.: Archon Books.

Yahoo Answers. (2009). I Would Like To Start a Million Man March With White Men Only, Will People Call It Racist? *Yahoo.com*. Retrieved 9/20/14 from https://answers.yahoo.com/question/index?qid=20090412065116AAZTUsN

Yahoo Answers. (2011). Proud To Be White??? Why Are Only Whites Called Racist? *Yahoo.com*. Retrieved 9/20/14, from https://answers.yahoo.com/question/index?qid=20071109110501AA2WoZo

Yemma J. (1997), "Whiteness Studies," an Attempt at Healing. *Boston globe*, December 21. A1.

Yeo, F.L. (1997a). *Inner-City Schools, Multiculturalism, and Teacher Education: A Professional Journey*. New York: Garland.

Yeo, F.L. (1997b). Teacher Preparation and Inner City Schools: Sustaining Educational Failure. *Urban Review* 29:127–143.

Zimmerman, J. (2002). *Whose America?: Culture Wars in the Public Schools*. Cambridge, Mass.: Harvard University Press.

Zimmerman, J. (2014, July 31). Donald Sterling vs. Ray Rice: Compare and Contrast. *New York Daily News*. Retrieved 9/20/14, from http://www.nydailynews.com/opinion/donald-sterling-ray-rice-compare-contrast-article-1.1887635

ABOUT THE AUTHOR

Aaron David Gresson III is Professor Emeritus at The Pennsylvania State University, where he taught education, human development, communications, and Africana studies. He previously taught at Brandeis, Colby, Brown, Hershey Medical School, and the State University of New York. His books include *Race and Education Primer* (2008), *The Recovery of Race in America* (1995), *Measured Lies: The Bell Curve Examined* (edited with Joe L. Kincheloe and Shirley R. Steinberg, 1996), *Black Amnesia* (1990), and *The Dialectics of Betrayal: Sacrifice, Violation, and the Oppressed* (1982). A licensed psychologist, Gresson currently resides in Maryland where he maintains a community mental health practice and teaches in the graduate Sociology program at Morgan State University.

INDEX

A

academia, and white pain, 13, 111
   and blackface, 80
   and whiteness, 93
"affective turn," xviii, 226, 228, 246n49
   and compassion, 230
   in cultural politics, 214
   defined, 214, 234n8
   in social justice pedagogy
affirmative action, 14–21, 28, 39–41, 50,
   64–65, 72–73, 81, 103, 151–153, 177,
   186–187, 196, 213
agency, xi, 37, 234, 246, 248
   as "dance," xi–xv, 231
   as empowerment, 5–7
   as *racialized dance*, 26, 32–37
   and white pain, 32–37, 45–54, 90, 109,
   112, 153
aggression, xix, 17, 44, 59–90
   blackface as, 79–83
   recovery as, 8–15

alienation, 14, 40, 81
   defined, 72
   in whiteness studies, 102–105
   see also white males
Alridge, Derrick, xxiii, 30, 114
America, and war, 118–147
America's "Atonement," 8–13
   as apologetics for racism, 11–12,
   19–23, 44, 127–128
   defined, 1
   as "non-apology," 8
   and white privilege, 15–18
   and white victimhood, 18
Anderson, David, 10–12, 221, 232
angry white male, 18–20, 50, 67,
   75, 234
   as masculinity crisis, 18
   see also white males
anti-oppression, as discourse, 85–88
   in education, 51–56, 88–92
apology, xviii, 8–11, 46, 55, 108, 200,
   229–230

and racial healing, 181–185
  see also non-apology
Apple, Michael, 62, 137, 187, 210
Arabs, 39, 202, 205
Armies of the Night, 48, 66–68, 251
  see also Norman Mailer
Asante, Molefi, 114
Asian American females, and white mates, 44–45
  and injustice, 175–176, 202
  and Jewish females, 46–47
  as "model minority," 84–85
Atwater, Deborah, 114
autobiography, 93, 96, 98
  and pedagogy, 163–176
  student, 107–113

B

backlash, 2, 70, 73–74, 170
  and blackface, 86
  and Obama, Barack, 76
Barthes, Roland, 113
Bederman, Gail, 8, 18, 81–82
  on Jack Johnson and "The Great White Hope," 75–78
Bergdahl, Bowe, as model of soldier, 50
Berlak, Ann, 162, 168
betrayal, dialectics of, 44, 51–52, 109, 116–117, 129, 216
  and Barack Obama as father figure, 87;
  and class, 86
blackface, 79–81, 128, 213, 244n43, 245n47
  and racial pain, 82–83
  and social recognition, 82–86
black males, 3–4, 45, 64, 75, 78
  and police, 62, 153, 219–224, 227
blackpain, 23, 54–56
  as self-deception, 55
  see also Debra Walker King
"black privilege," 152, 176
black women, racial pain and confusion, 33–35
  student narratives, 111–113

Blee, Kathleen M., 122
Bork, Robert H., 60–61
Boszormenyi-Nagy, Ivan, 215–217
Britzman, Deborah, 226–228, 237n25
Brown, Michael, xix, 218, 220
Brown, Richard, 52, 149
Bush, George H. W., 119–122, 143–146, 192
Bush, George W., xiii, 25, 79, 81, 112–114, 202
Butin, Dan W., 86–88, 90–91

C

Cheney, Dick, xiv
cinema, recovery themes, 69–79
  white pain and mediating function, 68
  see also *Forrest Gump*
  see also Magical Negro
coalitions, 70–71, 201, 216
Coates, Ta-Nehisi, 39
collusion, 22
  gender and race, 121–122
  in society, 131, 249n60
confusion, white male, 64–65
  as cultural pain, 53
  and racial identity, 33
contradiction, 17, 26, 34, 64, 74;
  9/11 and, xiv–xv
  in white male perceptions of race, 64–65
  in whiteness studies, 13, 32–34
cultural pain, 30, 52–53, 56
cultural turn, 10, 151–152, 234 n8, 248n59

D

Daly, Mary, 121, 125, 144
Davis, Jordan, 23, 218
dialectics, 46, 197, 214
  of "bad performance," 228–230
Dialectics of Betrayal, The, 109
  white student reflection on, 116–117

"difficult knowledge," 226–228, 237n25
Dinnerstein, Dorothy, 121
diversity, and white pain, 13, 22, 32, 62, 71–73, 102, 120–121, 212
Dr. Phil, 44–45, 222, 237n26
Du Bois, W.E.B., 74, 97, 177
Dumas, Rhetaugh Thomas, 143
Dunn, Michael, 23, 218
Dyer, Adam, 5–6

E

Emotion work, 163–167
existential moment, 43, 92
  defined, 14, 231–232

F

Fanon, Franz, 97, 121
Farrakhan, Louis, 3, 196
feminism, and white male anger, 82–83
  and mythmakers, 144
  and yellow ribbon ritual, 125–126
Ferguson, Missouri, and racial pain, 217–219
Fiddler on the Roof, 202, 249n65
Firefighters' Memorial scandal, xiv
Forrest Gump, 91–92, 96, 11–139, 142
Fortgang, Tal, 8–9
Frankenberg, Ruth, 23, 82, 122
Franklin, John Hope, 25, 196
Freire, Paulo, xx, 230
Fulton, Sabrina, 149, 219

G

gatekeepers in textbook publishing, 105–111
gaze, the, 92, 185, 205, 234n10
gender, identity confusion, 21–24, 33–35
  and race, 137–139
    romance and yellow ribbons, 128–131

George-Kanentiio, Douglas, 8
Gerzon, Mark, 128
Ginsburg, Mark, 166
Goodacre, Glenna, 144, 247n56
Gramsci, Antonio, 144, 249n60
guilt, black shame as, 96–97
  white, 98–101
Gulf Wars, see war

H

Haskell, Robert, on whiteness as problem, 91–96, 169, 188, 209
Hatch, John, 11–13; on atonement, 57
  on racial reconciliation, 119, 179, 181, 231
Healing, 179–214; group, 120–122
  the Internet and, 195–199
  loss and, 181
  and the Million Man March, 3–4
  mourning and, 179
  nonhealing, 195–199
  paradoxes of, 181–183
  phenomenology and, 183–186
  psychology of, 181–185
  Ronald Reagan on, 119
  white backlash as, 71–72
Heinemann, Larry, *Paco's Story*, 125–126
Here Comes Honey Boo-Boo, as racial pain, 52, 239n39
Higher Learning, 59–60, 62
Horowitz, David, on reparations, 201
humanity, 14, 21, 146, 194
  of black male youth, 219–222
  denial of in "the other," 97–102
  9/11 and discourse of, 199–200
  and white identity, 103
humiliation, and healing, 184–186
  and Asian Americans, 44–46, 85
  and black women, 35
  and President Barack Obama, 79
  and the South, 19
  and white manhood, 59, 79
  and the white middle class, 48–52

humility, 15, 36
  and healing, 183–185
Hussein, Saddam, 3, 126, 144, 213–214

I

identity, "non-spoiled," 9, 87
  spoiled, 6, 13, 37–40, 44–45, 51–52
  and trauma, 225
Identity crisis, Asian American, 44–46,
    84–85, 170
  black female, 35
  black male, 22
  white male, 74, 81–85, 169
identity threat, 137–139
  blackface and, 9/11 and, xiii–xv
  see also identity crisis
Iginla, Biodun, 233
Injustice, 13, 64, 66, 182, 189, 191,
    196, 223–231
  real and imagined among
    whites, 216
Ipsaro, Anthony, 21–22, 63–64
Iraqis, 146, 158
  see also Arabs
Israel, 54, 79, 201, 206, 237n25,
    241n38

J

Jackson, Jesse, x, 176
Jacobson, Gaye, 129
Jews, 146, 158, 237n25
  Bernie Madoff, 30–39
  Don Sterling, 36, 38, 53–54
  Freud on, 222
  and healing, 198–207
  narratives on Judaism, 101,
    105, 107
Johnson, Jack, 76–80
Johnson, Lyndon Baines, 66
Jurecic, Ann, 30–32

Justice
  see injustice
  social justice
  see also relational justice

K

Kazin, Alfred, 68
Kierkegaard, Søren, 91–92
Kimmel, Michael, 59, 81–82, 86
  on the "angry white male," 18–20
  on class and gender, 50
Kincheloe, Joe L., 19, 81, 111–112, 144,
    147, 225–226, 235n14, 251n70
King, Debra Walker, 2, 23, 38, 54
  see also *blackpain*
Kirk, H.D., 36, 162
Kirk, Russell, 104
Kumashrio, Kevin W., 156–162

L

Ladson-Billings, Gloria, 161
Laingen, Penne, 122–123, 129
Langer, Susan, 3, 7, 16, 51, 193, 223
La Spada, Camilla, 129–130
lesbians, 14, 194–195
Lifton, Robert Jay, 32, 218, 236n20
Lyman, Peter, 111, 190–195
Lynch, Frederick R., 41–42, 70–74, 206
Lynch, Jessica, 146
lynching, black males, 237n25, 244n43,
    245n44

M

Madoff, Bernie, 38–39
Magical Negro, 247–248
Mailer, Norman, on gender and class,
    48–50, 66–70, 241–242n36,
    251n69

Mandela, Nelson, 181, 197, 200, 211–212
Marable, Manning, 225
Martin, Trayvon, 23, 83, 219, 229
masculinity, 121, 206, 212, 242n39, 250n66
   as crisis, 18, 59, 81–82
   and Jack Johnson, 15–20
Mason, Susan, 114
Maternal, The, 139–142
McGarry, Susan Hallsten, 144
McGruder, Gail, 129
McPhail, Mark Lawrence, 34, 179–181
media: "embedded media," 24–24
   saturation, 21, 24–25
   stereotypes in, 21
mediation, defined, 120
   in cinema, 131–137
   and white pain, 120–144
   and yellow ribbons, 130–131
Million Man March, The, 3–6
   and white pride rhetoric, 9–10
Morris, David B., 50–52
   see also cultural pain
mourning, 144–148, 175–177
   as loss, 190–192
multiculturalism, 12–16, 20
   emotion work, 163–167
   and social justice, 151–177
   as source of racial pain, 12–16, 155
   and teacher education, 82–85
Murray, Charles, 26

N

narrative, as power, 9–10, 16, 104, 164
   and black female identity, 33–35
   and emotion work, 163–167
   and racial hurt, 40
   as rhetorical strategy, 43–44
   and Sergeant Bowe Bergdahl, 50–51
   and yellow ribbons, 126–128
Nash, Kate, 151, 153
   see also cultural turn
Native Americans, 43, 56

"non-apology," discourse defined, xviii, 8–10
   and "atonement," 15–18
Nouwen, Henri, xx, 226, 230
Novak, James, on white male backlash, 70–71

O

Obama, Barack, 50, 61, 192, 218, 243n40, 243n42, 246n52
   and Jack Johnson, 76–79
   and white pain, 5, 8, 27, 61, 88–89
O'Malley, Mike, 41
Orlando, Tony, and Dawn, 124
Owens, James, xviii

P

Pain, cultural, 52–56
   racial, 5–15
   social, 163–167
   and whiteness, 13–20, 91–117
Parsons, Gerald, 122–123
patriotism, and gender, 129–130
   and war, 119–147
Paul, Rand, on black male vulnerability, 224–225
pedagogy, and healing, defined, xxi–xiii, 157, 181, 193, 214
   anti-oppressive, 112–114, 139, 143
   and social justice, 153, 214–232
   see also teachers
People Magazine, on the yellow ribbon, 126
Pietà Embrace, The, defined, 24–25, 139–142
   photograph of Michelangelo's sculpture, 141
"Postracial," The, and racial pain, 25–28
Powell, Colin, 89
power, "atonement" as, 69–72
   in the academy, 105–111

blackface as, 80–83
and gender, 79, 84, 86, 143
symbolic, 119–144
psychological numbness, defined, 31

R

"racial dualism," 74, 177, 207
racial pain, 4–15
in the academy, 91–118
defined, 32–37
and traumatized relations, 30
white pain as racial, 30–37, 62–68
Rafferty, Max, 12–15, 41, 67, 74, 121, 176
Reagan, Ronald, and racial pain, 4, 128, 137, 211, 243n41
healing, 119–120
recognition, 225
and healing, 191, 206, 211, 213
and non-apology, xviii
and white identities, 187, 211
of white racial hurt, 40–42
see also social recognition
Recovery of Race in America, The, xii, 109
and *innocent whiteness*, 90
recovery climate, 24
Recovery project, defined, 21
redemption, and Million Man March, 3
and discourse, 127, 134
and the South, 122, 236n14
and Tea Party, 5
and white males, 139–144
see also ritualism
Reft, Ryan, 42–43
relational justice, 11
defined, 216–217
and the police, 217
reparations, and white anger, 200–202
repression, and healing, 194–195
retributive social dynamics, defined, 216
rhetorical condition, 114
rhetorical reversal, 6, 87
defined, 132
in *Forrest Gump*, 133–136

Rice, Condoleezza, xiv, 114
Rice, Ray, 55–56
Rich, Adrienne, 195
ritualism, redemptive, 122–130
in cinema, 131
ritual recovery, 119
see also ritualism
romance, as ideology,128
and *Forrest Gump*, 137–139
and yellow ribbon, 128–131
Romney, Ann, 140
Rossing, Jonathan, 26
Ryden, Wendy, 25, 27, 39, 163, 235n10

S

sacrifice, 3, 7, 88
and gender, 143
and healing, 193–194, 233n5
and loss, 15–16, 186
and working-class identity, 49–50
Santino, Jack, 127–129
Scheper-Hughes, Nancy, 6, 37, 88
Sebok, Anthony J., 201
see also reparations
Self-deception, 26, 54–55, 214
"societal," 216
September 11, 2001, xiii, xiv, xv, 30, 71, 145, 199, 202, 207
Slotkin, Richard, 212–213
Smith, David, on self-deception, 54–55, 214
social justice, 153–177, 214
social movements and racial pain, 12–13, 120
and social justice pedagogy, 153
social recognition, 82, 214
see also recognition
Sojourner Truth, 36–37
spoiled identities, defined, 6, 13, 32, 37
and healing, 183–186
the need for recognition, 3–7
racial pain, 29–36
and trauma, xix, 37–40
Spreen, Carol Anne, 30

Steinberg, Shirley, xii, xxiii, 75
Sterling, Donald, and NBA scandal, 47–48, 55
   on racism in Israel, 52–53
Subjectivity, defined, 41
   in *The Merchant of Venice*, 36–37
suffering, 9/11 and, xiii–xv

T

Taylor, Jared, 61–62
teachers, and non-alienated pedagogy, 167–175
   and "training for uncertainty," 208–211
Tea Party, The, 3, 6–7, 10, 61, 73, 246n50
   and "angry white men," 220–221
   and identity injury, 61
   and racial pain, 14
terrorism, xiv, 111–115, 120, 126, 202, 207–208
   see also war
Thompson, Audrey, 164–168, 210–211
Todd, Chuck, 89
trauma, xviii–xx, 234n9, 235n14, 236n20
   defined, 37–38
   identity and, 225–226
   injustice and, 37
   psychological numbing and, 31–32
   relations, 37–40
   and Tea Party, 5
Truth and Reconciliation Commission, The, 212, 216
Tutu, Bishop Desmond, 180–181, 200

V

Valli, Linda, 166–170
victims, white males as, 6–8,15–17, 23, 71, 82–83, 86–87, 186, 213
Vietnam, 12, 24, 30, 68–69, 111
   soldiers, 69–70
   yellow ribbons and, 119–147

vulnerability, 14, 23, 69, 238n27
   Israeli, 202–207
   male, 40–53
   racial pain and, 32–37, 40

W

war, George H.W. Bush and the Gulf War, 119–120, 144
   Vietnam, 119–126, 133, 143
   "war on terrorism," xiii–xv, 120, 126, 207
   "war on whites," 27
Weiner, Lois, 154–155
"white disprivilege," 70–72
white diversity leadership, 187–189
white females, complicity with white males, 82–83, 128
   humiliation and humility, 183–184
white identity crisis, 83–87
   in textbook episode, 105–111
"white innocence," xviii, 5, 13, 62–68
   as "color-blindness" and entitlement, 93–96
   ratio-legal aspects, 20–22
   see also apology
white males, alienation, 72–74
   "angry white males," 75–79
   blackface and, 80–83
   black male threat, 78–80
   fear, 18–19
   narratives, 170–175
   self-perceptions, 62–64
   working-class, 48–52, 210
whiteness, as problematic, 12, 24, 28, 35, 62
   as the desire to be loved, 164, 168
   gender and, 48–52
   as identity, 40, 82–87
   identity threat, 92–102
   and the need for self-display, 62
   as white pride, 20, 84
whiteness studies, teaching alienation, 42–45
   and anti-oppressive education, 156–163

white privilege, "atonement" and, 15–18
white students, 51–56
"white trash," defined, 50–52, 84, 103–104, 239n29, 242n39
Williams, Patricia, 161
Winant, Howard, 73–74, 176
Women's Vietnam Memorial, 131, 139, 141–144
   as romance, 76
   see also Pietà Embrace
Wortham, Stanton, 98–99
Wounded healer, 226–232
   defined, 226

Y

yellow ribbons, 119–141
   gender collusion, 139–140
   mediation of white pain, 120–122
   as redemptive ritual, 127–131
   as romance, 128–131
   see also Orlando, Tony, and Dawn

Z

Zimmerman, George, 23, 27, 56, 83, 218
Zimmerman, Jonathan, 55
Zuercher, Brent, 10–12

Studies in the Postmodern Theory of Education

General Editor
Shirley R. Steinberg

Counterpoints publishes the most compelling and imaginative books being written in education today. Grounded on the theoretical advances in criticalism, feminism, and postmodernism in the last two decades of the twentieth century, Counterpoints engages the meaning of these innovations in various forms of educational expression. Committed to the proposition that theoretical literature should be accessible to a variety of audiences, the series insists that its authors avoid esoteric and jargonistic languages that transform educational scholarship into an elite discourse for the initiated. Scholarly work matters only to the degree it affects consciousness and practice at multiple sites. Counterpoints' editorial policy is based on these principles and the ability of scholars to break new ground, to open new conversations, to go where educators have never gone before.

For additional information about this series or for the submission of manuscripts, please contact:

> Shirley R. Steinberg
> c/o Peter Lang Publishing, Inc.
> 29 Broadway, 18th floor
> New York, New York 10006

To order other books in this series, please contact our Customer Service Department:

> (800) 770-LANG (within the U.S.)
> (212) 647-7706 (outside the U.S.)
> (212) 647-7707 FAX

Or browse online by series:
> www.peterlang.com